D0939497

The Evolution of Desire

Books by David M. Buss

The Evolution of Desire:
Strategies of Human Mating

Sex, Power, Conflict:
Evolutionary and Feminist Perspectives
(Ed., with Neil Malamuth)

The Dangerous Passion:
Why Jealousy Is as Necessary as Love and Sex

Evolutionary Psychology:
The New Science of the Mind

Personality Psychology:
Domains of Knowledge About Human Nature
(with Randy Larsen)

The Evolution
of Desire

STRATEGIES OF

HUMAN MATING

REVISED EDITION

DAVID M. BUSS

BASIC
BOOKS

A Member of the Perseus Books Group

Library Resource Center
Renton Technical College
3000 N.E. 4th St.
Renton, WA 98056

For Cindy

306.7 BUSS-D 2003 c.2

Buss, David M.

The evolution of desire

Copyright © 1994 by David M. Buss
Revised edition © 2003 by David M. Buss

Published by Basic Books, A Member of the Perseus Books Group

All rights reserved. Printed in the United States of America. No part of
this book may be reproduced in any manner whatsoever without written
permission except in the case of brief quotations embodied in critical
articles and reviews. For information, address Basic Books, 387 Park
Avenue South, New York, NY 10016-8810.

Designed by Ellen Levine

Library of Congress Control Number: 2002111010
ISBN-13 978-0-465-00802-5
ISBN-10 0-465-00802-X

06 07 08 / 13 12 11 10 9 8

Library Resource Center
Renton Technical College
3000 N.E. 4th St.
Renton, WA 98056

Contents

Preface to the Revised Edition

SINCE THE publication of *The Evolution of Desire* in 1994, the field has witnessed an avalanche of new scientific research on human mating. Although neglected within mainstream psychology for decades, mating is beginning to command the attention it properly deserves. Nothing lies closer to the reproductive engine of the evolutionary process. Those who fail to mate fail to become ancestors. Each living human, therefore, has descended from a long and unbroken line of successful mateships stretching back millions of years. If any one of our ancestors had failed to traverse the complex hurdles posed by mating, we would not be alive to ponder these improbable feats. Our mating minds—the glory of romance, the flush of passion, the triumph of love—are fortunate products of this evolutionary process.

The original publication of *Desire* was greeted with a gratifying amount of attention, but it also provoked some emotions. The intensity of sentiment probably reflects the importance of the topic. Humans don't seem well-designed for dispassionate intellectual discourse about domains that have profound personal relevance. Some readers told me before the book was even published that the information it contained should be suppressed. Some refused to believe that sex differences in mating strategies existed, since the dominant dogma in social science for years has contended that women and men are essentially identical in sexual psychology. Others acknowledged the formidable body of scientific findings, but refused to believe that sex differences have evolutionary origins. It is encouraging that the hostility to this work has largely, although certainly not entirely, subsided. Mating research has entered the mainstream and is now known throughout the world—the first edition of *The Evolution of Desire* was translated into ten languages.

Although the publication of *The Evolution of Desire* shed some light on previous mysteries of human mating, it also pointed to gaps in knowledge, notably those surrounding the complexities of female sexuality. Because research since the book's publication has filled some of the gaps, I embraced the opportunity to provide an updated revised edition of *Desire*. The two new chapters in the current edition—Chapters 11 and 12—highlight these recent developments.

Chapter 11, "Women's Hidden Sexual Strategies," begins with new research and theory on the possible functions of female orgasm and then proceeds to examine why women have affairs. The two issues turn out to be linked in ways previous theorists never envisioned. The second half of this chapter centers on whether women's menstrual cycles influence sexual strategies and whether men can detect when women ovulate. These intriguing domains of female sexuality were virtually unexplored when *The Evolution of Desire* was first published; now they require a full chapter.

Chapter 12, "Mysteries of Human Mating," examines some of the enduring puzzles that have baffled scientists for centuries. Why does homosexuality exist? Can men and women be "just friends"? Do men have adaptations to rape? Do women have evolved anti-rape defenses? Are men and women hopelessly biased in reading each other's minds? Although these topics were briefly discussed in the original edition, recent theory and research dictate a deeper examination.

I owe a heavy thanks to my research collaborators and former graduate students for some of the discoveries showcased in the two new chapters: Heidi Greiling and I collaborated on a raft of studies on the hidden side of women's sexuality. Work with Martie Haselton revealed some of the cognitive biases men and women display in making inferences about each other's mating minds. Work with April Bleske exposed an intriguing new answer to the question of whether men and women can be "just friends." Work with David Schmitt provided the first systematic studies of human mate poaching. Work with Todd Shackelford, and also with Kevin Bennett, Bram Buunk, Jae Choe, Mariko Hasegawa, Toshi Hasegawa, Lee Kirkpatrick, and Randy Larsen, explored the defenses against sexual treachery.

Many friends and colleagues, in addition to those thanked in the acknowledgments to the first edition, helped me in various ways with the new material presented in this revision: Rosalind Arden, Mike Bailey, April Bleske, Ruth Buss, Greg Cochran, Josh Duntley, Trish Ellis,

Paul Ewald, Steve Gangestad, Heidi Greiling, Martie Haselton, Kim Hill, Owen Jones, Craig Palmer, David Schmitt, Todd Shackelford, John Gottschall, and Randy Thornhill. Basic Books Executive Editor Jo Ann Miller helped with enthusiasm and guidance. Steve Pinker and Don Symons deserve special thanks for extraordinary feedback on virtually every aspect of the two new chapters.

David M. Buss
July 8, 2002

Acknowledgments
to the First Edition

DON SYMONS, the author of the most important treatise on the evolution of human sexuality in the twentieth century, guided the evolution of this book through his writings, friendship, and insightful commentary on each chapter. Leda Cosmides and John Tooby were fledgling graduate students at Harvard when I first met them in 1981, but they were already developing a grand theory of evolutionary psychology that profoundly influenced my own thinking about human mating strategies. Martin Daly and Margo Wilson had a seminal influence through their work on the evolution of sex and violence. I had the great fortune to collaborate with Martin, Margo, Leda, and John at the Center for Advanced Study in the Behavioral Sciences in Palo Alto, California, on a special project called Foundations of Evolutionary Psychology. That project formed the basis of this book.

I owe a major debt to my superlative research collaborators: Alois Angleitner, Armen Asherian, Mike Barnes, Mike Botwin, Michael Chen, Lisa Chiodo, Ken Craik, Lisa Dedden, Todd DeKay, Jack Demarest, Bruce Ellis, Mary Gomes, Arlette Greer, Heidi Greiling, Dolly Higgins, Tim Ketelaar, Karen Kleinsmith, Liisa Kyl-Heku, Randy Larsen, Karen Lauterbach, Anne McGuire, David Schmitt, Jennifer Semmelroth, Todd Shackelford, and Drew Westen.

The fifty worldwide collaborators on the international study deserve special thanks: M. Abbott, A. Angleitner, A. Asherian, A. Biaggio, A. Blanco-VillaSeñor, M. Bruchon-Schweitzer, Hai-yuan Ch'u, J. Czapinski, B. DeRaad, B. Ekehammar, M. Fioravanti, J. Georgas, P. Gjerde, R. Guttman, F. Hazan, S. Iwawaki, N. Janakiramaiah, F. Khosroshani, S. Kreitler, L. Lachenicht, M. Lee, K. Liik, B. Little, N. Lohamy, S.

Makim, S. Mika, M. Moadel-Shahid, G. Moane, M. Montero, A. C. Mundy-Castle, T. Niit, E. Nsenduluka, K. Peltzer, R. Pienkowski, A. Pirtilla-Backman, J. Ponce De Leon, J. Rousseau, M. A. Runco, M. P. Safir, C. Samuels, R. Santioso, R. Serpell, N. Smid, C. Spencer, M. Tadinac, E. N. Todorova, K. Troland, L. Van den Brande, G. Van Heck, L. Van Langenhove, and Kuo-Shu Yang.

Many friends and colleagues read drafts of this book and provided suggestions. Geoffrey Miller offered creative commentary on the entire book. John Alcock, Dick Alexander, Laura Betzig, Leda Cosmides, Martin Daly, Bill Durham, Steve Gangestad, Elizabeth Hill, Kim Hill, Doug Jones, Doug Kenrick, Bobbi Low, Neil Malamuth, Kathleen Much, Dan Ozer, Colleen Seifert, Jennifer Semmelroth, Barb Smuts, Valerie Stone, Frank Sulloway, Nancy Thornhill, Randy Thornhill, Peter Todd, John Tooby, Paul Turke, and Margo Wilson provided outstanding help with particular chapters.

My first editor, Susan Arellano, gave encouragement and editorial advice during the early stages. Jo Ann Miller's keen judgment and editorial aplomb marshaled the book to completion. Every writer should have the great fortune to benefit from the intellectual and editorial powers of Virginia LaPlante, who helped me to transform disorganized scribbles into readable prose and a miscellany of chapters into a coherent book.

A bounty of institutional support has blessed me. Harvard University gave me the time and resources to launch the international study. The University of Michigan offered support from the Psychology Department, thanks to Al Cain and Pat Gurin; from the Evolution and Human Behavior Program, thanks to Dick Alexander, Laura Betzig, Kim Hill, Warren Holmes, Bobbi Low, John Mitani, Randy Nesse, Barb Smuts, Nancy Thornhill, and Richard Wrangham; and from the Research Center for Group Dynamics at the Institute for Social Research, thanks to Eugene Burnstein, Nancy Cantor, Phoebe Ellsworth, James Hilton, James Jackson, Neil Malamuth, Hazel Markus, Dick Nisbett, and Bob Zajonc. Grants from the National Institute of Mental Health (MH-41593 and MH-44206) greatly aided the research. A fellowship during 1989–90 from the Center for Advanced Study in the Behavioral Sciences, including grants from the Gordon P. Getty Trust and National Science Foundation Grant BNS98-00864, gave me the time and intellectual atmosphere I needed to complete the first draft of this book.

1

Origins of Mating Behavior

We have never quite outgrown the idea that somewhere, there are people living in perfect harmony with nature and one another, and that we might do the same were it not for the corrupting influences of Western culture.
—Melvin Konner, *Why the Reckless Survive*

HUMAN MATING BEHAVIOR delights and amuses us and galvanizes our gossip, but it is also deeply disturbing. Few domains of human activity generate as much discussion, as many laws, or such elaborate rituals in all cultures. Yet the elements of human mating seem to defy understanding. Women and men sometimes find themselves choosing mates who abuse them psychologically and physically. Efforts to attract mates often backfire. Conflicts erupt within couples, producing downward spirals of blame and despair. Despite their best intentions and vows of lifelong love, half of all married couples end up divorcing.

Pain, betrayal, and loss contrast sharply with the usual romantic notions of love. We grow up believing in true love, in finding our "one and only." We assume that once we do, we will marry in bliss and live happily ever after. But reality rarely coincides with our beliefs. Even a cursory look at the divorce rate, the 30 to 50 percent incidence of extramarital affairs, and the jealous rages that rack so many relationships shatters these illusions.

Discord and dissolution in mating relationships are typically seen as signs of failure. They are regarded as distortions or perversions of the natural state of married life. They are thought to signal personal inadequacy, immaturity, neurosis, failure of will, or simply poor judgment in the choice of a mate. This view is radically wrong. Conflict in mating is the norm and not the exception. It ranges from a man's anger at a woman who declines his advances to a wife's frustration with a husband who fails to help in the home. Such a pervasive pattern defies easy explanation. Something deeper, more telling about human nature is involved—something we do not fully understand.

The problem is complicated by the centrality of love in human life. Feelings of love mesmerize us when we experience them and occupy our fantasies when we do not. The anguish of love dominates poetry, music, literature, soap operas, and romance novels more than perhaps any other theme. Contrary to common belief, love is not a recent invention of the Western leisure classes. People in all cultures experience love and have coined specific words for it.[1] Its pervasiveness convinces us that love, with its key components of commitment, tenderness, and passion, is an inevitable part of the human experience, within the grasp of everyone.[2]

Our failure to understand the real and paradoxical nature of human mating is costly, both scientifically and socially. Scientifically, the dearth of knowledge leaves unanswered some of life's most puzzling questions, such as why people sacrifice years of their lives to the quest for love and the struggle for relationship. Socially, our ignorance leaves us frustrated and helpless when we are bruised by mating behavior gone awry in the workplace, on the dating scene, and in our home.

We need to reconcile the profound love that humans seek with the conflict that permeates our most cherished relationships. We need to square our dreams with reality. To understand these baffling contradictions, we must gaze back into our evolutionary past—a past that has grooved and scored our minds as much as our bodies, our strategies for mating as much as our strategies for survival.

Evolutionary Roots

More than a century ago, Charles Darwin offered a revolutionary explanation for the mysteries of mating.[3] He had become intrigued by the puzzling way that animals had developed characteristics that would appear to hinder their survival. The elaborate plumage, large antlers, and other conspicuous features displayed by many species seemed costly in the currency of survival. He wondered how the brilliant plumage of peacocks could evolve, and become more common, when it poses such an obvious threat to survival, acting as an open lure to predators. Darwin's answer was that the peacock's displays evolved because they led to an individual's reproductive success, providing an advantage in the competition for a desirable mate and continuing that peacock's genetic line. The evolution of characteristics because of their reproductive benefits, rather than survival benefits, is known as sexual selection.

Sexual selection, according to Darwin, takes two forms. In one form, members of the same sex compete with each other, and the outcome of their contest gives the winner greater sexual access to members of the opposite sex. Two stags locking horns in combat is the prototypical image of this intrasexual competition. The characteristics that lead to success in contests of this kind, such as greater strength, intelligence, or attractiveness to allies, evolve because the victors are able to mate more often and hence pass on more genes. In the other type of sexual selection, members of one sex choose a mate based on their preferences for particular qualities in that mate. These characteristics evolve in the other sex because animals possessing them are chosen more often as mates, and their genes thrive. Animals lacking the desired characteristics are excluded from mating, and their genes perish. Since peahens prefer peacocks with plumage that flashes and glitters, dull-feathered males get left in the evolutionary dust. Peacocks today possess brilliant plumage because over evolutionary history peahens have preferred to mate with dazzling and colorful males.

Darwin's theory of sexual selection begins to explain mating behavior by identifying two key processes by which evolutionary change can occur: preferences for a mate and competition for a mate. But the theory was vigorously resisted by male scientists for over a century, in part because the active choosing of mates seemed to grant too much power to females, who were thought to remain passive in the mating process. The theory of sexual selection was also resisted by mainstream social scientists because its portrayal of human nature seemed to depend on instinctive behavior, and thus to minimize the uniqueness and flexibility of humans. Culture and consciousness were presumed to free us from evolutionary forces. The breakthrough in applying sexual selection to humans came in the late 1970s and 1980s, in the form of theoretical advances initiated by my colleagues and me in the fields of psychology and anthropology.[4] We tried to identify underlying psychological mechanisms that were the products of evolution—mechanisms that help to explain both the extraordinary flexibility of human behavior and the active mating strategies pursued by women and men. This new discipline is called evolutionary psychology.

When I began work in the field, however, little was known about actual human mating behavior. There was a frustrating lack of scientific evidence on mating in the broad array of human populations, and practically no documented support for grand evolutionary theorizing. No one knew whether some mating desires are universal, whether certain sex differences are characteristic of all people in all cultures, or whether culture exerts a powerful enough influence to override the evolved preferences that might exist. So I departed from the traditional path of mainstream psychology to explore which characteristics of human mating behavior would follow from evolutionary principles. In the beginning, I simply wanted to verify a few of the most obvious evolutionary predictions about sex differences in mating preferences; for example, whether men desire youth and physical attractiveness in a mate and whether women desire status and economic security. Toward that end, I interviewed and administered questionnaires to 186 married adults and 100 unmarried college students within the United States.

The next step was to verify whether the psychological phenomena uncovered by this study were characteristic of our species. If mating desires and other features of human psychology are products of our evolutionary history, they should be found universally, not just in the United States. So I initiated an international study to explore how mates are selected in other cultures, starting with a few European countries, including Germany and the Netherlands. I soon realized, however, that since European cultures share many features, they do not provide the most rigorous test for the principles of evolutionary psychology. Over a period of five years, I expanded the study to include fifty collaborators from thirty-seven cultures located on six continents and five islands, from Australia to Zambia. Local residents administered the questionnaire about mating desires in their native language. We sampled large cities, such as Rio de Janeiro and São Paulo in Brazil, Shanghai in China, Bangalore and Ahmadabad in India, Jerusalem and Tel Aviv in Israel, and Tehran in Iran. We also sampled rural peoples, including Indians in the state of Gujarat and Zulus in South Africa. We covered the well educated and the poorly educated. We included respondents of every age from fourteen through seventy, as well as places in the entire range of political systems from capitalist to communist and socialist. All major racial groups, religious groups, and ethnic groups were represented. In all, we surveyed 10,047 persons worldwide.

This study, the largest ever undertaken on human mating desires, was merely the beginning. The findings had implications that reached into every sphere of human mating life, from dating to marriage, extramarital affairs, and divorce. They were also relevant to major social issues of the day, such as sexual harassment, domestic abuse, pornography, and patriarchy. To explore as many mating domains as possible, I launched over fifty new studies, involving thousands of individuals. Included in these studies were men and women searching for a mate in singles bars and on college campuses, dating couples at various stages of commitment, newlywed couples in the first five years of marriage, and couples who ended up divorced.

The findings from all of these studies caused controversy and confusion among my colleagues, because in many respects they contradicted conventional thinking. They forced a radical shift from the standard view of men's and women's sexual psychology. One of my aims in this book is to formulate from these diverse findings a unified theory of human mating, based not on romantic notions or outdated scientific theories but on current scientific evidence. Much of what I discovered about human mating is not nice. In the ruthless pursuit of sexual goals, for example, men and women derogate their rivals, deceive members of the opposite sex, and even subvert their own mates. These discoveries are disturbing to me; I would prefer that the competitive, conflictual, and manipulative aspects of human mating did not exist. But a scientist cannot wish away unpleasant findings. Ultimately, the disturbing side of human mating must be confronted if its harsh consequences are ever to be ameliorated.

Sexual Strategies

Strategies are methods for accomplishing goals, the means for solving problems. It may seem odd to view human mating, romance, sex, and love as inherently strategic. But we never choose mates at random. We do not attract mates indiscriminately. We do not derogate our competitors out of boredom. Our mating is strategic, and our strategies are designed to solve particular problems for successful mating. Understanding how people solve those problems requires an analysis of sexual strategies. Strategies are essential for survival on the mating battlefield.

Adaptations are evolved solutions to the problems posed by survival and reproduction. Over millions of years of evolution, natural selection has produced in us hunger mechanisms to solve the problem of providing nutrients to the organism; taste buds that are sensitive to fat and sugar to solve the problem of what to put into our mouths (nuts and berries, but not dirt or gravel); sweat glands and shivering mechanisms to solve the problems of extreme hot and cold; emotions such as fear and rage that motivate flight and fight to combat predators or aggressive competitors; and a complex immune system to combat diseases and parasites. These adaptations are human solutions to the problems of existence posed by the hostile forces of nature—they are our survival strategies. Those who failed to develop appropriate characteristics failed to survive.

Correspondingly, sexual strategies are adaptive solutions to mating problems. Those in our evolutionary past who failed to mate successfully failed to become our ancestors. All of us descend from a long and unbroken line of ancestors who competed successfully for desirable mates, attracted mates who were reproductively valuable, retained mates long enough to reproduce, fended off interested rivals, and solved the problems that could have impeded reproductive success. We carry in us the sexual legacy of those success stories.

Each sexual strategy is tailored to a specific adaptive problem, such as identifying a desirable mate or besting competitors in attracting a mate. Underlying each sexual strategy are psychological mechanisms, such as preferences for a particular mate, feelings of love, desire for sex, or jealousy. Each psychological mechanism is sensitive to information or cues from the external world, such as physical features, signs of sexual interest, or hints of potential infidelity. Our psychological mechanisms are also sensitive to information about ourselves, such as our ability to attract a mate who has a certain degree of desirability. The goal of this book is to peel back the layers of adaptive problems that men and women have faced in the course of mating and uncover the complex sexual strategies they have evolved for solving them.

Although the term *sexual strategies* is a useful metaphor for thinking about solutions to mating problems, it is misleading in the sense of connoting conscious intent. Sexual strategies do not require conscious planning or awareness. Our sweat glands are "strategies" for accomplishing the goal of thermal regulation, but they require neither conscious planning nor awareness of the goal. Indeed, just as a piano player's sudden awareness of her hands may impede performance, most human sexual strategies are best carried out without the awareness of the actor.

Selecting a Mate

Nowhere do people have an equal desire for all members of the opposite sex. Everywhere some potential mates are preferred, others shunned. Our sexual desires have come into being in the same way as have other kinds of desires. Consider the survival problem of what food to eat. Humans are faced with a bewildering array of potential objects to ingest—berries, fruit, nuts, meat, dirt, gravel, poisonous plants, twigs, and feces. If we had no taste preferences and ingested objects from our environment at random, some people, by chance alone, would consume ripe fruit, fresh nuts, and other objects that provide caloric and nutritive sustenance. Others, also by chance alone, would eat rancid meat, rotten fruit, and toxins. Earlier humans who preferred nutritious objects survived.

Our actual food preferences bear out this evolutionary process. We show great fondness for substances rich in fat, sugar, protein, and salt and an aversion to substances that are bitter, sour, and toxic.[5] These food preferences solve a basic problem of survival. We carry them with us today precisely because they solved critical adaptive problems for our ancestors.

Our desires in a mate serve analogous adaptive purposes, but their functions do not center simply on survival. Imagine living as our ancestors did long ago—struggling to keep warm by the fire; hunting meat for our kin; gathering nuts, berries, and herbs; and avoiding dangerous animals and hostile humans. If we were to select a mate who failed to deliver the resources promised, who had affairs, who was lazy, who lacked hunting skills, or who heaped physical abuse on us, our survival would be tenuous, our reproduction at risk. In contrast, a mate who provided abundant resources, who protected us and our children, and who devoted time, energy, and effort to our family would be a great asset. As a result of the powerful survival and reproductive advantages that were reaped by those of our ancestors who chose a mate wisely, clear desires in a mate evolved. As descendants of those people, we carry their desires with us today.

Many other species have evolved mate preferences. The African village weaverbird provides a vivid illustration.[6] When the male weaverbird spots a female in the vicinity, he displays his recently built nest by suspending himself upside down from the bottom and vigorously flapping his wings. If the male passes this test, the female approaches the nest, enters it, and examines the nest materials, poking and pulling them for as long as ten minutes. As she makes her inspection, the male sings to her from nearby. At any point in this sequence she may decide that the nest does not meet her standards and depart to inspect another male's nest. A male whose nest is rejected by several females will often break it down and start over. By exerting a preference for males who can build a superior nest, the female weaverbird solves the problems of protecting and provisioning her future chicks. Her preferences have evolved because they bestowed a reproductive advantage over other weaverbirds who had no preferences and who mated with any males who happened along.

Women, like weaverbirds, prefer men with desirable "nests." Consider one of the problems that women in evolutionary history had to face: selecting a man who would be willing to commit to a long-term relationship. A woman in our evolutionary past who chose to mate with a man who was flighty, impulsive, philandering, or unable to sustain relationships found herself raising her children alone, without benefit of the resources, aid, and protection that another man might have offered. A woman who preferred to mate with a reliable man who was willing to commit to her was more likely to have children who survived and thrived. Over thousands of generations, a preference for men who showed signs of being willing and able to commit to them evolved in women, just as preferences for mates with adequate nests evolved in weaverbirds. This preference solved key reproductive problems, just as food preferences solved key survival problems.

People do not always desire the commitment required of long-term mating. Men and women sometimes deliberately seek a short-term fling, a temporary liaison, or a brief affair. And when they do, their preferences shift, sometimes dramatically. One of the crucial decisions for humans in selecting a mate is whether they are seeking a short-term mate or a long-term partner. The sexual strategies pursued hinge on this decision. This book documents the universal preferences that men and women display for particular characteristics in a mate, reveals the evolutionary logic behind the different desires of each sex, and explores the changes that occur when people shift their goal from casual sex to a committed relationship.

Attracting a Mate

People who possess desirable characteristics are in great demand. Appreciating their traits is not enough for successful mating, just as spying a ripe berry bush down a steep ravine is not enough for successful eating. The next step in mating is to compete successfully for a desirable mate.

Among the elephant seals on the coast of California, males during the mating season use their sharp tusks to best rival males in head-to-head combat.[7] Often their contests and bellowing continue day and night. The losers lie scarred and injured on the beach, exhausted victims of this brutal competition. But the winner's job is not yet over. He must roam the perimeter of his harem, which contains a dozen or more females. This dominant male must hold his place in life's reproductive cycle by herding stray females back into the harem and repelling other males who attempt to sneak copulations.

Over many generations, male elephant seals who are stronger, larger, and more cunning have succeeded in getting a mate. The larger, more aggressive males control the sexual access to females and so pass on to their sons the genes conferring these qualities. Indeed, males now weigh roughly 4,000 pounds, or four times the weight of females, who appear to human observers to risk getting crushed during copulation.

Female elephant seals prefer to mate with the victors and thus pass on the genes conferring this preference to their daughters. But by choosing the larger, stronger winners, they also determine the genes for size and fighting abilities that will live on in their sons. The smaller, weaker, and more timid males fail to mate entirely. They become evolutionary dead ends. Because only 5 percent of the males monopolize 85 percent of the females, selection pressures remain intense even today.

Male elephant seals must fight not just to best other males but also to be chosen by females. A female emits loud bellowing sounds when a smaller male tries to mate with her. The alerted dominant male comes bounding toward them, rears his head in threat, and exposes a massive chest. This gesture is usually enough to send the smaller male scurrying for cover. Female preferences are one key to establishing competition among the males. If females did not mind mating with smaller, weaker males, then they would not alert the dominant male, and there would be less intense selection pressure for size and strength. Female preferences, in short, determine many of the ground rules of the male contests.

People are not like elephant seals in most of these mating behaviors. For example, whereas only 5 percent of the male elephant seals do 85 percent of the mating, more than 90 percent of men are able at some point in their lives to find a mate.[8] Male elephant seals strive to monopolize harems of females, and the winners remain victorious for only a season or two, whereas many humans form enduring unions that last for years and decades. But men and male elephant seals share a key characteristic: both must compete to attract females. Males who fail to attract females risk being shut out of mating.

Throughout the animal world, males typically compete more fiercely than females for mates, and in many species males are certainly more ostentatious and strident in their competition. But competition among females is also intense in many species. Among patas monkeys and gelada baboons, females harass copulating pairs in order to interfere with the mating success of rival females. Among wild rhesus monkeys, females use aggression to interrupt sexual contact between other females and males, occasionally winning the male consort for herself. And among savanna baboons, female competition over mates serves not merely to secure sexual access but also to develop long-term social relationships that provide physical protection.[9]

Competition among women, though typically less florid and violent than competition among men, pervades human mating systems. The writer H. L. Mencken noted: "When women kiss, it always reminds one of prize fighters shaking hands." This book shows how members of each sex compete with each other for access to members of the opposite sex. The tactics they use to compete are often dictated by the preferences of the opposite sex. Those who do not have what the other sex wants risk remaining on the sidelines in the dance of mating.

Keeping a Mate

Keeping a mate is another important adaptive problem; mates may continue to be desirable to rivals, who may poach, thereby undoing all the effort devoted to attracting, courting, and committing to the mate. Furthermore, one mate may defect because of the failure of the other to fulfill his or her needs and wants or upon the arrival of someone fresher, more compelling, or more beautiful. Mates, once gained, must be retained.

Consider the *Plecia nearctica,* an insect known as the lovebug. Male lovebugs swarm during the early morning and hover a foot or two off the ground, waiting for the chance to mate with a female.[10] Female lovebugs do not swarm or hover. Instead, they emerge in the morning from the vegetation and enter the swarm of males. Sometimes a female is captured by a male before she can take flight. Males often wrestle with other males, and as many as ten males may cluster around a single female.

The successful male departs from the swarm with his mate, and the couple glides to the ground to copulate. Perhaps because other males continue to attempt to mate with her, the male retains his copulatory embrace for as long as three full days—hence the nickname "lovebug." The prolonged copulation itself functions as a way of guarding the mate. By remaining attached to the female until she is ready to deposit her eggs, the male lovebug prevents other males from fertilizing her eggs. In reproductive currency, his ability to compete with other males and attract a female would be for naught if he failed to solve the problem of retaining his mate.

Different species solve this problem by different means. Humans do not engage in continuous copulatory embraces for days, but the problem of holding on to a mate is confronted by everyone who seeks a long-term relationship. In our evolutionary past, men who were indifferent to the sexual infidelities of their mates risked compromising their paternity. They risked investing time, energy, and effort in children who were not their own. Ancestral women, in contrast, did not risk the loss of parenthood if their mates had affairs, because maternity has always been 100 percent certain. But a woman with a philandering husband risked losing his resources, his commitment, and his investment in her children. One psychological strategy that evolved to combat infidelity was jealousy. Ancestral people who became enraged at signs of their mate's potential defection and who acted to prevent it had a selective advantage over those who were not jealous. People who failed to prevent infidelity in a mate had less reproductive success.[11]

The emotion of jealousy motivates various kinds of action in overt response to a threat to the relationship. Sexual jealousy, for example, may produce either of two radically different actions, vigilance or violence. In one case, a jealous man might follow his wife when she goes out, call her unexpectedly to see whether she is where she said she would be, keep an eye on her at a party, or read her mail. These actions represent vigilance. In the other case, a man might threaten a rival whom he spotted with his wife, beat the rival with his fists, get his friends to beat up the rival, or throw a brick through the rival's window. These actions represent violence. Both courses of action, vigilance and violence, are different manifestations of the same psychological strategy of jealousy. They represent alternative ways of solving the problem of the defection of a mate.

Jealousy is not a rigid, invariant instinct that drives robotlike, mechanical action. It is highly sensitive to context and environment. Many other behavioral options are available to serve the strategy of jealousy, giving humans a flexibility in tailoring their responses to the subtle nuances of a situation. This book documents the range of actions that are triggered by jealousy and the contexts in which they occur.

Replacing a Mate

Not all mates can be retained, nor should they be. Sometimes there are compelling reasons to get rid of a mate, such as when a mate stops providing support, withdraws sex, or starts inflicting physical abuse. Those who remain with a mate through economic hardship, sexual infidelity, and cruelty may win our admiration for their loyalty. But staying with a bad mate does not help a person successfully pass on genes. We are the descendants of those who knew when to cut their losses.

Getting rid of a mate has precedent in the animal world. Ring doves, for example, are generally monogamous from one breeding season to the next, but they break up under certain circumstances. The doves experience a divorce rate of about 25 percent every season; the major reason for breaking their bond is infertility.[12] When a ring dove fails to produce chicks with one partner during a breeding season, he or she leaves the mate and searches for another. Losing an infertile mate serves the goal of reproduction for ring doves better than remaining in a barren union.

Just as we have evolved sexual strategies to select, attract, and keep a good mate, we have also evolved strategies for jettisoning a bad mate. Divorce is a human universal that occurs in all known cultures.[13] Our separation strategies involve a variety of psychological mechanisms. We have ways to assess whether the costs inflicted by a mate outweigh the benefits provided. We scrutinize other potential partners and evaluate

Renton Tech Coll Library

whether they might offer more than our current mate. We gauge the likelihood of successfully attracting other desirable partners. We calculate the potential damage that might be caused to ourselves, our children, and our kin by the dissolution of the relationship. And we combine all this information into a decision to stay or leave.

Once a mate decides to leave, another set of psychological strategies is activated. Because such decisions have complex consequences for two sets of extended kin who often have keen interests in the union, breaking up is neither simple nor effortless. These complex social relationships must be negotiated, the breakup justified. The range of tactical options within the human repertoire is enormous, from simply packing one's bags and walking away to provoking a rift by revealing an infidelity.

Breaking up is a solution to the problem of a bad mate, but it opens up the new problem of replacing that mate. Like most mammals, humans typically do not mate with a single person for an entire lifetime. Humans often reenter the mating market and repeat the cycle of selection, attraction, and retention. But starting over after a breakup poses its own unique set of problems. People reenter the mating market at a different age and with different assets and liabilities. Increased resources and status may help one to attract a mate who was previously out of range. Alternatively, older age and children from a previous mateship may detract from one's ability to attract a new mate.

Men and women undergo predictably different changes as they divorce and reenter the mating market. If there are children, the woman often takes primary responsibility for child rearing. Because children from previous unions are usually seen as costs rather than benefits when it comes to mating, a woman's ability to attract a desirable mate often suffers relative to a man's. Consequently, fewer divorced women than men remarry, and this difference between the sexes gets larger with increasing age. This book documents the changing patterns of human mating over a lifetime and identifies circumstances that affect the likelihood of remating for men and women.

Conflict between the Sexes

The sexual strategies that members of one sex pursue to select, attract, keep, or replace a mate often have the unfortunate consequence of creating a conflict with members of the other sex. Among the scorpionfly, a female refuses to copulate with a courting male unless he brings her a substantial nuptial gift, which is typically a dead insect to be consumed.[14] While the female eats the nuptial gift, the male copulates with

Renton Tech Coll Library

her. During copulation, the male maintains a loose grasp on the nuptial gift, as if to prevent the female from absconding with it before copulation is complete. It takes the male twenty minutes of continuous copulation to deposit all his sperm into the female. Male scorpionflies have evolved the ability to select a nuptial gift that takes the female approximately twenty minutes to consume. If the gift is smaller and is consumed before copulation is completed, the female casts off the male before he has deposited all his sperm. If the gift is larger and takes the female more than twenty minutes to consume, the male completes copulation, and the two then fight over the leftovers. Conflict between male and female scorpionflies thus occurs over whether he gets to complete copulation when the gift is too small and over who gets to use the residual food resources when the gift is larger than needed.

Men and women also clash over resources and sexual access. In the evolutionary psychology of human mating, the sexual strategy adopted by one sex can trip up and conflict with the strategy adopted by the other sex in a phenomenon called strategic interference. Consider the differences in men's and women's proclivities to seek brief or lasting sexual relations. Men and women typically differ in how long and how well they need to know someone before they consent to sexual intercourse. Although there are many exceptions and individual differences, men generally have lower thresholds for seeking sex.[15] For example, men often express the desire and willingness to have sex with an attractive stranger, whereas women almost invariably refuse anonymous encounters and prefer some degree of commitment.

There is a fundamental conflict between these different sexual strategies: men cannot fulfill their short-term wishes without simultaneously interfering with women's long-term goals. An insistence on immediate sex interferes with the requirement for a prolonged courtship. The interference is reciprocal, since prolonged courting also obstructs the goal of ready sex. Whenever the strategy adopted by one sex interferes with the strategy adopted by the other sex, conflict ensues.

Conflicts do not end with the wedding vows. Married women complain that their husbands are condescending, emotionally constricted, and unreliable. Married men complain that their wives are moody, overly dependent, and sexually withholding. Both sexes complain about infidelities, ranging from mild flirtations to serious affairs. All of these conflicts become understandable in the context of our evolved mating strategies.

Although conflict between the sexes is pervasive, it is not inevitable. There are conditions that minimize conflict and produce harmony between the sexes. Knowledge of our evolved sexual strategies gives us tremendous power to better our own lives by choosing actions and contexts that activate some strategies and deactivate others. Indeed, understanding sexual strategies, including the cues that trigger them, is one step toward the reduction of conflict between men and women. This book explores the nature of conflict and offers some solutions for fostering harmony between the sexes.

Culture and Context

Although ancestral selection pressures are responsible for creating the mating strategies we use today, our current conditions differ from the historical conditions under which those strategies evolved. Ancestral people got their vegetables from gathering and their meat from hunting, whereas modern people get their food from supermarkets and restaurants. Similarly, modern urban people today deploy their mating strategies in singles bars, at parties, through computer networks, and by means of dating services rather than on the savanna, in protected caves, or around primitive campfires. Whereas modern conditions of mating differ from ancestral conditions, the same sexual strategies operate with unbridled force. Our evolved psychology of mating remains. It is the only mating psychology we have; it just gets played out in a modern environment.

To illustrate, look at the foods consumed in massive quantities at fast food chains. We have not evolved any genes for McDonald's, but the foods we eat there reveal the ancestral strategies for survival we carry with us today.[16] We consume in vast quantities fat, sugar, protein, and salt in the form of burgers, shakes, french fries, and pizzas. Fast food chains are popular precisely because they serve these elements in concentrated quantities. They reveal the food preferences that evolved in a past environment of scarcity. Today, however, we overconsume these elements because of their evolutionarily unprecedented abundance, and the old survival strategies now hurt our health. We are stuck with the taste preferences that evolved under different conditions, because evolution works on a time scale too slow to keep up with the radical changes of the past several hundred years. Although we cannot go back in time and observe directly what those ancestral conditions were, our current taste preferences, like our fear of snakes and our fondness for children, provide a window for viewing what those conditions must have been. We carry with us equipment that was designed for an ancient world.

Our evolved mating strategies, just like our survival strategies, may be currently maladaptive in the currencies of survival and reproduction. The advent of AIDS, for example, renders casual sex far more dangerous to survival than it ever was under ancestral conditions. Only by understanding our evolved sexual strategies, where they came from and what conditions they were designed to deal with, can we hope to change our current course.

One impressive advantage humans have over many other species is that our repertoire of mating strategies is large and highly sensitive to context. Consider the problem of being in an unhappy marriage and contemplating a decision to get divorced. This decision will depend upon many complex factors, such as the amount of conflict within the marriage, whether one's mate is philandering, the pressure applied by relatives on both sides of the family, the presence of children, the ages and needs of the children, and the prospects for attracting another mate. Humans have evolved psychological mechanisms that consider and weigh the costs and benefits of these crucial features of context.

Not only individual but also cultural circumstances vary in ways that are critical for evoking particular sexual strategies from the entire human repertoire. Some cultures have mating systems that are polygynous, allowing men to take multiple wives. Other cultures are polyandrous, allowing women to take multiple husbands. Still others are monogamous, restricting both sexes to one marriage partner at a time. And others are promiscuous, with a high rate of mate switching. Our evolved strategies of mating are highly sensitive to these legal and cultural patterns. In polygynous mating systems, for example, parents place tremendous pressure on their sons to compete for women in an apparent attempt to avoid the mateless state that plagues some men when others monopolize multiple women.[17] In monogamous mating cultures, in contrast, parents put less pressure on their sons' strivings.

Another important contextual factor is the ratio of the sexes, or the number of available men relative to available women. When there is a surplus of women, such as among the Ache Indians of Paraguay, men become more reluctant to commit to one woman, preferring instead to pursue many casual relationships. When there is a surplus of men, such as in contemporary cities of China and among the Hiwi tribe of Venezuela, monogamous marriage is the rule and divorce rates plummet.[18] As men's sexual strategies shift, so must women's, and vice versa. The two sets coexist in a complex reciprocal relation, based in part on the sex ratio.

From one perspective, context is everything. Contexts that recurred over evolutionary time created the strategies we carry with us now. Current contexts and cultural conditions determine which strategies get activated and which lie dormant. To understand human sexual strategies, this book identifies the recurrent selection pressures or adaptive problems of the past, the psychological mechanisms or strategic solutions they created, and the current contexts that activate some solutions rather than others.

Barriers to Understanding Human Sexuality

Evolutionary theory has appalled and upset people since Darwin first proposed it in 1859 to explain the creation and organization of life. Lady Ashley, his contemporary, remarked upon hearing about his theory of our descent from nonhuman primates: "Let's hope that it's not true; and if it is true, let's hope that it does not become widely known." Strenuous resistance continues to this day. These barriers to understanding must be removed if we are to gain real insight into our sexuality.

One barrier is perceptual. Our cognitive and perceptual mechanisms have been designed by natural selection to perceive and think about events that occur in a relatively limited time-span—over seconds, minutes, hours, days, sometimes months, and occasionally years. Ancestral humans spent most of their time solving immediate problems, such as finding food, maintaining a shelter, keeping warm, selecting and competing for partners, protecting children, forming alliances, striving for status, and defending against marauders, so there was pressure to think in the short term. Evolution, in contrast, occurs gradually over thousands of generations in tiny increments that we cannot observe directly. To understand events that occur on time scales this large requires a leap of the imagination, much like the cognitive feats of physicists who theorize about black holes and eleven-dimensional universes they cannot see.

Another barrier to understanding the evolutionary psychology of human mating is ideological. From Spencer's theory of social Darwinism onward, biological theories have sometimes been used for political ends—to justify oppression, to argue for racial or sexual superiority. The history of misusing biological explanations of human behavior, however, does not justify jettisoning the most powerful theory of organic life we have. To understand human mating requires that we face our evolutionary heritage boldly and understand ourselves as products of that heritage.

Another basis of resistance to evolutionary psychology is the naturalistic fallacy, which maintains that whatever exists should exist. The naturalistic fallacy confuses a scientific description of human behavior with a moral prescription for that behavior. In nature, however, there are diseases, plagues, parasites, infant mortality, and a host of other natural events which we try to eliminate or reduce. The fact that they do exist in nature does not imply that they should exist.

Similarly, male sexual jealousy, which evolved as a psychological strategy to protect men's certainty of their paternity, is known to cause damage to women worldwide in the form of wife battering and homicide.[19] As a society, we may eventually develop methods for reducing male sexual jealousy and its dangerous manifestations. Because there is an evolutionary origin for male sexual jealousy does not mean that we must condone or perpetuate it. Judgments of what should exist rest with people's value systems, not with science or with what currently exists.

The naturalistic fallacy has its reverse, the antinaturalistic fallacy. Some people have exalted visions of what it means to be human. According to one of these views, "natural" humans are at one with nature, peacefully coexisting with plants, animals, and each other. War, aggression, and competition are seen as corruptions of this essentially peaceful human nature by current conditions, such as patriarchy or capitalism. Despite the evidence, people cling to these illusions. When the anthropologist Napoleon Chagnon documented that 25 percent of all Yanomamö Indian men die violent deaths at the hands of other Yanomamö men, his work was bitterly denounced by those who had presumed the group to live in harmony.[20] The antinaturalistic fallacy occurs when we see ourselves through the lens of utopian visions of what we want people to be.

Opposition also arises to the presumed implications of evolutionary psychology for change. If a mating strategy is rooted in evolutionary biology, it is thought to be immutable, intractable, and unchangeable; we are therefore doomed to follow the dictates of our biological mandate, like blind, unthinking robots. This belief mistakenly divides human behavior into two separate categories, one biologically determined and the other environmentally determined. In fact, human action is inexorably a product of both. Every strand of DNA unfolds within a particular environmental and cultural context. Within each person's life, social and physical environments provide input to the evolved psychological mechanisms, and every behavior is without exception a joint product of those mechanisms and their environmental influences. Evolutionary psychology represents a true interactionist view, which identifies the historical, developmental, cultural, and situational features that formed human psychology and guide that psychology today.

All behavior patterns can in principle be altered by environmental intervention. The fact that currently we can alter some patterns and not others is a problem only of knowledge and technology. Advances in knowledge bring about new possibilities for change, if change is desired. Humans are extraordinarily sensitive to changes in their environment, because natural selection did not create in humans invariant instincts that manifest themselves in behavior regardless of context. Identifying the roots of mating behavior in evolutionary biology does not doom us to an unalterable fate.

Another form of resistance to evolutionary psychology comes from the feminist movement. Many feminists worry that evolutionary explanations imply an inequality between the sexes, support restrictions on the roles that men and women can adopt, encourage stereotypes about the sexes, perpetuate the exclusion of women from power and resources, and foster pessimism about the possibilities for changing the status quo. For these reasons, feminists sometimes reject evolutionary accounts.

Yet evolutionary psychology does not carry these feared implications for human mating. In evolutionary terms, men and women are identical in many or most domains, differing only in the limited areas in which they have faced recurrently different adaptive problems over human evolutionary history. For example, they diverge primarily in their preference for a particular sexual strategy, not in their innate ability to exercise the full range of human sexual strategies.

Evolutionary psychology strives to illuminate men's and women's evolved mating behavior, not to prescribe what the sexes could be or should be. Nor does it offer prescriptions for appropriate sex roles. It has no political agenda. Indeed, if I have any political stance on issues related to the theory, it is the hope for equality among all persons regardless of sex, regardless of race, and regardless of preferred sexual strategy; a tolerance for the diversity of human sexual behavior; and a belief that evolutionary theory should not be erroneously interpreted as implying genetic or biological determinism or impermeability to environmental influences.

A final source of resistance to evolutionary psychology comes from the idealistic views of romance, sexual harmony, and lifelong love to which we all cling. I cleave tightly to these views myself, believing that love has a central place in human sexual psychology. Mating relationships provide some of life's deepest satisfactions, and without them life would seem empty. After all, some people do manage to live happily ever after. But we have ignored the truth about human mating for too long. Conflict, competition, and manipulation also pervade human mating, and we must lift our collective heads from the sand to see them if we are to understand life's most engrossing relationships.

2

What Women Want

We are walking archives of ancestral wisdom.
—Helena Cronin, *The Ant and the Peacock*

WHAT WOMEN ACTUALLY WANT in a mate has puzzled male scientists and other men for centuries, for good reason. It is not androcentric to propose that women's preferences in a partner are more complex and enigmatic than the mate preferences of either sex of any other species. Discovering the evolutionary roots of women's desires requires going far back in time, before humans evolved as a species, before primates emerged from their mammalian ancestors, back to the origins of sexual reproduction itself.

One reason women exert choice about mates stems from the most basic fact of reproductive biology—the definition of sex. It is a remarkable circumstance that what defines biological sex is simply the size of the sex cells. Males are defined as the ones with the small sex cells, females as the ones with the large sex cells. The large female gametes remain reasonably stationary and come loaded with nutrients. The small male gametes are endowed with mobility and swimming speed.[1] Along with differences in the size and mobility of sex cells comes a difference between the sexes in quantity. Men, for example, produce millions of sperm, which are replenished at a rate of roughly twelve million per hour, while women produce a fixed and unreplenishable lifetime supply of approximately four hundred ova.

Women's greater initial investment does not end with the egg. Fertilization and gestation, key components of human parental investment, occur internally within women. One act of sexual intercourse, which requires minimal male investment, can produce an obligatory and energy-consuming nine-month investment by the woman that forecloses other mating opportunities. Women then bear the exclusive burden of lactation, an investment that may last as long as three or four years.

No biological law of the animal world dictates that women invest more than men. Indeed, among some species, such as the Mormon cricket, pipefish seahorse, and Panamanian poison arrow frog, males invest more.[2] The male Mormon cricket produces through great effort a large spermatophore that is loaded with nutrients. Females compete with each other for access to the males that hold the largest spermatophores. Among these so-called sex-role reversed species, it is the males who are more discriminating about mating. Among all four thousand species of mammals, including the more than two hundred species of primates, however, females bear the burden of internal fertilization, gestation, and lactation.

The great initial parental investment of women makes them a valuable, but limited, resource.[3] Gestating, bearing, nursing, nurturing, and protecting a child are exceptional reproductive resources that cannot be allocated indiscriminately. Nor can one woman dispense them to many men.

Those who hold valuable resources do not give them away cheaply or unselectively. Because women in our evolutionary past risked enormous investment as a consequence of having sex, evolution favored women who were highly selective about their mates. Ancestral women suffered severe costs if they were indiscriminate—they experienced lower reproductive success, and fewer of their children survived to reproductive age. A man in human evolutionary history could walk away from a casual coupling having lost only a few hours of time. His reproductive success was not seriously compromised. A woman in evolutionary history could also walk away from a casual encounter, but if she got pregnant as a result, she bore the costs of that decision for months, years, and even decades afterward.

Modern birth control technology has altered these costs. In today's industrial nations, women can have short-term dalliances with less fear of pregnancy. But human sexual psychology evolved over millions of years to cope with ancestral adaptive problems. We still possess this underlying sexual psychology, even though our environment has changed.

Components of Desire

Consider the case of an ancestral woman who is trying to decide between two men, one of whom shows great generosity with his resources to her and one of whom is stingy. Other things being equal, the generous man is more valuable to her than the stingy man. The generous man may share his meat from the hunt, aiding her survival.

He may sacrifice his time, energy, and resources for the benefit of the children, furthering the woman's reproductive success. In these respects, the generous man has higher value as a mate than the stingy man. If, over evolutionary time, generosity in men provided these benefits repeatedly and the cues to a man's generosity were observable and reliable, then selection would favor the evolution of a preference for generosity in a mate.

Now consider a more complicated and realistic case in which men vary not just in their generosity but also in a bewildering variety of ways that are significant to the choice of a mate. Men vary in their physical prowess, athletic skill, ambition, industriousness, kindness, empathy, emotional stability, intelligence, social skills, sense of humor, kin network, and position in the status hierarchy. Men also differ in the costs they impose on a mating relationship: some come with children, bad debts, a quick temper, a selfish disposition, and a tendency to be promiscuous. In addition, men differ in hundreds of ways that may be irrelevant to women. Some men have navels turned in, others have navels turned out. A strong preference for a particular navel shape would be unlikely to evolve unless male navel differences were somehow adaptively relevant to ancestral women. From among the thousands of ways in which men differ, selection over hundreds of thousands of years focused women's preferences laser-like on the most adaptively valuable characteristics.

The qualities people prefer, however, are not static characteristics. Because characteristics change, mate seekers must gauge the future potential of a prospective partner. A young medical student who lacks resources now might have excellent future promise. Or a man might be very ambitious but have already reached his peak. Another man might have children from a previous marriage, but because they are about to leave the nest, they will not drain his resources. Gauging a man's mating value requires looking beyond his current position and evaluating his potential.

Evolution has favored women who prefer men who possess attributes that confer benefits and who dislike men who possess attributes that impose costs. Each separate attribute constitutes one component of a man's value to a woman as a mate. Each of her preferences tracks one component.

Preferences that favor particular components, however, do not completely solve the problem of choosing a mate. Women face further adaptive hurdles. First, a woman must evaluate her unique circumstances and personal needs. The same man might differ in value for different women. A man's willingness to do a lot of direct child care, for example, might be more valuable to a woman who does not have kin around to help her than to a woman whose mother, sisters, aunts, and uncles eagerly participate. The dangers of choosing a man with a volatile temper may be greater for a woman who is an only child than for a woman with four strapping brothers around to protect her. The value of potential mates, in short, depends on the individualized, personalized, and contextualized perspective of the person doing the choosing.

In selecting a mate, women must identify and correctly evaluate the cues that signal whether a man indeed possesses a particular resource. The assessment problem becomes especially acute in areas where men are apt to deceive women, such as pretending to have higher status than they do or feigning greater commitment than they are willing to give.

Finally, women face the problem of integrating their knowledge about a prospective mate. Suppose that one man is generous but emotionally unstable. Another man is emotionally stable but stingy. Which man should a woman choose? Choosing a mate calls upon psychological mechanisms that make it possible to evaluate the relevant attributes and give each its appropriate weight in the whole. Some attributes are granted more weight than others in the final decision about whether to choose or reject a particular man. One of these heavily weighted components is the man's resources.

Economic Capacity

The evolution of the female preference for males who offer resources may be the most ancient and pervasive basis for female choice in the animal kingdom. Consider the gray shrike, a bird that lives in the Negev Desert of Israel.[4] Just before the start of the breeding season, male shrikes begin amassing caches of edible prey, such as snails, and other useful objects, such as feathers and pieces of cloth, in numbers ranging from 90 to 120. They impale these items on thorns and other pointed projections within their territory. Females look over the available males and prefer to mate with those having the largest caches. When the biologist Reuven Yosef arbitrarily removed portions of some males' caches and added edible objects to others, females shifted to the males with the larger bounties. Females avoided entirely males without resources, consigning them to bachelorhood. Wherever females show a mating preference, the male's resources are often the key criterion.

Among humans, the evolution of women's preference for a permanent mate with resources would have required three preconditions. First, resources would have had to be accruable, defensible, and controllable by men during human evolutionary history. Second, men would have had to differ from each other in their holdings and their willingness to invest those holdings in a woman and her children—if all men possessed the same resources and showed an equal willingness to commit them, there would be no need for women to develop the preference for them. Constants do not count in mating decisions. And third, the advantages of being with one man would have to outweigh the advantages of being with several men.

Among humans, these conditions are easily met. Territory and tools, to name just two resources, are acquired, defended, monopolized, and controlled by men worldwide. Men vary tremendously in the quantity of resources they command—from the poverty of the street bum to the riches of Trumps and Rockefellers. Men also differ widely in how willing they are to invest their time and resources in long-term mateships. Some men are cads, preferring to mate with many women while investing little in each. Other men are dads, channeling all of their resources to one woman and her children.[5]

Women over human evolutionary history could often garner far more resources for their children through a single spouse than through several temporary sex partners. Men provide their wives and children with resources to an extent that is unprecedented among primates. Among most other primate species, for example, females must rely solely on their own efforts to acquire food, because males usually do not share food with their mates.[6] Men, in contrast, provide food, find shelter, and defend territory. Men protect children. They tutor them in the art of hunting, the craft of war, the strategies of social influence. They transfer status, aiding offspring in forming reciprocal alliances later in life. Such benefits are unlikely to be secured by a woman from a temporary sex partner. Not all potential husbands can confer all of these benefits, but over thousands of generations, when some men were able to provide some of these benefits, women gained a powerful advantage by preferring them as mates.

So the stage was set for women to evolve a preference for men with resources. But women needed cues to signal a man's possession of those resources. These cues might be indirect, such as personality characteristics that signaled a man's upward mobility. They might be physical, such as a man's athletic ability or health. They might include reputational information, such as the esteem in which a man was held by his peers. Economic resources, however, provide the most direct cue.

Women's current mate preferences provide a window for viewing our mating past, just as our fears of snakes and heights provide a window for viewing ancestral hazards. Evidence from dozens of studies documents that modern American women indeed value economic resources in mates substantially more than men do. In a study conducted in 1939, for example, American men and women rated eighteen characteristics for their relative desirability in a mate or marriage partner, ranging from irrelevant to indispensable. Women did not view good financial prospects as absolutely indispensable, but they did rate them as important. Men rated them as merely desirable but not very important. Women in 1939 valued good financial prospects in a mate about twice as highly as men, and this finding was replicated in 1956 and again in 1967.[7]

The sexual revolution of the late 1960s and early 1970s failed to change this sex difference. In an attempt to replicate the studies from earlier decades, I surveyed 1,491 Americans in the mid-1980s using the same questionnaire. Women and men from Massachusetts, Michigan, Texas, and California rated eighteen personal characteristics for their value in a marriage partner. As in the previous decades, women still value good financial prospects in a mate roughly twice as much as men do.[8]

The premium that women place on economic resources has been revealed in many contexts. The psychologist Douglas Kenrick and his colleagues devised a useful method for revealing how much people value different attributes in a marriage partner; they asked men and women to indicate the "minimum percentiles" of each characteristic that they would find acceptable.[9] The percentile concept was explained with such examples as: "A person at the 50th percentile would be above 50% of the other people on earning capacity, and below 49% of the people on this dimension." American college women indicate that their minimum acceptable percentile for a husband on earning capacity is the 70th percentile, or above 70 percent of all other men, whereas men's minimum acceptable percentile for a wife's earning capacity is only the 40th.

Personal ads in newspapers and magazines confirm that women who are actually in the marriage market desire financial resources. A study of 1,111 personal ads found that female advertisers seek financial resources roughly eleven times as often as male advertisers do.[10] In short, sex differences in a preference for resources are not limited to college students and are not bound by the method of inquiry.

Nor are these female preferences restricted to America, or to Western societies, or to capitalist countries. The international study on choosing a mate conducted by my colleagues and me documented the universality of women's preferences. For over five years from 1984 to 1989, in thirty-seven cultures on six continents and five islands, we investigated populations that varied on many demographic and cultural characteristics. The participants came from nations that practice polygyny, such as Nigeria and Zambia, as well as nations that are more monogamous, such as Spain and Canada. The countries included those in which living together is as common as marriage, such as Sweden and Finland, as well as countries in which living together without marriage is frowned upon, such as Bulgaria and Greece. In all, the study sampled 10,047 individuals.[11]

Male and female participants in the study rated the importance of eighteen characteristics in a potential mate or marriage partner, on a scale from unimportant to indispensable. Women across all continents, all political systems (including socialism and communism), all racial groups, all religious groups, and all systems of mating (from intense polygyny to presumptive monogamy) place more value than men on good financial prospects. Overall, women value financial resources about 100 percent more than men do, or roughly twice as much. There are some cultural variations. Women from Nigeria, Zambia, India, Indonesia, Iran, Japan, Taiwan, Colombia, and Venezuela value good financial prospects a bit more than women from South Africa (Zulus), the Netherlands, and Finland. In Japan, for example, women value good financial prospects roughly 150 percent more than men do, whereas women from the Netherlands deem financial prospects only 36 percent more important than their male counterparts do, or less than women from any other country. Nonetheless, the sex difference remained invariant—women worldwide desire financial resources in a marriage partner more than men.

These findings provide the first extensive cross-cultural evidence supporting the evolutionary basis for the psychology of human mating. Because ancestral women faced the tremendous burdens of internal fertilization, a nine-month gestation, and lactation, they would have benefited tremendously by selecting mates who possessed resources. These preferences helped our ancestral mothers solve the adaptive problems of survival and reproduction.

Social Status

Traditional hunter-gatherer societies, which are our closest guide to what ancestral conditions were probably like, suggest that ancestral men had clearly defined status hierarchies, with resources flowing freely to those at the top and trickling slowly to those at the bottom.[12] Traditional tribes today, such as the Tiwi, an aboriginal group residing on two small islands off the coast of Northern Australia; the Yanomamö of Venezuela; the Ache of Paraguay; and the !Kung tribe of Botswana, are replete with people described as "head men" and "big men" who wield great power and enjoy the resource privileges of prestige. Therefore, an ancestral man's social status would provide a powerful cue to his possession of resources.

Henry Kissinger once remarked that power is the most potent aphrodisiac. Women desire men who command a high position in society because social status is a universal cue to the control of resources. Along with status come better food, more abundant territory, and superior health care. Greater social status bestows on children social opportunities missed by the children of lower-ranked males. For male children worldwide, access to more mates and better quality mates typically accompanies families of higher social status. In one study of 186 societies ranging from the Mbuti Pygmies of Africa to the Aleut Eskimos, high-status men invariably had greater wealth, better nourishment for children, and more wives.[13]

Women in the United States do not hesitate to express a preference for mates who have high social status or a high-status profession, qualities that are viewed as only slightly less important than good financial prospects.[14] Using a rating scale from irrelevant or unimportant to indispensable, American women from Massachusetts, Michigan, Texas, and California rate social status as between important and indispensable, whereas men rate it as merely desirable but not very important. In one study of 5,000 college students, women list status, prestige, rank, position, power, standing, station, and high place as important considerably more frequently than men do.[15]

David Schmitt and I conducted a study of temporary and permanent mating in order to discover which characteristics people especially value in potential spouses, as contrasted with potential sex partners. Participants were female and male college students from the University of Michigan, a population for which both casual and marital mating issues are highly relevant. Several hundred individuals rated sixty-seven characteristics for their desirability or undesirability in the short or long term. Women judge the likelihood of success in a profession and the possession of a promising career to be highly desirable in a spouse. Significantly, these cues to future status are seen by women as more desirable in spouses than in casual sex partners.

American women also place great value on education and professional degrees in mates—characteristics that are strongly linked with social status. The same study found that women rate lack of education as highly undesirable in a potential husband. The cliché that women prefer to marry doctors, lawyers, professors, and other professionals seems to correspond with reality. Women shun men who are easily dominated by other men or who fail to command the respect of the group.

Women's desire for status shows up in everyday occurrences. A colleague overheard a conversation among four women at a restaurant. They were all complaining that there were no eligible men around. Yet these women were surrounded by male waiters, none of whom was wearing a wedding ring. Waiters, who do not have a high-status occupation, were apparently not even considered by these women. What they meant was not that there were no eligible men, but that there were no eligible men of acceptable social status.

Women on the mating market look for "eligible" men. The word *eligible* is a euphemism for "not having his resources already committed elsewhere." The frequency with which the word appears in the combination "eligible bachelor" reveals the mating desires of women. When women append an adverb to this phrase, it becomes "most eligible bachelor," referring not to the man's eligibility but rather to his social status and the magnitude of his resources. It is a euphemism for the highest-status, most resource-laden unattached man around.

The importance that women grant to social status in mates is not limited to America or even to capitalist countries. In the vast majority of the thirty-seven cultures included in the international study on choosing a mate, women value social status more than men in a prospective mate—in both communist and socialist countries, among blacks and orientals, among Catholics and Jews, in the tropics and the northern climes.[16] For example, in Taiwan, women value status 63 percent more than men; in Zambia, women value it 30 percent more; in West Germany, women value it 38 percent more; and in Brazil, women value it 40 percent more.

Because hierarchies are universal features among human groups and resources tend to accumulate to those who rise in the hierarchy, women solve the adaptive problem of acquiring resources in part by preferring men who are high in status. Social status gives a woman a strong indicator of the ability of a man to invest in her and her children. The contemporary evidence across many cultures supports the evolutionary prediction that women key onto this cue to the acquisition of resources. Women worldwide prefer to marry up. Those women in our evolutionary past who failed to marry up tended to be less able to provide for themselves and their children.

Age

The age of a man also provides an important cue to his access to resources. Just as young male baboons must mature before they can enter the upper ranks in the baboon social hierarchy, human adolescents and young men rarely command the respect, status, or position of more mature older men. This tendency reaches an extreme among the Tiwi tribe, a gerontocracy in which the very old men wield most of the power and prestige and control the mating system through complex networks of alliances. Even in American culture, status and wealth tend to accumulate with increasing age.

In all thirty-seven cultures included in the international study on choosing a mate, women prefer men who are older than they are.[17] Averaged over all cultures, women prefer men who are roughly three and a half years older. The smallest preferred age difference is seen in French Canadian women, who seek husbands who are not quite two years older, and the largest is found among Iranian women, who seek husbands who are more than five years older. The worldwide average age difference between actual brides and grooms is three years, suggesting that women's marriage decisions often match their mating preferences.

To understand why women value older mates, we must turn to the things that change with age. One of the most consistent changes is access to resources. In contemporary Western societies, income generally increases with age.[18] American men who are thirty years old, for example, make fourteen thousand dollars more than men who are twenty; men who are forty make seven thousand dollars more than men who are thirty. These trends are not limited to the Western world. Among traditional nonmodernized societies, older men have more social status. Among the Tiwi tribe, men are typically at least thirty years of age before they acquire enough social status to acquire a first wife.[19] Rarely does a Tiwi man under the age of forty attain enough status to acquire more than one wife. Older age, resources, and status are coupled across cultures.

In traditional societies, part of this linkage may be related to physical strength and hunting prowess. Physical strength increases in men as they get older, peaking in their late twenties and early thirties. Although there have been no systematic studies of the relationship between age and hunting ability, anthropologists believe that ability may peak when a man is in his thirties, at which point his slight decline in physical prowess is more than compensated for by his increased knowledge, patience, skill, and wisdom.[20] So women's preference for older men may stem from our hunter-gatherer ancestors, for whom the resources derived from hunting were critical to survival.

Women may prefer older men for reasons other than tangible resources. Older men are likely to be more mature, more stable, and more reliable in their provisioning. Within the United States, for example, men become somewhat more emotionally stable, more conscientious, and more dependable as they grow older, at least up through the age of thirty.[21] In a study of women's mate preferences, one woman noted that "older men [are] better looking because you [can] talk to them about serious concerns; younger men [are] silly and not very serious about life."[22] The status potential of men becomes clearer with increasing age. Women who prefer older men are in a better position to gauge how high they are likely to rise.

Twenty-year-old women in all thirty-seven cultures in the international study typically prefer to marry men only a few years older, not substantially older, in spite of the fact that men's financial resources generally do not peak until their forties or fifties. One reason that young women are not drawn to substantially older men may be that older men have a higher risk of dying and hence are less likely to be around to continue contributing to the provisioning and protection of children. Furthermore, the potential incompatibility created by a large age discrepancy may lead to strife, thus increasing the odds of divorce. For these reasons, young women may be drawn more to men a few years older who have considerable promise, rather than to substantially older men who already have attained a higher position but have a less certain future.

Not all women, however, select older men. Some select younger men. A study of a small Chinese village found that women who were seventeen or eighteen sometimes married "men" who were only fourteen or fifteen. The contexts in which this occurred, however, were highly circumscribed in that all the "men" were already wealthy, came from a high-status family, and had secure expectations through inheritance.[23] Apparently the preference for slightly older men can be overridden when the man possesses other powerful cues to status and resources and when his resource expectations are guaranteed.

Other exceptions occur when women mate with substantially younger men. Many of these cases occur not because of strong preferences by women for younger men but rather because both older women and younger men lack bargaining power on the mating market. Older women often cannot secure the attentions of high-status men and so must settle for younger men, who themselves have not acquired much status or value as mates. Among the Tiwi, for example, a young man's first wife is typically an older woman—sometimes older by decades—because older women are all he is able to secure with his relatively low status.

Still other exceptions occur among women who already have high status and plentiful resources of their own and then take up with much younger men. Cher and Joan Collins are striking celebrity examples; they became involved with men who were two decades younger. But these cases are rare, because most women with resources prefer to mate with men at least as rich in resources as they are, and preferably more so.[24] Women may mate temporarily with a younger man, but typically they seek an older man when they decide to settle down in marriage. Neither Cher's nor Joan Collins's romance with a younger man proved to be stable over time.

All these cues—economic resources, social status, and older age—add up to one thing: the ability of a man to acquire and control resources that women can use for themselves and for their children. A long history of evolution by selection has fashioned the way in which women look at men as success objects. But the possession of resources is not enough. Women also need men who possess traits that are likely to lead to the sustained acquisition of resources over time.

In cultures where people marry young, often the economic capacity of a man cannot be evaluated directly but must be deduced indirectly. Indeed, in hunter-gatherer groups that lack a cash economy, the target of selection cannot be financial resources per se. Among the Tiwi tribe, for example, young men are scrutinized carefully by both women and older men to evaluate which ones are "comers," destined to acquire status and resources, and which are likely to remain in the slow lane, based in part on their personality. The young men are evaluated for their promise, the key signs being good hunting skills, good fighting skills, and especially a strong proclivity to ascend the hierarchy of tribal power and influence. Women in all cultures, past and present, can select men for their apparent ability to accrue future resources, based on certain personality characteristics. And women who value the personality characteristics likely to lead to status and sustained resource acquisition are far better off than women who ignore these vital characterological cues.

Ambition and Industriousness

Liisa Kyl-Heku and I conducted a study of getting ahead in everyday life. Our goal was to identify the tactics that people use to elevate their position within hierarchies in the workplace and in social settings. We asked eighty-four individuals from California and Michigan to think about people whom they knew well, then to write down the acts they had observed these people using to get ahead in status or dominance hierarchies. Using various statistical procedures, we discovered twenty-six distinct tactics, including deception, social networking, sexual favors, education, and industriousness. The industriousness tactic included actions such as putting in extra time and effort at work, managing time efficiently, prioritizing goals, and working hard to impress others. We then asked 212 individuals who were in their middle to late twenties to indicate which tactics they use to get ahead. Separately, we asked their spouses to indicate which tactics their partners use to get ahead. Next, we correlated this information with their past income and promotions and with their anticipated income and promotions to see which tactics for getting ahead were most successfully linked with actual measures of getting ahead.

Among all the tactics, sheer hard work proved to be one of the best predictors of past and anticipated income and promotions. Those who said that they worked hard, and whose spouses agreed that they worked hard, achieved higher levels of education, higher annual salaries, and anticipated greater salaries and promotions than those who failed to work hard. Industrious and ambitious men secure a higher occupational status than lazy, unmotivated men do.[25]

American women seem to be aware of this connection, because they indicate a desire for men who show the characteristics linked with getting ahead. In the 1950s, for example, 5,000 undergraduates were asked to list characteristics they desired in a potential mate. Women far more often than men desire mates who enjoy their work, show career orientation, demonstrate industriousness, and display ambition.[26] The 852 single American women and 100 married American women in the international study on choosing a mate unanimously rate ambition and industriousness as important or indispensable. Women in the study of temporary and permanent mating regard men who lack ambition as extremely undesirable, whereas men view the lack of ambition in a wife as neither desirable nor undesirable. Women are likely to discontinue a long-term relationship with a man if he loses his job, lacks career goals, or shows a lazy streak.[27]

Women's preference for men who show ambition and industry is not limited to the United States or to Western society. Women in the overwhelming majority of cultures value ambition and industry more than men do, typically rating it as between important and indispensable. In Taiwan, for example, women rate ambition and industriousness as 26 percent more important than men do; women from Bulgaria rate it as 29 percent more important; and women from Brazil rate it as 30 percent more important.

This cross-cultural and cross-time evidence supports the key evolutionary expectation that women have evolved a preference for men who show signs of the ability to acquire resources and a disdain for men who lack ambition. This preference helped ancestral women to solve the critical adaptive problem of obtaining reliable resources. It helped them to gauge the likelihood of obtaining future resources from a man when direct and easily observable signs of current resources were absent. Even if directly observable resources were present, a man's ambition and industriousness provided a guarantee of the continuation of those resources. Hard work and ambition, however, are not the only available cues to potential resources. Two others, dependability and stability, provide further information about how steady or erratic such resources will be.

Dependability and Stability

Among the eighteen characteristics rated in the worldwide study on choosing a mate, the second and third most highly valued characteristics, after love, are a dependable character and emotional stability or maturity. In twenty-one out of thirty-seven cultures, men and women have the same preference for dependability in a partner. Of the sixteen cultures where there is a sex difference, women in fifteen of the cultures value dependability more than men. Averaged across all thirty-seven cultures, women rate dependable character 2.69 where a 3.00 signifies indispensable; men rate it nearly as important, with an average of 2.50. In the case of emotional stability or maturity, the sexes differ more. Women in twenty-three cultures value this quality significantly more than men do; in the remaining fourteen cultures, men and women value emotional stability equally. Averaging across all cultures, women give this quality a 2.68, whereas men give it a 2.47. In all cultures, in effect, women place a tremendous value on these characteristics, judging them to be anywhere from important to indispensable in a potential spouse.

These characteristics may possess such a great value worldwide because they are reliable signals that resources will be provided consistently over time. Undependable people, in contrast, provide erratically and inflict heavy costs on their mates. In a study of newlyweds, my colleagues and I contacted 104 couples at random from the public records of all marriages that had been licensed in a large county in Michigan during a six-month period. These couples completed a six-hour battery of personality tests and self-evaluations of their marital relationship, and evaluations of their spouse's character, and they were each interviewed by both a male and a female interviewer. Among these tests was a instrument that asked the participants to indicate which among 147 possible costs their partner had inflicted on them over the past year. Emotionally unstable men—as defined by themselves, their spouses, and their interviewers—are especially costly to women. First, they tend to be self-centered and monopolize shared resources. Furthermore, they tend to be possessive, monopolizing much of the time of their wives. They show higher than average sexual jealousy, becoming enraged when their wives even talk with someone else. They show dependency, insisting that their mates provide for all of their needs. They tend to be abusive both verbally and physically. They display inconsiderateness, such as by failing to show up on time. And they are moodier than their more stable counter-parts, often crying for no apparent reason. They have more affairs than average, which suggests a further diversion of time and resources.[28] All of these costs indicate that such spouses will absorb their partner's time and resources, divert their own time and resources elsewhere, and fail to channel resources consistently over time. Dependability and stability are personal qualities that signal increased likelihood that a woman's resources will not be drained by the man.

The unpredictable aspects of emotionally unstable men inflict additional costs by impeding solutions to critical adaptive problems. The erratic supply of resources can wreak havoc with accomplishing the goals required for survival and reproduction. Meat that is suddenly not available because an undependable mate decided at the last minute to take a nap rather than to go on the hunt is a resource that was counted on but not delivered. Its absence creates problems for nourishment and sustenance. Resources prove most beneficial when they are predictable. Erratically provided resources may even go to waste when the needs they were intended to meet are met through other, more costly means. Resources that are supplied predictably can be more efficiently allocated to the many adaptive hurdles that must be overcome in everyday life.

Emotional stability and dependability are broad categories. In order to identify with more precision the meaning of these global traits, Michael Botwin and I asked 140 persons to name specific examples of emotionally stable and unstable behavior. Some behavior that reflects emotional stability involves resiliency, such as not complaining or showing consideration for others in a trying situation. Other emotionally stable behavior relates to work, such as staying home to finish work when everyone else is going out or putting all one's energy into a job rather than expressing anxiety about it. This kind of behavior signals an ability to work steadily, to rely on personal resources to cope with stresses and setbacks, and to expend personal resources for the benefit of others even under adverse conditions.

These acts contrast markedly with the behavior of people who are emotionally unstable. Unstable behavior reflects an inability to command personal resources, such as worrying over something that one can do nothing about, breaking down when a problem arises, or getting upset about the work that needs to be done instead of doing it. This behavior signals inefficiency in working, difficulty in handling stress, a proclivity to inflict costs on others, and a lack of personal reserve to channel benefits to others.

Women place a premium on dependability and emotional stability to avoid incurring these costs and to reap the benefits that a mate can provide to them consistently over time. In human ancestral times, women who chose stable, dependable men had a greater likelihood of ensuring the man's ability to acquire and maintain resources for use by them and their children. Women who made these wise choices avoided many of the costs inflicted by undependable and unstable men.

Intelligence

Dependability, emotional stability, industriousness, and ambition are not the only personal qualities that signal the acquisition and steadiness of resources. The ephemeral quality of intelligence provides another important cue. No one knows for sure what intelligence tests measure, but there is clear evidence of what high scorers can do. Intelligence is a good predictor of the possession of economic resources within the United States.[29] People who test high go to better schools, get more years of education, and ultimately get higher paying jobs. Even within particular professions, such as construction and carpentry, intelligence predicts who will advance more rapidly to positions of power and who will command higher incomes. In tribal societies, the head men or leaders are almost invariably among the more intelligent members of the group.[30]

If intelligence has been a reliable predictor of economic resources over human evolutionary history, then women could have evolved a preference for this quality in a potential marriage partner. The international study on choosing a mate found that women indeed rate education and intelligence fifth out of eighteen desirable characteristics. Ranked in a smaller list of thirteen desirable characteristics, intelligence emerges in second place worldwide. Women value intelligence more than men in ten out of the thirty-seven cultures. Estonian women, for example, rank intelligence third out of thirteen desired characteristics, whereas Estonian men rank it fifth. Norwegian women value it second, whereas Norwegian men rank it fourth. In the remaining twenty-seven cultures, however, both sexes place the same high premium on intelligence.

The quality of intelligence signals many potential benefits. These are likely to include good parenting skills, capacity for cultural knowledge, and adeptness at parenting.[31] In addition, intelligence is linked with oral fluency, ability to influence other members of a group, prescience in forecasting danger, and judgment in applying health remedies. Beyond these specific qualities, intelligence conveys the ability to solve problems. Women who select more intelligent mates are more likely to become the beneficiaries of all of these critical resources.

To identify some of the actions that intelligent people perform, Mike

Botwin and I asked 140 men and women to think of the most intelligent people they knew and to describe five actions that reflect their intelligence. All these actions imply benefits that will flow to someone fortunate enough to choose an intelligent person as a mate. Intelligent people tend to have a wide perspective and to see an issue from all points of view, suggesting better judgment and decision making. They communicate messages well to other people and are sensitive to signs of how others are feeling, suggesting good social skills. They know where to go to solve problems, implying good judgment. Intelligent people manage money well, suggesting that resources will not be lost or frittered away. They accomplish tasks they have never before attempted with few mistakes, suggesting an efficiency in problem solving and allocating time. By selecting an intelligent mate, women increase their chances of receiving all these benefits.

Contrast these benefits with the costs imposed by the behavior of less intelligent people. Their behavior includes failing to pick up subtle hints from others, missing a joke that everyone else gets, and saying the wrong thing at the wrong time, all of which suggest a lack of social adeptness. Less intelligent people repeat mistakes, suggesting that they have less ability to learn from experience. They also fail to follow simple verbal instructions, fail to grasp explanations, and argue when they are obviously wrong. This behavior implies that unintelligent mates are poor problem solvers, unreliable workers, and social liabilities. All these costs are incurred by those who choose less intelligent partners.

Ancestral women who preferred intelligent mates would have raised their odds of securing social, material, and economic resources for themselves and for their children. Since intelligence is moderately heritable, these favorable qualities would have been passed on genetically to their sons and daughters, providing an added benefit. Modern women across all cultures display these preferences.

A mate who is too discrepant from oneself in intelligence, however, is less desirable than a mate who is matched for intelligence. A person of average intelligence typically does not desire a brilliant mate, for example. Similarity, therefore, is critical for successful mating.

Compatibility

Successful long-term mating requires a sustained cooperative alliance with another person for mutually beneficial goals. Relationships riddled with conflict impede the attainment of those goals. Compatibility between mates entails a complex mesh between two different kinds of characteristics. One kind involves complementary traits, or a mate's possession of resources and skills that differ from one's own, in a kind of division of labor between the sexes. Both persons benefit through this specialization and division.

The other kinds of traits crucial to compatibility with a mate, however, are those that are most likely to mesh cooperatively with one's own particular personal characteristics and thus are most similar to one's own. Discrepancies between the values, interests, and personalities of the members of a couple produce strife and conflict. The psychologist Zick Rubin and his colleagues studied 202 dating couples over several years to see which ones stayed together and which broke up.[32] They found that couples who were mismatched in these regards tend to break up more readily than their matched counterparts. The 103 couples who broke up had more dissimilar values on sex roles, attitudes toward sex among acquaintances, romanticism, and religious beliefs than did the 99 couples who stayed together.

One solution to the problem of compatibility is thus to search for the similar in a mate. Both in the United States and worldwide, men and women who are similar to each other on a wide variety of characteristics tend to get married. The tendency for like people to mate shows up most obviously in the areas of values, intelligence, and group membership.[33] People seek mates with similar political and social values, such as their views on abortion or capital punishment, for which couples are correlated +.50. Mismatches on these values are likely to lead to conflict. People also desire mates who are similar in race, ethnicity, and religion. Couples desire and marry mates of similar intelligence, on which spouses correlate +.40. In addition, similarity matters in personality characteristics such as extraversion, agreeableness, and conscientiousness, which show correlations between spouses of +.25. People like mates who share their inclination toward parties if they are extraverted and toward quiet evenings at home if they are introverted. People who are characteristically open to experience prefer mates who share their interest in fine wines, art, literature, and exotic foods. Conscientious people prefer mates who share their interest in paying bills on time and saving for the future. Less conscientious people prefer mates who share their interest in living for the moment.

The similarity in compatible couples is in part a byproduct of the fact that people tend to marry others who are in close proximity, and those who are nearby tend to be similar to oneself. Similarity of intelligence in modern marriages, for example, may be an incidental outcome of the fact that people of similar intelligence tend to go to the same educational institutions. The incidental outcome explanation, however, cannot account for the widespread preference that people express for mates who are similar.[34] In a study conducted on dating couples in Cambridge, Massachusetts, I measured the personalities and intelligence levels of 108 individuals who were involved in a dating relationship. Separately, they completed a questionnaire that asked for their preferences in an ideal mate for the same qualities. The study found that women express a preference for mates who are similar to themselves in many respects, including boldness, dominance, and activeness; warmth, agreeableness, and kindness; responsibility, conscientiousness, and industriousness; and especially intelligence, perceptiveness, and creativity. Those who judge themselves to be low in these personality traits express a desire for mates who are also low in them.

The search for a similar other provides an elegant solution to the adaptive problem of creating compatibility within the couple so that their interests are maximally aligned in the pursuit of mutual goals. Consider a woman who is an extravert and loves wild parties and who is married to an introvert who prefers quiet evenings at home. Although they may decide to go their separate ways evening after evening, the mismatch causes strife. Couples in which both members are introverted or both are extraverted are not at loggerheads about mutually pursued activities. The marriage of a Democrat and a Republican or an abortion rights advocate with an abortion opponent can make for interesting discussions, but the ensuing conflict wastes valuable energy because their goals are incompatible and their efforts cancel each other out.

Perhaps more important, matched couples maximize the smooth coordination of their efforts when pursuing mutual goals such as child rearing, maintaining kin alliances, and social networking. A couple at odds over how to rear their child wastes valuable energy and also confuses the child, who receives contradictory messages. The search for similarity prevents couples from incurring these costs.

Another adaptive benefit to seeking similarity comes from securing a good bargain and avoiding wasteful mating effort, given what a person's mating assets are on the marriage market. Because personality characteristics such as agreeableness, conscientiousness, and intelligence are all highly desirable on the mating market, those who possess more of them can command more of them in a mate.[35] Those who lack these valuable personal assets can command less and so must limit their search to those with assets that are similar to their own. By seeking similarity, individuals avoid wasting time and money courting people who are out of their reach. Competing for a mate who exceeds one's own value entails the risk of eventual abandonment by the partner whose mating options are more expansive. Dissimilar relationships tend to break up because the more desirable partner can strike a better bargain elsewhere.

The search for similarity thus solves several adaptive problems simultaneously. It maximizes the value one can command on the mating market, leads to the coordination of efforts, reduces conflict within the couple, avoids the costs of mutually incompatible goals, maximizes the likelihood of achieving success, and reduces the risk of later abandonment or dissolution of the relationship.

Resources, personality, intelligence, and similarity provide important information about the benefits a potential partner can bestow. Physical characteristics of a potential mate provide additional adaptively significant information. These, too, have joined the array of preferences that women hold.

Size and Strength

When the great basketball player Magic Johnson revealed that he had slept with thousands of women, he inadvertently revealed women's preference for mates who display physical and athletic prowess. The numbers may be shocking, but the preference is not. Physical characteristics, such as athleticism, size, and strength, convey important information that women use in making a mating decision.

The importance of physical characteristics in the female choice of a mate is prevalent throughout the animal world. In the species called the gladiator frog, males are responsible for creating nests and defending the eggs.[36] In the majority of courtships, a stationary male is deliberately bumped by a female who is considering him. She strikes him with great force, sometimes enough to rock him back or even scare him away. If the male moves too much or bolts from the nest, the female hastily leaves to examine alternative mates. Most females mate with males who do not move or who move minimally when bumped. Only rarely does a female reject a male who remains firmly planted after being bumped. Bumping helps a female frog to decide how successful the male will be at defending her clutch. The bump test reveals the male's physical ability to perform the function of protection.

Women sometimes face physical domination by larger, stronger men, which can lead to injury and sexual domination by preventing them from exercising choice. Such domination undoubtedly occurred regularly during ancestral times. Indeed, studies of many nonhuman primate groups reveal that male physical and sexual domination of females has been a recurrent part of our primate heritage. The primatologist Barbara Smuts lived among baboons in the savanna plains of Africa while studying their mating patterns. She found that females frequently form enduring "special friendships" with males who offer physical protection to themselves and their infants. In return, these females grant their "friends" preferential sexual access during times of estrus. In essence, female baboons exchange sex for protection.

Analogously, one benefit to women of permanent mating is the physical protection a man can offer. A man's size, strength, and physical prowess are cues to solutions to the problem of protection. The evidence shows that women's preferences in a mate embody these cues. In the study of temporary and permanent mating, American women rated the desirability or undesirability of a series of physical traits. Women judge short men to be undesirable as a permanent mate.[37] In contrast, they find it very desirable for a potential permanent mate to be tall, physically strong, and athletic. Another group of American women consistently indicates a preference for men of average or greater than average height, roughly five feet and eleven inches, as their ideal marriage partner. Tall men are consistently seen as more desirable dates and mates than men who are short or of average height.[38] Furthermore, the two studies of personal ads described earlier revealed that, among women who mention height, 80 percent want a man who is six feet or taller. Perhaps even more telling is the finding that ads placed by taller men receive more responses from women than those placed by shorter men. Tall men date more often than short men and have a larger pool of potential mates. Women solve the problem of protection from aggressive men at least in part by preferring a mate who has the size, strength, and physical prowess to protect them.

Tall men tend to have a higher status in nearly all cultures. "Big men" in hunter-gatherer societies—men high in status—are literally big men physically.[39] In Western cultures, tall men make more money, advance in their professions more rapidly, and receive more and earlier promotions. Few American presidents have been less than six feet tall. Politicians are keenly aware of voters' preference. Following the televised presidential debate in 1988, George Bush made a point of standing very close to his shorter competitor, Michael Dukakis, in a strategy of highlighting their disparity in size. As the evolutionary psychologist Bruce Ellis notes:

Height constitutes a reliable cue to dominance in social interactions . . . shorter policemen are likely to be assaulted more than taller policemen . . . suggesting that the latter command more fear and respect from adversaries . . . taller men are more sought after in women's personal advertisements, receive more responses to their own personal advertisements, and tend to have prettier girlfriends than do shorter men.[40]

This preference for taller men is not limited to Western cultures. Among the Mehinaku tribe of the Brazilian Amazon, the anthropologist Thomas Gregor notes the importance of men's wrestling skills as an arena where size differences become acute:

> A heavily muscled, imposingly built man is likely to accumulate many girlfriends, while a small man, deprecatingly referred to as a *peritsi*, fares badly. The mere fact of height creates a measurable advantage. . . . A powerful wrestler, say the villagers, is frightening . . . he commands fear and respect. To the women, he is "beautiful" (awitsiri), in demand as a paramour and husband. Triumphant in politics as well as in love, the champion wrestler embodies the highest qualities of manliness. Not so fortunate the vanquished! A chronic loser, no matter what his virtues, is regarded as a fool. As he wrestles, the men shout mock advice. . . . The women are less audible as they watch the matches from their doorways, but they too have their sarcastic jokes. None of them is proud of having a loser as a husband or lover.[41]

Barbara Smuts believes that during human evolutionary history physical protection was one of the most important things a man could offer a woman. The presence of aggressive men who tried to dominate women physically and to circumvent their sexual choices may have been an important influence on women's mate selection in ancestral times. Given the alarming incidence of sexual coercion and rape in many cultures, a mate's protection value may well remain relevant to mate selection in modern environments. Many women simply do not feel safe on the streets, and a strong, tall, athletic mate acts as a deterrent for sexually aggressive men.

Attributes such as size, strength, and athletic prowess are not the only physical attributes that signal high mating value. Another physical quality critical for survival is good health.

Good Health

Women worldwide prefer mates who are healthy.[42] In all thirty-seven cultures included in the international study on choosing a mate, women judge good health to be anywhere from important to indispensable in a marriage partner. In another study on American women, poor physical conditions, ranging from bad grooming habits to a venereal disease, are regarded as extremely undesirable characteristics in a mate. The biologists Clelland Ford and Frank Beach found that signs of ill health, such as open sores, lesions, and unusual pallor, are universally regarded as unattractive.[43]

In humans, good health may be signaled by behavior as well as by physical appearance. A lively mood, high energy level, and sprightly gait, for example, may be attractive precisely because they are calorically costly and can be displayed only by people brimming with good health.

The tremendous importance we place on good health is not unique to our species. Some animals display large, loud, and gaudy traits that are costly and yet signal great health and vitality. Consider the bright, flamboyant, ostentatious plumage of the peacock. It is as if the peacock is saying: "Look at me; I'm so fit that I can carry these large, cumbersome feathers, and yet still I'm thriving." The mystery of the peacock's tail, which seems so contrary to utilitarian survival, is finally on the verge of being solved. The biologists William D. Hamilton and Marlena Zuk propose that the brilliant plumage serves as a signal that the peacock carries a light load of parasites, since peacocks who carry more than the average number of parasites have duller plumage.[44] The burdensome plumage provides a cue to health and robustness. Peahens prefer the brilliant plumage because it provides clues to the male's health.

In ancestral times, four bad consequences were likely to follow if a woman selected a mate who was unhealthy or disease-prone. First, she put herself and her family at risk of being contaminated by the disease. Second, her mate was less able to perform essential functions and provide crucial benefits to her and her children, such as food, protection, health care, and child rearing. Third, her mate was at increased risk of dying, prematurely cutting off the flow of resources and forcing her to incur the costs of searching for a new mate and courting all over again. And fourth, if health is partly heritable, she would risk passing on genes for poor health to her children. A preference for healthy mates solves the problem of mate survival and ensures that resources are likely to be delivered over the long run.

Love and Commitment

A man's possession of such assets as health, status, and resources, however, still does not guarantee his willingness to commit them to a particular woman and her children. Indeed, some men show a tremendous reluctance to marry, preferring to play the field and to seek a series of temporary sex partners. Women deride men for this hesitancy, calling them "commitment dodgers," "commitment phobics," "paranoid about commitment," and "fearful of the M word."[45] And women's anger is reasonable. Given the tremendous costs women incur because of sex, pregnancy, and childbirth, it is reasonable for them to require commitment from a man in return.

The weight women attach to commitment is revealed in the following true story (the names are changed). Mark and Susan had been going out with each other for two years and had been living together for six months. He was a well-off forty-two-year-old professional, she a medical student of twenty-eight. Susan pressed for a decision about marriage—they were in love, and she wanted to have children within a few years. But Mark balked. He had been married before; if he ever married again, he wanted to be absolutely sure it would be for good. As Susan continued to press for a decision, Mark raised the possibility of a prenuptial agreement. She resisted, feeling that this violated the spirit of marriage. Finally they agreed that by a date four months in the future he would have decided one way or another. The date came and went, and still Mark could not make a decision. Susan told him that she was leaving him, moved out, and started dating another man. Mark panicked. He called her up and begged her to come back, saying that he had changed his mind and would marry her. He promised a new car. He promised that there would be no prenuptial agreement. But it was too late. Mark's failure to commit was too strong a negative signal to Susan. It dealt the final blow to their relationship. She was gone forever.

Women past and present face the adaptive problem of choosing men who not only have the necessary resources but also show a willingness to commit those resources to them and their children. This problem may be more difficult than it seems at first. Although resources can often be directly observed, commitment cannot be. Instead, gauging commitment requires looking for cues that signal the likelihood of fidelity in the channeling of resources. Love is one of the most important cues to commitment.

Feelings and acts of love are not recent products of particular Western views. Love is universal. Thoughts, emotions, and actions of love are experienced by people in all cultures worldwide—from the Zulu in the southern tip of Africa to the Eskimos in the north of Alaska. In a survey of 168 diverse cultures from around the world, the anthropologist William Jankowiak found strong evidence for the presence of romantic love in nearly 90 percent of them. For the remaining 10 percent, the anthropological records were too sketchy to definitely verify the presence of love. When the sociologist Sue Sprecher and her colleagues interviewed 1,667 men and women in Russia, Japan, and the

United States, they found that 61 percent of the Russian men and 73 percent of the Russian women were currently in love. Comparable figures for the Japanese were 41 percent of the men and 63 percent of the women. Among Americans, 53 percent of the men and 63 percent of the women acknowledged being in love. Clearly, love is not a phenomenon limited to Western cultures.[46]

To identify precisely what love is and how it is linked to commitment, I initiated a study of acts of love.[47] First, I asked fifty women and fifty men from the University of California and the University of Michigan to think of people they knew who were currently in love and to describe actions performed by those people that reflect or exemplify their love. A different group of forty college men and women evaluated each of the 115 acts named for how typical it was of love in their estimation. Acts of commitment top the women's and men's lists, being viewed as most central to love. Such acts include giving up romantic relations with others, talking of marriage, and expressing a desire to have children with the person. When performed by a man, these acts of love signal the intention to commit resources to one woman and her children.

Commitment, however, has many facets. One major component of commitment is fidelity, exemplified by the act of remaining faithful to a partner when they are separated. Fidelity signals the exclusive commitment of sexual resources to a single partner. Another aspect of commitment is the channeling of resources to the loved one, such as buying her an expensive gift or ring. Acts such as this signal a serious intention to commit economic resources to a long-term relationship. Emotional support is yet another facet of commitment, revealed by such behavior as being available in times of trouble and listening to the partner's problems. Commitment entails a channeling of time, energy, and effort to the partner's needs at the expense of fulfilling one's own personal goals. Acts of reproduction also represent a direct commitment to one's partner's genes. All these acts, which are viewed as central to love, signal the commitment of sexual, economic, emotional, and genetic resources to one person.

Since love is a worldwide phenomenon, and since a primary function of acts of love is to signal commitment of reproductively-relevant resources, then women should place a premium on love in the process of choosing a mate. To find out, Sue Sprecher and her colleagues asked American, Russian, and Japanese students whether they would marry someone who had all the qualities they desired in a mate if they were not in love with that person.[48] Fully 89 percent of American women and 82 percent of Japanese women say they would still require love for marriage, even if all other important qualities are present.

Among Russians, only 59 percent of women will not marry someone with whom they are not in love, no matter how many desirable qualities that person has. Although a clear majority of Russian women require love, the lower threshold may reflect the tremendous difficulty Russian women have in finding a mate because of the severe shortage of men and especially men capable of investing resources. These variations reveal the effects of cultural context on mating. Nonetheless, the majority of women in all three cultures see love as an indispensable ingredient in marriage.

Direct studies of preferences in a mate confirm the centrality of love. In a study of 162 Texas women college students, out of one hundred characteristics examined, the quality of being loving is the most strongly desired in a potential husband.[49] The international study on choosing a mate confirmed the importance of love across cultures. Among eighteen possible characteristics, mutual attraction or love proved to be the most highly valued in a potential mate by both sexes, being rated a 2.87 by women and 2.81 by men. Nearly all women and men from the tribal enclaves of South Africa to the bustling streets of Brazilian cities give love the top rating, indicating that it is indispensable for marriage. Women place a premium on love in order to secure the commitment of men's economic, emotional, and sexual resources.

Two additional personal characteristics, kindness and sincerity, are critical to securing long-term commitment. In one study of 800 personal advertisements, sincerity was the single most frequently listed characteristic sought by women.[50] Another analysis of 1,111 personal advertisements again showed that sincerity is the quality most frequently sought by women—indeed, women advertisers seek sincerity nearly four times as often as men advertisers.[51] Sincerity in personal advertisements is a code word for commitment, used by women to screen out men seeking casual sex without any commitment.

People worldwide depend on kindness from their mates. As shown by the international study on choosing a mate, women have a strong preference for mates who are kind and understanding. In thirty-two out of the thirty-seven cultures, in fact, sexes are identical in valuing kindness as one of the three most important qualities out of a possible thirteen in a mate. Only in Japan and Taiwan do men give greater emphasis than women to kindness. And only in Nigeria, Israel, and France do women give greater emphasis than men to kindness. In no culture, for either sex, however, is kindness in a mate ranked lower than third out of thirteen.

Kindness is an enduring personality characteristic that has many components, but at the core of all of them is the commitment of resources. The trait signals an empathy toward children, a willingness to put a mate's needs before one's own, and a willingness to channel energy and effort toward a mate's goals rather than exclusively and selfishly to one's own goals.[52] Kindness, in other words, signals the ability and willingness of a potential mate to commit energy and resources selflessly to a partner.

The lack of kindness signals selfishness, an inability or unwillingness to commit, and a high likelihood that costs will be inflicted on a spouse. The study of newlyweds, for example, identified unkind men on the basis of their self-assessment, their wives' assessment, and the judgment of male and female interviewers, and then examined the wives' complaints about these husbands. Women married to unkind men complain that their spouses abuse them both verbally and physically by hitting, slapping, or spitting at them. Unkind men tend to be condescending, putting down their wife's opinions as stupid or inferior. They are selfish, monopolizing shared resources. They are inconsiderate, failing to do any housework. They are neglectful, failing to show up as promised. Finally, they have more extramarital affairs, suggesting that these men are unable or unwilling to commit to a monogamous relationship.[53] Unkind men look out for themselves, and have trouble committing to anything much beyond that.

Because sex is one of the most valuable reproductive resources women can offer, they have evolved psychological mechanisms that cause them to resist giving it away indiscriminately. Requiring love, sincerity, and kindness is a way of securing a commitment of resources commensurate with the value of the resource that women give to men. Requiring love and kindness helps women to solve the critical adaptive mating problem of securing the commitment of resources from a man that can aid in the survival and reproduction of her offspring.

When Women Have Power

A different explanation has been offered for the preferences of women for men with resources, based on the so-called structural powerlessness of women.[54] According to this view, because women are typically excluded from power and access to resources, which are largely controlled by men, women seek mates who have power, status, and earning capacity. Women try to marry upward in socioeconomic status to gain access to resources. Men do not value economic resources in a mate as much as women do because they already have control over these resources and because women have no resources anyway.

The society of Bakweri, from Cameroon in West Africa, casts doubt on this theory by illustrating what happens when women have real power. Bakweri women hold greater personal and economic power because they have more resources and are in scarcer supply than men.[55] Women secure resources through their own labors on plantations, but also from casual sex, which is a lucrative source of income. There are roughly 236 men for every 100 women, an imbalance that results from the continual influx of men from other areas of the country to work on the plantations. Because of the extreme imbalance in numbers of the sexes, women have considerable latitude to exercise their choice in a mate. Women thus have more money than men and more potential mates to choose from. Yet Bakweri women persist in preferring to have a mate with resources. Wives often complain about receiving insufficient support from their husbands. Indeed, lack of sufficient economic provisioning is the most frequently cited divorce complaint of women. Bakweri women change husbands if they find a man who can offer them more money and pay a larger bride price. When women are in a position to fulfill their evolved preference for a man with resources, they do so. Having the dominant control of economic resources does not circumvent this key mate preference.

Professionally and economically successful women in the United States also value resources in men. The newlywed study identified women who were financially successful, measured by their salary and income, and contrasted their preferences in a mate with those of women with lower salaries and income. The financially successful women often made more than $50,000 a year, and a few made more than $100,000. These women were well educated, tended to have professional degrees, and had high self-esteem. As the study showed, successful women place an even greater value than less successful women on mates who have professional degrees, high social status, and greater intelligence, as well desiring mates who are tall, independent, and self-confident. Perhaps most tellingly, these women express an even stronger preference for high-earning men than do women who are less financially successful. In a separate study the psychologists Michael Wiederman and Elizabeth Allgeier found that college women who expect to earn the most after college place more importance on the financial prospects of a potential husband than do women who expect to earn less. Professionally successful women, such as medical students and law students, also assign great importance to a mate's earning capacity.[56] Furthermore, men low in financial resources and status do not value economic resources in a mate any more than financially successful men do.[57] Taken together, these results not only fail to support the structural powerlessness hypothesis but directly contradict it.

Structural powerlessness has an element of truth in that men in most cultures do control resources and exclude women from power. But the theory cannot explain the fact that men strive to exclude other men from power at least as much as women, that the origins of the male control of resources remain unexplained, that women have not evolved bigger, stronger bodies to acquire resources directly, and that men's preferences in a mate remain entirely mysterious. Evolutionary psychology accounts for this constellation of findings. Men strive to control resources and to exclude other men from resources to fulfill women's mating preferences. In human evolutionary history, men who failed to accumulate resources failed to attract mates. Men's larger bodies and more powerful status drives are due, at least in part, to the preferences that women have expressed over the past few million years.

Women's Many Preferences

We now have the outlines of an answer to the enigma of what women want. Women are judicious, prudent, and discerning about the men they consent to mate with because they have so many valuable reproductive resources to offer. Those with valuable resources rarely give them away indiscriminately. The costs in reproductive currency of failing to exercise choice were too great for ancestral women, who would have risked beatings, food deprivation, disease, abuse of children, and abandonment. The benefits of choice in nourishment, protection, and paternal investment for children were abundant.

Permanent mates may bring with them a treasure trove of resources. Selecting a long-term mate who has the relevant resources is clearly an extraordinarily complex endeavor. It involves at least a dozen distinctive preferences, each corresponding to a resource that helps women to solve critical adaptive problems.

That women seek resources in a permanent mate may be obvious. But because resources cannot always be directly discerned, women's mating preferences are keyed to other qualities that signal the likely possession, or future acquisition, of resources. Indeed, women may be less influenced by money per se than by qualities that lead to resources, such as ambition, status, intelligence, and age. Women scrutinize these personal qualities carefully because they reveal a man's potential.

Potential, however, is not enough. Because many men with a high resource potential are themselves discriminating and are at times content with casual sex, women are faced with the problem of commitment. Seeking love and sincerity are two solutions to the commitment problem. Sincerity signals that the man is capable of commitment. Acts of love signal that he has in fact committed to a particular woman.

To have the love and commitment of a man who could be easily downed by other men in the physical arena, however, would have been a problematic asset for ancestral women. Women mated to small, weak men lacking in physical prowess would have risked damage from other men and loss of the couple's joint resources. Tall, strong, athletic men offered ancestral women protection. In this way, their resources and commitment could be secured against incursion. Women who selected men in part for their strength and prowess were more likely to be successful at surviving and reproducing.

Resources, commitment, and protection do a woman little good if her husband becomes diseased or dies or if the couple is so mismatched that they fail to function as an effective team. The premium that women place on a man's health ensures that husbands will be capable of providing these benefits over the long haul. And the premium that women place on similarity of interests and traits with their mate helps to ensure the convergence of mutually pursued goals. These multiple facets of current women's mating preferences thus correspond perfectly with the multiple facets of adaptive problems that were faced by our women ancestors thousands of years ago.

Ancestral men, however, were confronted with a different set of adaptive problems. So we must now shift perspective to gaze at ancestral women as potential mates through the eyes of our male forebears.

3

Men Want Something Else

Beauty is in the adaptations of the beholder.
                    —Donald Symons, "What Do Men Want?"

WHY MEN MARRY poses a puzzle. Since all an ancestral man needed to do to reproduce was to impregnate a woman, casual sex without commitment would have sufficed for him. For evolution to have produced men who desire marriage and who are willing to commit years of investment to a woman, there must have been powerful adaptive advantages, at least under some circumstances, to that state over seeking casual sex partners.

One solution to the puzzle comes from the ground rules set by women. Since it is clear that many ancestral women required reliable signs of male commitment before consenting to sex, men who failed to commit would have suffered selectively on the mating market. Men who failed to fulfill women's standards typically would have failed to attract the most desirable women and perhaps even failed to attract any women at all. Women's requirements for consenting to sex made it costly for most men to pursue a short-term mating strategy exclusively. In the economics of reproductive effort, the costs of not pursuing a permanent mate may have been prohibitively high for most men.

A further cost of failing to seek marriage was impairment of the survival and reproductive success of the man's children. In human ancestral environments, it is likely that infants and young children were more likely to die without prolonged investment from two parents or related kin.[1] Even today, among the Ache Indians of Paraguay, when a man dies in a club fight, the other villagers often make a mutual decision to kill his children, even when the children have a living mother. In one case reported by the anthropologist Kim Hill, a boy of thirteen was killed after his father had died in a club fight. Overall, Ache children whose fathers die suffer a death rate more than 10 percent higher than children whose fathers remain alive. Such are the hostile forces of nature among the Ache.

Over human evolutionary history, even children who did survive without the father's investment would have suffered from the absence of his teaching and political alliances, since both of these assets help to solve mating problems later in life. Fathers in many cultures past and present have a strong hand in arranging beneficial marriages for their sons and daughters. The absence of these benefits hurts children without fathers. These evolutionary pressures, operating over thousands of generations, gave an advantage to men who married.

Another benefit of marriage is an increase in the quality of the mate a man is able to attract. The economics of the mating marketplace typically produce an asymmetry between the sexes in their ability to obtain a desirable mate in a committed as opposed to a temporary relationship.[2] Most men can obtain a much more desirable mate if they are willing to commit to a long-term relationship. The reason is that women typically desire a lasting commitment, and highly desirable women are in the best position to get what they want. In contrast, most women can obtain a much more desirable temporary mate by offering sex without requiring commitment, since high-status men are willing to relax their standards and have sex with a variety of women if the relationship is only short-term and carries no commitment. Men of high status typically insist on more stringent standards for a spouse than most women are able to meet.

The puzzle remains as to precisely what characteristics were desired by ancestral men when they sought a long-term mate. To be reproductively successful, ancestral men had to marry women with the capacity to bear children. A woman with the capacity to bear many children was more valuable in reproductive currencies than a woman who was capable of bearing few or none. Men needed some basis, however, on which to judge a woman's reproductive capacity.

The solution to this problem is more difficult than it first might appear. Ancestral men had few obvious aids for figuring out which women possessed the highest reproductive value. The number of children a woman is likely to bear in her lifetime is not stamped on her forehead. It is not imbued in her social reputation. Her family is clueless. Even women themselves lack direct knowledge of their reproductive value.

A preference nevertheless evolved for this quality that cannot be discerned directly. Ancestral men evolved mechanisms to sense cues to a woman's underlying reproductive value. These cues involve observable features of females. Two obvious cues are youth and health.[3] Old or unhealthy women clearly could not reproduce as much as young, healthy women. Ancestral men solved the problem of finding reproductively valuable women in part by preferring those who are young and healthy.

Youth

Youth is a critical cue, since women's reproductive value declines steadily with increasing age after twenty. By the age of forty, a woman's reproductive capacity is low, and by fifty it is close to zero. Thus, women's capacity for reproduction is compressed into a fraction of their lives.

Men's preferences capitalize on this cue. Within the United States men uniformly express a desire for mates who are younger than they are. Among college students surveyed from 1939 through 1988 on campuses coast to coast, the preferred age difference hovers around 2.5 years.[4] Men who are 21 years old prefer, on average, women who are 18.5 years old.

Men's preoccupation with a woman's youth is not limited to Western cultures. When the anthropologist Napoleon Chagnon was asked which females are most sexually attractive to Yanomamö Indian men of the Amazon, he replied without hesitation, "Females who are *moko dude*."[5] The word *moko,* when used with respect to fruit, means that the fruit is harvestable, and when used with respect to a woman, it means that the woman is fertile. Thus, *moko dude,* when referring to fruit, means that the fruit is perfectly ripe and, when referring to a woman, means that she is postpubescent but has not yet borne her first child, or about fifteen to eighteen years of age. Comparative information on other tribal peoples suggests that the Yanomamö men are not atypical in their preference.

Nigerian, Indonesian, Iranian, and Indian men are similarly inclined. Without exception, in every one of the thirty-seven societies examined in the international study on choosing a mate, men prefer wives who are younger than themselves. Nigerian men who are 23.5 years old, for example, express a preference for wives who are six and a half years younger, or just over 17 years old. Yugoslavian men who are 21.5 years old express a desire for wives who are approximately 19 years old. Chinese, Canadian, and Colombian men share with their Nigerian and Yugoslavian brethren a powerful desire for younger women. On average, men from the thirty-seven cultures express a desire for wives approximately 2.5 years younger than themselves.

Although men universally prefer younger women as wives, the strength of this preference varies somewhat from culture to culture. Scandinavian men in Finland, Sweden, and Norway prefer their brides to be only one or two years younger. Men in Nigeria and Zambia prefer their brides to be 6.5 and 7.5 years younger, respectively. In Nigeria and

Zambia, which practice polygyny, like many cultures worldwide, men who can afford it are legally permitted to marry more than one woman. Since men in polygynous mating systems are typically older than men in monogamous systems by the time they have acquired sufficient resources to attract wives, the larger age difference preferred by Nigerian and Zambian men may reflect their greater age when they acquire wives.[6]

A comparison of the statistics derived from personal advertisements in newspapers reveals that a man's age has a strong effect on his preferences. As men get older, they prefer as mates women who are increasingly younger than they are. Men in their thirties prefer women who are roughly five years younger, whereas men in their fifties prefer women ten to twenty years younger.[7]

Actual marriage decisions confirm the preference of men for women who are increasingly younger as they age. American grooms exceed their brides in age by roughly three years at first marriage, five years at second marriage, and eight years at third marriage.[8] Men's preference for younger women also translates into actual marriage decisions worldwide. In Sweden during the 1800s, for example, church documents reveal that men who remarried following a divorce selected new brides 10.6 years younger on average. In all countries around the world where information is available on the ages of brides and grooms, men on average exceed their brides in age.[9] Among European countries, the age difference ranges from about two years in Poland to roughly five years in Greece. Averaged across all countries, grooms are three years older than their brides, or roughly the difference expressly desired by men worldwide. In polygynous cultures, the age difference runs even larger. Among the Tiwi of Northern Australia, for example, high-status men often have wives who are two and three decades younger than they are.[10] In short, contemporary men prefer young women because they have inherited from their male ancestors a preference that focused intently upon this cue to a woman's reproductive value. This psychologically based preference translates into everyday mating decisions.

Standards of Physical Beauty

A preference for youth, however, is merely the most obvious of men's preferences linked to a woman's reproductive capacity. Evolutionary logic leads to an even more powerful set of expectations for universal standards of beauty. Just as our standards for attractive landscapes embody cues such as water, game, and refuge, mimicking our ancestors' savanna habitat, so our standards for female beauty embody cues to women's reproductive capacity.[11] Beauty may be in the eyes of the beholder, but those eyes and the minds behind the eyes have been shaped by millions of years of human evolution.

Our ancestors had access to two types of observable evidence of a woman's health and youth: features of physical appearance, such as full lips, clear skin, smooth skin, clear eyes, lustrous hair, and good muscle tone, and features of behavior, such as a bouncy, youthful gait, an animated facial expression, and a high energy level. These physical cues to youth and health, and hence to reproductive capacity, constitute the ingredients of male standards of female beauty.

Because physical and behavioral cues provide the most powerful observable evidence of a woman's reproductive value, ancestral men evolved a preference for women who displayed these cues. Men who failed to prefer qualities that signal high reproductive value—men who preferred to marry gray-haired women lacking in smooth skin and firm muscle tone—would have left fewer offspring, and their line would have died out.

Clelland Ford and Frank Beach discovered several universal cues that correspond precisely with this evolutionary theory of beauty.[12] Signs of youth, such as clear skin and smooth skin, and signs of health, such as the absence of sores and lesions, are universally regarded as attractive. Any cues to ill health or older age are seen as less attractive. Poor complexion is always considered sexually repulsive. Pimples, ringworm, facial disfigurement, and filthiness are universally repugnant. Cleanliness and freedom from disease are universally attractive.

Among the Trobriand Islanders in northwestern Melanesia, for example, the anthropologist Bronislaw Malinowski reports that "sores, ulcers, and skin eruptions are naturally held to be specially repulsive from the viewpoint of erotic contact."[13] The "essential conditions" for beauty, in contrast, are "health, strong growth of hair, sound teeth, and smooth skin." Specific features, such as bright eyes and full, well-shaped lips rather than thin or pinched lips, are especially important to the islanders.

Cues to youth are also paramount in the aesthetics of women's attractiveness. When men and women rate a series of photographs of women differing in age, judgments of facial attractiveness decline with the increasing age of the woman.[14] The decline in ratings of beauty occurs regardless of the age or sex of the judge. The value that men attach to women's faces, however, declines more rapidly than do women's ratings of other women's faces as the age of the woman depicted in the photograph increases, highlighting the importance to men of age as a cue to reproductive capacity.

Most traditional psychological theories of attraction have assumed that standards of attractiveness are learned gradually through cultural transmission, and therefore do not emerge clearly until a child is at least three or four years old. The psychologist Judith Langlois and her colleagues have overturned this conventional wisdom by studying infants' social responses to faces.[15] Adults evaluated color slides of white and black female faces for their attractiveness. Then infants of two to three months of age and six to eight months of age were shown pairs of these faces that differed in their degree of attractiveness. Both younger and older infants looked longer at the more attractive faces, suggesting that standards of beauty apparently emerge quite early in life. In a second study, Langlois and her colleagues found that twelve-month-old infants showed more observable pleasure, more play involvement, less distress, and less withdrawal when interacting with strangers who wore attractive masks than when interacting with strangers who wore unattractive masks.[16] In a third study, they found that twelve-month-old infants played significantly longer with attractive dolls than with unattractive dolls. No training seems necessary for these standards to emerge. This evidence challenges the common view that the idea of attractiveness is learned through gradual exposure to current cultural standards.

The constituents of beauty are neither arbitrary nor culture bound. When the psychologist Michael Cunningham asked people of different races to judge the facial attractiveness of photographs of women of various races, he found great consensus about who is and is not good looking.[17] Asian and American men, for example, agree with each other on which Asian and American women are most and least attractive. Consensus has also been found among the Chinese, Indian, and English; between South Africans and Americans; and between black and white Americans.[18]

Recent scientific breakthroughs confirm the evolutionary theory of female beauty. To find out what makes for an attractive face, composites of the human face were generated by means of the new technology of computer graphics. These faces were then superimposed upon each other to create new faces. The new composite faces were made up of a differing number of individual faces—four, eight, sixteen, or thirty-two. People were asked to rate the attractiveness of each composite face, as well as the attractiveness of each individual face that made up the composite. A startling result emerged. The composite faces were uniformly judged to be more physically attractive than any of the individual ones. The sixteen-face composite was more attractive than the four-face or eight-face composites, and the thirty-two–face composite was the most attractive of all. Because superimposing individual faces tends to eliminate their irregularities and make them more symmetrical, the average or symmetrical faces are more attractive than actual faces.[19]

One explanation for why symmetrical faces are considered more attractive comes from research conducted by the psychologist Steve Gangestad and the biologist Randy Thornhill, who examined the relationship between facial and bodily asymmetries and judgments of attractiveness.[20] Repeated environmental insults produce asymmetries during development. These include not just injuries and other physical insults, which may provide a cue to health, but also the parasites that inhabit the human body. Because parasites cause physical asymmetries, the degree of asymmetry can be used as a cue to the health status of the individual and as an index of the degree to which the individual's development has been perturbed by various stressors. In scorpionflies and swallows, for example, males prefer to mate with symmetrical females and tend to avoid those that show asymmetries. In humans as well, when Gangestad and Thornhill measured people's features, such as foot breadth, hand breadth, ear length, and ear breadth, and independently had these people evaluated on attractiveness, they found that less symmetrical people are seen as less attractive. Human asymmetries also increase with age. Older people's faces are far more asymmetrical than younger people's faces, so that symmetry provides another cue to youth as well. This evidence provides yet another confirmation of the theory that cues to health and cues to youth are embodied in standards of attractiveness—standards that emerge remarkably early in life.

Body Shape

Facial beauty is only part of the picture. Features of the rest of the body provide an abundance of cues to a woman's reproductive capacity. Standards for female bodily attractiveness vary from culture to culture, along such dimensions as a plump versus slim body build or light versus dark skin. Emphasis on particular physical features, such as eyes, ears, or genitals, also varies by culture. Some cultures, such as the Nama, a branch of Hottentots residing in Southwest Africa, consider an elongated labia majora to be sexually attractive, and they work at pulling and manipulating the vulvar lips to enhance attractiveness. Men in many cultures prefer large, firm breasts, but in a few, such as the Azande of Eastern Sudan and the Ganda of Uganda, men view long, pendulous breasts as the more attractive.[21]

The most culturally variable standard of beauty seems to be in the preference for a slim versus plump body build. This variation is linked with the social status that body build conveys. In cultures where food is scarce, such as among the Bushmen of Australia, plumpness signals wealth, health, and adequate nutrition during development.[22] In cultures where food is relatively abundant, such as the United States and many western European countries, the relationship between plumpness and status is reversed, and the rich distinguish themselves through thinness.[23] Men apparently do not have an evolved preference for a particular amount of body fat per se. Rather, they have an evolved preference for whatever features are linked with status, which vary in predictable ways from culture to culture. Clearly such a preference does not require conscious calculation or awareness.

Studies by the psychologist Paul Rozin and his colleagues reveal a disturbing aspect of women's and men's perceptions of the desirability of plump versus thin body types.[24] American men and women viewed nine female figures that varied from very thin to very plump. The women were asked to indicate their ideal for themselves, as well as their perception of what men's ideal female figure was. In both cases, women selected a figure slimmer than average. When men were asked to select which female figure they preferred, however, they selected the figure of average body size. American women erroneously believe that men desire thinner women than is the case. These findings refute the belief that men desire women who are emaciated.

While men's preferences for a particular body size vary, the psychologist Devendra Singh has discovered one preference for body shape that is invariant—the preference for a particular ratio of waist size to hip size.[25] Before puberty, boys and girls show a similar fat distribution. At puberty, however, a dramatic change occurs. Boys lose fat from their buttocks and thighs, while the release of estrogen in pubertal girls causes them to deposit fat in their lower trunk, primarily on their hips and upper thighs. Indeed, the volume of body fat in this region is 40 percent greater for women than for men.

The waist-to-hip ratio is thus similar for the sexes before puberty. After puberty, however, women's hip fat deposits cause their waist-to-hip ratio to become significantly lower than men's. Healthy, reproductively capable women have a waist-to-hip ratio between 0.67 and 0.80, while healthy men have a ratio in the range of 0.85 to 0.95. Abundant evidence now shows that the waist-to-hip ratio is an accurate indicator of women's reproductive status. Women with a lower ratio show earlier pubertal endocrine activity. Married women with a higher ratio have more difficulty becoming pregnant, and those who do become pregnant do so at a later age than women with a lower ratio. The waist-to-hip ratio is also an accurate indication of long-term health status. Diseases such as diabetes, hypertension, heart problems, previous stroke, and gallbladder disorders have been shown to be linked with the distribution of fat, as reflected by the ratio, rather than with the total proportion of body fat. The link between the waist-to-hip ratio and both health and reproductive status makes it a reliable cue for ancestral men's preferences in a mate.

Singh discovered that waist-to-hip ratio is a powerful cue to women's attractiveness. In a dozen studies conducted by Singh, men rated the attractiveness of female figures, which varied in both their waist-to-hip ratio and their total amount of fat. Men find the average figure to be more attractive than a thin or fat figure. Regardless of the total amount of fat, however, men find women with a low waist-to-hip ratio to be the most attractive. Women with a ratio 0.70 are seen as more attractive than women with a ratio of 0.80, who in turn are seen as more attractive than women with a ratio of 0.90. Studies with line drawings and with computer-generated photographic images produced the same results. Finally, Singh's analysis of *Playboy* centerfolds and winners of beauty contests within the United States over the past thirty years confirmed the invariance of this cue. Although both centerfolds and beauty contest winners got thinner over that period, their waist-to-hip ratio remained exactly the same at 0.70.

There is one more possible reason for the importance of waist-to-hip ratio in men's evolved preferences. Pregnancy alters this ratio dramatically. A higher ratio mimics pregnancy and therefore may render women less attractive as mates or sexual partners. A lower ratio, in turn, signals health, reproductive capacity, and lack of current pregnancy. Men's standards of female attractiveness have evolved over thousands of generations to pick up this reliable cue.

Importance of Physical Appearance

Because of the many cues conveyed by a woman's physical appearance, and because male standards of beauty have evolved to correspond to these cues, men place a premium on physical appearance and attractiveness in their mate preferences. Within the United States mate preferences for physical attractiveness, physical appearance, good looks, or beauty have been lavishly documented. When five thousand college students were asked in the 1950s to identify the characteristics they wanted in a future husband or wife, what men listed far more often than women was physical attractiveness.[26] The sheer number of terms that men listed betrays their values. They wanted a wife who was pretty, attractive, beautiful, gorgeous, comely, lovely, ravishing, and glamorous. American college women, at that time at least, rarely listed physical appearance as paramount in their ideal husband.

A cross-generational mating study, spanning a fifty-year period within the United States from 1939 to 1989, gauged the value men and women place on different characteristics in a mate. The same eighteen characteristics were measured at roughly one-decade intervals to determine how mating preferences have changed over time within the United States. In all cases, men rate physical attractiveness and good looks as more important and desirable in a potential mate than do women.[27] Men tend to see attractiveness as important, whereas women tend to see it as desirable but not very important. The sex difference in the importance of attractiveness remains constant from one generation to the next. Its size does not vary throughout the entire fifty years. Men's greater preference for physically attractive mates is among the most consistently documented psychological sex differences.[28]

This does not mean that the importance people place on attractiveness is forever fixed by our genes. On the contrary, the importance of attractiveness has increased dramatically within the United States in this century alone.[29] For nearly every decade since 1930, physical appearance has gone up in importance for men and women about equally, corresponding with the rise in television, fashion magazines, advertising, and other media depictions of attractive models. For example, the importance attached to good looks in a marriage partner on a scale of 0.00 to 3.00 increased between 1939 and 1989 from 1.50 to 2.11 for men and from 0.94 to 1.67 for women. These shifts show that mate preferences can change. But the sex difference so far remains invariant. The gap between men and women has been constant since the late 1930s.

These sex differences are not limited to the United States, or even to Western cultures. Regardless of the location, habitat, marriage system, or cultural living arrangement, men in all thirty-seven cultures included in the international study on choosing a mate value physical appearance in a potential mate more than women. China typifies the average difference in importance attached to beauty, with men giving it a 2.06 and women giving it a 1.59. This internationally consistent sex difference persists despite variations in ranking, in wording, and in race, ethnicity, religion, hemisphere, political system, and mating system. Men's preference for physically attractive mates is a species-wide psychological mechanism that transcends culture.

Men's Status and Women's Beauty

The importance that men assign to a woman's attractiveness has reasons other than her reproductive value. The consequences for a man's social status are critical. Everyday folklore tells us that our mate is a reflection of ourselves. Men are particularly concerned about status, reputation, and hierarchies because elevated rank has always been an important means of acquiring the resources that make men attractive to women. It is reasonable, therefore, to expect that a man will be concerned about the effect that his mate has on his social status—an effect that has consequences for gaining additional resources and mating opportunities.

A person's status and resource holdings, however, often cannot be observed directly. They must instead be inferred from tangible characteristics. Among humans, one set of cues is people's ornamentation. Gold chains, expensive artwork, or fancy cars may signal to both sexes an abundance of resources that can be directed toward parental investment.[30] Men seek attractive women as mates not simply for their reproductive value but also as signals of status to same-sex competitors and to other potential mates.[31]

This point was vividly illustrated by the real-life case of Jim, who complained to a friend about his wife, an unusually attractive woman. "I'm thinking about getting a divorce," he said. "We are incompatible, have different values, and argue all the time." His friend, though sympathetic, offered this counsel: "In spite of your troubles, Jim, you might want to reconsider. She looks great on your arm when you walk into a party." Although Jim and his wife eventually divorced, he delayed the split for several years, in part because of his friend's advice. Jim felt that he would be losing a valuable social asset if he divorced his attractive wife. "Trophy" wives are not just the perquisites of high status, but in fact increase the status of the man who can win them.

Experiments have documented the influence of attractive mates on men's social status. When people are asked to evaluate men on a variety of characteristics, based on photographs of the men with "spouses" of differing physical attractiveness, the consequences are especially great for evaluations of men's status. Unattractive men paired with attractive spouses are rated most favorably on criteria related to status, such as occupational prestige, in comparison with all other possible pairings, such as attractive men with unattractive women, unattractive women with unattractive men, and even attractive men with attractive women. People suspect that a homely man must have high status if he can interest a stunning woman, presumably because people know that attractive women have high value as mates and hence usually can get what they want in a mate.

Another indication of the consequences of an attractive mate comes from a comparison of the effects of different kinds of mating behavior on the status and reputation of men and women.[32] In my study of human prestige criteria, American men and women evaluated the relative influence of experiences such as dating someone who is physically attractive, having sex with a date on the first night, and treating a date to an expensive dinner on the status and reputation of both men and women. Dating someone who is physically attractive greatly increases a man's status, whereas it increases a woman's status only somewhat. In contrast, a man who dates an unattractive woman experiences a moderate decrease in status and reputation, whereas a woman who dates a physically unattractive man experiences only a trivial decrease in status. On a scale of +4.00 (great increase in status) to −4.00 (great decrease in status), going out with someone who was not physically attractive affected men's status by −1.47, whereas it affected women's status by only −0.89.

These trends occur in different cultures. When my research collaborators and I surveyed native residents of China, Poland, Guam, and Germany in parallel studies of human prestige criteria, we found that in each of these countries, acquiring a physically attractive mate enhances a man's status more than a woman's. In each country, having an unattractive mate hurts a man's status more than a woman's. And in each country dating an unattractive person hurts a man's status moderately but has only a slight or inconsequential effect on a woman's status. Men across cultures today value attractive women not only because attractiveness signals a woman's reproductive capacity but also because it signals status.

Homosexual Mate Preferences

The premium that men place on a mate's appearance is not limited to heterosexuals. Homosexual relationships provide an acid test for the evolutionary basis of sex differences in the desires for a mate.[33] The issues are whether homosexual men show preferences more or less like those of other men, differing only in the sex of the person they desire; whether they show preferences similar to those of women; or whether they have unique preferences unlike the typical preferences of either sex.

No one knows what the exact percentage of homosexuals is in any culture, past or present. Part of the difficulty lies with definitions. The sexologist Alfred Kinsey estimated that more than a third of all men engaged at some point in life in some form of homosexual activity, typically as part of adolescent experimentation. Far fewer people, however, express a strong preference for the same sex as a mate. Conservative estimates put the figure at about 3 to 4 percent for men and 1 percent for women.[34] The discrepancy between the percentages of people who have engaged in some kinds of homosexual acts and people who express a core preference for partners of the same sex suggests an important distinction between the underlying psychology of preference and the outward manifestation of behavior. Many men who prefer women as mates may nonetheless substitute a man as a sex partner, either because of an inability to attract women or because of a temporary situational constraint that precludes access to women, such as being in prison.

No one knows why some people have a strong preference for members of their own sex as mates, although this lack of knowledge has not held back speculation. One suggestion is the so-called kin selection theory of homosexuality, which holds that homosexuality evolved when some people served better as an aide to their close genetic relatives than as a reproducer.[35] For example, an ancestral man who had difficulty in attracting a woman might have been better off investing effort in his sister's children than in trying to secure a mate himself. A related theory is that some parents manipulate particular children, perhaps those who might have a lower value on the mating market, to become homosexual in order to aid other family members, even if it would be in the child's best reproductive interest to reproduce directly.[36] No current evidence exists to support either of these theories. The origins of homosexuality remain a mystery.

Homosexual preferences in a mate, in contrast, are far less mysterious. Studies document the great importance that homosexual men place on the youth and physical appearance of their partners. William Jankowiak and his colleagues asked homosexual and heterosexual individuals, both men and women, to rank sets of photographs of men and women differing in age on physical attractiveness.[37] Homosexual and heterosexual men alike rank the younger partners as consistently more attractive. Neither lesbian nor heterosexual women, on the contrary, place any importance on youth in their ranking of attractiveness. These results suggest that lesbian women are very much like heterosexual women in their mate preferences, except with respect to the sex of the person they desire. And homosexual men are similar to heterosexual men in their mate preferences.

The psychologists Kay Deaux and Randel Hanna conducted the most systematic study of homosexual mate preferences.[38] They collected eight hundred ads from several East Coast and West Coast newspapers, equally sampling male heterosexuals, female heterosexuals, male homosexuals, and female homosexuals. Using a coding scheme, they calculated the frequency with which each of these groups offers and seeks particular characteristics, such as physical attractiveness, financial security, and personality traits.

Lesbians tend to be similar to heterosexual women in placing little emphasis on physical appearance, with only 19.5 percent of the heterosexual women and 18 percent of the lesbians mentioning this quality. In contrast, 48 percent of heterosexual men and 29 percent of homosexual men state that they are seeking attractive partners. Among all groups, lesbians list their own physical attractiveness less often than any other group; mentions appear in only 30 percent of their ads. Heterosexual women, in contrast, offer attractiveness in 69.5 percent of the ads, male homosexuals in 53.5 percent of the ads, and male heterosexuals in 42.5 percent of the ads. Only 16 percent of the lesbians request a photograph of respondents to their ads, whereas 35 percent of heterosexual women, 34.5 percent of homosexual men, and 37 percent of heterosexual men make this request.

Lesbians are distinct from the other three groups in specifying fewer physical characteristics, such as weight, height, eye color, or body build. Whereas only 7 percent of lesbian women mention their desire for specific physical attributes, 20 percent of heterosexual women, 38 percent of homosexual men, and 33.5 percent of heterosexual men request particular physical traits. And as with overall attractiveness, lesbians stand out in that only 41.5 percent list physical attributes among their assets offered, whereas 64 percent of heterosexual women, 74 percent of homosexual men, and 71.5 percent of heterosexual men offer particular physical assets. It is clear that homosexual men are similar to heterosexual men in the premium they place on physical appearance. Lesbians are more like heterosexual women in their desires, but where they differ, they place even less value on physical qualities, both in their offerings and in the qualities they seek.

Less formal studies confirm the centrality of youth and physical appearance for male homosexuals. Surveys of the gay mating market consistently find that physical attractiveness is the key determinant of the desirability of a potential partner. Male homosexuals place great emphasis on dress, grooming, and physical condition. And youth is a key ingredient in judging attractiveness: "Age is the monster figure of the gay world."[39]

The sociologists Philip Blumstein and Pepper Schwartz found that the physical beauty of a partner is critical to the desires of homosexual and heterosexual men more than to lesbian or heterosexual women, even among already coupled individuals.[40] All members of their sample were in relationships. They found that 57 percent of gay men and 59 percent of heterosexual men feel that it is important that their partner be sexy looking. In contrast, only 31 percent of the heterosexual women and 35 percent of the lesbians state that sexy looks are important in a partner. Male homosexuals and male heterosexuals seem to have indistinguishable mating preferences, except with respect to the sex of their preferred partner. Both place a premium on appearance, and youth is a central ingredient in their definition of beauty.

Men Who Achieve Their Desires

Although most men place a premium on youth and beauty in a mate, it is clear that not all men are successful in achieving their desires. Men who lack the status and resources that women want, for example, generally have the most difficult time attracting pretty young women and must settle for less than their ideal. Evidence for this possibility comes from men who have historically been in a position to get exactly what they prefer, such as kings and other men of unusually high status. In the 1700s and 1800s, for example, wealthier men from the Krummerhörn population of Germany married younger brides than did men lacking wealth. Similarly, high-status men, from the Norwegian farmers of 1700 to 1900 to the Kipsigis in contemporary Kenya, consistently secured younger brides than did their lower-status counterparts.[41]

Kings and despots routinely stocked their harems with young, attractive, nubile women and had sex with them frequently. The Moroccan emperor Moulay Ismail the Bloodthirsty, for example, acknowledged having sired 888 children. His harem had 500 women. But when a woman reached the age of thirty, she was banished from the emperor's harem, sent to a lower-level leader's harem, and replaced by a younger woman. Roman, Babylonian, Egyptian, Incan, Indian, and Chinese emperors all shared the tastes of Emperor Ismail and enjoined their trustees to scour the land for as many young pretty women as could be found.[42]

Marriage patterns in modern America confirm the fact that the men with the most resources are the best equipped to actualize their preferences. High-status men, such as the aging rock stars Rod Stewart and Mick Jagger and the movie stars Warren Beatty and Jack Nicholson, frequently select women two or three decades younger. One study examined the impact of a man's occupational status on the woman he marries. Men who are high in occupational status are able to marry women who are considerably more physically attractive than are men who are low in occupational status.[43] Indeed, a man's occupational status seems to be the best predictor of the attractiveness of the woman he marries. Men in a position to attract younger women often do.

Men who enjoy high status and income are apparently aware of their ability to attract women of higher value. In a study of a computer dating service involving 1,048 German men and 1,590 German women, the ethologist Karl Grammer found that as men's income goes up, they seek younger partners.[44] Men earning more than 10,000 deutsche marks, for example, advertised for mates who were between five and fifteen years younger, whereas men earning less than 1,000 deutsche marks advertised for mates who were up to five years younger. Each increment in income is accompanied by a decrease in the age of the woman sought.

Not all men, however, have the status, position, or resources to attract young women, and some men end up mating with older women. Many factors determine the age of the woman at marriage, including the woman's preferences, the man's own age, the man's mating assets, the strength of the man's other mating preferences, and the woman's appearance. Mating preferences are not invariably translated into actual mating decisions for all people all of the time, just as food preferences are not invariably translated into actual eating decisions for all people all of the time. But men who are in a position to get what they want often marry young, attractive women. Ancestral men who actualized these preferences enjoyed greater reproductive success than those who did not.

Media Effects on Standards

Advertisers exploit the universal appeal of beautiful, youthful women. Madison Avenue is sometimes charged with inflicting pain on people by advancing a single, arbitrary standard of beauty that everyone must live up to.[45] Advertisements are thought to convey unnatural images of beauty and to tell people to strive to embody those images. This interpretation is at least partially false. The standards of beauty are not arbitrary but rather embody reliable cues to reproductive value. Advertisers have no special interest in inculcating a particular set of beauty standards and merely want to use whatever sells most easily. Advertisers perch a clear-skinned, regular-featured young woman on the hood of the latest model car because the image exploits men's evolved psychological mechanisms and therefore sells cars, not because they want to promulgate a single standard of beauty.

The media images we are bombarded with daily, however, have a potentially pernicious consequence. In one study, after groups of men looked at photographs of either highly attractive women or women of average attractiveness, they were asked to evaluate their commitment to their current romantic partner.[46] Disturbingly, the men who had viewed pictures of attractive women thereafter judged their actual partner to be less attractive than did the men who had viewed analogous pictures of women who were average in attractiveness. Perhaps more important, the men who had viewed attractive women thereafter rated themselves as less committed, less satisfied, less serious, and less close to their actual partners. Parallel results were obtained in another study in which men viewed physically attractive nude centerfolds—they rated themselves as less attracted to their partners.[47]

The reason for these distressing changes are found in the unrealistic nature of the images. The few attractive women selected for advertisements are chosen from thousands of applicants. In many cases, literally thousands of pictures are taken of a chosen woman. *Playboy*, for example, is reputed to shoot roughly six thousand pictures for its centerfold each month. From thousands of pictures, a few are selected for advertisements and centerfolds. So what men see are the most attractive women in their most attractive pose with the most attractive background in the most attractive airbrushed photographs. Contrast these photographs with what you would have witnessed in ancestral times, living in a band of a few score individuals. It is doubtful that you would see hundreds or even dozens of attractive women in that environment. If there were plenty of attractive and hence reproductively valuable women, however, a man might reasonably consider switching mates, and hence he would decrease his commitment to his existing mate.

We carry with us the same evaluative mechanisms that evolved in ancient times. Now, however, these mechanisms are artificially stimulated by the dozens of attractive women we witness daily in our visually saturated culture in magazines, billboards, television, and movies. These images do not represent real women in our actual social environment. Rather, they exploit mechanisms designed for a different environment. But they may create sources of unhappiness by interfering with existing real-life relationships.

As a consequence of viewing such images, men become dissatisfied and less committed to their mates. The potential damage inflicted by these images affects women as well, because they create a spiraling and unhealthy competition with other women. Women find themselves competing with each other to embody the images they see daily—images desired by men. The unprecedented rates of anorexia nervosa and radical cosmetic surgery may stem in part from these media images; some women go to extreme lengths to fulfill men's desires. But the images do not cause this unfortunate result by creating standards of beauty that were previously absent. Rather, they work by exploiting men's existing evolved standards of beauty and women's competitive mating mechanisms on an unprecedented and unhealthy scale.

Facial and bodily beauty, as important as they are in men's mating preferences, solve for men only one set of adaptive problems, that of identifying and becoming aroused by women who show signs of high reproductive capacity. Selecting a reproductively valuable woman, however, provides no guarantee that her value will be monopolized exclusively by one man. The next critical adaptive problem is to ensure paternity.

Chastity and Fidelity

Mammalian females typically enter estrus only at intervals. Vivid visual cues and strong scents often accompany estrus and powerfully attract males. Sexual intercourse occurs primarily in this narrow envelope of time. Women, however, do not have any sort of genital display when they ovulate. Nor is there evidence that women secrete detectable olfactory cues. Indeed, women are rare among primates in possessing the unusual adaptation of concealed or cryptic ovulation.[48] Cryptic female ovulation obscures a woman's reproductive status.

Concealed ovulation dramatically changed the ground rules of human mating. Women became attractive to men not just during ovulation but throughout their ovulatory cycles. Cryptic ovulation created a special adaptive problem for men by decreasing the certainty of their paternity. Consider a primate male who monopolizes a female for the brief period that she is in estrus. In contrast to human males, he can be fairly confident of his paternity. The period during which he must guard her and have sex with her is sharply constrained. Before and after her estrus, he can go about his other business without running the risk of cuckoldry.

Ancestral men did not have this luxury. Our human ancestors never knew when a woman was ovulating. Because mating is not the sole activity that humans require to survive and reproduce, women could not be guarded around the clock. And the more time a man spent in guarding, the less time he had available for grappling with other critical adaptive problems. Ancestral men, therefore, were faced with a unique paternity problem not faced by other primate males—how to be certain of their paternity when ovulation was concealed.

Marriage provided one solution.[49] Men who married would benefit reproductively relative to other men by substantially increasing their certainty of paternity. Repeated sexual contact throughout the ovulation cycle raised a man's odds that a woman would bear his child. The social traditions of marriage function as public ties about the couple. Fidelity is enforced by family members as well as by the couple. Marriage also provides opportunities to learn intimately about the mate's personality, making it difficult for her to hide signs of infidelity. These benefits of marriage would have outweighed the costs of forgoing the sexual opportunities available to ancestral bachelors, at least under some conditions.

For an ancestral man to reap the reproductive benefits of marriage, he had to seek reasonable assurances that his wife would indeed remain sexually faithful to him. Men who failed to be aware of these cues would have suffered in reproductive success because they lost the time and resources devoted to searching, courting, and competing. Failure to be sensitive to these cues would have diverted years of the woman's parental investment to another man's children. Perhaps even more devastating in reproductive terms, failure to ensure fidelity meant that a man's efforts would be channeled to another man's gametes. Men who were indifferent to the potential sexual contact between their wives and other men would not have been successful at passing on their genes.

Our forebears solved this uniquely male adaptive problem by seeking qualities in a potential mate that might increase the odds of securing their paternity. At least two preferences in a mate could solve the problem for males: the desire for premarital chastity and the quest for post-marital sexual loyalty. Before the use of modern contraceptives, chastity provided a cue to the future certainty of paternity. On the assumption that a woman's proclivities toward chaste behavior would be stable over time, her premarital chastity signaled her likely future fidelity. A man who did not obtain a chaste mate risked becoming involved with a woman who would cuckold him.

In modern times men value virgin brides more than women value virgin grooms. Within the United States, a cross-generational mating study found that men value chastity in a potential mate more than women do. But the value they place on it has declined over the past half century, coinciding with the increasing availability of birth control and probably as a consequence of this cultural change.[50] In the 1930s, men viewed chastity as close to indispensable, but in the past two decades men have rated it as desirable but not crucial. Among the eighteen characteristics rated, chastity declined from the tenth most valued in 1939 to the seventeenth most valued in the late 1980s. Furthermore, not all American men value chastity equally. Regions differ. College students in Texas, for example, desire a chaste mate more than college students in California, rating it a 1.13 as opposed to 0.73 on a 3.00 scale. Despite the decline in the value of chastity in the twentieth century and despite regional variations, the sex difference remains—men more than women emphasize chastity in a potential committed mateship.

The trend for men to value chastity more than women holds up worldwide, but cultures vary tremendously in the value placed on chastity. At one extreme, people in China, India, Indonesia, Iran, Taiwan, and the Palestinian Arab areas of Israel attach a high value to chastity in a potential mate. At the opposite extreme, people in Sweden, Norway, Finland, the Netherlands, West Germany, and France believe that virginity is largely irrelevant or unimportant in a potential mate.

In contrast to the worldwide consistency in the different preferences by sex for youth and physical attractiveness, only 62 percent of the cultures in the international study on choosing a mate place a significantly different value by sex on chastity in a committed mateship. Where sex differences in the value of virginity are found, however, men invariably place a greater value on it than women do. In no case do women value chastity more than men do.

The cultural variability in the preference of each sex for chastity is explained by several factors, including the prevailing incidence of premarital sex, the degree to which chastity can be demanded in a mate, the economic independence of women, and the reliability with which chastity can be evaluated. Chastity differs from other attributes, such as a woman's physical attractiveness, in that it is less directly observable. Even physical tests of female virginity are unreliable, whether from variations in the structure of the hymen, rupture due to nonsexual causes, or deliberate alteration.[51] In Japan, for example, there is currently a booming medical business in "remaking virgins" by surgically reconstructing the hymen, because Japanese men continue to place a relatively high value on chaste brides, rating it 1.42 on a scale of 0.00 to 3.00; American men rate chastity only 0.85, and German men rate it only 0.34.

Variation in the value people place on chastity may be traceable in part to variability in the economic independence of women and in women's control of their own sexuality. In some cultures, such as Sweden, premarital sex is not discouraged and practically no one is a virgin at marriage. One reason may be that women in Sweden are far less economically reliant on men than women in most other cultures. The legal scholar Richard Posner notes that marriage provides few benefits for Swedish women relative to women in most other cultures.[52] The Swedish social welfare system includes day care for children, long paid maternity leaves, and many other material benefits. The Swedish taxpayers effectively provide what husbands formerly provided, freeing women from their economic dependence on men. Women's economic independence from men lowers the cost to them of a free and active sex life before marriage, or as an alternative to marriage. Thus, practically no Swedish women are virgins at marriage, and hence the value men place on chastity has commensurately declined to a worldwide low of 0.25.[53]

Differences in the economic independence of women, in the benefits provided by husbands, and in the intensity of competition for husbands all drive the critical cultural variation.[54] Where women benefit from marriage and where competition for husbands is fierce, women compete to signal chastity, causing the average amount of premarital sex to go down. Where women control their economic fate, do not require so much of men's investment, and hence need to compete less, women are freer to disregard men's preferences, which causes the average amount of premarital sex to go up. Men everywhere might value chastity if they could get it, but in some cultures they simply cannot demand it of their brides.

From a man's reproductive perspective, a more important cue to the certainty of paternity than virginity per se is the assurance of future fidelity. If men cannot reasonably demand that their mates be virgins, they can require of them sexual loyalty or fidelity. In fact, the study of temporary and permanent mating found that American men view the lack of sexual experience as desirable in a spouse. Furthermore, men see promiscuity as especially undesirable in a permanent mate, rating it –2.07 on a scale of –3.00 to +3.00. The actual amount of prior sexual activity in a potential mate, rather than virginity per se, would have provided an excellent guide for ancestral men who sought to solve the problem of uncertainty of paternity. Indeed, contemporary studies show that the single best predictor of extramarital sex is premarital sexual permissiveness—people who have many sexual partners before marriage are more unfaithful than those who have few sexual partners before marriage.[55]

Modern men place a premium on fidelity. When American men in the study of temporary and permanent partners evaluated sixty-seven possible characteristics for their desirability in a committed mateship, faithfulness and sexual loyalty emerged as the most highly valued traits.[56] All men give these traits the highest rating possible, an average of +2.85 on a scale of –3.00 to +3.00. Men regard unfaithfulness as the least desirable characteristic in a wife, rating it a –2.93, reflecting the high value that men place on fidelity. Men abhor promiscuity and infidelity in their wives. Unfaithfulness proves to be more upsetting to men than any other pain a spouse can inflict on her mate. Women also become extremely upset over an unfaithful mate, but several other factors, such as sexual aggressiveness, exceed infidelity in the grief they cause women.[57]

The sexual revolution of the 1960s and 1970s, with its promises of sexual freedom and lack of possessiveness, apparently has had a limited impact on men's preferences for sexual fidelity. Cues to fidelity still signal that the woman is willing to channel all of her reproductive value exclusively to her husband. A woman's future sexual conduct looms large in men's marriage decisions.

Evolutionary Bases of Men's Desires

The great emphasis that men place on a woman's physical appearance is not some immutable biological law of the animal world. Indeed, in many other species, such as the peacock, it is the females who place the greater value on physical appearance. Nor is men's preference for youth a biological universal in the animal world. Some primate males, such as orangutans, chimpanzees, and Japanese macaques, prefer older females, who have already demonstrated their reproductive abilities by giving birth; they show low sexual interest in adolescent females because they have low fertility.[58] But human males have faced a unique set of adaptive problems and so have evolved a unique sexual psychology. They prefer youth because of the centrality of marriage in human mating. Their desires are designed to gauge a woman's future reproductive potential, not just immediate impregnation. They place a premium on physical appearance because of the abundance of reliable cues it provides to the reproductive potential of a potential mate.

Men worldwide want physically attractive, young, and sexually loyal wives who will remain faithful to them until death. These preferences cannot be attributed to Western culture, to capitalism, to white Anglo-Saxon bigotry, to the media, or to incessant brainwashing by advertisers. They are universal across cultures and are absent in none. They are deeply ingrained, evolved psychological mechanisms that drive our mating decisions, just as our evolved taste preferences drive our decisions on food consumption.

Homosexual mate preferences, ironically, provide a testament to the depth of these evolved psychological mechanisms. The fact that physical appearance figures centrally in homosexual men's mate preferences, and that youth is a key ingredient in their standards of beauty, suggests that not even variations in sexual orientation alter these fundamental mechanisms.

These circumstances upset some people, because they seem unfair. We can modify our physical attractiveness only in limited ways, and some people are born better looking than others. Beauty is not distributed democratically. A woman cannot alter her age, and a woman's reproductive value declines more sharply with age than a man's; evolution deals women a cruel hand, at least in this regard. Women fight the decline through cosmetics, through plastic surgery, through aerobics classes—an eight billion dollar cosmetics industry has emerged in America to exploit these trends.

After a lecture of mine on the subject of sex differences in mate preferences, one woman suggested that I should suppress my findings because of the distress they would cause women. Women already have it hard enough in this male-dominated world, she felt, without having scientists tell them that their mating problems may be based in men's evolved psychology. Yet suppression of this truth is unlikely to help, just as concealing the fact that people have evolved preferences for succulent, ripe fruit is unlikely to change their preferences. Railing against men for the importance they place on beauty, youth, and fidelity is like railing against meat eaters because they prefer animal protein. Telling men not to become aroused by signs of youth and health is like telling them not to experience sugar as sweet.

Many people hold an idealistic view that standards of beauty are arbitrary, that beauty is only skin deep, that cultures differ dramatically in the importance they place on appearance, and that Western standards stem from brainwashing by the media, parents, culture, or other agents of socialization. But standards of attractiveness are not arbitrary—they reflect cues to youth and health, and hence to reproductive value. Beauty is not merely skin deep. It reflects internal reproductive capabilities. Although fertility technology may grant women greater latitude for reproducing across a wider age span, men's preferences for women who show apparent signs of reproductive capacity continue to operate today, in spite of the fact that they were designed in an ancestral world that may no longer exist.

Cultural conditions, economic circumstances, and technological inventions, however, play a critical role in men's evaluation of the importance of chastity. Where women are less economically dependent on men, as in Sweden, sexuality is highly permissive, and men do not desire or demand chastity from potential wives. These shifts highlight the sensitivity of some mate preferences to features of culture and context.

Despite cultural variations, sexual fidelity tops the list of men's long-term mate preferences. Although many men in Western culture cannot require virginity, they do insist on sexual loyalty. Even though birth control technology may render this mate preference unnecessary for its original function of ensuring paternity, the mate preference perseveres. A man does not relax his desire for fidelity in his wife just because she takes birth control pills. This constant demonstrates the importance of our evolved sexual psychology—a psychology that was designed to deal with critical cues from an ancestral world but that continues to operate with tremendous force in today's modern world of mating.

That world of mating, however, involves more than marriage. If ancestral couples had always remained faithful, there would have been no selection pressure for the intense concern with fidelity. The existence of this concern means that both sexes must also have engaged in short-term mating and casual sex. So we must turn to this dark and shrouded region of human sexuality.

4

Casual Sex

The biological irony of the double standard is that males could not have been selected for promiscuity if historically females had always denied them opportunity for expression of the trait.
—Robert Smith, *Sperm Competition and the Evolution of Mating Systems*

IMAGINE THAT AN ATTRACTIVE PERSON of the opposite sex walks up to you on a college campus and says: "Hi, I've been noticing you around town lately, and I find you very attractive. Would you go to bed with me?" How would you respond? If you are like 100 percent of the women in one study, you would give an emphatic no. You would be offended, insulted, or plain puzzled by the request out of the blue. But if you are a man, the odds are 75 percent that you would say yes.[1] You would most likely feel flattered by the request. Men and women react differently when it comes to casual sex.

Casual sex typically requires the consent of two persons. Ancestral men could not have carried out temporary affairs unaided. At least some ancestral women must have practiced the behavior some of the time, because if all women historically had mated for life with a single man and had no premarital sex, the opportunities for casual sex with consenting women would have vanished.[2]

In ancestral environments, one of the keys to extramarital sexual opportunities for a woman was a lapse in scrutiny by the woman's regular mate—a temporary failure of the man to guard her. Hunting opened wide gaps in scrutiny, because men went off for hours, days, or weeks to procure meat. Hunting left a man's wife either unguarded or less vigilantly guarded by the kin left behind to watch her.

In spite of the prevalence and evolutionary significance of casual sex, practically all research on human mating has centered on marriage. The fact that temporary mating is by definition transient and often cloaked in greater secrecy makes it difficult to study. In Kinsey's research on sexual behavior, for example, the question about extramarital sex caused many people to refuse to be interviewed altogether. Among those who did consent to an interview, many declined to answer questions about extramarital sex.

Our relative ignorance of casual mating also reflects deeply held values. Many shun the promiscuous and scorn the unfaithful because they often interfere with our own sexual strategies. From the perspective of a married woman or man, for example, the presence of promiscuous people endangers marital fidelity. From the perspective of a single woman or man seeking marriage, the presence of promiscuous people lowers the likelihood of finding someone willing to commit. We derogate short-term strategists as cads, tramps, or womanizers because we want to discourage casual sex, at least among some people. It is a taboo topic. But it fascinates us. We must look closer and ask why it looms so large in our mating repertoire.

Physiological Clues to Sexual Strategies

Existing adaptations in our psychology, anatomy, physiology, and behavior reflect prior selection pressures. Just as our current fear of snakes betrays an ancestral hazard, so our sexual anatomy and physiology reveal an ancient story of short-term sexual strategies. That story has just recently come to light through careful studies of men's testes size, ejaculate volume, and variations in sperm production.

There are a number of physiological clues to our history of multiple matings. One clue comes from the size of men's testes. Large testes typically evolve as a consequence of intense sperm competition, when the sperm from two or more males occupy the reproductive tract of the female at the same time because she has copulated with them.[3] Sperm competition exerts a selection pressure on males to produce large ejaculates containing numerous sperm. In the race to the valuable egg, the more voluminous sperm-laden ejaculate has an advantage in displacing the ejaculate of other men inside the woman's body.

The testes size of men, relative to their body weight, is far larger than that of gorillas and orangutans. Male testes account for 0.018 percent of body weight in gorillas and 0.048 percent in orangutans. In contrast, men's testes account for 0.079 percent of body weight, or 60 percent more than that of orangutans and more than four times the percentage of gorillas. Men's relatively large testes provide one solid piece of evidence that women in human evolutionary history sometimes had sex with more than one man within a time span of a few days. The attribution made in many cultures that a man has "big balls" may be a metaphorical expression that has a literal referent. But humans do not possess the largest testes of all the primates. Human testicular volume is substantially smaller than that of the highly promiscuous chimpanzee, whose testes account for 0.269 percent of body weight, which is more than three times the percentage of men. These findings suggest that our human ancestors rarely reached the chimpanzee's extreme of promiscuity.[4]

Another clue to the evolutionary existence of casual mating comes from variations in sperm production and insemination.[5] In a study to determine the effect of separating mates from each other on sperm production, thirty-five couples agreed to provide ejaculates resulting from sexual intercourse, either from condoms or from the flowback, or gelatinous mass of seminal fluid that is spontaneously ejected by a woman at various points after intercourse. All the couples had been separated from each other for varying intervals of time.

Men's sperm count increased dramatically with the increasing amount of time the couple had been apart. The more time spent apart, the more sperm the husbands inseminated in their wives when they finally had sex. When the couples spent 100 percent of their time together, men inseminated only 389 million sperm per ejaculate. But when the couples spent only 5 percent of their time together, men inseminated 712 million sperm per ejaculate, or almost double the amount. Sperm insemination increases when other men's sperm might be inside the wife's reproductive tract at the same time, as a consequence of the opportunity provided for extramarital sex by the couple's separation. This increase in sperm is precisely what would be expected if humans had an ancestral history of some casual sex and marital infidelity.

The increase in sperm insemination by the husband upon prolonged separation ensures that his sperm will stand a greater chance in the race to the egg, by crowding out or displacing the interloper's sperm. A man appears to inseminate just enough sperm to replace the sperm that have died inside the woman since his last sexual episode with her, thereby "topping off" his wife to a particular level to keep the population of his sperm inside her relatively constant. Men carry a physiological mechanism that elevates sperm count when their wives may have had opportunities to be unfaithful.

The physiology of women's orgasm provides another clue to an evolutionary history of short-term mating. Once it was thought that a woman's orgasm functions to make her sleepy and keep her reclined, thereby decreasing the likelihood that sperm will flow out and increasing the likelihood of conceiving. But if the function of orgasm were to keep the woman reclined so as to delay flowback, then more sperm would be retained when flowback is delayed. That is not the case. Rather, there is no link between the timing of the flowback and the number of sperm retained.[6]

Women on average eject roughly 35 percent of the sperm within thirty minutes of the time of insemination. If the woman has an orgasm, however, she retains 70 percent of the sperm and ejects only 30 percent. Lack of an orgasm leads to the ejection of more sperm. This evidence is consistent with the theory that women's orgasm functions to suck up the sperm from the vagina into the cervical canal and uterus, increasing the probability of conception.

The number of sperm a woman retains is also linked with whether she is having an affair. Women time their adulterous liaisons in a way that is reproductively detrimental to their husbands. In a nationwide sex survey of 3,679 women in Britain, the women recorded their menstrual cycles as well as the timing of their copulations with their husbands and, if they were having affairs, with their lovers. It turned out that women who are having affairs appear to time their copulations to coincide with the point in their ovulatory cycle when they are most likely to be ovulating and hence are most likely to conceive.[7]

This may not be good news for husbands, but it suggests that women have evolved strategies that function for their own reproductive benefit in the context of extramarital affairs, perhaps by securing superior genes from a high-status man and investment from their regular mate. Most of us could not have imagined that human physiological mechanisms approached this level of complex functionality. These mechanisms suggest a long evolutionary history of casual mating.

Lust

But anatomy and physiology yield only one set of clues to a human history of casual mating. In addition to anatomical and physiological features, there are psychological mechanisms that point to a human past of casual sex. Because the adaptive benefits of temporary liaisons differ for each sex, however, evolution has forged different psychological mechanisms for men and women. The primary benefit of casual sex to ancestral men was a direct increase in the number of offspring, so that men faced a key adaptive problem of gaining sexual access to a variety of different women. As a solution to this adaptive problem, men have evolved a number of psychological mechanisms that cause them to seek a variety of sexual partners.

One psychological solution to the problem of securing sexual access to a variety of partners is old-fashioned lust. Men have evolved a powerful desire for sexual access to a variety of women. When President Jimmy Carter told a reporter that he "had lust in his heart," he expressed honestly a universal male desire for sexual variety. Men do not always act on this desire, but it is a motivating force. "Even if only one impulse in a thousand is consummated, the function of lust nonetheless is to motivate sexual intercourse."[8]

To find how many sexual partners people in fact desire, the study of temporary and permanent mating asked unmarried American college students to identify how many sex partners they would ideally like to have within various time periods, ranging from the next month to their entire lifetime.[9] Men desire more sex partners than women at each of the different time intervals. Within the next year, for example, men state on average that ideally they would like to have more than six sex partners, whereas women say that they would like to have only one. Within the next three years, men desire ten sex partners, whereas women want only two. The differences between men and women in the ideal number desired of sex partners continue to increase as the time becomes longer. For the lifetime, men on average would like to have eighteen sex partners and women only four or five. Men's inclination to count their "conquests" and to "put notches on their belt," long erroneously attributed in Western culture to male immaturity or masculine insecurity, instead signals an adaptation to brief sexual encounters.

Another psychological solution to the problem of gaining sexual access to a variety of partners is to let little time elapse before seeking sexual intercourse. The less time that he permits to elapse before obtaining sexual intercourse, the larger the number of women a man can successfully mate with. Large time investments absorb more of a man's mating effort and interfere with solving the problem of number and variety. In the business world, time is money. In the mating world, time is sexual opportunity.

College men and women in the study of temporary and permanent mating rated how likely they would be to consent to sex with someone they viewed as desirable if they had known the person for only an hour, a day, a week, a month, six months, a year, two years, or five years. Both men and women say that they would probably have sex upon knowing a desirable potential mate for five years. At every shorter interval, however, men exceed women in their reported likelihood of having sex. Five years or six months—it's all the same for men. They express equal eagerness for sex with women they have known for either length of time. In contrast, women drop from probable consent to sex after five years' acquaintance to neutral feelings about sex after knowing a person for six months.

Having known a potential mate for only one week, men are still on average positive about the possibility of consenting to sex. Women, in sharp contrast, are highly unlikely to have sex after knowing someone for just a week. Upon knowing a potential mate for merely one hour, men are slightly disinclined to consider having sex, but the disinclination is not strong. For most women, sex after just one hour is a virtual impossibility. As with men's desires, men's inclination to let little time elapse before seeking sexual intercourse offers a partial solution to the adaptive problem of gaining sexual access to a variety of partners.

Standards for Short-Term Mates

Yet another psychological solution to securing a variety of casual sex partners is men's relaxation of their standards for acceptable partners. High standards for attributes such as age, intelligence, personality, and marital status function to exclude the majority of potential mates from consideration. Relaxed standards ensure the presence of more eligible players.

College students in the study provided information about the minimum and maximum acceptable ages of a partner for a temporary and permanent sexual relationship. College men accept an age range that is roughly four years wider than women do for a temporary liaison. Men are willing to mate in the short run with members of the opposite sex who are as young as sixteen and as old as twenty-eight, whereas women require men to be at least eighteen but no older than twenty-six. This relaxation of age restrictions by men does not apply to committed mating, for which the minimum age is seventeen and the maximum is twenty-two, whereas for women the minimum age for committed mating is nineteen and the maximum is twenty-five.

Men relax their standards for a wide variety of other characteristics as well. Out of the sixty-seven characteristics nominated as potentially desirable in a casual mate, men in the study express significantly lower standards than the women do on forty-one of the characteristics. For brief encounters, men require a lower level of such assets as charm, athleticism, education, generosity, honesty, independence, kindness, intellectuality, loyalty, sense of humor, sociability, wealth, responsibility, spontaneity, cooperativeness, and emotional stability. Men thus relax their standards in relation to a range of attributes, which helps to solve the problem of gaining access to a variety of sex partners.

When the college students rated sixty-one undesirable characteristics, women rated roughly one-third of them as more undesirable than men did in the context of casual sex. Men have less objection in short-term relations to drawbacks such as mental abuse, violence, bisexuality, dislike by others, excessive drinking, ignorance, lack of education, possessiveness, promiscuity, selfishness, lack of humor, and lack of sensuality. In contrast, men rate only four negative characteristics as significantly more undesirable than women do: a low sex drive, physical unattractiveness, need for commitment, and hairiness. Men clearly relax their standards more than women do for brief sexual encounters.

Relaxed standards, however, are still standards. Indeed, men's standards for sexual affairs reveal a precise strategy to gain sexual access to a variety of partners. Compared with their long-term preferences, men who seek casual sex partners dislike women who are prudish, conservative, or have a low sex drive. In contrast to their long-term preferences, men value sexual experience in a potential temporary sex partner, which reflects a belief that sexually experienced women are more sexually accessible to them than women who are sexually inexperienced. Men abhor promiscuity or indiscriminate sexuality in a potential wife but believe that promiscuity is either neutral or even mildly desirable in a potential sex partner. Promiscuity, high sex drive, and sexual experience in a woman probably signal an increased likelihood that a man can gain sexual access for the short run. Prudishness and low sex drive, in contrast, signal a difficulty in gaining sexual access and thus interfere with men's short-term sexual strategy.

The distinguishing feature of men's relaxation of standards for a temporary sex partner involves the need for commitment. In contrast to the tremendous positive value of +2.17 that men place on commitment when seeking a marriage partner, men seeking a temporary liaison dislike a woman's seeking a commitment, judging it −1.40, or undesirable, in a short-term partner.[10] Furthermore, men are not particularly bothered by a woman's marital status when they evaluate casual sex partners, because a woman's commitment to another man reduces the odds that she will try to extract a commitment from them. These findings confirm that men shift their desires to minimize their investment in a casual mating, providing an additional clue to an evolutionary history in which men sometimes sought casual, uncommitted sex.

The Coolidge Effect

Another psychological solution to the problem of gaining sexual access to a number of women has to do with men's own arousal by women and is known as the Coolidge effect. The story is told that President Calvin Coolidge and the first lady were being given separate tours

of newly formed government farms. Upon passing the chicken coops
and noticing a rooster vigorously copulating with a hen, Mrs. Coolidge
inquired about how often the rooster performed this duty. "Dozens of
times each day," replied the guide. Mrs. Coolidge asked the guide to
"please mention this fact to the president." When the president passed
by later and was informed of the sexual vigor of the rooster, he asked,
"Always with the same hen?" "Oh, no," the guide replied, "a different
one each time." "Please tell *that* to Mrs. Coolidge," said the president.
And so the Coolidge effect was named, referring to the tendency of
males to be sexually rearoused upon the presentation of novel females,
giving them a further impulse to gain sexual access to multiple women.

The Coolidge effect is a widespread mammalian trait that has been
documented many times.[11] Male rats, rams, cattle, and sheep all show
the effect. In a typical study, a cow is placed in a bull pen, and after
copulation the cow is replaced with another cow. The bull's sexual
response continues unabated with each new cow but diminishes quickly
when the same cow is left in the pen. Males continue to become
aroused to the point of ejaculation in response to novel females, and the
response to the eighth, the tenth, or the twelfth female is nearly as
strong as the response to the first.

Sexual arousal to novelty occurs despite a variety of attempts to
diminish it. For example, when ewes with whom mating had already
occurred are disguised with a canvas covering, the rams are never
fooled. Their response to a female with whom they had already copulated is always lower than with a novel female. The diminished drive is
not a result of the female's having had sex per se; the renewed drive
occurs just as often if the novel female has already copulated with
another male. And the male remains uninterested if the original female
is merely removed and reintroduced. Males are not fooled by this ploy.

Men across cultures also show the Coolidge effect. In Western culture, the frequency of intercourse with one's partner declines steadily
as the relationship lengthens, reaching roughly half the frequency after
one year of marriage as it was during the first month of marriage, and
declining more gradually thereafter. As Donald Symons notes, "the
waning of lust for one's wife is adaptive . . . because it promotes a roving eye."[12] Human roving takes many forms. Men in most cultures pursue extramarital sex more often than do their wives. The Kinsey study,
for example, found that 50 percent of men but only 26 percent of
women had extramarital affairs. Some studies show that the gap may
be narrowing. One study of 8,000 married men and women found that
40 percent of the men and 36 percent of the women reported at least
one affair. The Hite reports on sexuality suggest figures as high as 75

percent for men and 70 percent for women, although these samples are acknowledged not to be representative. More representative samples, such as Hunt's survey of 982 men and 1,044 women, yielded an incidence of 41 percent for men and 18 percent for women.[13] Despite these varying estimates, and a possible narrowing of the gap between the sexes, all studies show sex differences in the incidence and frequency of affairs, with more men having affairs more often and with more partners than women.[14]

Spouse swapping in America is nearly always initiated by husbands, not by wives.[15] Group sex is sought out mainly by men. A Muria male from India summarized the male desire for variety succinctly: "You don't want to eat the same vegetable every day."[16] A Kgatla man from South Africa describes his sexual desires about his two wives: "I find them both equally desirable, but when I have slept with one for three days, by the fourth day she has wearied me, and when I go to the other I find that I have greater passion, she seems more attractive than the first, but it is not really so, for when I return to the latter again there is the same renewed passion."[17]

The anthropologist Thomas Gregor described the sexual feelings of Amazonian Mehinaku men in this way: "Women's sexual attractiveness varies from 'flavorless' (*mana*) to the 'delicious' (*awirintya*) . . . sad to say, sex with spouses is said to be mana, in contrast with sex with lovers, which is nearly always *awirintyapa*."[18] Gustav Flaubert wrote of Madame Bovary that she was "like any other mistress; and the charm of novelty, gradually slipping away like a garment, laid bare the eternal monotony of passion, whose forms and phrases are forever the same." And Kinsey summed it up best: "There seems to be no question but that the human male would be promiscuous in his choice of sexual partners throughout the whole of his life if there were no social restrictions. . . . The human female is much less interested in a variety of partners."[19]

Sexual Fantasies

Sexual fantasies provide still another psychological clue to the evolutionary basis of men's proclivity for casual mating. One of several videos targeted to adolescent men shows a male rock star cavorting across a beach peopled with dozens of beautiful bikini-clad women. Another shows a male rock star caressing the shapely legs of one woman after another as he sings. Yet another shows a male rock star gazing at dozens of women who are wearing only underwear. Since these videos are designed to appeal to adolescent male audiences, the implication is clear. A key male sexual fantasy is to have sexual access to dozens of fresh, beautiful women who respond eagerly.

There are huge differences between men and women with regard to sexual fantasy. Studies from Japan, Great Britain, and the United States show that men have roughly twice as many sexual fantasies as women.[20] In their sleep men are more likely than women to dream about sexual events. Men's sexual fantasies more often include strangers, multiple partners, or anonymous partners. Most men report that during a single fantasy episode they sometimes change sexual partners, whereas most women report that they rarely change sexual partners. Forty-three percent of women but only 12 percent of men report that they never substitute or switch sexual partners during a fantasy episode. Thirty-two percent of men but only 8 percent of women report having imagined sexual encounters with over a thousand different partners in their lifetime. Fantasies about group sex occur among 33 percent of the men but only 18 percent of the women.[21] A typical male fantasy, in one man's description, is having "six or more naked women licking, kissing, and fellating me."[22] Another man reported the fantasy of "being the mayor of a small town filled with nude girls from 20 to 24. I like to take walks, and pick out the best-looking one that day, and she engages in intercourse with me. All the women have sex with me any time I want."[23] Numbers and novelty are key ingredients of men's fantasy lives.

Men focus on body parts and sexual positions stripped of emotional context. Male sexual fantasies are heavily visual, focusing on smooth skin and moving body parts. During their sexual fantasies, 81 percent of men but only 43 percent of women focus on visual images rather than feelings. Attractive women with lots of exposed skin who show signs of easy access and no commitment are frequent components of men's fantasies. As Bruce Ellis and Donald Symons observe, "The most striking feature of [male fantasy] is that sex is sheer lust and physical gratification, devoid of encumbering relationships, emotional elaboration, complicated plot lines, flirtation, courtship, and extended foreplay."[24] These fantasies betray a psychology attuned to seeking sexual access to a variety of partners.

Women's sexual fantasies, in contrast, often contain familiar partners. Fifty-nine percent of American women but only 28 percent of American men report that their sexual fantasies typically focus on someone with whom they are already romantically and sexually involved. Emotions and personality are crucial for women. Forty-one percent of the women but only 16 percent of the men report that they focus most heavily on the personal and emotional characteristics of the fantasized partner. And 57 percent of women but only 19 percent of men report that they focus on feelings as opposed to visual images. As one woman observed: "I usually think about the guy I am with. Sometimes I realize that the feelings will overwhelm me, envelop me, sweep me away."[25] Women emphasize tenderness, romance, and personal involvement in their sexual fantasies. Women pay more attention to the way their partners respond to them than to visual images of the partner.[26]

Perceptions of Attractiveness

Another psychological clue to men's strategy of casual sex comes from studies that examine shifts in judgments of attractiveness over the course of an evening at a singles bar. In one study, 137 men and 80 women were approached at nine o'clock, ten thirty, and twelve midnight and asked to rate the attractiveness of members of the opposite sex in the bar using a 10-point scale.[27] As closing time approached, men viewed women as increasingly attractive. The judgments at nine o'clock were 5.5, but by midnight they had increased to over 6.5. Women's judgments of men's attractiveness also increased over time. But women's ratings overall of the male bar patrons were lower than men's ratings of women. Women rate the men at the bar as just below the average of 5.0 at nine o'clock, increasing near the midnight closing time to only 5.5.

Men's shift in perceptions of attractiveness near closing time occurs regardless of how much alcohol has been consumed. Whether a man has consumed a single drink or six drinks has no effect on the shift in viewing women as more attractive near closing time. The often noted "beer goggles" phenomenon, whereby women are presumed to be viewed as more attractive with increasing intoxication, may instead be attributable to a psychological mechanism sensitive to decreasing opportunities for casual sex over the course of the evening. As the evening progresses and a man has not yet been successful in picking up a woman, he views the remaining women in the bar as increasingly attractive, a shift that will presumably increase his attempts to solicit sex from the remaining women in the bar.

Another perceptual shift may take place after men have an orgasm with a casual sex partner with whom they wish no further involvement. Some men report viewing a sex partner as highly attractive before his orgasm, but then a mere ten seconds later, after orgasm, viewing her as less attractive or even homely. There have been no systematic studies of these shifts in emotions and perceptions, and further research must determine whether they exist commonly, and, if so, under which conditions. Based on the cumulative evidence of men's sexual strategies, one may speculate that the perceptual shift will occur most frequently when a man is motivated primarily by the desire for casual sex rather than a committed relationship, and when the woman with whom he has sex is below him in her desirability on the mating market. The negative shift in attraction following orgasm may function to prompt a hasty departure to reduce risks to the man such as getting involved in an unwanted commitment or incurring reputational damage if others become aware of the affair. The notion that male desire elevates a man's judgments of beauty prior to orgasm and then lowers his judgments of beauty following orgasm is a speculation. Nonetheless, it is not unreasonable to believe that mechanisms attuned to reaping the benefits of casual sex without paying the costs have evolved and will be discovered within the next decade of research on men's and women's strategies of casual sex.

Sexual Variations

A further clue to the significant role of casual mating in men's sexual repertoire comes from the sexual variation known as homosexuality. Donald Symons notes that male homosexual sexuality is unconstrained by women's dictates of romance, involvement, and commitment. Similarly, lesbian sexuality is unconstrained by men's dictates and demands. The actual behavior of homosexuals, therefore, provides a window for viewing the nature of men's and women's sexual desires, unclouded by the compromises imposed by the sexual strategies of the opposite sex.

The most frequent manifestation of male homosexuality is casual sex between strangers.[28] Whereas male homosexuals often cruise the bars, parks, and public rest rooms for brief encounters, lesbians rarely do. Whereas male homosexuals frequently search for new and varied sex partners, lesbians are far more likely to settle into intimate, lasting, committed relationships. One study found that 94 percent of male homosexuals had more than fifteen sex partners, whereas only 15 percent of lesbians had that many.[29] The more extensive Kinsey study conducted in San Francisco in the 1980s found that almost one-half of the male homosexuals had over five hundred different sex partners, mostly strangers met in baths or bars.[30] This evidence suggests that when men are unconstrained by the courtship and commitment requirements typically imposed by women, they freely satisfy their desires for casual sex with a variety of partners.

In their casual mating proclivities, the same as in their permanent mating preferences, homosexual males are similar to heterosexual males and lesbians are similar to heterosexual women. Homosexual proclivities reveal fundamental differences between men and women in the centrality of casual sex. Symons notes that "heterosexual men would be as likely as homosexual men to have sex most often with strangers, to participate in anonymous orgies in public baths, and to stop off in public rest rooms for five minutes of fellatio on the way home from work if women were interested in these activities. But women are not interested."[31]

Prostitution, the relatively indiscriminate exchange of sexual services for economic profit, is another reflection of men's greater desire for casual sex.[32] Prostitution occurs in nearly every society that has been studied. Within the United States, estimates of the number of active prostitutes range from 100,000 to 500,000. Tokyo has more than 130,000 prostitutes, Poland 230,000, and Addis Ababa in Ethiopia 80,000. In western Germany, there are 50,000 legally registered prostitutes and triple that number working illegally. In all cultures, men are overwhelmingly the consumers. Kinsey found that 69 percent of American men had been to a prostitute, and for 15 percent prostitution was a regular sexual outlet. The corresponding numbers for women were so low that they are not even reported as significant sexual outlets for women.

The prevalence of prostitution does not imply that it is an adaptation, something that was the target of evolutionary selection. Rather, it can be understood as a consequence of two factors operating simultaneously— men's desire for low-cost casual sex and women's either choosing or being forced by economic necessity to offer sexual services for material gain.

The greater male interest in short-term, opportunistic sex is also reflected in the patterns of incest. Father–daughter incest is far more common than mother–son incest. Girls are two to three times as likely to be incest victims as boys, and men are the predominant perpetrators in both cases. Furthermore, the men who commit incest are heavily concentrated among stepfathers rather than genetic fathers, suggesting that they do not incur the genetic costs typically linked with the offspring of incest, such as intellectual deficits and a higher frequency of recessive diseases. Estimates of the proportion of stepfather–stepdaughter incest range from 48 percent to 75 percent of all reported incest cases.[33] Men's quest for sexual variety and for attractive casual partners is revealed in the patterns of incest.

Sexual fantasy, the Coolidge effect, lust, the inclination to seek intercourse rapidly, the relaxation of standards, shifts in judgments of attractiveness, homosexual proclivities, prostitution, and incestuous tendencies are all psychological clues that betray men's strategies for casual sex. These psychological clues reveal an evolutionary past that favored men who had short-term mating in their sexual repertoire. But heterosexual men need consenting women for casual sex.

The Hidden Side of Women's Short-Term Sexuality

Perhaps because the reproductive benefits to men of casual sex are so large and direct, the benefits that women reap from short-term mating have been almost totally neglected. Although women cannot increase the number of children they bear by having sex with multiple partners, they can gain other important advantages from casual sex as one strategy within a flexible sexual repertoire.[34] Ancestral women must have sought casual sex for its benefits in some contexts at some times at least, because if there had been no willing women, men could not possibly have pursued their own interest in brief affairs. Men could not have evolved the psychological mechanisms attuned to short-term opportunities.

For ancestral women, unlike men, seeking sex as an end in itself is unlikely to have been a powerful goal of casual mating, for the simple reason that sperm have never been scarce. Access to more sperm would not have increased a woman's reproductive success. Minimal sexual access is all a woman needs, and there is rarely a shortage of men willing to provide the minimum. Additional sperm are superfluous for fertilization.

One key benefit of casual sex to women, however, is immediate access to resources. Imagine a food shortage hitting an ancestral tribe thousands of years ago. Game is scarce. The first frost has settled ominously. Bushes no longer yield berries. A lucky hunter takes down a deer. A woman watches him return from the hunt, hunger pangs gnawing. She makes him an offer for a portion of the prized meat. Sex for resources, or resources for sex—the two have been exchanged in millions of transactions over the millennia of human existence.

In many traditional societies, such as the Mehinaku of Amazonia and the natives of the Trobriand Islands, men bring food or jewelry, such as tobacco, betel nuts, turtle shell rings, or armlets, to their mistresses. Women deny sex if the gifts stop flowing. A girl might say, "You have no payment to give me—I refuse."[35] A Trobriand man's reputation among women suffers if he fails to bring gifts, and this interferes with his future ability to attract mistresses. Trobriand women benefit materially through their affairs.

Modern women's preferences in a lover provide psychological clues to the evolutionary history of women's material and economic benefits from brief sexual encounters. Women in the study on temporary and permanent mating especially value four characteristics in temporary lovers more than in committed mates—spending a lot of money on them from the beginning, giving them gifts from the beginning, having an extravagant life style, and being generous with their resources.[36] Women judge these attributes to be only mildly desirable in husbands but quite desirable in casual sex partners. Women dislike frugality and early signs of stinginess in a lover because these qualities signal that the man is reluctant to devote an immediate supply of resources to them. These psychological preferences reveal that the immediate extraction of resources is a key adaptive benefit that women secure through affairs.

The benefit of economic resources from casual sex is most starkly revealed in extreme cases such as prostitution. In cross-cultural perspective, many women who become prostitutes do so out of economic necessity because they lack suitable opportunities for marriage. Women who have been divorced by a man because of adultery, for example, are often unmarriageable among cultures such as Taiwan Hokkien or the Somalis.[37] Women among the Chinese, Burmese, and Pawnee may be unmarriageable if they are not virgins. Women among the Aztec and Ifugao are unmarriageable if they have diseases. In all these societies, unmarriageable women sometimes resort to prostitution to gain the economic benefits needed for survival.

Some women, however, say that they turn to prostitution to avoid the drudgery of marriage. Maylay women in Singapore, for example, become prostitutes to avoid the hard work expected of wives, which includes the gathering of firewood and the laundering of clothes. And among the Amhara and Bemba, prostitutes earn enough through casual sex to hire men to do the work that is normally expected of wives. Immediate economic resources, in short, remain a powerful benefit to women who engage in temporary sexual liaisons.

Affairs also provide an opportunity to evaluate potential husbands, supplying additional information that is unavailable through mere dating without sexual intercourse. Given the tremendous reproductive importance of selecting the right husband, women devote great effort to evaluation and assessment. Affairs prior to marriage allow a woman to assess the intentions of the prospective mate—whether he is seeking a brief sexual encounter or a marriage partner and hence the likelihood that he will abandon her. It allows her to evaluate his personality characteristics—how he holds up under stress and how reliable he is. It allows her to penetrate any deception that might have occurred—whether he is truly free or already involved in a serious relationship. And it allows her to assess his value as a mate or to learn how attractive he is to other women.

Sexual intercourse gives a couple the opportunity to evaluate how compatible they are sexually, providing important information about the long-term viability of the relationship. Through sex women can gauge such qualities as a man's sensitivity, his concern with her happiness, and his flexibility. Sexually incompatible couples divorce more often and are more likely to be plagued by adultery.[38] Twenty-nine percent of men and women questioned by the sex researchers Samuel Janus and Cynthia Janus state that sexual problems were the primary reason for their divorce, which makes that reason the most often mentioned. The potential costs inflicted by an unfaithful mate and by divorce potentially can be avoided by assessing sexual compatibility before making a commitment.

Women's preferences for short-term mates reveal hints that they use casual sex to evaluate possible marriage partners. If women sought short-term mates simply for opportunistic sex, as many men do, certain characteristics would not be particularly bothersome, such as a man's preexisting committed relationship or his promiscuity. Women, like men, would find promiscuity in a prospective lover to be neutral or mildly desirable.[39] In truth, however, women regard a preexisting relationship or promiscuous tendencies in a prospective lover as highly undesirable, since they signal unavailability as a marriage partner or the repeated pursuit of a short-term sexual strategy. These characteristics thus decrease the woman's odds of entering a long-term relationship with the man. They convey powerfully that the man cannot remain faithful and is a poor long-term mating prospect. And they interfere with the function of extracting immediate resources, since men who are promiscuous or whose resources are tied up in a serious relationship have fewer unencumbered assets to allocate.

Women's desires in a short-term sex partner strongly resemble their desires in a husband.[40] In both cases, women want someone who is kind, romantic, understanding, exciting, stable, healthy, humorous, and generous with his resources. In both contexts, women desire men who are tall, athletic, and attractive. Men's preferences, in marked contrast, shift abruptly with the mating context. The constancy of women's preferences in both scenarios is consistent with the theory that women see casual mates as potential husbands and thus impose high standards for both.

A more accurate self-assessment of their own desirability is another potential benefit that women gain from casual sex. In human evolutionary history, reproductive penalties would have been imposed on women and men who failed to assess their own value accurately. Underestimates would have been especially detrimental. A woman who settled for a less desirable mate because she underestimated her own value would have secured fewer resources, less paternal investment, and perhaps inferior genes to pass on to her children. A woman who overestimated her own value also suffered costs on the mating market. By setting her standards too high, she ensured that fewer men would reach her threshold, and those who did might not desire her because they could obtain more desirable women. If a woman's excessive self-estimate persisted too long, her actual mating value would decline as she aged. By engaging in brief affairs with several men, either simultaneously or sequentially, a woman can more accurately assess her own mating value. She obtains valuable information about the quality of the men she can potentially attract.

Through casual sex, women may also secure back-up protection against conflicts that arise with other men or with competitors. Having a second mate who will defend and protect her may be especially advantageous for women in societies where they are at considerable risk of attack or rape. In some societies, such as the Yanomamö of Venezuela, women are vulnerable to male violence, including physical abuse, rape, and even the killing of their children when they lack the protection of a mate.[41] This vulnerability is illustrated by the account of a Brazilian woman who was kidnapped by Yanomamö men.[42] When men from another village tried to rape her, not a single Yanomamö man came to her defense because she was not married to any of them and had no special male friends to protect her.

The use of such special friendships for protection has a primate precedent among savanna baboons.[43] Female baboons form special friendships with one or more males other than their primary mates, and these friends protect them against harassment from other males. Females show a marked preference for mating with their friends when they enter estrus, suggesting a strategy of exchanging sex for protection. As Robert Smith points out:

> A primary mate cannot always be available to defend his wife and children and, in his absence, it may be advantageous for a female to consort with another male for the protection he may offer. . . . absence of the primary mate [for example, when he is off hunting] may create the opportunity and need for extrabond mating. . . . a male may be inclined to protect the children of a married lover on the chance that his genes are represented among them.[44]

A lover may also serve as a potential replacement for the woman's regular mate if he should desert, become ill or injured, prove to be infertile, or die, which were not unusual events in ancestral environments. A permanent mate may fail to return from the hunt, for example, or be killed in a tribal war. Men's status may change over time—the head man to whom a woman is married might be deposed, his position usurped, his resources co-opted. Women benefit by positioning themselves to replace a mate quickly, without having to start over again. A woman who must delay the replacement by starting over is forced to incur the costs of a new search for a mate while her own desirability declines. Women benefit from having men waiting in reserve.

The mate-switching function has been observed in the spotted sandpiper (*Actitis macularia*), a polyandrous shorebird studied on Little Pelican Island in Leech Lake, Minnesota.[45] Biologists Mark Colwell and Lewis Oring, through four thousand hours of field observation, discovered that a female spotted sandpiper who engages in extra-pair copulations with another male has an increased likelihood of becoming an enduring mate with that male in the future. The females use the copulation as a way to test the receptivity and availability of the male. Male spotted sandpipers, however, sometimes foil these attempts at mate switching. Some males were observed to move several territories away from their home base when seeking extra-pair copulations, apparently so that the female will not detect that they are already mated. Despite this conflict between the sexes, the fact that the adulterers often end up as mates suggests that the extra-pair matings function as a means to switch mates.

Evidence for the mate-switching function of casual sex comes from two sources. The first study found that women have affairs primarily when they are dissatisfied with their current relationship; in contrast, men who have affairs are no more unhappy with their marriage than men who refrain from affairs. A second study, by Heidi Greiling and me, revealed that women sometimes have affairs when they are trying to replace their current mate or in order to make it easier to break off with a current mate.[46]

Casual sex partners sometimes bestow elevated status on their temporary mates. The affair of the model Marla Maples with the business tycoon Donald Trump made the headlines. She received tremendous publicity, monetary offers, and access to new social circles. Women sometimes elevate their status by mating with a prestigious man, even if it is just an affair. In the economics of the mating marketplace, people assume that the woman must be special, since prestigious men generally have their pick of the most desirable women. Women may gain temporary access to a higher social stratum, from which they can potentially secure a permanent mate. Women also can elevate their status within their own social circles and potentially secure a more desirable husband.

It is theoretically possible through casual sex for women to gain superior genes which are passed on to their children. Given men's proclivities with regard to a temporary sex partner, the economics of the mating marketplace render it far easier for a woman to get a man from a higher stratum or with better genes to have sex with her than it is for her to get him to marry her. A woman might try to secure the investment of a lower-ranking man by marrying him, for example, while simultaneously securing the genes of a higher-ranking man by cuckolding her husband.

This dual strategy exists in Great Britain, where the biologists Robin Baker and Mark Bellis have discovered that women typically have affairs with men who are higher in status than their husbands.[47]

One version of the better genes theory has been labeled the "sexy son hypothesis."[48] According to this theory, women prefer to have casual sex with men who are attractive to other women because they will have sons who possess the same charming characteristics. Women in the next generation will therefore find these sons attractive, and the sons will enjoy greater mating success than the sons of women who mate with men who are not regarded as attractive by most women.

Evidence for this theory comes from the temporary and permanent mating study, which identified a key exception to women's more stringent selection criteria for permanent partners. Women are more exacting with regard to physical attractiveness in a casual encounter than they are in a permanent mate.[49] This preference for physically attractive casual sex partners may be a psychological clue to a human evolutionary history in which women benefited through the success of their sexy sons.

Although we can never know for sure, anthropologists believe that many women during human evolutionary history did not contract their own marriages; the evidence is that marriages arranged by fathers and other kin are common in today's tribal cultures, which are assumed to resemble the conditions under which humans evolved.[50] The practice of arranged marriage is still common in many parts of the world as well, such as India, Kenya, and the Middle East. Arranged marriages restrict the opportunities for women to reap the benefits of short-term mating. Even where matings are arranged by parents and kin, however, women often exert considerable influence over their sexual and marital decisions by manipulating their parents, carrying on clandestine affairs, defying their parents' wishes, and sometimes eloping. These forms of personal choice open the window to the benefits for women of short-term mating, even when marriage is arranged by others.

Costs of Casual Sex

All sexual strategies carry costs, and casual sex is no exception. Men risk contracting sexually transmitted diseases, acquiring a poor reputation as a womanizer, or suffering injury from a jealous husband. A significant proportion of murders across cultures occurs because jealous men suspect their mates of infidelity.[51] Unfaithful married men risk retaliatory affairs by their wives and costly divorces. Short-term sexual strategies also take time, energy, and economic resources.

Women sometimes incur more severe costs than men do. Women risk impairing their desirability if they develop reputations for promiscuity since men prize fidelity in potential wives. Because of men's abhorrence of promiscuity in a permanent partner, casual sex for women becomes a risky venture for their reputations. Women known as promiscuous suffer reputational damage even in relatively promiscuous cultures, such as among the Swedes and the Ache Indians.[52]

Lacking a permanent mate to offer physical protection, a woman who adopts an exclusively short-term sexual strategy is at greater risk of physical and sexual abuse. Although women in marriages are also subjected to battering and even rape from husbands, the alarming statistics on the incidence of date rape, which run as high as 15 percent in studies of college women, support the contention that women who are not in long-term relationships are at considerable risk.[53] The fact that women in the study of temporary and permanent partners abhor lovers who are physically abusive, violent, and psychologically abusive suggests that women may be aware of the risks of abuse. Mate preferences, if judiciously applied in order to avoid potentially dangerous men, can minimize these risks.

Unmarried women in the pursuit of casual sex risk getting pregnant and bearing a child without the benefits of an investing man. In ancestral times, such children would likely have been at much greater risk of disease, injury, and death.[54] Some women commit infanticide in the absence of an investing man. In Canada, for example, single women delivered only 12 percent of the babies born between 1977 and 1983, but they committed just over 50 percent of the sixty-four maternal infanticides reported to the police.[55] This trend occurs across cultures as well, such as among the Baganda of Africa. But even this solution does not cancel the substantial costs that women incur of nine months of gestation, reputational damage, and lost mating opportunities.

An unfaithful married woman risks the withdrawal of resources by her husband. From a reproductive standpoint, she may be wasting valuable time in an extramarital liaison, obtaining sperm that are unnecessary for reproduction.[56] Furthermore, she risks increasing the sibling competition among her children, who may have weaker ties because they were fathered by different men.[57]

Short-term mating thus poses hazards for both sexes. But because there are powerful benefits as well, women and men have evolved psychological mechanisms to select contexts in which costs are minimized and benefits increased.

Favorable Contexts for Casual Sex

Everyone knows some men who are womanizers, others who would never stray. Everyone knows some women who enjoy casual sex and others who would not dream of sex without commitment. Individuals differ in their proclivities for casual mating. Individuals also shift their proclivities at different times and in different contexts. These variations in sexual strategy depend on a range of social, cultural, and ecological conditions.

The absence of an investing father during childhood is one context that increases the incidence of casual sex. Women whose parents were divorced, for example, are far more promiscuous than women whose families were intact. Furthermore, women whose fathers were absent attain menarche, or the onset of menstruation, earlier than women who grow up with their fathers present.[58] Their father's absence may lead women to conclude that men are not reliable investors; such women may pursue a strategy of extracting immediate resources from a number of short-term partners, rather than trying to secure the continued investment of one.

Casual sex is also related to people's developmental stage in life. Adolescents in many cultures are more likely to use temporary mating as a means of assessing their value on the mating market, experimenting with different strategies, honing their attraction skills, and clarifying their own preferences. After they have done so, they are ready for marriage. The fact that premarital adolescent sexual experimentation is tolerated and even encouraged in some cultures, such as the Mehinaku of Amazonia, provides a clue that short-term mating is related to one's stage in life.[59]

The transitions between committed matings offer additional opportunities for casual sex. Upon divorce, for example, it is crucial to reassess one's value on the current mating market. The existence of children from the marriage generally lowers the desirability of divorced people. The elevated status that comes with being more advanced in their career, on the other hand, may raise their desirability. Precisely how all these changed circumstances affect a particular person is often best evaluated by brief affairs, which allow a person to gauge more precisely how desirable he or she currently is, and hence to decide how to direct his or her mating efforts.

The abundance or dearth of eligible men relative to eligible women is another critical context for temporary mating. Many factors affect this sex ratio, including wars, which kill larger numbers of men than women; risky activities such as fights, which more frequently affect men; intentional homicides, in which roughly seven times more men than women die; and differential remarriage rates by age, whereby women remarry less and less often than men with increasing age. Men shift to brief encounters when many women are sexually available because the sex ratio is in their favor and they are better able to satisfy their desire for variety. Among the Ache, for example, men are highly promiscuous because there are 50 percent more women than men. Women shift to casual sex when there is a dearth of investing men available for marriage or when there are few benefits to marriage.[60] In some subcultures, notably inner-city ghettos, men often lack the resources that women desire in a permanent mate. Where men do not have resources, women have less reason to mate with only one man. Similarly, when women receive more resources from their kin than from their husbands, they are more likely to engage in extramarital sex.[61] Women in these contexts mate opportunistically with different men, securing greater benefits for themselves and their children.

In cultures where food is shared communally, women have less incentive to marry and often shift to temporary sex partners. The Ache of Paraguay, for example, communally share food secured from large game hunting. Good hunters do not get a larger share of meat than poor hunters. Women receive the same allotment of food, regardless of whether they have a husband and regardless of the hunting skill of their husband. Hence, there is less incentive for Ache women to remain mated with one man, and about 75 percent of them favor short-term relationships.[62] The socialist welfare system of Sweden provides another example. Since food and other material resources are provided to everyone, women have less incentive to marry. As a result, only half of all Swedish couples who live together get married, and members of both sexes pursue temporary relationships.[63]

Another factor that is likely to foster brief sexual encounters— although differently for men and women—is one's future desirability as a mate. A man at the apprenticeship stage of a promising career may pursue only brief affairs, figuring that he will be able to attract a more desirable permanent mate later on, when his career is closer to its peak. A woman whose current desirability is low may reason that she cannot attract a husband of the quality she desires and so may pursue carefree short-term relationships as an alternative.

Certain legal, social, and cultural sanctions encourage short-term mating. Roman kings, for example, were permitted to take hundreds of concubines, who were cycled out of the harem by the time they reached the age of thirty.[64] In Spain and France, it is an accepted cultural tradition that men who can afford it keep mistresses in apartments, a short-term arrangement outside the bounds and bonds of marriage. The ideologies of some communes and isolated groups, living arrangements that were especially popular during the late 1960s and early 1970s, encourage sexual experimentation with short-term relationships.

The sexual strategies pursued by other people affect the likelihood of casual sex. When many men pursue temporary relationships, as in Russia in the 1990s, then women are forced de facto into casual mating because fewer men are willing to commit. Or when one spouse has an extramarital affair, then the other may feel inclined to even the score. Casual sex is never pursued in a vacuum. It is influenced by development, personal appeal, sex ratio, cultural traditions, legal sanctions, and the strategies pursued by others. All of these contexts affect the likelihood that a person will choose casual sex from the entire repertoire of human sexual strategies.

Casual Sex as a Source of Power

The scientific study of mating in the twentieth century has focused nearly exclusively on marriage. Human anatomy, physiology, and psychology, however, betray an ancestral past filled with affairs. The obvious reproductive advantages of such affairs to men may have blinded scientists to the benefits for women. Affairs involve willing women. Willing women demand benefits.

This picture of human nature may be disturbing to many. Women may not be comforted by the ease with which men sometimes hop into bed with near strangers. Men may not be comforted by the knowledge that their wives continue to scan the mating terrain, encourage other men with hints of sexual accessibility, and sometimes cuckold husbands with impunity. Human nature can be alarming.

But viewed from another perspective, our possession of a complex repertoire of potential mating strategies gives us far more power, far more flexibility, and far more control of our own destiny. We choose from a large mating menu and are not doomed to a single, invariant strategy. We tailor our mating strategies to the contexts we encounter. Moreover, modern technology and contemporary living conditions allow people to escape many of the costs of casual sex that our ancestors experienced. Effective birth control, for example, allows many people to avoid the costs of an unwanted or ill-timed pregnancy. The relative anonymity of urban living diminishes the reputational damage incurred by casual sex. Geographic mobility lowers the restrictive influences that parents often impose on the mating decisions of their children. And survival safety nets provided by governments lower the survival costs to children produced by short-term liaisons. These reduced costs foster a fuller expression of the range of human mating within our complex repertoire.

Acknowledging the full complexity of our mating strategies may violate our socialized conceptions of matrimonial bliss. But simultaneously this knowledge gives us greater power to design our own mating destiny than any other humans have ever possessed.

5

Attracting a Partner

Hearts have as many changing moods as the face has expressions. To cap-
ture a thousand hearts demands a thousand devices.
> —Ovid, *The Erotic Poems: The Art of Love*

KNOWING WHAT YOU DESIRE in a mate provides no guarantee that you will succeed in getting what you want. Success hinges on providing signals that you will deliver the benefits desired by a member of the opposite sex. Because ancestral women desired high status in men, for example, men have evolved motivation for acquiring and displaying status. Because ancestral men desired youth and health in potential mates, women have evolved motivation to appear young and healthful. Competition to attract a mate, therefore, involves besting one's rivals in the characteristics most keenly sought by the opposite sex.

In this co-evolutionary cycle, psychological mechanisms evolve in one sex to solve the adaptive problems imposed by the other sex. Just as the successful fisherman uses the lure that most closely resembles food that fits the fish's evolved preferences, so the successful competitor employs psychological tactics that most closely fit the evolved desires of the opposite sex. The characteristics that men and women value are thus keys to understanding the means of attracting a mate.

Attracting a mate, however, does not occur in a social vacuum. Desirable partners elicit intense social competition for their favors. Successful attraction therefore depends not merely upon providing signals that one will fulfill a potential mate's desires, but also on counter-acting the seductive signals of rivals. Humans have evolved a method for running interference that is unique in the animal kingdom—the verbal derogation of competitors. The put-down, the slur, and the insinuation that damage a rival's reputation are all part of the process of successfully attracting a mate.

Derogatory tactics, like tactics of attraction, work because they exploit the psychological mechanisms that predispose persons of the opposite sex to be sensitive to certain valuable qualities in possible mates, such as their resources or appearance. A man's communication to a woman that his rival lacks ambition can be effective only if the woman is predisposed to reject men who have a low potential for acquiring resources. Similarly, a woman's remark to a man that her rival is sexually promiscuous can work only if men are predisposed to reject women who do not devote themselves sexually to one man.

The success of both attractive and derogatory tactics hinges on whether the target of desire is seeking a casual sex partner or a marital partner. Consider the case of a woman who denigrates a rival by mentioning that she has slept with many men. If the man is seeking a spouse, this tactic is highly effective, because men dislike promiscuity in a potential wife. If the man is seeking a temporary sex partner, however, the woman's tactic backfires, because most men are not bothered by promiscuity in short-term mates. Similarly, overt displays of sexuality are effective as temporary tactics for women but are ineffective in the long run. The effectiveness of attraction, in short, depends critically on the temporal context of the mating. Men and women tailor their attraction techniques to the length of the relationship they seek.

The rules of play on the sexual field differ substantially from those of the marriage market. In long-term mating, both men and women prefer a lengthy courtship, in a process that permits evaluation of the nature and magnitude of the assets the person possesses and the costs they carry. Initial exaggerations of status or resources are revealed. Prior commitments to other mates surface. Children by former mates pop up.

Casual affairs truncate this kind of assessment, dramatically increasing the opportunities for deception. Exaggeration of prestige, status, and income may go undetected. Prior commitments remain concealed. Information that damages a reputation comes too late. Casual mating, in short, is a rocky terrain where manipulation and deception can trip the unwary with every step. To compound this problem, deception occurs in the domains that are most important to members of the opposite sex, namely status, resources, and commitment for women and appearance and sexual fidelity for men.

The battle for casual sex is joined by both sexes, but not equally. The fact that more men than women seek casual sex partners creates a hurdle for men, in that there are fewer willing women. Women therefore tend to be more in control in short affairs than in the marital arena. For every sexually willing woman there are usually dozens of men who would consent to have sex with her. Women can be very choosy in these cases because they have so many men to choose from. In committed relationships, in contrast, this level of choosiness is a luxury that only very desirable women can afford.

Attracting a committed or casual mate requires display. Just as weaver-birds display their nests and scorpionflies display their nuptial gifts, men and women must advertise their wares on the mating market. Because men's and women's desires differ, the qualities they must display differ.

Displaying Resources

The evolution of male strategies for accruing and displaying resources pervades the animal kingdom. The male roadrunner, for example, catches a mouse or baby rat, pounds it into a state of shock or death, and offers it to a female as her next meal, but without actually handing it over.[1] Rather, the male holds it away from her while croaking and waving his tail. Only after the birds have copulated does he release his gift to the female, who uses it to nourish the eggs that the male has just fertilized. Males that fail to offer this food resource fail in the effort to court and attract females.

Men, too, go to great lengths to display their resources to attract mates. The mate attraction studies conducted by my colleagues and me identified dozens of tactics that men and women use to attract a mate. We asked several hundred college students from the University of California at Berkeley, Harvard University, and the University of Michigan to describe all such tactics they had observed in others or had used themselves. Their examples included bragging about accomplishments, talking about their importance at work, showing sympathy for the problems of others, initiating visual contact, and wearing sexy clothes. A team of four researchers reduced the larger set of more than one hundred actions into twenty-eight relatively distinct categories. The category "display athletic prowess," for example, includes actions such as working out with weights, impressing someone by twisting open difficult jars, and talking about success at sports. Subsequently, 100 adult married couples and 200 unmarried university students evaluated each tactic for how effective it is in attracting a mate, whether it is more effective when employed in casual or permanent relationships, and how frequently they, their close friends, and their spouses employ it.[2]

One of men's techniques is to display tangible resources, showing a high earning potential, flashing a lot of money to impress women, driving an expensive car, telling people how important they are at work, and bragging about their accomplishments. Another technique is for men to deceive women about their resources by misleading the women about their career expectations, for example, and exaggerating their prestige at work. Like the male roadrunner offering up his kill, men offer women resources as a primary method of attraction.

Men also derogate their rival's resources. In the studies of derogation, we first secured eighty-three nominations from college students about the ways in which men and women put down or denigrate a member of their own sex to make the person less attractive to members of the opposite sex. Typical behavior includes spreading false rumors about a rival, making fun of a rival's appearance, scoffing at a rival's achievements, and telling others that a rival has a sexually transmitted disease. As it did with the attraction tactics, our research team classified these actions into twenty-eight categories. For example, the category of derogating a competitor's intelligence includes the actions of making the rival seem dumb, telling others that the rival is stupid, and mentioning that a rival is an "airhead." Subsequently, 100 married couples and 321 unmarried university students evaluated each tactic for its overall effectiveness, its effectiveness in temporary versus committed relationships, and its frequency of use by themselves, their friends, and their spouses.

Men counteract the attraction tactics of other men by derogating a rival's resource potential. Typically men tell women that their rivals are poor, have no money, lack ambition, and drive cheap cars. Women are far less likely to derogate a rival's resources; when they do, the tactic is less effective than men's practice.[3]

Timing plays a key role in determining the effectiveness of different types of resource display. The immediate display of wealth, such as flashing money, buying a woman gifts, or taking her out to an expensive restaurant on the first date, proves more effective for attracting casual sex partners than long-term mates. In bars, where opportunities for imparting resources are limited, men frequently initiate contact with prospective sex partners by offering to buy them drinks. Mixed drinks, being more expensive than beer or wine, are reputed to work better, as is giving the waitress a large tip, since these acts indicate not just the possession of wealth but also the critical willingness to impart it immediately.[4]

Showing the potential for having resources by exhibiting studiousness at college or describing ambitious goals to a woman is more effective for attracting permanent mates than casual sex partners. Derogation tactics also reveal the importance of timing. Putting down the economic potential of a rival is most effective in the context of long-term mating. Telling a woman that the other man will do poorly in his profession or lacks ambition is highly effective in the marital market but relatively ineffective when it comes to casual sex. These findings mesh perfectly with the preferences that women express in the same two contexts—desiring immediate resources from brief affairs and reliable future resources from permanent bonds.

Wearing costly clothing works equally well in both contexts. One study found that women who are shown slides of different men are more attracted to men who wear expensive clothing, such as three-piece suits, sports jackets, and designer jeans, than to men who wear cheap clothing, such as tank tops and T-shirts.[5] This effect occurs whether the woman is evaluating the man as a marital partner or as a sex partner, perhaps because expensive clothing signals both immediate resources and future resource potential. The anthropologists John Marshall Townsend and Gary Levy verified that the effect of the expense and status of clothing in attracting women is robust across any sort of involvement, from merely having coffee with a man to marriage. The same men were photographed wearing either a Burger King uniform with a blue baseball cap and a polo-type shirt or a white dress shirt with a designer tie, a navy blazer, and a Rolex watch. Based on these photographs, women state that they are unwilling to date, have sex with, or marry the men in the low-status costumes, but are willing to consider all these relationships with men in high-status garb.

The importance of resources to attraction is not limited to Western cultures. Among the Siriono of eastern Bolivia, one man who was a particularly unsuccessful hunter and had lost several wives to men who were better hunters suffered a loss of status within the group. The anthropologist A. R. Holmberg began hunting with this man, gave him game that others were told he had killed, and taught him the art of killing game with a shotgun. Eventually, as a result of the man's increased hunting prowess, he "was enjoying the highest status, had acquired several new sex partners, and was insulting others, instead of being insulted by them."[6]

The power of imparting resources is no recent phenomenon. Ovid observed precisely the same phenomenon two thousand years ago, testifying to the longstanding nature of this tactic over human written history: "Girls praise a poem, but go for expensive presents. Any illiterate oaf can catch their eye provided he's rich. Today is truly the Golden Age: gold buys honor, gold procures love."[7] We still live in that golden age.

Displaying Commitment

Displays of love, commitment, and devotion are powerful attractions to a woman. They signal that a man is willing to channel his time, energy, and effort to her over the long run. Showing commitment is difficult and costly to fake, because commitment is gauged from repeated signals over a period of time. Men who are interested simply in casual sex are unlikely to invest this much effort. The reliability of the display of commitment as a signal renders it an especially effective technique for attracting women.

The mate attraction studies confirm the power of displaying commitment in the marital market. Discussing marriage signals that a man would like to integrate the woman into his social and family life, commit his resources to her, and, in many cases, have children with her. Offering to change his religion in order to be with her shows a willingness to accommodate to her needs. Showing a deep concern for her problems communicates emotional support and a commitment to be there in times of need. The 100 newlywed women all report that their husbands displayed these signals during their courtship, confirming that they are highly effective when used.

One strong signal of commitment is a man's persistence in courtship. It can take the form of spending a lot of time with the woman, seeing her more often than other women, dating her for an extended period of time, calling her frequently on the phone, and writing her numerous letters. These tactics are extremely effective in courting women as permanent mates, with average effectiveness ratings of 5.48 on a 7-point scale, but only a moderately effective 4.54 at courting casual sex partners. Furthermore, persistence in courtship proves to be more effective for a man than for a woman because it signals that he is interested in more than casual sex.

The effectiveness of sheer persistence in courtship is illustrated by a story told by one newlywed: "Initially, I was not interested in John at all. I thought he was kind of nerdy, so I kept turning him down and turning him down. But he kept calling me up, showing up at my work, arranging to run into me. I finally agreed to go out with him just to get him off my back. One thing led to another, and six months later, we got married."

Persistence also worked for a German university professor. While returning to Germany by train from a professional conference in Poland, he started talking to an attractive physician, twelve years his junior. The conversation became animated as their attraction for one another grew. The physician was on her way to Amsterdam, not Germany, and before long, the station where she had to change trains was upon them. The physician said goodbye to the professor, but he insisted on helping her with her luggage and carried it to a station locker for her. As his train pulled away from the station, the professor berated himself for failing to seize the moment, and he decided to take action. At the next station he got off and boarded another train back to where he had left the physician. He searched the station in vain—there were no signs of her. On foot, he searched all the stores and shops surrounding the station. No luck. Finally he went back to the station and planted himself in front of the locker into which he had loaded her luggage. Eventually she returned, was surprised to see him, and was impressed by his persistence in tracking her down. A year later she left her native Poland to marry him in Germany. Without tenacity, the professor would have lost her irretrievably. Persistence pays.

Displays of kindness, which also signal commitment, figure prominently in successful attraction techniques. Men who demonstrate an understanding of a woman's problems, show sensitivity to her needs, act compassionately toward her, and perform helpful deeds succeed in attracting women as long-term mates. Kindness works because it signals that the man cares for the woman, will be there for her in times of need, and will channel resources to her. It signals a long-term romantic interest rather than a casual sexual interest.

Some men exploit this tactic to attract women as casual sex partners. The psychologists William Tooke and Lori Camire studied exploitative and deceptive attraction tactics in a university population.[8] From a nomination procedure parallel to the one used in the attraction studies, they assembled a list of eighty-eight ways in which men and women deceive one another in the service of attracting a mate. College students reported misleading the opposite sex about career expectations, sucking in their stomachs when walking near members of the opposite sex, appearing to be more trusting and considerate around members of the opposite sex than is actually the case, and acting uninterested in having sex when it is really on their minds. These techniques were then evaluated by 252 university students for their frequency and effectiveness when used by a man and by a woman. The deception study discovered that men, in order to attract women, act more polite than they really are, appear to be more considerate than they really are, and seem more vulnerable than they really are.

The singles bar study produced similar results. Four researchers spent approximately one hundred person-hours sitting in singles bars in Washtenaw county in Michigan, writing down each attraction tactic they witnessed. Through this procedure, they detected 109 attraction tactics, such as sucking seductively on a straw, offering to buy someone a drink, sticking out one's chest, and staring at someone's body. Then a different sample of 100 university students evaluated the tactics for their probable effectiveness at attracting them when employed by a person of the opposite sex. Women stated that the most effective tactics for attracting them are displaying good manners, offering help, and acting sympathetic and caring. Mimicking what women want in a husband by showing kindness and sincere interest, in short, is also an effective technique for luring women into brief sexual liaisons.

Another tactic for revealing kindness is to display nurturance toward children. In one study, women were shown slides of the same man in three different conditions—standing alone, interacting positively with a baby, and ignoring a baby in distress.[9] Women were most attracted to the man when he acted kindly toward the baby, and were least attracted to him when he ignored the baby in distress. When men were shown analogous slides of a woman standing alone, showing positive feelings toward a baby, and ignoring the baby, however, their attraction to her was identical in all these contexts. Showing nurturance toward the young is apparently an attraction tactic that is effective mainly for men—a tactic that works by signaling a proclivity to commit to, and care for, children.

Men also signal their commitment by showing loyalty and fidelity. Signs of promiscuity, in contrast, indicate that the man is pursuing a short-term strategy of casual sex. Short-term strategists, in contrast to their more committed counterparts, typically distribute their resources over several women. Out of 130 possible ways for men to attract a mate, women regard showing fidelity as the second most effective act, just a shade behind displaying an understanding of the woman's problems.

Because fidelity signals commitment, an effective tactic for denigrating a rival is for a man to question the rival's sexual intentions. For a man to tell a woman that his rival just wants casual sex, for example, is deemed by women to be far more effective in decreasing that rival's attractiveness in the long run than in the short run. Similarly, saying that a rival cheats on women and cannot stay loyal to just one woman are highly effective tactics for men in decreasing a rival's long-term attractiveness to women.[10]

Displays of love provide another sign of commitment. A man can attract a woman by doing special things for her, showing a loving devotion to her, and saying "I love you." Men and women rate these tactics among the top 10 percent of all tactics for attracting a permanent female mate. Demonstrations of love convey cues to long-term commitment.

In 1991, the television comedian Roseanne Barr made a deal with her husband, the actor Tom Arnold. Roseanne wanted Tom to change his religion to Judaism as a sign of his love for her. He wanted her to take his last name to signal her love for him. After a brief test of wills, he converted and she changed her name. These acts of love entail personal sacrifice and, perhaps more important, they signal the kind of public commitment that raises the odds of securing a lasting relationship as opposed to a brief encounter.

While signals of commitment prove highly effective in attracting long-term mates, the simulation of commitment can be effective in attracting and seducing a woman. Men looking for casual liaisons compete by mimicking what women desire in a permanent mate. This tactic is especially potent when women use casual sex to evaluate prospective husbands. Women are more receptive, even in the short term, to men who appear to embody their ideals for a long-term mate.

The deception study found that men use several tactics in an attempt to deceive women about their intentions. Men, significantly more often than women, pretend to be interested in starting a relationship when they are not really interested and act as if they care about a woman even though they really do not care. Feigning long-term intentions is judged by both sexes to be a more effective attraction tactic for men than for women. Men are aware that simulating commitment is an effective tactic for gaining access to short-term sex, and they admit to deceiving women by this means.

As the biologist Lynn Margulis notes: "Any animal that can perceive can be deceived." "Deception consists of mimicking the truth," comments the biologist Robert Trivers in describing how the technique works. "[It is] a parasitism of the preexisting system for communicating correct information." Whenever females look for investing males, some males deceive about their willingness to invest. Certain male insects offer females food, only to take it back after the copulation is complete.[11] They then use the same resources to court another female. For females, this strategy poses the problem of detecting deception, discovering insincerity, and penetrating disguise. One of the human solutions to this problem is to place a premium on honesty.

Displays of honesty by a man are in fact powerful tactics for obtaining a permanent mate. They convey to the woman that the man is not simply seeking a transient sex partner. Of the 130 identified tactics to attract a female mate, three of the top ones suggest openness and honesty—acting honest with the woman, communicating feelings to her directly and openly, and acting himself. All of these tactics are judged to be among the most effective 10 percent of all attraction tactics that men can use.

Because of the adaptive problem historically imposed on women by men's dual sexual strategy of short- and long-term relationships, tactics that allow women a clear window for evaluating the man's actual characteristics and intentions prove to be highly attractive. Signals of dishonesty conceal those characteristics and intentions, rendering that assessment window opaque and hence interfering with the process of attracting a mate.

While signs of commitment are highly effective for attracting women, signals that resources are already committed elsewhere undermine attraction. Among the men who patronize singles bars, many are married or have steady relationships. Furthermore, some have children who command large shares of their resources. These men report removing their wedding rings before entering the bars. After the intensive grilling of men at one singles bar, researchers found that "12 people admitted that they were married . . . we suspected that others were married, by somewhat rather undefinable qualities, sometimes connected with a rather mysterious withholding of various kinds of information about everyday life styles."[12] Because having a marital commitment clearly interferes strategically with attracting for casual sex women who seek permanent mates, it becomes a liability for men who fail to conceal it.

University students confirm that knowledge of prior commitments hinders a man's efforts to attract a woman. Indeed, out of eighty-three tactics that men can perform to render a rival less attractive to women, mentioning that a rival has a serious girlfriend is judged to be the single most effective one.

Signals of commitment help men to attract women because they signal that the man is pursuing a long-term sexual strategy. They signal that the resources he has will be channeled exclusively to the woman. And they signal that she will gain greater assets over the long run in exchange for her own assets. Signals of commitment, like signals of resources, are effective at attracting women because they match what women want.

Displaying Physical Prowess

Men display physical and athletic prowess in modern times as part of their tactical arsenal for attracting women. Newlywed couples and undergraduate dating couples alike report that men display their strength roughly twice as often as women and display athletic prowess roughly 50 percent more often than women as part of their courtship tactics. Furthermore, displays of strength and athleticism are judged to be significantly more effective for attracting mates when used by men than by women. Flexing muscles, showing off strength by opening jars, playing sports, boasting about one's athletic prowess, and lifting weights all figure more prominently in men's attraction tactics.

College students' evaluations of derogation tactics confirm that displays of physical and athletic prowess are significantly more effective for attracting casual sex partners than for attracting spouses. The derogation tactics that stand out as being more effective in casual than in permanent contexts include putting down a rival's strength and athletic ability. Mentioning that a rival is physically weak, outshining a competitor in sports, and physically dominating a rival are all viewed as more effective short-term than long-term tactics. The studies support the common belief that male athletes enjoy greater than average success at attracting women for casual sex.

Among the Yanomamö, a man's status is heavily determined by his physical feats, which include chest-pounding duels, ax fights, combat against neighboring villages, and physically vanquishing rivals. The status gained through physical prowess translates into greater reproductive success through the greater sexual access that such men have to women. Indeed, men who have demonstrated their prowess through killing other men (*unoka*) have more wives and more children than same-aged non-*unoka* men.[13]

Displays of physical and athletic prowess, in short, remain powerful attractions in traditional societies and among modern Western cultures. The fact that physical displays are more effective for attracting casual sex partners than for attracting long-term mates supports the hypothesis that women may be seeking the back-up protection that short-term mating can offer. The effectiveness of this tactic from the male menu of tactics thus hinges on the context of women's desires.

Displaying Bravado and Self-Confidence

Displays of masculine self-confidence prove effective for men at attracting mates, but are significantly more effective for attracting casual than committed mates. Acting conceited or macho, bragging about one's accomplishments, and showing off are all judged by college students to be more effective for men in attracting sex partners than wives.

The effectiveness of bravado and confidence is reflected in a story told by a woman in a singles bar:

I was sitting at a corner table talking to my girlfriend and sipping on a gin and tonic. Then Bob walked in. He walked into the bar like he owned the place, smiling broadly and very confident. He caught my eye, and I smiled. He sat down and started talking about how horses were his hobby. He casually mentioned that he owned a horse farm. When the last call for alcohol came, he was still talking about how expensive his horses were, and said that we should go riding together. He said, 'In fact, we could go riding right now.' It was 2:00 A.M., and I left the bar and had sex with him. I never did find out whether he owned horses.

Self-confidence in a man signals status and resources.[14] Among newlyweds, for example, men scoring high on self-confidence earn significantly more money than men with lower self-confidence. Self-confidence then translates into success in finding temporary sex partners. A woman at a singles bar put it this way: "Some guys just seem to know what they are doing. They know how to approach you and just make you feel good. Then you get those nerds . . . who can't get anything right. They come on strong at first, but can't keep it together. . . . they just hang around until you dump them by going to the rest room or over to a friend to talk."[15] Women frequently distinguish false bravado from real self-confidence; the genuine article is more successful at attracting them. Furthermore, two other studies have demonstrated that men who are high in self-esteem tend to approach physically attractive women and ask them for dates, regardless of their own physical attractiveness. Men who are low in self-esteem, in contrast, avoid approaching attractive women, believing that their chances are too slim.[16]

The degree of self-confidence a man displays, however, is responsive to feedback. In singles bars, men rebuffed by women in their first few attempts produce successively less confident approaches. Rejection produces a downward cycle of resentment, hostility, and sometimes a cessation of all tactics. One man in a singles bar commented after a third woman had rebuffed him, "You need steel balls to make it in this place." Apparently the psychological pain and lowered confidence experienced by rejected men trigger psychological mechanisms that cause them to reevaluate their sexual techniques, lower their sights to women who have lower appeal, and wait until circumstances are more propitious for further attempts.[17]

Another tactic used by men to attract a mate is to feign confidence. According to the deception study, men boast and brag to make themselves appear better, act more masculine than they really feel, and behave more assertively around women than they really are, in order to attract temporary partners. Men strut for a reason: to increase their odds of securing casual sex.

Not all displays of bravado and confidence are directed toward attracting the opposite sex. These displays are also directed toward other men in an attempt to elevate status and prestige within the group. College men overstate the numbers of their sexual partners, mislead others about how many women express a desire for them, exaggerate their own sexual adeptness and sexual conquests, and act more dominant, more confident, and braver than they really feel.

Men boast about their sexual exploits, exaggerate their desirability to women, and express a bravado that they might not even feel because of status competition. Men compete for position; access to prized resources, particularly sexual resources, signals an elevated position. If a man can obtain the deference of other men by elevating his position in the sexual domain, his status will typically translate into greater access to desirable women.

The fact that men select this tactic primarily in casual mating contexts provides circumstantial support for the sexy son hypothesis. Men who display their bravado and sexual conquests signal to women that they are sexually attractive to women in general. Like the peacock displaying his plumage, these strutting men may be more likely to have sons that are attractive to women in the next generation. Displays of bravado and confidence are key components of a man's menu of attraction tactics.

This kind of attraction display, like the others, is subject to exploitation by other males. To attract females, for example, male bullfrogs sit at the edge of a pond and emit loud, resonant croaks. Females listen carefully to the chorus of male sounds and select one to move toward. The louder and more resonant the croak, the more attractive it is to females. The larger, healthier, and more dominant the male, the more resonant his croaks. The dominant male strategy, therefore, is to emit the loudest and most resonant croaks possible. Sitting silently nearby a dominant male is a smaller, weaker male. He emits no croaks and attracts no attention. But as a female approaches the sounds of the dominant male, the silent male darts from his hiding place, intercepts her, and quickly copulates. This strategy, called a satellite or sneak strategy, illustrates the exploitation of the attraction strategies of rivals.[18]

Humans also use this strategy, which is humorously depicted in a Woody Allen film of men dressed up as male sperm who are fighting over access to an egg. The macho male sperm battle it out in physical combat. When they have defeated each other and lie down exhausted, a diminutive sperm played by Woody Allen steps out cautiously from behind a curtain, where he has been cowering, and proceeds to hop onto the egg.

College men sometimes use this sneak or satellite strategy, as we found in studies of mate poaching. We asked fifty men and fifty women what strategies they would use to attract someone who was already mated with someone else.[19] One of the most frequent tactics is pretending to be friends with the couple and then switching to a mating mode when the opportunity arises.

A less frequent male poaching tactic is to feign femaleness. Among the sunfish in the lakes of Ontario, for example, a small male mimics a female and enters the nesting site of the dominant male. This mimicry reduces the likelihood of his being attacked. Once inside the territory, however, the small male quickly fertilizes the eggs that have already been deposited by the females, thus cuckolding the territory-holding male. Feigning homosexuality so as not to incur the suspicion of the dominant man and then attempting to have sex with the woman when the dominant man is not around is a rare tactic among humans. Nonetheless, it is interesting that a few college men reported having observed this strategy. Like bullfrogs and sunfish, humans sometimes use sneak or satellite strategies that exploit the attraction tactics of others of their own sex.

Enhancing Appearance

Just as men's successful tactics for attracting women depend on women's desires in a mate, women's attraction tactics depend on men's preferences. Women who succeed in this endeavor appear reproductively valuable by embodying physical and behavioral cues that signal their youth and physical attractiveness. Women who fail to fulfill these qualities lose a competitive edge.

Because men place a premium on appearance, competition among women to attract men centers heavily on enhancing their physical attractiveness along youthful and healthful lines. The cosmetics industry verifies this practice. The cosmetics industry is supported mainly by women, and women on average devote far more time and effort to enhancing their appearance than men. Women's magazines depict an avalanche of advertisements for beauty products. Men's magazines, in contrast, advertise for cars, stereo equipment, and alcoholic beverages. When advertisements in men's magazines offer appearance enhancement, it is typically for muscle-building devices rather than cosmetics.

Women do not compete to communicate accurate information to men. Rather, they compete to activate men's evolved psychological standards of beauty, keyed to youth and health. Because flushed cheeks and high color are cues that men use to gauge a woman's health, women rouge their cheeks artificially to trigger men's attraction. Because smooth, clear skin is one of men's evolved desires, women cover up blemishes, use moisture cream, apply astringents, and get facelifts. Because lustrous hair is one of men's evolved desires, women highlight, bleach, tint, or dye their hair, and they give it extra body with conditioners, egg yolks, or beer. Because full red lips trigger men's evolved desires, women apply lipstick skillfully and even get collagen injections to enlarge their lips. And because firm, youthful breasts stimulate men's desires, women obtain breast implants and reconstructive surgery.

The heavy reliance of women on enhancing their appearance is lavishly documented by the studies. Both undergraduate and newlywed women report that they use makeup to accentuate their looks twenty times as often as men, and they learn how to apply cosmetics ten times as often as men. Women go on diets to improve their figures twice as often as men. Women, more than twice as often as men, spend over an hour a day on their appearance. Women get a new and interesting haircut twice as often as men and lie out in the sun to achieve a healthy-looking glow 50 percent more often than men. Furthermore, improvements in appearance that are designed for attracting a mate are twice as effective for women as for men.[20] In contrast, men who devote a lot of attention to enhancing their appearance can hurt their competitive chances. People sometimes infer that they are homosexual or narcissistic.[21]

There is more to improving women's appearance than meets the eye. Women perform a number of deceptive tactics to manipulate their appearance, such as wearing false fingernails to make their hands appear longer, wearing heels to appear taller and thinner, wearing dark clothing to appear thinner, wearing vertical stripes to appear thinner, going to a tanning salon to appear darker, pulling in their stomach to appear slimmer, padding their clothes to appear more full-figured, and dying their hair to appear more youthful. Physical appearance can be deceptive.

Improving one's appearance is more effective for women in attracting sex partners than marital partners, mirroring the finding that men value appearance more in casual than in permanent mates. College students judge it to be extremely effective in the short-term context but only moderately effective in the context of commitment. Whereas men's efforts to enhance their appearance are more effective in attracting casual sex partners than spouses, in both contexts men's use of these tactics is significantly less effective than women's.

Women are well aware of the importance of appearance on the singles scene. After interviews with women in singles bars, the researchers concluded that "many women said that they went home from work before going out to the bars to do a 'whole revamping': often, they would take a bath, wash their hair, put on fresh makeup and go through three changes of outfits before they went out to the bars—'primping for us counts more than for guys—they don't need to worry about their looks as much.'"[22] The "ability to make men's heads turn" signals a highly desirable mate and elicits overtures from a wide pool of male prospects.

The larger the pool of suitors, the greater the choice a woman can exercise and the higher the quality of the mate she can attract.

Women do not merely strive to improve their own looks; they also denigrate the looks of other women. Women in the derogation study say their rivals are fat, ugly, physically unattractive, and that their bodies have no shape. Making fun of a rival's appearance is perceived to be significantly more effective for women in temporary than in long-term contexts, and it is more effective for women than for men in both sexual and marital contexts.

Women derogate other women's appearance both to the desired men and directly to the rivals themselves. One woman in a singles bar study described her habit of looking at a rival's elaborately done-up hair and, without saying anything, taking out a hairbrush and handing it to her. Often the practice succeeded in driving away her competition. Damaging the self-image of a rival is one way to clear the field.

Making public the disapproval of another woman's appearance enhances its effectiveness. The knowledge that others believe a woman to be unattractive elevates the costs of copulation in terms of the damage it can do to the man's reputation. One man from a fraternity reported being ridiculed mercilessly by his brothers after it became known that he had sex with a particularly unattractive woman. Men who are discovered having sex with unattractive women suffer social humiliation. They lose status and prestige in the eyes of their peers.[23] Whereas for women the derogation of a rival's physical appearance is effective in casual mating contexts that are public and observable by one's social circles, such tactics are far less deterring to a man if he can secure a private mating without anyone else's knowledge, so that he will not suffer any costs to his reputation. But given the fascination that people have about who is sleeping with whom, one can rarely count on such information remaining hidden from public view.

Since physical attractiveness is an attribute that is easy for men to observe directly, this form of derogation works by guiding men's perceptions of women. Women can draw attention to flaws that are otherwise unobserved or not salient, such as heavy thighs, a long nose, short fingers, and an asymmetrical face, and make them salient. No human is without defects, and drawing attention to those defects magnifies their importance, especially if attention is drawn to efforts to conceal or disguise a defect. Women also exploit the fact that our judgments of attractiveness are influenced by other people's judgments.[24] Knowledge that others find a woman unattractive causes a downward shift in our view of that woman's appearance. Moreover, knowledge that other people in our social environment do not believe that a woman is attractive actually renders her a less valuable asset as a mate. Even with easily observed qualities, such as physical appearance and stature, there is plenty of room for the effective use of belittling tactics.

Modern cosmetology exploits women's evolved psychology of competing for mates. If some women make effective use of methods to enhance their appearance, others who do not are at a selective disadvantage in attracting mates. This situation has created a runaway beauty competition, in which the time, effort, and money expended on appearance have reached proportions unprecedented in human evolutionary history. Women in all cultures alter their appearance, but perhaps none so much as those in the "civilized" West because it has the technology to exploit women's desire to appear attractive through visual media unavailable to more traditional societies. The cosmetics industry does not create desires so much as it exploits the desires that are already there.

The journalist Naomi Wolf has described the media advertisements as creating a false ideal, called the beauty myth, in order to subjugate women sexually, economically, and politically, and hence to turn back the clock on feminism. The beauty myth is presumed to have taken on causal properties, covertly undoing all the accomplishments of feminism in improved conditions for women. The surgical technologies of breast implants and facelifts are believed to be designed to institute medical control of women.[25] The diet, cosmetics, and cosmetic surgery industries combined, totaling some 53 billion dollars a year, are said to stem from the need to keep women in line. Standards of beauty, the argument goes, are arbitrary—capriciously linked with age, highly variable across cultures, not universal in nature, and hence not a function of evolution. Myths, however, cannot have causal force—only the individuals who carry myths can. Power structures cannot have causal force—only the individuals who wield power can. The story depicted by this view of the beauty myth is therefore unflattering to women. It implies that women are unsuspecting dupes, passive receptacles, with no preferences and no individuality, buffeted and brainwashed by the powerful forces of entities like "power structures" and "myths" that seek to subjugate them.

In contrast, an evolutionary psychological approach shows that women have far more autonomy and choice in their deployment of attraction tactics than proponents of the beauty myth would have us believe. Women who seek a lasting mate, for example, have at their disposal a wide range of tactics, including displays of loyalty, signals of common interests, and acts of intelligence. Moreover, women purchase beauty products not because they have been brainwashed by the media, but rather because they determine that their power to get what they want will be increased. Women are not unsuspecting dupes buffeted about by the evil forces of Madison Avenue, but rather determine through their preferences the products that are offered.

Advertisements do damage women, however. Women are bombarded with exploitative images of unattainable beauty. These magnify a woman's focus on appearance and at the same time fail to highlight the deeper personal qualities that are also critical to men's desires, such as intelligence, personality, and fidelity. The cosmetics industry exploits women's evolved concern over appearance and then increases women's insecurity by raising the standards of attractiveness to which women aspire with a deluge of seemingly flawless world-class models. This deception increases the apparent beauty of other women and may lower women's self-esteem. It may also distort women's and men's understanding of the actual mating pool and mating market.

All women today are unique, distinctive winners of a five million year Pleistocene beauty contest of sexual selection. Every female ancestor of the readers of these words was attractive enough to obtain enough male investment to raise at least one child to reproductive age. Every male ancestor was attractive enough to obtain a woman to have his child. So we are all the products of a long and unbroken line of successes. Every living human is an evolutionary success story.

Displaying Fidelity

In light of men's emphasis on fidelity in a committed relationship, displays of fidelity should in evolutionary terms be paramount in women's tactics of attraction. These tactics would signal that the woman is pursuing a long-term rather than a short-term sexual goal and that she is pursuing it without deception and exclusively with one man.

Newlyweds and college students confirmed the effectiveness of displays of fidelity. Out of 130 tactics of attraction, remaining faithful, avoiding sex with other men, and showing devotion prove to be the three most effective tactics for attracting a permanent mate. All are rated over 6.5, with 7.0 indicating the highest possible effectiveness. Signals of fidelity communicate a potential for commitment to the relationship. To the man, this offers a solution to one of the most important reproductive problems confronted in ancestral times—the problem of ensuring his paternity.

The centrality of fidelity in the context of committed mating shows up indirectly in the tactics employed by women to derogate a rival. Saying that a rival cannot stay loyal to one man was judged by university students to be the single most effective tactic for a woman to use against a competitor in the marriage market. Similarly, calling a rival a tramp, saying that a rival is loose, or telling others that a rival sleeps around a lot emerge in the top 10 percent of effective derogation tactics for women. Newlywed couples also maintain that women are significantly more likely than men to derogate their rival's promiscuity.[26]

This tactic can backfire, however, if a man is seeking casual sex. Mae West once noted that "men like women with a past because they hope history will repeat itself." Men who are seeking short-term partners typically are not bothered by promiscuity in a woman, and in fact find it mildly desirable since it increases their chances of success. Calling another woman promiscuous, therefore, does not have the intended effect of dissuading men who are pursuing a short-term goal. Calling a rival promiscuous and questioning her fidelity, however, are highly effective for women if the man is seeking a spouse. The effectiveness of the derogatory tactics women select from their arsenal thus depends heavily on the context. Women who mistakenly gauge a man's intentions fail in their quest to render their rivals undesirable.

Men's dual sexual strategy of short-term and long-term mating complicates women's choice of tactics. A woman must judge a man's interest in another woman as brief or lasting and adjust her derogatory and attraction tactics accordingly. If she guesses wrong, she will do exactly the opposite of what she intends to do. The risks are high. Furthermore, most women are not merely worried that their men might marry their rivals; they also do not want their men to have sex with their rivals. Thus, denigrating the promiscuity of a woman may be an extremely risky tactic unless the woman is confident that the man is looking solely for a permanent mate—which can be a doubtful prospect.

The fact that female promiscuity is abhorred by men in committed mates and is exploited by women to undermine rivals is reinforced by the prevalence of derogatory terms for this activity in the language. Although there are words for men who are promiscuous, such as Lothario and Don Juan, they are fewer in number and less derogatory than the words for women. Indeed, such terms applied to men are sometimes not intended to be derogatory at all but are said with admiration or envy. In contrast, John Barth's *The Sot Weed Factor* illustrates the range of insults hurled by women.[27] An English woman competes against a French woman by using these labels to cast aspersions on her character: harlot, whore, sow, bawd, strawgirl, tumbler, mattressback, windowgirl, galleywench, fastfanny, nellie, nightbird, shortheels, bumbessie, furrowbutt, coxswain, conycatcher, tart, arsebender, canvasback, hipflipper, hardtonguer, bedbug, breechdropper, giftbox, craterbutt, pisspallet, narycherry, poxbox, flapgap, codhopper, bellylass, trollop, joygirl, bumpbacon, strumpet, slattern, chippie, pipecleaner, hotpot, back-bender, leasepiece, spreadeagle, sausage-grinder, cornergirl, codwinker, nutcracker, hedgewhore, fleshpot, cotwarmer, hussy, stumpthumper. The French woman uses a comparably long list of counterderogations in her native language. In literature as in life, denigrating a competitor's promiscuity decreases her attractiveness to a man in the marital market.

The importance of context is also shown by the attraction tactic of acting coy or unavailable. Appearing indifferent to a person one likes and playing hard to get are judged to be more effective for women than for men. Furthermore, these forms of coyness are more effective for women in the context of permanent as opposed to casual mates.[28]

This outcome meshes perfectly with the sexual strategies of both women and men. The coyness tactic works for women in the marital context because it signals to the man both desirability and fidelity. Men think that if a woman is easy for them to get, then she may be easy for other men to get, and hence her signals of fidelity are compromised. College men, for example, point out that women who are easy to get are probably desperate for a mate and might also have a disease—signals, respectively, of low desirability and high promiscuity.[29]

Another study found that playing hard to get is most successful as a mate-attracting tactic when it is used selectively, that is, when a woman is hard to get in general but is selectively accessible to a particular man.[30] For example, a woman might publicly spurn the advances of all men except the particular man who is the target of her attraction efforts. In this case the coyness tactic effectively implies to a man that he is obtaining an excellent bargain on the mating market and also that the woman is likely to be faithful in the long run. Successful women convey being hard to get and discriminating without turning off the particular men they desire.

Playing hard to get signals great desirability, tests a man's willingness to invest resources, and communicates fidelity to the man. If a woman is hard to get, then a man can be more certain that other men will fail to attract her once she becomes his wife. The effectiveness of playing hard to get as a long-term attraction technique stems from providing men with two key reproductive assets: desirability on the mating market and a signal that he alone will have sexual access.

When a woman has a long history of casual sex, it may be difficult to appear faithful, loyal, and devoted. Mate-attracting tactics are not deployed in a social vacuum, and people are keenly interested in information about the sexual reputation of others. Gossip columnists, talk show hosts, and their audiences dwell on who is sleeping with whom, savoring each detail. Women strive to avoid acquiring a reputation as sexually promiscuous because of the damage they would suffer in the currency of desirability as a mate.

In the context of the small social groups in which humans evolved, damage to one's reputation would have been lasting. Concealing sexual information from others in a small tribe is virtually impossible. Among the Ache Indians, for example, everyone knows who has slept with whom, so there is little room for deception. When a male anthropologist queried Ache men about who had slept with whom, and a female anthropologist did likewise with Ache women, there was perfect correspondence in their accounts.[31] In modern Western culture, with its great mobility and anonymous urban living, there is considerably more room for rehabilitating one's reputation and starting fresh in a new social environment where one's past is unknown. Having a history of promiscuity in these circumstances may not preclude the subsequent use of signs of fidelity to attract a mate.

Employing Sexual Signals

Most men want primarily one benefit from casual mating relationships: sex with attractive women. Initiating a sexual overture and signaling sexual availability, therefore, are powerful tactics for women in these contexts.

College men reveal that accepting a man's sexual invitations is the single most effective act that a woman can perform to attract a man for a casual liaison. Also rated near the top of the 7-point effectiveness scale are asking a man if he will have sex, making him think of having sex with her, acting promiscuous, talking seductively, and making a sexual advance. All these attraction tactics are judged to be more effective for women in casual than in permanent contexts, and they are substantially more effective for women than for men in the short term.

Men in singles bars corroborated these findings. When they evaluated 103 mate-attracting tactics for their effectiveness, men singled out such actions as a woman's rubbing her chest or pelvis against a man, looking at him seductively, putting her arms around his neck, running her hands through his hair, puckering her lips and blowing kisses, sucking on a straw or finger, leaning forward to expose her chest, and bending over to accentuate her curves. In sharp contrast, women do not judge these same actions to be effective in attracting them when performed by men. The more overt the sexual advances by men, the less attractive women find them. On a 7-point scale, men place a woman's act of rubbing her chest or pelvis up against a man at 6.07, the second most effective act of all 103 acts, exceeded only by agreeing to have sex with him. Women, however, place a man's use of this act at only 1.82, suggesting that this behavior is extremely ineffective, perhaps even repulsive, to women. Because men seek sex as an end in itself in brief matings, direct sexual overtures and signals of immediate sexual access are extraordinarily effective as female tactics.

Another highly effective tactic for a woman who seeks short-term relations is sexualizing her appearance. Men in the single bars stated that wearing sexy, revealing, tight clothes; wearing a shirt with a low-cut back or a low-cut front; letting the shirt slip off her shoulders; wearing a short skirt; walking seductively; dancing seductively; and walking with a strut all place in the top 25 percent of the tactics most likely to attract them. Sexualizing her appearance and behavior succeed for a woman in eliciting overtures from men.

The anthropologist Elizabeth Cashdan found remarkably similar results in her study of cads and dads, which focused on variations in the display of resources, willingness to invest, fidelity, and sexuality according to whether the person is pursuing a temporary or a permanent partner. Women who are pursuing a mating strategy of casual sex more often wear revealing clothes than women who are pursuing a strategy of long-term commitment.[32]

The power of sexualizing appearance is further shown by a study of clothing style and skin exposure. Men and women watched slides of the opposite sex in which models differed in the amount of skin exposed and the tightness of their clothing. After each slide, the subjects judged the model's attractiveness as a dating partner, marital partner, and sex partner. Men find women in tight-fitting and revealing clothing more attractive than fully clothed women as dating partners and sex partners, but not as marriage partners. Women, in contrast, judge men in tight-fitting and revealing clothes to be less attractive than fully clothed men in either case, perhaps because relative undress signals that the man is primarily interested in short-term sex.[33]

Sexualizing one's appearance becomes quite overt in singles bars. The researchers report that women "often walked around the room, standing tall, protruding their chests, holding in their stomachs, stroking their own arms or hair—they seemed to exhibit themselves on public display." Sometimes, a woman's appearing sexy is so effective that it preempts all other male thoughts. The same researchers described one woman who was very thin, attractive, and large-breasted:

She often tended to say things that were scatterbrained and she had a nervous giggle. Her talk and her erratic laughter seemed quite secondary in the singles bar, as most men who talked to her were preoccupied with her chest and the way she displayed her chest by twisting and turning. Some men commented to us that they hardly heard what this woman said—or for that matter, even cared what she said. Such men seemed to prefer to look at this woman's chest than to listen to her.[34]

Initiating visual contact also proves to be a highly effective tactic for women who seek to attract a sex partner. Looking intensely into a man's eyes and allowing a man to see her staring are judged to be among the top 15 percent of effective tactics women can use to attract short-term sex partners. In contrast, this tactic proves only moderately effective in attracting committed mates, scoring near the midpoint of the 7-point scale.

Men are highly sensitive to signals of an increased probability of obtaining casual sex. A woman who initiates visual contact provides a powerful cue to men of this probability shift. In one study, men and women were videotaped interacting.[35] After a brief period of time, the woman looked into the man's eyes and smiled at him. Men and women witnessed the videotape and then made judgments about the woman's intentions. Men interpret this kind of behavior as a sign of sexual interest and seductive intent. Women who observe the same actions by other women interpret the behavior as a signal of friendliness rather than sexiness or seductiveness. Clearly, eye contact and smiles are often ambiguous—sometimes they signal sexual interest, and sometimes they do not.

Initiating visual contact may be less effective for a woman who seeks a long-term rather than short-term mate because the contact is interpreted by men as a sign that the woman may be desperate or low in desirability. In contrast, acting coy, aloof, and hard to get signals high desirability and hence is more effective for women who want to attract committed mates. Initiating visual contact activates men's psychological mechanisms to signal sexual accessibility. Being readily accessible backfires for a woman as a tactic for seeking a husband because it signals low desirability and perhaps gives a cue to future infidelity.

While women convey sexual availability as a tactic, they also question the sexual availability of other women as a means of derogating them. When a college woman derogates a rival in a short-term context, she mentions that her rival is merely a tease, indicates that her rival leads men on, and tells the man that her rival is frigid. All of these acts imply that the other woman will not be sexually accessible to the man and that he is likely to waste his time and energy in courting her as a casual partner.

Women are more likely than men to derogate their rivals by questioning their sexual accessibility. They call their competitors prudish, priggish, or puritanical. This tactic is effective for women primarily in context of the brief affair but is less effective for the purpose of committed mating. Questioning the sexual accessibility of rivals is an effective female strategy, because inaccessible women are costly for men who seek casual sex—they risk channeling time and resources toward doubtful sexual prospects. Men also risk damage to their reputation by being rebuffed by such women publicly.

Some acts that women use to question a rival's sexual accessibility, such as calling a competitor a tease and saying that she leads men on, seem extraordinarily clever, because at the same time they do not imply that the woman is loyal, faithful, or a good long-term prospect. Rather, they imply an exploitative strategy of feigning sexual accessibility, perhaps to obtain resources and attention, but then failing to deliver. Furthermore, saying that a rival is frigid or prudish implies that she is a problematic casual sex partner without implying that she is also a desirable marriage partner, because men also dislike sexual coldness in a wife. Tactics that simultaneously derogate a rival's short-term and long-term value on the mating market are especially effective.

Mae West once commented, "Brains are an asset, if you hide them." That may indeed be true in the case of casual sex. Women sometimes act submissive, helpless, and even stupid to attract short-term mates. Women report pretending to be helpless, letting the man control the conversation, acting dumb, acting "dizzy," and pretending to be meek and helpless.

College students consider the helplessness tactic to be moderately effective for women on the 7-point scale in attracting short-term mates (3.35) but not at all effective in attracting long-term mates (1.62). Helplessness and submissiveness are highly ineffective for men in both contexts—1.60 in casual sex and 1.31 in committed relationships.

Submissiveness by women conveys to the man that he need not expect hostile reactions to his advances.[36] Subservient signals implicitly give men permission to approach. Since men are more likely to initiate approaches, signs of submissiveness and helplessness lower barriers to approach. Acting submissive is likely to elicit approaches from a larger number of men, expand the pool of potential mates, create greater opportunities for choice, and ultimately increase the quality of the mate obtained.

Acting submissive, helpless, or dumb may also signal that the man will be able to control or manipulate the woman easily for his own ends. Because these ends in brief mating are primarily sexual, submissiveness may signal increased sexual accessibility. A woman's apparent helplessness may signal ease of sexual exploitation, in that sex can be had without the cost of commitment. Manipulability of a target increases the odds of sexual access, and acting helpless, submissive, or not too bright signals ease of control. The stereotype of the "bubble-headed blond" may be misleading; this public presentation is intended as a strategic signal of approachability or even sexual accessibility rather than of actual intellectual ineptness.

Signals of sexual accessibility, in fact, sometimes are part of a larger strategy to lure a man into a long-term relationship. Sometimes the only way a woman can gain the attention and interest of a man is by offering herself as a sexual commodity with no apparent strings attached. In principle, if the costs in resources and commitment are made low enough, many men would succumb to a sexual opportunity. Once a woman gains sexual access to a man of her choice, her proximity offers opportunities for insinuating herself, for making the man depend on her for various functions, and for gradually escalating both the benefits he will receive by staying in the relationship and the costs he will incur if he leaves her. What seems initially like a benefit without strings attached ends up as a benefit purchased in the coin of commitment.

Men employ a similar tactic when they seek a permanent mate by attempting to minimize the costs they carry in order to increase their overall attractiveness. If women bait with sex, men bait with investment. But because men's psychological mechanisms orient them so vigilantly to short-term sexual opportunities, women can exploit these mechanisms as a first step toward luring the man into a committed relationship.

The Sexes at Cross Purposes

Success at attracting a mate depends on more than grasping the context and the intentions of a potential partner. It also hinges on besting the competition. For this reason, men and women do not merely enhance their own attractiveness; they also derogate their rivals. While making themselves appear attractive by exhibiting the characteristics sought by the opposite sex, people also denigrate their rivals by making them appear to lack the characteristics sought by the opposite sex.

Perhaps more than in any other part of the mating arena, in casual sex men and women suffer from the strategies of the opposite sex. Men deceive women by feigning an interest in commitment to achieve a quick sexual gain. Men also feign confidence, status, kindness, and resources that they lack for the goal of brief encounters. Women who succumb to this deception give up a valuable sexual benefit at bargain-basement prices. But women battle back by insisting on stronger cues to commitment and by feigning interest in casual sex as a means of concealing their long-term intentions. Some men take the bait and risk becoming ensnared in a web of hidden costs.

But offering the sexual bait poses risks for women. To suggest sexual availability is, without question, the most effective way for a woman to lure a man into a casual relationship. But because men abhor signs of promiscuity or indiscriminate sexual activity in a lasting mate, the sexual strategy that works so well for the woman in the short run often backfires if she is seeking a husband. Because men use similar strategies in both contexts, they can determine at a later stage, with more information in hand, whether they want the woman as a short-term or long-term partner. Women often have more to lose if they make errors in sexual strategies.

Men and women both are alert to deception at the hands of the opposite sex. Women hold out sexually, require the demonstration of honorable intentions and commitment, and penetrate possible deceptions to discover hidden commitments. Men conceal their emotions, disguise their external commitments, and remain uncommunicative and noncommittal. They try to abscond with the sexual benefit without paying the cost of commitment.

The ratio of available women to men affects the prevailing tactics used to attract a partner. The typical ratio in a singles bar, for example, favors women, because many more men than women are seeking short-term sex partners, and so those women who are looking for a brief encounter can exercise a great deal of choice. The sex ratio imbalance pressures men to best other men with better lines, better deceptions, and better simulations of the criteria that women impose. The losers typically outnumber the winners, and most men go home alone.

Where the sex ratio is reversed and there are many more available women than men, the balance of power shifts to men because they can more easily attract women for casual sex. This imbalance becomes especially pronounced in inner-city contexts, where crime convictions and homicides often take even more men out of the available mating pool.[37] These conditions are extremely unfavorable to women who seek long-term mates, taxing their attraction tactics and rendering competition among women commensurately fiercer.

This trend is exacerbated by women's high standards for a mate: their choosiness dramatically shrinks the effective pool of eligible men. Many men are dismissed for failing to pass even the preliminary trials. This leaves just a few survivors—men of high status, high self-confidence, and high resource potential—over whom women then do battle. Those who succeed in attracting a lasting mate then face the next adaptive problem—staying together.

6

Staying Together

When two people are first together, their hearts are on fire and their passion is very great. After a while . . . they continue to love each other, but in a different way—warm and dependable.
          —Marjorie Shostak, *Nisa: The Life and Words of a !Kung Woman*

TREMENDOUS BENEFITS flow to couples who remain committed. From this unique alliance comes the efficiency of acquiring a complementarity of skills, a division of labor, a sharing of resources, a unified front against mutual enemies, a stable home environment for rearing children, and a more extended kin network. To reap these benefits, people must be able to retain the mates they have won.

People who fail to stay together incur severe costs. Bonds between extended kin become ripped apart. Essential resources are lost. Children are forced to forsake a stable home environment. Failure to keep a committed mate can mean wasting all the effort expended in the selection, attraction, courting, and commitment process. Men who fail to prevent the defection of their mate risk losing access to valuable childbearing capabilities and maternal investment. Women who fail to retain their mate risk losing the mate's resources, protection, and paternal investment. Both sexes incur costs from failing to keep a mate because of the lost opportunities for exploring other possibilities of mating.

Given the high rate of divorce in Western cultures, and the existence of divorce in all cultures, it is obvious that staying together is neither automatic nor inevitable. Rivals loom on the periphery, waiting for an opportunity to lure someone away from a mate. Existing mates sometimes fail to provide the promised benefits. Some start imposing costs that are difficult to sustain. Couples are surrounded by people with interests and agendas at odds with their own and who attempt to loosen their bond. Staying together can be a fragile proposition unless the couple undertakes the strategies that are evolutionarily designed to ensure a successful, committed union.

Mate-keeping tactics occupy an important place in animal mating systems. Although they are phylogenetically far removed from humans, insects offer instructive contrasts with humans because of the great diversity of their tactics and because humans' ways of solving the adaptive problem of keeping a mate are strikingly analogous to insects'.[1] One of the most frequent strategies used by insects is to conceal the mate from competitors. Among the many possible tactics are physically removing a mate from an area that is dense with competitors, concealing the attractive cues offered by a mate, and reducing the conspicuousness of the courtship display. Male wasps who successfully track the scents of a female to her perch immediately whisk her away from the spot to prevent the mating attempts of other males who may also be tracking her scent.[2] If the male wasp fails to remove the female, he risks a physical battle with other males who converge on the perch. Male beetles release a scent that reduces their mates' attractiveness, thus preventing other males from noticing the female or making it more likely that other males will search for uncontested females rather than persist in a possibly costly attempt to mate with one who is already taken. A male cricket starts out with loud calls, but he softens them as he gets close to the female in order to prevent interference from other males.[3] All of these concealment tactics reduce a mate's contact with same-sex rivals.

Another strategy is the physical prevention of a takeover by other males. Many insects maintain close contact with the mate and repel interfering competitors. The male veliid water strider, for example, grasps his mate and sometimes rides on her back for hours or days, even while not engaged in copulation, to prevent encroachment by other males. Faced with rival males, insects may use their antennae to lash out at them, turn and wrestle with them, or simply chase them off.[4] Perhaps the most unusual form of physical interference with the designs of rival males is the insertion of copulatory plugs. One species of worm, for example, adds a special substance to the seminal fluid that coagulates once deposited in the female, thus preventing other males from inseminating her and literally cementing his own reproductive bond with her. And in one species of fly, the *Johannseniella nitida*, males leave their genitalia broken off from their own bodies after copulation to seal the reproductive opening of the female. Such are the lengths that some males go to in order to forestall reproductive takeovers from rivals.[5]

Although the phylogenetic distance between humans and insects is vast, the basic adaptive logic behind holding on to a mate shows striking parallels. Males in both cases strive to inseminate females and to prevent cuckoldry. Females in both cases strive to secure investments in return for sexual access. But human tactics to retain a mate take on uniquely intricate forms of psychological manipulation which set them apart from the rest of the animal kingdom.

Humans differ from most other animals in that both sexes reap reproductive rewards from staying together. Remaining committed to a spouse, therefore, becomes crucial for women as well as for men. Although mate-keeping tactics among insects are performed primarily by males, among humans they are performed by both sexes. Indeed, women are equal to men in the effort they channel toward the adaptive problem of staying together. This equality follows from the evolutionary logic of the value of the reproductive resources that would be lost by a breakup compared with the potential gains an individual could accrue by a breakup. Because men and women who embark on a committed relationship tend on average to couple with individuals of equivalent desirability, both sexes lose equally on average as a result of a breakup.[6]

Humans have evolved their own special strategies for mate keeping. One of the most important is continuing to fulfill the desires of one's mate—the desires that led to the mate selection to begin with. But merely fulfilling these desires may not be enough if rivals are attempting the same thing. Ancestral humans needed a psychological mechanism specifically designed to alert them to potential threats from the outside, a mechanism that would regulate when to swing into action in deploying mate-guarding strategies. That mechanism is sexual jealousy.

The Functions of Sexual Jealousy

Whenever males contribute to their offspring, they confront the problem of uncertain paternity. This problem occurs whenever fertilization and gestation occur inside the female's body, and it becomes exacerbated whenever males invest in offspring after they are born. Compared with many other male mammals, men invest tremendously in their offspring. Cuckoldry is therefore a serious adaptive problem that men throughout human evolutionary history have had to solve. The prevalence of the problem in the animal kingdom is reflected in the fact that so few mammalian males invest at all in their young.[7] Among chimpanzees, our closest primate relatives, males defend their troop against conspecific aggressors, but they invest nothing in their own offspring. Men's investment in their children without certainty of paternity would be extremely unlikely to have evolved, since males would incur a double penalty. Their parental effort would not only be wasted but might also get channeled to a rival's offspring. The general mammalian failure of males to invest in their young suggests that most male mammals have not solved the problem of ensuring paternity. The fact that men do invest heavily in their young provides powerful circumstantial evidence that our ancestors evolved effective psychological mechanisms for solving the paternity problem and for reducing the likelihood of cuckoldry. Studies of sexual jealousy, in all its diverse manifestations, provide direct evidence that jealousy is that mechanism.

Imagine getting off work early and returning home. As you enter the house, you hear sounds coming from the back room. You call your partner's name, but no one answers. As you approach the back room, sounds of heavy breathing and moaning become louder. You open the bedroom door. On the bed is a stranger, naked and in the act of sexual intercourse with your partner. What emotions would you experience? If you are a woman, you would be likely to experience sadness and feelings of abandonment. If you are a man, you would be likely to experience rage. If you are human, you would most likely experience humiliation.[8]

Sexual jealousy consists of emotions that are evoked by a perceived threat to a sexual relationship. The perception of a threat leads to actions designed to reduce or eliminate that threat.[9] These can range from vigilance, which functions to monitor the mate for signs of extra-pair involvement, to violence, which inflicts a heavy cost on the mate or rival for signs of defection or poaching. Sexual jealousy is activated when one is confronted either with signs that someone else has an interest in one's mate or with signs of defection by one's mate, such as flirting with someone else. The rage, sadness, and humiliation following these cues motivate action typically intended either to cut off a rival or to prevent the mate's defection.

Men who fail to solve this adaptive problem risk not only suffering direct reproductive costs but also losing status and reputation, which can seriously impair their ability to attract other mates. Consider the reaction in Greek culture to cuckoldry: "The wife's infidelity . . . brings disgrace to the husband who is then a Keratas—the worst insult for a Greek man—a shameful epithet with connotations of weakness and inadequacy. . . . While for the wife it is socially acceptable to tolerate her unfaithful husband, it is not socially acceptable for a man to tolerate his unfaithful wife and if he does so, he is ridiculed as behaving in an unmanly manner."[10] Cuckolded men are universal objects of derision. The penalties for failure to keep a mate for oneself thus include the loss of social status, which can diminish future success in the dangerous game of mating.

Most research on jealousy has focused on male sexual jealousy, probably because of the asymmetry between men's and women's confidence about their parenthood. Nonetheless, women also experience jealousy; a mate's contact with other women can lead him to redirect his resources and commitment away from her and her children and toward another woman and her children. Men and women do not differ in either the frequency or the magnitude of their jealousy experience. In one study, 300 individuals who were partners in 150 romantic relationships were asked to rate how jealous they are in general, how jealous they are of their partner's relationships with members of the opposite sex, and the degree to which jealousy is a problem in their relationship. Men and women admitted to equal amounts of jealousy, confirming that both sexes experience jealousy and overall do not differ in the intensity of their jealous feelings.[11]

These reactions are not limited to the United States. Over 2,000 individuals from Hungary, Ireland, Mexico, the Netherlands, the Soviet Union, the United States, and Yugoslavia were asked their reactions to a variety of different sexual scenarios. Men and women in all seven countries express identically negative emotional reactions to thoughts of their partner's flirting with someone else or having sexual relations with someone else. The sexes are also identical in their jealous reactions to a sexual partner's hugging someone else or dancing with someone else, although their responses to these events are less negative than to flirting and sexual relations. As in the United States, both men and women worldwide have jealousy as a key psychological mechanism that becomes activated in response to a threat to a valued relationship.[12]

Despite these similarities, there are intriguing sexual differences in the content and focus of jealousy, or the specific events that trigger jealousy in men and women. In one study, twenty men and twenty women were asked to play a role in a scenario in which they became jealous.[13] But first the subjects were asked individually to choose their scenario from among a group of possible scenarios, which typically involved either jealousy over a partner's sexual involvement with someone else or jealousy over a partner's devotion of time and resources to someone else. Seventeen of the women chose infidelity over either resources or time as the jealousy-inducing event, whereas only three women chose sexual infidelity. In marked contrast, sixteen of the twenty men chose sexual infidelity as the jealousy-inducing event, and only four men chose the diversion of time or resources. This study provides the first clue that, although both men and women have the psychological mechanism of jealousy, it is triggered by different events, which correspond to the adaptive problems of ensuring paternity for men and ensuring resources and commitment for women.

In another study, fifteen couples were asked to list situations that would make them jealous. Men identified sexual involvement between their partner and a third party as the primary cause of jealousy, and secondarily comparison between themselves and a rival. Women, in contrast, indicated that they would have jealous reactions primarily to their partner's spending time with other women, talking with a competitor, and kissing a female competitor.[14] Women's jealousy, in short, is triggered by cues to the possible diversion of their mate's investment to another women, whereas men's jealousy is triggered primarily by cues to the possible diversions of their mate's sexual favors to another man.

These sex differences manifest themselves both psychologically and physiologically. In a study of sex differences in jealousy, my colleagues and I asked 511 college men and women to compare two distressing events—if their partner had sexual intercourse with someone else and if their partner formed a deep emotional attachment to someone else.[15] Fully 83 percent of the women found their partner's emotional infidelity more upsetting, whereas only 40 percent of the men did. In contrast, 60 percent of the men experienced their partner's sexual infidelity as more upsetting, whereas only 17 percent of the women did.

To evaluate a different group of sixty men and women with regard to their physiological distress to sexual and emotional infidelity, we placed electrodes on the corrugator muscle in the brow, which contracts when people frown; on the first and third fingers of the right hand to measure skin conductance, or sweating; and on the thumb to measure pulse or heart rate. Then we asked the subjects to imagine the same two types of infidelity, sexual and emotional. The men became more physiologically distressed by the sexual infidelity. Their heart rates accelerated by nearly five beats per minute, equivalent to drinking three cups of coffee at one sitting. Their skin conductance increased 1.5 microSiemens with the thought of sexual infidelity, but showed little change from baseline in response to the thought of emotional infidelity. And their frowning increased, showing 7.75 microvolt units of contraction to sexual infidelity, as compared with only 1.16 units in response to emotional infidelity. Women tended to show the opposite pattern, exhibiting greater physiological distress at the thought of emotional infidelity. Women's frowning, for example, increased to 8.12 microvolt units of contraction in response to emotional infidelity, from only 3.03 units of contraction in response to sexual infidelity. The coordination of psychological reactions of distress with physiological arousal patterns in men and women illustrates the precision with which humans have adapted over time to the particular threats they have faced to keeping a mate.

Sex differences in the causes of jealousy are not limited to Americans.

In one study of jealous men and women in central Europe, 80 percent of the men expressed fears of a sexual nature, such as worrying about their mate's having intercourse with another man or worrying about their own sexual adequacy.[16] Only 22 percent of the jealous women expressed sexual concerns, the majority focusing instead on the emotional relationship, such as the degree of closeness between their mate and another woman. Men in Hungary, Ireland, Mexico, the Netherlands, the Soviet Union, the United States, and Yugoslavia all show more intense jealousy than women in response to their partner's having sexual fantasies about another person.[17] These sexual differences in the causes of jealousy appear to characterize the entire human species.

The Consequences of Jealousy

The sexual jealousy of men is neither a trivial nor a peripheral emotion in human life. It sometimes becomes so powerful that it causes the person who experiences it to kill a mate or an interloper. In one case a wife killing was apparently fueled by an awareness of the reproductive damage of cuckoldry, as the husband explained:

> You see, we were always arguing about her extramarital affairs. That day was something more than that. I came home from work and as soon as I entered the house I picked up my little daughter and held her in my arms. Then my wife turned around and said to me: "You are so damned stupid that you don't even know she is someone else's child and not yours." I was shocked! I became so mad. I took the rifle and shot her.[18]

A wife's infidelity is sometimes viewed as so extreme a provocation that a "reasonable man" may legally respond with lethal violence. In Texas until 1974, for example, it was legal for a husband to kill his wife and her lover if he did so while the adulterers were engaging in the act of intercourse; their murder was considered a reasonable response to a powerful provocation. Laws exonerating men from killing adulterous wives are found worldwide and throughout human history. Among the Yaps, for example, rules permit husbands to kill wives and their lovers and to burn them up in the house if caught in the act of adultery. Similar provisions are made for offended husbands among the Toba-Batak of Sumatra. Old Roman law granted the husband the right to homicide only if the adultery occurred in his own house, and many similar laws remain in effect in Europe today.[19]

Male sexual jealousy is the single most frequent cause of all types of violence directed at wives, including beatings and actual murder. In one study of forty-four battered wives seeking refuge, 55 percent stated that jealousy was the key motive behind assaults from their husband.[20] Sexual jealousy is a major motive for murder. In a study of homicides among the Tiv, Soga, Gisu, Nyoro, Luyia, and Luo in British colonial Africa, of seventy homicides of wives by their husbands, 46 percent were explicitly over sexual matters, including adultery, the woman's abandonment of the husband, and the woman's refusal of sex with the husband.

Many of the homicides perpetrated by women also appear to have male sexual jealousy at their root. Women who kill men frequently do so to defend themselves against an enraged, threatening, and abusive husband from whom they fear bodily harm. In a sample of forty-seven homicide cases precipitated by a jealous man, sixteen women were killed by men for real or suspected infidelity, seventeen male rivals were killed by enraged men, and nine men were killed, in self-defense, by women whom the men had accused of infidelity.[21]

This behavior is by no means limited to American or even to Western cultures. Sexual jealousy is a leading motive behind homicide in Sudan, Uganda, and India.[22] One study in the Sudan, for example, found that the leading motive for 74 of 300 male-perpetrated murders was sexual jealousy.[23] Most cases of spousal homicide in every society studied are apparently precipitated by male accusations of adultery or by the woman's leaving or threatening to leave the husband. Furthermore, about 20 percent of the homicides of men by men have as their motive rivalry over a woman or a man's taking offense at advances made to a spouse, daughter, or female relative.[24]

The adaptive functions of jealousy to prevent infidelity and ensure paternity are hard to reconcile with the seemingly maladaptive act of killing one's wife, which interferes with reproductive success by destroying a key reproductive resource. There are several possible explanations. Because the overwhelming majority of unfaithful wives are not killed, the actual killing of a wife might represent an accidental slip of the mechanism, in which violent jealousy becomes pathological, is carried too far, and intentionally or accidentally results in death.[25] Yet, while this explanation fits some cases, it does not square with the seeming intentionality of many acts of wife killing, where men acknowledge that they intended to kill their partner and even hunted the woman down to do so.

An alternative explanation is that the killings that stem from jealousy represent extreme but nonetheless evolved manifestations of the mechanism. Killing one's wife would not necessarily have been reproductively damaging under all conditions during human evolutionary history. In the first place, if a wife is going to abandon her husband, not only will he lose her reproductive resources anyway but he also may suffer the additional cost of finding that those resources are channeled to a competitor, which is a double blow to relative reproductive success.

Furthermore, men who allow themselves to be cuckolded are subject to ridicule and damage to their reputation, especially if they take no retaliatory action. In a polygynous marriage, for example, killing an unfaithful wife might salvage a man's honor and also serve as a powerful deterrent to infidelity by his other wives. Polygynous men who took no action may have risked being cuckolded with impunity in the future. In some circumstances in our evolutionary past, killing a wife may have represented an effort at damage containment designed to stop the hemorrhaging of reproductive resources.

In the face of the conflicting costs and benefits of homicide, it is reasonable to speculate that in some circumstances, killing a spouse who was unfaithful or was determined to leave would have been reproductively more beneficial than allowing oneself to be cuckolded or abandoned with impunity. Thoughts of killing and occasional actual killings may have been adaptive over human evolutionary history and hence may be part of men's evolved mechanisms. This is a disconcerting and even horrifying possibility, but if society is ever going to grapple successfully with the serious problem of spousal homicide, it must confront the psychological mechanisms that give rise to it, especially the contexts and conditions that activate the mechanisms and make them especially dangerous.

In the overwhelming majority of cases, jealousy leads not to homicide but to a more benign set of tactics designed to keep the mate. Perhaps the most important of these tactics are efforts to fulfill the desires of one's mate.

The Value of Fulfilling a Mate's Desires

Once jealousy has become activated by threats to the security of one's mateship, it can motivate tactics directed at the mate, at the rival, or at oneself. Men and women can use a variety of tactics to keep a mate. Their original desires in a mate form the basis for one major strategy. In evolutionary terms, fulfilling the preferences held by a mate, or providing that mate with the sorts of resources he or she initially sought, should be a highly effective method of preserving the relationship.

To investigate this possibility, I initiated the mate-keeping studies.[26] First, I asked dating men and women to describe specific behaviors that they had observed in people trying to hold on to a partner and prevent that partner from becoming involved with someone else. They came up with 104 identifiable acts, which a team of four investigators classified into nineteen discrete clusters. The cluster called vigilance, for example, included the actions of calling a partner at unexpected times to see who the person was with, having one's friends check up on the partner, snooping through personal belongings, and dropping by unexpectedly to see what the partner was doing. Finally, I asked 102 college students who were involved in dating relationships and 210 newlyweds to rate how frequently they performed each of these acts. In their fifth year of marriage, the newlywed couples again reported on their use of the tactics to keep a mate. A separate group of forty-six college students then judged each of the tactics for its effectiveness in keeping a mate when performed by a man and when performed by a woman.

Fulfilling the initial mating desires of the partner indeed proved to be an effective mate-keeping tactic. Because women desire love and kindness in their initial selection of a mate, continuing to provide love and kindness is a highly effective tactic for men who want to keep their mates. Men who tell their mates that they love them, show helpfulness when their mates need it, and display kindness and affection regularly succeed in retaining their mates. These acts are judged to be the most effective men can perform, with an effectiveness rating of 6.23 on a 7-point scale, and significantly more effective than analogous acts performed by women, which received an effectiveness rating of 5.39. Furthermore, the performance of these acts is directly linked with the length of the relationship among dating couples and with the duration of marriage after five years. Husbands who fail to perform acts of love and commitment have wives who contemplate or seek divorce more than the wives of husbands who are kind and loving. Acts of love and kindness succeed because they signal an emotional commitment to the relationship, they bestow a benefit rather than inflicting a cost, and they fulfill women's psychological preferences in a mate.

Because women also value economic and material resources, continuing to provide them is another highly effective tactic for men to keep their mates. In the service of this goal, men in the study report spending a lot of money on their mates and buying them expensive gifts. Among committed dating couples, men provide these external resources more often than women do. Furthermore, the provision of resources is the second most effective tactic for men in retaining a mate, with an average effectiveness rating of 4.50, in contrast to a rating of 3.76 when used by women. Men more than women provide resources in the service of keeping their mates during the newlywed phase of marriage, and they continue to use this tactic more often than their wives after five years of marriage.[27] Like successful tactics for attracting a mate, successful tactics to keep a mate fulfill the desires of the opposite sex—in this case, the premium that women place on economic and material resources.

Analogously, because men value physical attractiveness in a mate, it is not surprising that women report that enhancing their appearance is one of their primary tactics for keeping their mates. After love and kindness, enhancing appearance is the second most effective tactic of the nineteen clusters evaluated. Women go out of their way to make themselves attractive to their partners, making up their faces to look nice, dressing to maintain a partner's interest, and acting sexy to distract a partner's attention from other women. Not only newlywed women but also women married for five years enhance their physical appearance in the service of keeping a mate, which shows that continuing to fulfill men's initial mating desires is a key to staying together.

The importance of appearance was dramatically illustrated by a study in which men and women watched a videotape of a couple sitting on a couch, talking.[28] After forty-five seconds, during which the couple cuddled, kissed, and touched one another, one of the partners got up and left the room to refill their wine glasses. Seconds later, an inter-loper entered and was introduced as the old girlfriend or boyfriend of the partner who had remained on the couch. The men watched the version with an old boyfriend as the interloper and the women watched the version with an old girlfriend as the interloper. The partner then stood up and briefly hugged the interloper, then the two sat down on the couch. Over the next minute they performed intimate actions, such as kissing and touching. The absent partner then returned, stopped, and looked down at the two people who were showing affection to each other on the couch. The tape ended there. Women who see the tape are nearly twice as likely as men to report that, in response to this threat to keeping a mate, they would try to make themselves more attractive to their partner. Men, in contrast, are more likely to say that they would become angry, suggesting a more aggressive strategy of keeping a mate. Women enhance their appearance because it exploits men's existing desires.

The Uses of Emotional Manipulation

When other tactics, such as providing resources, love, and kindness, fail, people sometimes resort to increasingly desperate emotional tactics to retain their mates, particularly if they are lower in desirability than their partners. Included in this cluster are tactics such as crying when the partner indicates interest in others, making the partner feel guilty about such interest, and telling the partner that one is hopelessly dependent upon him or her.

Submission or self-abasement is another tactic of emotional manipulation. For example, people may go along with everything a mate says, let a mate have his or her way, and promise to change in order to please a mate. In spite of the common stereotype that women are more submissive than men, the mate-keeping studies show precisely the opposite. Men submit to and abase themselves before their mates roughly 25 percent more than women in order to keep their mates. This sex difference shows up among college dating couples, among newlywed couples, and even among couples after several years of marriage. Furthermore, the sex difference in self-abasement cannot be attributed to a male reporting bias, because the spouses of those men report the same sex difference. The sex difference is robust and transcends the different kinds of couples.

Precisely why men would use the tactic of submission and self-abasement more than women remains a puzzle, given the stereotype of women as the more submissive sex. Perhaps men who perceive themselves to be relatively lower in desirability than their wives or girlfriends use submission to try to prevent a woman from defecting to another relationship. Perhaps the tactic represents an attempt to satisfy or placate a woman who is on the verge of leaving. But these speculations are not satisfactory because they beg the question of why men need to resort to this tactic more than women. Only future research can reveal the answer to this mystery.

Another emotional manipulation is intentionally trying to provoke sexual jealousy with the goal of keeping a mate. This tactic includes actions such as dating others to make a mate jealous, talking with people of the opposite sex at parties to incite jealousy, and showing an interest in people of the opposite sex to make a mate angry. These tactics are all judged to be nearly twice as effective for women as for men in retaining their mates. Women who flirt with other men in order to elicit jealousy and thereby hold on to a mate, however, walk a delicate balance. If a woman elicits jealousy injudiciously, her mate may perceive promiscuity and actually abandon her.

One study has identified a key context in which women intentionally elicit jealousy. This study examined discrepancies between a man's and a woman's admitted involvement in a relationship. These discrepancies signal differences in desirability of the partners, since the less involved person is generally more desirable. Although women admit to inducing jealousy more than men overall, not all women resort to this tactic. Whereas 50 percent of the women who view themselves as more involved than their partner in the relationship intentionally provoke jealousy, only 26 percent of the women who are equally or less involved resort to provoking jealousy. Women acknowledge that they are motivated to elicit jealousy in order to increase the closeness of the relationship, to test the strength of the relationship, to see if the partner still cares, and to inspire possessiveness. Discrepancies between partners in desirability, as indicated by differences in involvement in the relationship, apparently cause women to provoke jealousy as a tactic to gain information about, and to elevate, men's levels of commitment.

Ways to Keep Competitors at Bay

Humans, like many species, show proprietary attitudes toward their possessions and toward their mates. One method for signaling ownership is some public marking that tells intrasexual competitors to stay away. Public signals of possession can be verbal, as in introducing a person as a spouse or lover and bragging about a mate to friends. Public signals can also be physical, such as holding hands with or putting one's arm around a mate in front of other people. Public signals can also be ornamental, such as asking a mate to wear one's jacket, giving jewelry that signifies that the person is taken, and displaying a picture to signify that the person is taken.

Although men and women do not differ in how often they employ these public measures, the signals were judged by our panel of forty-six raters to be significantly more effective at keeping a mate when used by men than by women. The reason may be that public signals provide a strong cue to the woman of a man's intent to commit. Verbal, physical, and ornamental displays attain their effectiveness by dissuading potential competitors, just as the male insect who mingles his scent with that of the female causes rivals to seek other mates who are uncontested. These displays also communicate a commitment that fulfills women's long-term desires.

Maintaining vigilance is an additional means that both sexes use to keep their mates. An animal analogue occurs among the male elephant seals on the California coast, who patrol the perimeter of their harem to maintain a vigil against rivals or female defections. Calling mates at unexpected times to see if they are home or reading letters addressed to them are two human forms of exercising vigilance. Vigilance represents an effort to detect whether there are any signs of defection in the mate. Vigilance also conveys a message to a mate that evidence of consorting with rivals will be detected and acted upon. Other things being equal, it is reasonable to infer that people in our evolutionary past who were not vigilant experienced more defections, and hence lower reproductive success, than people who were vigilant.

The tactic of concealing mates is closely related to vigilance. Just as the male wasp whisks his mate away from the path that might be tracked by other males, men and women conceal their mates by refusing to take them to parties where competitors will be present, refusing to introduce them to friends of the same sex, taking them away from gatherings where other members of the same sex are present, and preventing them from talking with competitors. Concealment attains its effectiveness by reducing the contact of mates with rivals, decreasing the chances for poaching on mates, and reducing the opportunities for mates to assess other mating prospects.

Monopolizing a mate's time is a close cousin of concealment. It includes spending all one's free time with a mate so that he or she cannot meet anyone else, monopolizing his or her time at social gatherings, and insisting that the couple spend all its free time together. Monopolizing mates prevents them from having contact with potential rivals who could poach or provide an attractive alternative to an existing relationship.

These forms of manipulating mates for the goal of keeping them in the relationship have historical and cross-cultural precedents. Claustration, or the concealment of women to prevent their contact with potential sexual partners, provides a vivid example of mate monopolization. Historically, Indian men have secluded women in the interior of dwellings, Arabic men have veiled the faces and bodies of women, and Japanese men have bound the feet of women to restrict their contact with men. In societies that practice veiling, the most extreme veiling rituals, those in which the greatest surface area of the skin gets covered, occur at weddings, when women are generally at or close to peak reproductive value. Young prepubescent girls and older postmenopausal women are less severely concealed, perhaps because they are viewed as less enticing to rivals.[29]

Another common practice throughout human history was for men to gather women in guarded harems. The term *harem* means "forbidden." Indeed, it was as difficult for women to leave harems as it was for outside men to get in. Men used eunuchs to guard their harems. In India during the sixteenth century, merchants supplied rich men with a steady supply of Bengali slave eunuchs, who not only were castrated but had their entire genitalia cut off.[30]

The number of women collected into harems is staggering by any standard. The Indian emperor Bhuponder Singh had 332 women in his harem when he died, "all of [whom] were at the beck and call of the

Maharaja. He could satisfy his sexual lust with any of them at any time of day or night."[31] In India, estimates of the harems of sixteenth-century kings ranged between four and twelve thousand occupants.[32] In Imperial China, emperors around 771 B.C. kept one queen, three consorts or wives of the first rank, nine wives of the second rank, twenty-seven wives of the third rank, and eighty-one concubines.[33] In Peru, an Inca lord kept a minimum of seven hundred women "for the service of his house and on whom to take his pleasure . . . [having] many children by these women."[34]

All of these public signals of keeping a mate serve the single goal of preventing contact between the mates and potential rivals. Because men historically have been in a position of power, their ability to apply dramatic tactics has reduced women's freedom of choice. In modern industrial societies, with greater sexual equality, both sexes deploy public signals to retain their mates, albeit typically less drastic ones than used by medieval lords.

Destructive Mate-Keeping Measures

A final method for keeping mates is to inflict costs either on the competitors or on the mates themselves through derogation, threats, and violence. These tactics contrast sharply with such benefit-conferring tactics as providing resources or bestowing love and kindness. Destructive tactics acquire their effectiveness by both deterring rivals from poaching on mates and deterring mates from straying.

One set of destructive tactics is aimed at would-be rivals. Verbal denigration of competitors is perhaps the mildest form, although in Ecclesiasticus (28:17) it is noted, "The blow of a whip raises a welt, but a blow of the tongue crushes the bones." To dissuade mates from becoming attracted to rivals, men and women may belittle the appearance or intelligence of a competitor or start damaging rumors about a competitor. Derogation of competitors continues even after the wedding vows, because mate switching is always a possibility. When used judiciously, it is an effective method for rendering rivals less attractive, lowering the odds of a mate's defection, and increasing the chances that the couple will remain together.

A more costly tactic to rivals occurs when they are subjected to verbal threats and violence. Just as chimpanzees bare their teeth in a threat that sends rivals scurrying from a female, newlywed men yell at rivals who look at their brides, threaten to strike rivals who make passes at their mates, and stare coldly at men who look too long at their mates.

These destructive retention tactics are performed almost exclusively by men. Although they are not performed often, about 46 percent of the married men in the mate-keeping study had threatened an intrasexual competitor within the past year, whereas only 11 percent of the married women had done so. These tactics function by conveying a message to other men that they will incur a heavy cost if they show interest in a mate.

Men can inflict even more extreme costs on their rivals. Married men may hit men who make passes at their wives, get their friends to beat up a rival, slap men who show too much interest in their wives, and vandalize the property of rivals. These acts impose heavy costs in the form of bodily injury or, in rare cases, death on other men for poaching on mates. The reputation that these acts earn for their perpetrator can also act as a deterrent to other men. Most men would think twice before flirting with the girlfriend of a rough-looking, large, or violent man.

Destructive tactics are not directed only at rivals. Many are directed at mates to deter them from straying. Male baboons and other primates literally wound females who consort with other males.[35] Married men and women become angry when their partners flirt with others, yell after the partners show interest in others, and threaten to break up if their partners ever cheat. Furthermore, they may threaten never to speak with their partners again if they catch them with someone else, and occasionally they hit their partners when they flirt with others. Men in committed dating relationships and men who are married inflict these costs nearly twice as often as men who do not expect to be with their current mates in the future.

Punishing a mate who shows signs of interest in others acquires its effectiveness from the deterrent value of the threatened costs. Some of these costs are physical, such as bodily injury. Other costs are psychological, such as the lowered self-esteem that comes from being yelled at or otherwise verbally abused.[36] Perhaps the most important cost is the threat of terminating the relationship itself, which could involve losing everything that has been expended in the selection, attraction, and courtship of the mate.

A culturally sanctioned preventive strike may be attempted. Several ways have been developed to prevent extramarital sexual activity through genital mutilation in various cultures across northern and central Africa, Arabia, Indonesia, and Malaysia. Clitoridectomy, the surgical removal of the clitoris to prevent a woman from experiencing sexual pleasure, is practiced on millions of African women. Another practice common in Africa is infibulation, the sewing shut of the labia majora. According to one estimate, sixty-five million women living today in twenty-three countries from Northern and Central Africa have been genitally mutilated through infibulation.[37]

Infibulation effectively prevents sexual intercourse. It is sometimes performed by the woman's kin as a guarantee to a potential husband that the bride is intact. After marriage, infibulated women must be cut open to allow for sexual intercourse. If the husband goes away for a while, his wife may be reinfibulated. In the Sudan, the woman is reinfibulated after she bears a child and then must be reopened to allow for intercourse. Although the decision to reinfibulate a woman usually rests with her husband, some women demand reinfibulation after delivery, believing the practice to increase the husband's pleasure. A Sudanese woman who fails to please her husband risks being divorced, thus losing her children, losing economic support, and bringing disgrace upon her entire family.[38]

Men sometimes inflict extreme costs on women to keep them. Cross-cultural studies of the Baiga reveal cases in which husbands have attacked their wives with blazing logs as punishment for flirting with another man, violence against women in which jealousy is the key motive. Studies of battered women in Canada show that 55 percent of the women report that jealousy was one of the reasons for their husband's assault on them; half of the women reporting jealousy as a motive acknowledged that their sexual infidelity had provoked the violence.[39]

There are no cultures in which men are not sexually jealous. In every supposedly nonjealous culture previously thought to contain no bar to sexual conduct beyond the incest taboo, there is now evidence for sexual jealousy. The Marquesa Islanders, for example, were once thought to impose no bars to adultery. This notion is contradicted by an ethnographic report: "When a woman undertook to live with a man, she placed herself under his authority. If she cohabited with another man without his permission, she was beaten or, if her husband's jealousy was sufficiently aroused, killed."[40]

Another presumed example of the absence of sexual jealousy involves the practice of wife sharing by Eskimo men. Contrary to popular myth, however, male sexual jealousy is a leading cause of spousal homicide among the Eskimos, and these homicides occur at an alarmingly high rate.[41] Eskimo men share their wives only under highly circumscribed conditions, when there is a reciprocal expectation that the favor will be returned in kind. Wife swapping apparently can mitigate the onset of men's jealousy. All of these findings demonstrate that there are no paradises populated with sexually liberated people who share mates freely and do not get jealous.

Some societies require the cuckolder to pay reparation to the husband when caught having intercourse with his wife. Even in the United States, monetary payments to the husband have been imposed on cuckolders for the "alienation of affection." In North Carolina, for example, an ophthalmologist was required to pay a woman's ex-husband $200,000 for having enticed her away from her husband. These legal strictures reflect an intuitive understanding of human evolutionary psychology: cuckoldry represents the unlawful stealing of another man's resources. Men everywhere seem to regard wives as chattel to be owned and controlled. Men everywhere react to cuckoldry as they would to theft, and sometimes leave a trail of destruction in their wake.[42]

The Fragile Union

It is a remarkable human achievement that a man and a woman who have no genes in common can stay together in a union of solidarity over years, decades, or a lifetime. Because of the many forces that pull couples apart, however, staying together is a fragile proposition that poses a unique set of adaptive problems. Successful solutions typically incorporate several ingredients. First, the mate is supplied with the adaptively relevant resources needed to prevent defection. Second, competitors are kept at bay, for example, by public signals of possession or through concealing the mate from others. Third, emotional manipulation may be used, for example, by provoking jealousy to increase perceptions of desirability, submitting or abasing oneself to the mate, or convincing the mate that alternatives are undesirable. Fourth, unfortunately for the victims, destructive measures may come into play, such as punishing a mate for signals of defection or physically assaulting a rival.

These diverse tactics for keeping mates succeed by exploiting the psychological mechanisms of mates and rivals. The beneficial tactics, such as giving love and resources, work for a man because they fulfill the psychological desires that led the woman to choose him to begin with. For a woman, enhancing her physical appearance succeeds because it matches a man's psychology of desire that places a premium on attractiveness.

Unfortunately, the tactics of threats and violence, which inflict costs on a mate for defecting and on rivals for poaching, also work by exploiting the psychological mechanisms of others. Just as physical pain leads people to avoid the environmental hazards that can harm them, psychological fear causes people to avoid the wrath of an angry mate. Aggression sometimes pays.

Male sexual jealousy, the master mechanism underlying many methods for staying together, is also responsible for a majority of men's acts of violence against their mates. It may seem ironic that this mechanism, which is designed to keep a mate, causes so much destruction. It does so because the reproductive stakes are so high and the reproductive interests of the players fail to converge. The goals of a married man conflict with those of his rival, who seeks to lure his desirable wife away. The goals of a married man also can conflict with those of his wife or girlfriend, who may become the victim of violent sexual jealousy. And when one partner wants to stay together while the other wants to break up, both parties are in for suffering. Tactics of staying together can thus lead to conflict between the sexes.

7

Sexual Conflict

As we learn more about the patterns and structures that have shaped us today, it sometimes seems men are the enemy, the oppressors, or at the very least an alien and incomprehensible species.

—Carol Cassell, *Swept Away*

NOVELS, POPULAR SONGS, soap operas, and tabloids tell us about battles between men and women and the pain they inflict on each other. Wives bemoan their husbands' neglect; husbands are bewildered by their wives' moodiness. "Men are emotionally constricted," say women. "Women are emotional powder kegs," say men. Men want sex too soon, too fast; women impose frustrating delays.

When I first started exploring the topic of conflict between the sexes, I wanted to conduct a broad survey of the terrain. Toward this end, I asked several hundred women and men simply to list all the things that members of the opposite sex did that upset, angered, annoyed, or irritated them.[1] People were voluble on the topic. They listed 147 distinct things that someone could do to upset or anger a member of the opposite sex. These range from condescension, insults, and physical abuse to sexual aggression, sexual withholding, sexism, and sexual infidelity. With this basic list of conflicts in hand, my colleagues and I conducted studies of more than 500 individuals in dating couples and married couples to identify which sources of conflict occur most often and which produce the greatest distress. The findings from these studies present a framework for understanding conflict between the sexes as stemming from our evolved mating strategies.

Conflict between the sexes is best understood in the broader context of social conflict. Social conflict occurs whenever one person interferes with the achievement of the goal of another person. Interference can take various forms. Among men, for example, conflict occurs when they compete for precisely the same resources, such as position in a hierarchy or access to a desirable woman. Because young, attractive women are in scarcer supply than men who seek them, some men get shut out. One man's gain becomes other men's loss. Similarly, two women who desire the same responsible, kind, or achieving man come into conflict; if one woman get what she wants, the other woman cannot.

Conflict also erupts between men and women whenever one sex interferes with the goals and preferences of the other sex. In the sexual arena, for example, a man who seeks sex without investing in his partner short circuits a mating goal of many women, who want greater emotional commitment and higher material investment. This kind of interference runs both ways. A woman who requires a long courtship and heavy investment interferes with a man's sexual strategy, which involves acquiring sex with a minimum of obligation.

Whatever the nature of the intersexual strife, conflict per se serves no evolutionary purpose. It is generally not adaptive for individuals to get into conflicts with the opposite sex as an end in itself. Rather, conflict is more often an undesirable outcome of the fact that people's sexual strategies are different. Men and women often cannot simultaneously reach their goals without coming into conflict. Conflict stemming from the pursuit of mating goals has created recurrent adaptive problems over human evolutionary history, however, and so our ancestors evolved psychological mechanisms that alerted them to and helped them solve these problems. We have inherited from our ancestors these psychological solutions to conflict management.

The negative emotions of anger, distress, and upset are key human psychological solutions that have evolved in part to alert people to interference with their sexual and other adaptive goals. These emotions serve several related functions. They draw our attention to the problematic events, focusing attention on them and momentarily screening out less relevant events. They mark those events for storage in memory and easy retrieval from memory. Emotions also lead to action, causing people to strive to eliminate the source of the problem.

Because men and women have different sexual strategies, they differ in which events activate negative emotions. Men who seek casual sex without commitment or involvement, for example, often anger and upset women, whereas women who lead men to invest for a period of time and then withhold the sex that was promised or implied will cause men to get angry and upset.

Sexual Accessibility

Disagreements about sexual access or availability may be the most common sources of conflict between men and women. In a study of 121 college students who kept daily diaries of their dating activities for four weeks, 47 percent reported having one or more disagreements about the desired level of sexual intimacy.[2] Men sometimes seek sexual access with a minimum of investment. Men guard their resources jealously and are extraordinarily choosy about whom they invest in. They are "resource coy" in order to preserve their investment for a long-term mate or for a series of casual sex partners. Because women's long-term sexual strategies loom large in their repertoire, they often seek to obtain investment, or signals of investment, before giving a man sexual access. The investment that women covet is precisely the investment that men most jealously guard. The sexual access that men seek is precisely the resource that women are so selective about giving.

Conflict over perceived desirability, where one person feels resentment because the other ignores him or her as a potential mate, is often where the first battle line is drawn. People with higher desirability have more resources to offer and so can attract a mate with a higher value. Those with a low value must settle for less. Sometimes, however, a person may feel that he or she is worthy of consideration, and yet the other person disagrees.

This point is illustrated by a woman who frequents singles bars. She reports that she is sometimes approached by a beer-drinking, T-shirted, baseball-capped, stubble-faced truck driver or construction worker who asks her to dance. When she declines, the men sometimes get verbally abusive, saying, for example, "What's the matter, bitch, I'm not good enough for you?" Although she simply turns her back, that is precisely what she thinks: they are not good enough for her. Her unspoken message is that she can obtain someone better, given her own desirability, and this message infuriates the rebuffed men. Differences between people's perceptions of their value as mates cause conflict.

A major psychological source of such conflicts is the fact that men sometimes infer sexual interest on the part of a woman when it may not exist. Laboratory experiments have documented this phenomenon. In one study, 98 men and 102 women from a midwestern university watched a ten-minute videotape of a conversation between a male professor and a female student.[3] The student visits the professor's office to ask for a deadline extension for a term paper. The actors in the film were a female drama student and a male drama professor. Neither the student nor the professor acted flirtatious or provocative, although both were instructed to behave in a friendly manner. People who witnessed the tape then rated the likely intentions of the woman using 7-point scales. Women watching the interaction were more likely to say that the student was trying to be friendly, with a rating of 6.45, and not sexy (2.00) or seductive (1.89). Men, while also perceiving friendliness (6.09), were significantly more likely than women to infer seductive (3.38) and sexual (3.84) intentions. Similar results were obtained when 246 university students rated the intentions of women in photographs of a man and women studying together.[4] Men rate the photographed women as showing moderate intent to be sexy (4.87) and seductive (4.08), whereas women rating identical photographs see considerably less sexual intent (3.11) and less seductive intent (2.61). Men apparently interpret simple friendliness and mere smiling by women as indicating some level of sexual interest, even when women report no such interest.[5]

When in doubt, men seem to infer sexual interest. Men act on their inferences, occasionally opening up sexual opportunities. If over evolutionary history even a tiny fraction of these "misperceptions" led to sex, then men would have evolved lower thresholds for inferring women's sexual interest. It is impossible to state unequivocally that males are misperceiving women's sexual interest, because it is impossible to determine with certainty what someone's interests and intentions actually are. But we can say with certainty that men have lower thresholds than women for reading in sexual interest.

Once this male mechanism is in place, it is susceptible to manipulation. Women sometimes use their sexuality as a tactic of manipulation. In one study of 200 university students, women significantly more than men report smiling and flirting as a means for eliciting special treatment from members of the opposite sex, even though they have no interest in having sex with those men.[6]

Men's perception of sexual interest in women combines with women's intentional exploitation of this psychological mechanism to create a potentially volatile mix. These sexual strategies lead to conflict over desired level of sexual intimacy, over men's feelings that women lead them on, and over women's feelings that men are too pushy in the sexual sphere.

Sexual pushiness sometimes slips over the line into sexual aggressiveness, the vigorous pursuit of sexual access despite a woman's reluctance or resistance. Sexual aggressiveness is one strategy men use to minimize the costs they incur for sexual access, although this strategy carries its own costs in the possibility of retaliation and damage to their reputation. Acts of sexual aggression can be defined, for example, as the man's demanding or forcing sexual intimacy, failing to get mutual agreement for sex, and touching a woman's body without her permission. In one study, we asked women to evaluate 147 potentially upsetting actions that a man could perform. Women rate sexual aggression on average to be 6.50, or close to the 7.00 maximum of distress. No other kinds of acts that men can perform, including verbal abuse and nonsexual physical abuse, are judged by women to be as upsetting as sexual aggression. Contrary to a view held by some men, women do not want forced sex. Women sometimes have fantasies that involve forced sex with a man who turns out to be rich and handsome, and sometimes the theme of forced sex occurs in romance novels, but neither of these circumstances means that women actually desire forced or nonconsensual sex.[7]

Men, in sharp contrast, seem considerably less bothered if a woman is sexually aggressive; they see it as relatively innocuous compared with other sources of discomfort. On the same 7-point scale, for example, men judge the group of sexually aggressive acts to be only 3.02, or only lightly upsetting, when performed by a woman. A few men spontaneously wrote in the margins of the questionnaire that they would find such acts sexually arousing if a woman performed them. Other sources of distress, such as a mate's infidelity and verbal or physical abuse, are seen by men are far more upsetting—6.04 and 5.55, respectively—than sexual aggression by a woman.

A disturbing difference between men and women is that men consistently underestimate how unacceptable sexual aggression is to women. When asked to judge its negative impact on women, men rate it only 5.80 on the 7-point scale, which is significantly lower than women's own rating of 6.50. This is an alarming source of conflict between the sexes because it implies that some men may be inclined to use aggressive sexual acts because they fail to comprehend how distressing such acts really are to women. In addition to creating conflict between individuals in their heterosexual interactions, men's failure to correctly understand the psychological pain that women experience from sexual aggression may be one of the mechanisms causing men to lack empathy for rape victims.[8] The case of the Texas politician who callously said that if a woman cannot escape a rape, she should just lie back and enjoy it, is something that only someone who fails to understand the magnitude of the trauma experienced by women who are victims of sexual aggression could utter.

Women, in contrast, overestimate how upsetting sexual aggression by a woman is to a man, judging it to be 5.13, or moderately upsetting, in contrast to men's rating of only 3.02.[9] Men and women both fail to evaluate correctly how serious this source of conflict is for the other sex. This sexual bias in perception may result from erroneous beliefs about the other sex based on one's own reactions. That is, men think women are more like them than they really are and women think men are more like them than they really are in their reactions to sexual aggression. Dissemination of knowledge about sex differences in perceptions of the same events may be one small step toward reducing conflict between the sexes.

The flip side of the coin of sexual aggression is sexual withholding. Men consistently complain about women's sexual withholding, defined by such acts as being sexually teasing, saying no to having sex, and leading a man on and then turning him off. On the same 7-point scale of magnitude of upset, men judge sexual withholding to be 5.03, whereas women judge it to be 4.29. Both sexes are bothered by sexual withholding, but men significantly more so than women.

For women, sexual withholding fulfills several possible functions. One is to preserve their ability to choose men of high quality, who are willing to commit emotionally and to invest materially. Women withhold sex from certain men and selectively allocate it to others of their own choosing. Moreover, by withholding sex, women increase its value. They render it a scarce resource. Scarcity bumps up the price that men are willing to pay for it. If the only way men can gain sexual access is by heavy investment, then they will make that investment. Under conditions of sexual scarcity, men who fail to invest fail to mate. This circumstance creates another conflict between a man and a woman, since her withholding interferes with his strategy of gaining sexual access sooner and with fewer emotional strings attached.

Another function of sexual withholding is to manipulate a man's perception of a woman's value as a mate. Because highly desirable women are less sexually accessible to the average man by definition, a woman may exploit a man's perception of her desirability by withholding sexual access. Finally, sexual withholding, at least initially, may encourage a man to evaluate a woman as a permanent rather than a temporary mate. Granting sexual access early often causes a man to see a woman as a casual mate. He may perceive her as too promiscuous and too sexually available, characteristics that men avoid in committed mates.

Since men generally pursue casual sex with a variety of women, yet typically commit to only one, women's sexual withholding can create conflict by interfering with men's sexual strategy. By withholding sex, women impose a cost on men. They circumvent the component of men's mating strategy that involves obtaining low-cost sex. Certainly, women have a right to choose when, where, and with whom they want to have sex. But unfortunately, the exercise of that choice interferes with one of men's deep-seated sexual strategies and is therefore experienced by men as upsetting; hence, it is one of the key sources of conflict between the sexes.

Emotional Commitment

In the most abstract sense, adaptive problems get solved by one of two means—by one's own labor or by securing the labor of others. In principle, people who can successfully secure the labor of others, with a minimal commitment on their part, can be far more successful in solving life's adaptive problems. It is often in a woman's best interest, for example, to have a man so devoted to her that all of his energies are channeled to her and her children. It is often in a man's best interest, however, to allocate only a portion of his resources to one woman, reserving the rest for additional adaptive problems, such as seeking additional mating opportunities or achieving higher social status. Hence, the sexes are often at odds over each other's commitments.

A key sign of conflict over commitment centers on the irritation women express about men's tendency not to express their feelings openly. One of the most frequent complaints women have about men is that they are emotionally constricted. Among newlyweds, for example, 45 percent of women, in contrast to only 24 percent of the men, complain that their mates fail to express their true feelings.

These findings are mirrored in complaints about partners who ignore one's feelings. During the dating phase, roughly 25 percent of women complain that their partners ignore their feelings; this increases to 30 percent in the first year of marriage. By the fourth year of marriage, 59 percent of women complain that their husbands ignore their feelings. In contrast, only 12 percent of newlywed men and 32 percent of men in their fourth year of marriage make that same complaint.

The sex difference in these complaints must be examined from both women's and men's perspectives. From a woman's vantage point, what are the benefits she gains by getting a man to express his emotions, and what are the costs she incurs if he fails to express them? From a man's vantage point, are there benefits to withholding the expression of emotions and costs to expressing them?

One source of this sex difference is the fact that men's reproductive resources are more easily fractionated than women's. Within any one-year period, for example, a woman can only get pregnant by one man, and so the bulk of her reproductive resources cannot be partitioned. Within that same year, a man can fraction his resources by investing in two or more women.

One reason that men fail to express their emotions is that investing less emotionally in a relationship frees up resources that can be channeled toward other women or other goals. As in many negotiable exchanges, it is often in a man's best interest not to reveal how strong his desires are, how much he is willing to pay, how intensely he is willing to commit. Turkish rug dealers wear dark glasses to conceal their interest. Gamblers strive for a poker face to disguise telltale emotions that give away their hands. Emotions often betray the degree of investment. If emotions are concealed, one's sexual strategies remain concealed as well. The lack of information causes women to agonize, to sift through the available signs trying to discern where men really stand. College women, far more than college men, report that they spend time recalling and dissecting conversations with the people they are dating and that they try to analyze their partner's "real" inner states, intentions, and motivations.[10] Conflict over commitment resides at the core of complaints about men's emotional constrictedness.

Concealment of sexual strategies is not the only force driving men to remain stoic, nor are men necessarily inept at expressing emotions under different circumstances. Similarly, women sometimes conceal their emotions for strategic reasons. In the mating arena, however, discerning the long-term intentions of a potential partner is less critical for men than for women. Women in ancestral times who erred in their assessment suffered severe costs by granting sexual access to men who failed to commit to them. Getting a man to express himself emotionally represents one tactic that women use to gain access to the important information they need to discern a man's degree of commitment.

While women complain that men are emotionally constricted, men commonly complain that women are too moody and emotional. Roughly 30 percent of dating men, in contrast to 19 percent of dating women, complain about their partner's moodiness. These figures jump to 34 percent of men during the first year of marriage and 49 percent of men by the fourth year of marriage, in contrast with married women, of whom only 25 percent make these complaints.

Moody partners can be costly because they absorb time and effort. Palliative procedures, such as efforts to get the partner out of the bad mood and putting one's own plans aside temporarily, absorb energy at the expense of other goals. Women impose these costs on men as a tactic for eliciting commitment. A moody woman may be saying: "You had better increase your commitment to me, or else I will impose costs on you with emotional volatility." It is one tactic in women's repertoire for eliciting male commitment. Men dislike it because it absorbs effort that could be allocated elsewhere.

Moodiness also functions as an assessment device to test the strength of the bond.[11] Women use moodiness to impose small costs on their mates and then use men's reactions to the costs as a gauge of their degree of commitment. Men's unwillingness to tolerate these costs signals that their commitment is low. Men's willingness to tolerate the costs, and to be responsive to the increasing demands for investment, signals a greater level of commitment to the relationship. Either way, the woman gains valuable information about the strength of the bond.

Neither the functions of moodiness nor the functions of reserve require conscious thought on the part of the actor. Women need not be aware that they are attempting to test the strength of the man's commitment. Men need not be aware that they are trying to minimize their commitment to reserve some for efforts outside the couple. Like most psychological mechanisms, the functions of conflict over emotional constriction and expression remain hidden from view.

Investment of Resources

In addition to emotional commitment, couples also conflict directly over the investment of time, energy, and resources. Neglect and unreliability are manifestations of investment conflicts. More than a third of all dating and married women complain that their partners neglect them, reject them, and subject them to unreliable treatment. Among their common complaints are that men do not spend enough time with them, fail to call when they say they will, show up late, and cancel dates or other arrangements at the last minute. Roughly twice as many women as men complain about these events, suggesting that they are a cost inflicted by men on women. Approximately 38 percent of dating women, for example—but only 12 percent of dating men—complain that their partners sometimes fail to call them when they say they will.

Upset over neglect and unreliability reflects a conflict over investment of time and effort. It takes effort to be on time. Reliability requires relinquishing resources that could be channeled toward another goal. Neglect signals a low investment, indicating that the man lacks the depth of commitment necessary to perform acts that require even minimal cost for the woman's benefit.

Complaints about neglect and unreliability do not end when people marry because the skirmishing about investment continues. Partners continue to test each other periodically to determine what costs each is willing to bear.[12] Defection from the relationship lurks in the background as an option for someone who becomes dissatisfied.

Marriage does not extinguish conflict over investments. Indeed, as the marriage progresses from the newlywed year to the fourth year, women's complaints about neglect and unreliability continue unabated, signaling an ongoing source of conflict. Roughly 41 percent of newlywed women and 45 percent of women married for four years complain that their partners do not spend enough time with them. The analogous figures for men are only 4 percent during the newlywed year and 12 percent during the fourth year of marriage.

The flip side of the coin of neglect is dependency and possessiveness. Conflict develops when one mate absorbs so much energy that the partner's freedom is restricted. A common complaint of married men, far more than of married women, is that their spouses absorb too much of their time and energy. Thirty-six percent of married men, in contrast with only 7 percent of married women, complain that their spouses demand too much of their time. Twenty-nine percent of married men, but only 8 percent of married women, complain that their mates demand too much attention from them.

These sex differences in demands on time and attention reflect a continuing conflict about investment. Women try to sequester their mate's investment. Some men resist monopolization, striving to channel a portion of their effort toward other adaptive problems such as raising their status or acquiring additional mates. More than three times as many men as women voice complaints about this form of possessiveness because of differences in the benefits each sex derives by diverting surplus resources into additional matings, or into increased status that opens up mating opportunities. For men, the reproductive payoff historically was large and direct. For women, the benefits were smaller, less direct, and often more costly because they risked the loss of the existing mate's investment of time and resources. Wives may be possessive and demanding because they do not want their husband's investment to be diverted.

Another manifestation of conflict over investment centers on complaints about a partner's selfishness. Among married couples, 38 percent of men and 39 percent of women complain that their partners act selfishly. Similarly, 37 percent of married women and 31 percent of married men complain that their partners are self-centered. Self-centeredness involves allocating resources to oneself at the expense of others, such as a spouse or children. Complaints about self-centeredness rise dramatically during the course of marriage. During the first year of marriage, only 13 percent of women and 15 percent of men complain that their partners are self-centered. By the fourth year of marriage, the numbers more than double.

To understand these dramatic increases in complaints about selfishness, consider the critical signals of investment during the courting stage. Effective courting signals to a potential mate one's selfless willingness to put that mate's interests before one's own, or at least on par with one's own. These cues are powerful tactics for attracting a mate and are displayed most floridly while courting. After the marriage is reasonably secure, the tactics signaling selflessness subside because their initial function of attracting a mate recedes in importance. Each sex becomes freer to indulge the self and to channel less effort toward the partner. Perhaps this is what married couples mean when they complain that their spouses "take them for granted."

The picture is not a very pretty one, but humans were not designed by natural selection to coexist in niceness and matrimonial bliss. They were designed for individual survival and genetic reproduction. The psychological mechanisms fashioned by these ruthless criteria are often selfish ones.

The final manifestation of conflict over investment is fights over the allocation of money. It has become a cliche that married couples fight over money more than practically anything else. There is some truth to this. A study of American couples found that money is indeed one of the most frequent sources of conflict. Seventy-two percent of married couples fight about money at least once a year, with 15 percent fighting more than once a month.[13] Interestingly, these couples fight more about how the money they have is to be allocated than about how much money they have.

Because the interests of spouses are rarely identical, men's best allocation decisions sometimes differ from women's. Disagreements may center on how much one spouse spends of the mutually held resources and on how much one spouse earns.

American men, far more often than women, complain that their spouses spend too much money on clothes. The percentage of men who express this complaint starts at 12 percent during the newlywed year and increases to 26 percent by the fourth year of marriage. In contrast, among women, only 5 percent during the newlywed year and 7 percent during the fifth year of marriage complain about their husband's spending on clothes. Both sexes, however, complain equally that their spouses spend too much money in general. Nearly one-third of men and women by the fourth year of marriage complain about their spouses' overexpenditure of mutual resources.

More women than men complain that their spouses fail to channel the money they do earn to them, especially noting their failure to buy them gifts. By the fifth year of marriage, roughly one-third of married women voice this complaint; in contrast, only 10 percent of husbands express similar complaints. Conflict between the sexes corresponds remarkably well with the initial sex-linked preferences in a mate. Women select mates in part for their external resources, and once married, complain more than men that those resources are not forthcoming enough.

Deception

Conflicts between the sexes over sexual access, emotional commitment, and investment of resources become exacerbated when one deceives the other. Forms of deception abound in the plant and animal world. Some orchids, for example, have brilliantly colored petals and centers that mimic the colors, shapes, and scents of female wasps of the species *Scolia ciliata*.[14] Male wasps, powerfully attracted by these scents and colors, land on the orchids the way they would land on a female's back. This event is followed by a pseudocopulation, in which the male moves rapidly over the rigid hairs of the upper surface of the flower, which mimic the hairs on a female wasp's abdomen. He probes the orchid in an apparent search for complementary female genital structures, at the same time picking up the pollen. Failing to find the exact structures needed for ejaculation, however, the male moves on to another pseudofemale. In this manner, orchids deceive the male wasp for the function of cross-pollination.

Among humans, men and women sometimes deceive each other to gain access to resources that the other possesses. In one instance of sexual deception, a colleague used to go to up-scale bars and pick up men who would take her out to dinner. During dinner, she was friendly, flirtatious, sexy, and engaging. Toward the end of dinner, she would excuse herself to go to the women's room, then slip out the back door and disappear into the night. Sometimes she did this alone, sometimes with a girlfriend. Her targets were often businessmen from out of town, whom she would be unlikely to encounter again. Although she spoke no lies, she was a sexual deceiver. She led men to believe that they had a reasonable probability of having sex, she used sexual cues to elicit resources, and then she absconded without delivering sex.

Although this scene may appear to be unusual or even Machiavellian, its underlying theme occurs repeatedly in ordinary behavior in various guises. Women are apparently aware of the sexual effects they have on men. When 104 college women were asked how often they flirted with a man to get something they wanted, such as a favor or special treatment, knowing that they did not want to have sex with him, they gave it on average a frequency of 3 on a 4-point scale, where 3 signified "sometimes" and 4 signified "often," whereas the comparable figure for men was 2. Women gave similar responses to questions about using sexual hints to gain favors and attention, yet admitted they had no intention of having sex with the targets of these hints. Women admit to being sexual deceivers part of the time.

While women are more likely to be sexual deceivers, men are more likely to be commitment deceivers. Consider what a thirty-three-year-old man had to say about the commitment implied by declarations of love:

> You would think saying "I love you" to a woman to thrill and entice her isn't necessary anymore. But that's not so. These three words have a toniclike effect. I blurt out a declaration of love whenever I'm in the heat of passion. I'm not always believed, but it adds to the occasion for both of us. It's not exactly a deception on my part, I have to feel *something* for her. And, what the hell, it usually seems like the right thing to say at the time.[15]

Men in fact do report intentionally deceiving women about emotional commitment. When 112 college men were asked whether they had ever exaggerated the depth of their feelings for a woman in order to have sex with her, 71 percent admitted to having done so, compared with only 39 percent of the women who were asked a parallel question. When the women were asked whether a man had ever deceived them by his exaggeration of the depth of his feelings in order to have sex with her, 97 percent admitted that they had experienced this tactic at the hands of men; in contrast, only 59 percent of the men had experienced this tactic at the hands of women.

Among married couples, deception about the depth of commitment continues in the form of sexual infidelity. The motivations for male infidelity are clear, since ancestral men who had extramarital affairs had the possibility of siring additional offspring and thereby gaining a reproductive advantage over their more loyal counterparts. Women get extremely upset by male infidelity because it signals that the man might divert resources to other women or even defect from their relationship. Women stand to lose the entire investment secured through the marriage. Based on this prospect, women should be far more upset by an affair that contains emotional involvement than about one that does not, because emotional involvement typically signals outright defection rather than the less costly siphoning off of a fraction of resources. This proves to be the case, because women are more forgiving and less upset if no emotional involvement accompanies their husband's affair.[16] Men seem to know this. When caught having an affair, men often plead that the other woman "means nothing."

In human courtship, the costs of being deceived about a potential mate's resources and commitment are shouldered more heavily by women. An ancestral man who made a poor choice in sex partners risked losing only a small portion of time, energy, and resources, although he may also have evoked the rage of a jealous husband or a protective father. An ancestral woman, however, who made a poor choice of a casual mate, allowing herself to be deceived about the man's long-term intentions or willingness to devote resources to her, risked enduring pregnancy, childbirth, and child care unaided.

Because the deceived can suffer tremendous losses, there must have been great selection pressures for the evolution of a form of psychological vigilance to detect cues to deception and to prevent its occurrence. The modern generation is merely one more cycle in the endless spiral of an evolutionary arms race between deception perpetrated by one sex and detection accomplished by the other. As the deceptive tactics get more subtle, the ability to penetrate deception becomes more refined.

Women have evolved strategies to guard against deception. When they are seeking a committed relationship, the first line of defense is imposing courtship costs by requiring extended time, energy, and commitment before consenting to sex. More time buys more assessment. It allows a woman greater opportunity to evaluate a man, to assess how committed he is to her, and to detect whether he is burdened by prior commitments to other women and children. Men who seek to deceive women about their ultimate intentions typically tire of extended courtship. They go elsewhere for sex partners who are more readily accessible.

To guard against deception, women spend hours discussing with their friends the details of interactions they have had with their mates or with potential mates. Conversations are recounted and scrutinized. When asked, for example, whether they talk with their friends to try to figure out the intentions of someone they have gone out with, most women admit that they do. Men, in contrast, are significantly less inclined to devote effort to this problem of assessment.[17] Women must separate men who seek casual sex from those who seek marriage. Ancestral men generally had less need than women to channel time and effort to assessing a potential mate's long-terms intentions.

Although women have developed strategies for penetrating men's deception, men clearly cannot ignore deception at the hands of women.

This is especially true when men seek spouses. Accurate assessments of women's reproductive value, resources, kin group or other alliances, and prospective faithfulness become paramount. This is vividly illustrated in a scene from Tennessee Williams's play *A Streetcar Named Desire:* Mitch is on a date with Blanche DuBois, a former high school teacher to whom he is engaged to be married but who has deceived him about her sexual past with other men, including a sexual relationship with a student which caused her expulsion from the school. A friend has just alerted Mitch to Blanche's past, so he aggressively tells her that evening that he has always seen her only at night under a dim light, never in a well-lit room. He turns on a bright light, from which Blanche recoils, but he sees that she is older than she had led him to believe she was. He confronts her with what he has heard about her florid sexual past. She plaintively asks Mitch whether he will still marry her. He says, "No, I don't think I'll marry you now," as he approaches her menacingly for sex.

Given the tremendous importance that men assign to physical appearance and sexual exclusivity in a potential mate, they are especially sensitive to deception about a woman's age and sexual history. Men seek out information about women's sexual reputation. Psychological alertness guards men against deception by women about two of the most reproductively important considerations for a man in a permanent mate—her reproductive value and the likelihood that this value will be channeled exclusively to him.

Both sexes are sensitive to deception at the hands of the other sex, but the forms of deception about which men and women are vigilant differ, because the costs that they suffer at the hands of the other sex differ. The psychological mechanisms underlying human mating strategies gauge these costs. Anger at a member of the opposite sex over particular forms of deception provides a window into the nature of these sexually differentiated strategies.

Unfortunately, conflict between the sexes does not end with skirmishing about sexual access. It does not end with disagreement over commitment or investment. It does not even end with deception suffered at the hands of the other sex. It takes on more violent forms.

Abuse

Abuse can take several forms. One form is psychological abuse, which causes partners to feel less valuable in the relationship, to lower their sense of desirability, to make them feel lucky to have secured the partners, and to diminish their perceived prospects on the mating market were they to defect.[18] Condescension to, and derogation of, a mate, abhorrent though they seem, represent tactics for accomplishing these goals. Unfortunately, women are more often the victims and men are more often the perpetrators of condescension and other forms of psychological abuse.

Condescension takes several forms. In one, a man places more value on his opinions than on the mate's simply because he is male. In another, a man treat his mate as if she were stupid or inferior. Newlywed men perform these acts of condescension roughly twice as often as their wives do. These acts have the effect of lowering the wife's sense of her own desirability relative to that of the husband.[19] In effect, abuse may function to increase the victim's investment and commitment to the relationship and to bend the victim's energies toward the goals of the abuser. Victims often feel that, because their mating alternatives are not rosy, they must strive valiantly to placate the current mate by increasing their investment. They also may devote increased effort and more placating gestures to the mate in an attempt to avoid incurring further wrath.

Men's motives for physically battering women center heavily on coercive control. One researcher attended the trials of 100 Canadian couples engaged in litigation over the husband's violence toward the wife. Although no quantitative analyses were performed, the researcher concluded that the core of nearly all cases involved the husband's frustration about his inability to control his wife, with frequent accusations of her being a whore or having sex with other men.[20] A more systematic study of thirty-one battered American women found that jealousy was the main topic of the argument between the husband and wife that led to the physical abuse in 52 percent of the cases, with 94 percent listing it as a frequent cause of a history of battering.[21] Yet another study of sixty battered wives who sought the assistance of a clinic in North Carolina found that "morbid jealousy," such as jealousy if the wife left the house for any reason or if she maintained friendships with other men or women, evoked violent reactions in 95 percent of the cases.[22] The coercive constraint of women, particularly in sexual matters, underlies the majority of cases of physical abuse.

Spouse abuse is obviously a dangerous game to play. The abuser may be seeking an increased commitment and investment, but the tactic may backfire and produce a defection instead. Alternatively, this form of abuse may increase precisely as a last-ditch attempt to hold on to mates by inflicting costs on them for signs of defection. In this sense, the abuser treads on thin ice. He risks triggering in the victim the decision that the relationship is too costly and that a better partnership can be had elsewhere. Perhaps this is why abusers are often profusely apologetic after the abuse, crying, pleading, and promising that never again will they inflict such costs.[23] These actions may be attempts to avoid the risks of defection inherent in using abuse as a tactic of control.

Wife abuse is not a Western invention. It occurs cross-culturally. Among the Yanomamö, for example, husbands regularly strike their wives with sticks for offenses as slight as serving tea too slowly.[24] Interestingly, Yanomamö wives often regard physical abuse as a sign of the depth of their husband's love for them—an interpretation probably not shared by their modern American counterparts. Whatever the interpretation, these beatings have the effect of subordinating Yanomamö women to their husbands.

Another form of abuse that men sometimes heap on their mates is insults about their physical appearance. Although only 5 percent of newlywed men inflict this form of insult on their mates, the percentage triples by the fourth year of marriage. In marked contrast, only 1 percent of newlywed women insult their husband's appearance, and only 5 percent of women married for four years make these insults. Given that a woman's physical appearance is typically a larger part of her desirability, women find derogations in this domain to be especially distressing. Men may derogate women's appearance as a means of lowering women's perception of their own desirability, thereby securing a more favorable power balance within the relationship.

As with other destructive tendencies, the fact that the use of abuse has an adaptive logic behind it does not mean that we should accept it, desire it, or be lax about curtailing it. On the contrary, greater understanding of the logic behind such tactics as abuse and about the contexts in which they occur may eventually lead to more effective means to reduce or eliminate them. The means for reducing abuse may come from the recognition that abuse is not a uniform and unmodifiable feature of male biology but is rather a response that depends on particular contexts. Among newlyweds, for example, men who have certain personality dispositions, such as lacking trust in others and being emotionally unstable, were four times as likely to abuse their wives as were emotionally stable and trusting men. Discrepancies in the desirability of the two spouses which make the husband fear losing his wife, the distance of the wife's kin, and the absence of legal and other costs to abuse are additional contexts likely to affect the incidence of wife battering. Identifying the contexts will be crucial for ameliorating the problems.

Sexual Harassment

Disagreements over sexual access occur not just in the context of dating and marital relationships, but also in the workplace, where people often seek casual and permanent mates. The search may cross a line and become sexual harassment, which is defined as "unwanted and unsolicited sexual attention from other individuals in the workplace."[25] It can range from mild forms such as unwanted staring and sexual comments, to physical violations, such as the touching of breasts, buttocks, or crotch. Sexual harassment clearly produces conflict between the sexes.

Evolutionary psychology offers the possibility of identifying some of the key psychological mechanisms that underlie the behavior and some of the crucial contexts that activate those mechanisms. The message of evolutionary psychology is not that these problems are biologically determined, unmodifiable, or inevitable. Rather, by identifying key contexts that foster the occurrence of harassment, evolutionary psychology offers hope for understanding and intervention.

Sexual harassment is typically motivated by the desire for short-term sexual access, although this does not exclude the possibility that it is sometimes motivated by the desire to exercise power or to seek lasting romantic relationships. The view that sexual harassment is a product of the evolved sexual strategies of men and women is supported by the profiles of typical victims, including such features as their sex, age, marital status, and physical attractiveness; their reactions to unwanted sexual advances; and the conditions under which they were harassed.

Victims of sexual harassment are not random with respect to sex. In one study of complaints filed with the Illinois Department of Human Rights over a two-year period, seventy-six complaints were filed by women and only five by men.[26] Another study of 10,644 federal government employees found that 42 percent of the women, but only 15 percent of the men, had experienced sexual harassment at some point in their careers.[27] Among the complaints filed in Canada under human rights legislation, ninety-three cases were filed by women and only two by men. In both cases filed by men, the harassers were men rather than women. It seems clear that women are generally the victims of sexual harassment and men are the perpetrators. Nonetheless, given the previously documented tendency of women to experience greater distress in response to acts of sexual pushiness or aggressiveness, it is likely that the same acts of sexual harassment are experienced as more upsetting by women than by men, and hence women might be more likely to file official complaints than men when harassed.

Although any woman may be the target of sexual harassment, the victims are disproportionately young, physically attractive, and single. Women over forty-five are far less likely than younger women to experience sexual harassment of any type.[28] One study found that women between the ages of twenty and thirty-five filed 72 percent of the complaints of harassment, whereas they represented only 43 percent of the labor force at the time. Women over forty-five, who represented 28 percent of the work force, filed only 5 percent of the complaints.[29] In none of the many studies of sexual harassment have older women had a risk of harassment that was as great as that of younger women. The targets of sexual harassment seem very much like the women of male sexual interest in general in their relative youth.

Single and divorced women are subjected to more sexual harassment than married women. In one study, 43 percent of women filing complaints were single, whereas they represented only 25 percent of the labor force; married women, comprising 55 percent of the labor force, filed only 31 percent of the complaints.[30] There may be several reasons for this phenomenon. The costs that might be imposed on a sexual harasser by a jealous husband are absent when the victim is single. Moreover, single women may be perceived to be more receptive than married women to sexual advances. Finally married women are indeed generally less receptive to sexual advances than are single or divorced women, because they risk losing the commitment and resources they currently secure from their husbands. Single women are thus more vulnerable targets.

Reactions to sexual harassment tend to follow evolutionary psychological logic. When men and women were asked how they would feel if a co-worker of the opposite sex asked them to have sex, 63 percent of the women would be insulted, whereas only 17 percent of the women would feel flattered.[31] Men's reactions were just the opposite—only 15 percent would be insulted, whereas 67 percent would feel flattered. These reactions fit with the evolutionary logic of human mating, with men having positive emotional reactions to the prospect of casual sex and women having more negative reactions to being treated merely as sex objects.

The degree of chagrin that women experience upon sexual advances, however, depends in part on the status of the harasser. Jennifer Semmelroth and I asked 109 college women how upset they would feel if a man they did not know, whose occupational status varied from low to high, persisted in asking them out on a date despite repeated refusals, in a relatively modest form of harassment. On a 7-point scale, women would be most upset by advances from construction workers (4.04), garbage collectors (4.32), cleaning men (4.19), and gas station attendants (4.13), and

least upset by persistent advances by premedical students (2.65), graduate students (2.80), or successful rock stars (2.71). When a different
group of 104 women were asked how flattered they would feel by outright sexual propositions from variously occupied men, the responses
were similar. The same acts of harassment from men who differ in status
are not equally upsetting.

Women's reactions to sexual harassment also depend heavily on
whether the motivation of the harasser is perceived to be sexual or
romantic. Sexual bribery, attaching job promotions to sex, and other cues
that the person is interested only in casual sex, are more likely to be
labeled as harassment than are signals of potential interest that may
transcend the purely sexual, such as nonsexual touching, complimentary
looks, or flirting.[32] When 110 college women used a 7-point scale to rate
how sexually harassing a series of actions were, acts such as a fellow co-
worker's putting his hand on a woman's crotch (6.81) or trying to corner
a woman when no one else is around (6.03) were seen as extremely
harassing. In contrast, acts such as a co-worker's telling a woman that he
sincerely likes her and would like to have coffee with her after work was
judged to be only 1.50, where a 1.00 signified no harassment at all.
Clearly, short-term sexual and coercive intentions are more harassing
than sincere romantic intentions.

Not all women, however, label even coercive behavior as harassment.
For example, some 17 percent of women in a study of sexual harassment in the workplace did not consider sexual touching to be harassment. Women's evolved sexual strategy may be conditional in that
women sometimes can benefit from, or take advantage of, men's sexual
advances. It is clear, for example, that women as well as men often seek
and find romantic and sexual relationships in the workplace. Some
women are even willing to exchange sex for good positions and privileges at work. One woman reported that she did not consider the
expectation that she would have sex with her foreman as harassment,
because "all the women were treated the same way" and because she
was able to get "easy work" that way.[33] Just as material benefits sometimes accrue to women in casual mating outside the workplace, there
may be circumstances in which women gain benefits from casual mating within the workplace.

All these findings about the profiles of sexual harassment victims, the
sex differences in emotional reactions, and the importance of the status
of the harasser follow from the evolutionary logic of human mating
strategies. Men have evolved lower thresholds for seeking casual sex
without commitment and lower thresholds for perceiving sexual intent
in others, and these evolved sexual mechanisms operate in the work con-

text perhaps no less than in any other social context. This information does not mean that we should condone sexual harassment or overlook its pernicious effects. Rather, it provides us with the key causes and underlying psychological principles needed to lessen the occurrence of this regrettable behavior.

Rape

Rape may be defined as the use of force, or the threat to use force, to obtain sexual intercourse. Estimates of the number of women who have been raped vary, depending on how inclusive a definition the researcher has used. Some researchers use broad definitions that include instances in which a woman did not perceive that she was raped at the time but admitted later that she did not really want to have intercourse. Other researchers use stricter definitions that delimit rape to forced intercourse against the woman's will. One large-scale study of 2,016 university women, for example, found that 6 percent had been raped.[34] Another study of 380 college women, however, found that almost 15 percent had been involved in sexual intercourse against their will.[35] Given the tremendous social stigma attached to rape victims, these figures may underestimate the actual numbers of women who have been raped.

The issue of rape has a bearing on human mating strategies, in part because many rapes occur within the context of mating relationships. Dating is a common context for rape. One study found that almost 15 percent of college women had experienced unwanted sexual intercourse in the context of dating situations. Another study of 347 women found that 63 percent of all instances of sexual victimization were perpetrated by dates, lovers, husbands, or de facto partners.[36] The most extensive study of rape in marriage found that of nearly a thousand married women, 14 percent had been raped by their husbands.[37] It is clear that rape cannot be considered solely as a behavior perpetrated by strangers in dark alleys. It occurs in the context of other forms of mating activities and mating relationships.

As with sexual harassment, men are almost invariably the perpetrators and women are almost invariably the victims. These facts points to a continuity with other conflicts between the sexes. This continuity suggests that clues to understanding rape may be discovered within the mating strategies of men and women. The view that there is a continuity, however, does not imply that rape per se is an evolved strategy in men's sexual repertoire or was ever adaptive in human evolutionary history.

Indeed, it is a matter of controversy within evolutionary psychology today whether rape represents an evolved sexual strategy of men or is better understood as a horrifying side effect of men's general sexual strategy of seeking low-cost casual sex.[38] The key issue is whether the evidence shows that rape is a distinct evolved strategy within the human arsenal of strategies, as it clearly is among some insect and bird species. Among scorpionflies, for example, the males have a special anatomical clamp that functions solely in the context of raping a female and not in normal mating, for which a male offers a nuptial gift.[39] Experiments that seal the clamp with wax literally prevent the male from achieving a forced copulation.

Although men are not like scorpionflies, psychological and physiological experiments have revealed some disturbing findings. Laboratory studies that expose men to audio and visual depictions of rape versus mutually consenting sexual encounters find that men display sexual arousal, assessed both by self-report and by penile tumescence, to both consenting and nonconsenting situations. Men apparently are sexually aroused when exposed to sexual scenes, whether or not consent is involved, although other conditions, such as the presence of violence and a disgust reaction from the woman, appear to inhibit the sexual arousal of the men.[40]

These findings, however, cannot differentiate between the two alternative possibilities: either that men have only a general tendency to be sexually aroused in response to witnessing sexual encounters and hence have no distinct adaptation to forced sex, or that men have evolved a distinct rape psychology. Consider a food analogy. Humans, like dogs, salivate when they smell or see appetizing food, especially if they have not eaten for a while. Suppose that a scientist hypothesized that humans have a specific adaptation to take food forcibly from others. The scientist then conducted studies in which people were deprived of food for twenty-four hours and thereafter were exposed visually to one of two scenes: appetizing food that was given willingly by one person to another person, or equally appetizing food that was forcibly taken from one person by another.[41] If this hypothetical experiment yielded the result that people salivate an equal volume to both food scenes, we could not conclude that people have a distinct adaptation to "take food forcibly." All we could conclude is that, when hungry, people seem to salivate when exposed to scenes of food, regardless of the circumstances surrounding the form of procurement. This hypothetical example is analogous to the data that indicate sexual arousal in men in response to sexual scenes, regardless of whether those scenes depict mutually consenting sex or forced sex. The data do not constitute evidence that rape is a distinct evolved strategy of men.

Correspondences between rape and human mating strategies are found, however, in the profiles of rape victims. Despite the fact that some women of all ages are raped, the victims of rape are heavily concentrated among young women. In one study of 10,315 rape victims, women between the ages of sixteen and thirty-five were far more likely to be raped than women in any other age category.[42] Eighty-five percent of all rape victims are less than thirty-six years old. By way of comparison, victims of other crimes, such as aggravated assault and murder, show a radically different age distribution. Women between forty and forty-nine, for example, are just as likely to suffer an aggravated assault as women between twenty and twenty-nine, but the older women are far less likely to be raped. Indeed, the age distribution of rape victims corresponds almost perfectly to the age distribution of women's reproductive value, in marked contrast to the age distribution of victims of other violent crimes. This evidence strongly suggests that rape is not independent of men's evolved sexual psychology.

Rape victims, like most individuals of male sexual desire, are by and large young and physically attractive. Men have evolved psychological mechanisms that respond with attraction and arousal to physical cues of youth and health, which are powerful determinants of standards of beauty. The fact that rapists also find these cues attractive and select their victims partly on the basis of them does not provide evidence of an evolved strategy in males for rape that is distinct from their strategy of casual uncommitted sex. This evidence simply provides further support for men's general desire for women who are young and attractive.

In the current state of knowledge, there is no direct evidence to suggest that men have evolved a distinct sexual strategy of rape. Rather, men seem to use force and violence to achieve a variety of goals. Because obtaining sexual access to young women is often one of these goals, some men employ force to achieve it, just as they use violence to vanquish rivals or to steal other people's resources.

The suggestion that men use coercion of one form or another in a wide variety of sexual contexts, however, has considerable credibility.[43] In attitude studies, men are more likely than women to see sexual coercion as acceptable. College women report that men often persevere to excess in their sexual requests, frequently initiate sexual advances even after the women say no, occassionally use verbal or physical threats, and sometimes use physical violence, such as slapping or hitting.[44] One study of college women, for example, found that of those women who had been raped, 55 percent reported that the man did it even after she had said no; 14 percent used physical coercion, such as holding her down; and 5 percent used threats.[45] Coercion is part of many sexual encounters.

The use of coercion by men is not limited to sexual encounters, however; men use coercion in a variety of contexts. Men coerce other men, perpetrate violence against other men, and kill other men four times as often as they kill women. Men are clearly the more coercive and violent sex and are responsible for most of the socially unacceptable, illegal, and repugnant behavior in the world.[46] Coercion and violence may be weapons that men use in a wide range of interpersonal contexts, both sexual and nonsexual.

Feminist investigations have been critical in illuminating the abhorrence of rape from the victim's point of view. Contrary to what some men think, the evidence clearly shows that women do not want to be raped and do not experience rape as a sexual act. The psychological trauma experienced by rape victims—including rage, fear, self-loathing, humiliation, shame, and disgust—must surely rank among the most horrendous experiences anyone can suffer.

One important source of evidence about the evolutionary context of rape is studies that evaluate the psychological pain experienced by rape victims. The evolutionary biologists Nancy Thornhill and Randy Thornhill propose that psychological pain is an evolved mechanism that focuses an individual's attention on the events surrounding the pain, promoting the elimination and avoidance of the pain-causing events.[47] In a study of 790 rape victims in Philadelphia, women of reproductive age were more severely traumatized by rape than either prepubescent girls or older women, as indicated by having trouble sleeping, suffering nightmares, being afraid of unknown men, and having a fear of being home alone. Because the intensity of psychological pain is presumably a function of the reproductive costs that ancestral women would have experienced as a result of a rape, a woman of reproductive age would have experienced rape as a more severe cost than pre- or postreproductive women with regard to such factors as the inability to choose the father of her offspring. The fact that women of reproductive age appear to experience more psychological pain supports the view that women have evolved mechanisms that are sensitive to their own reproductive condition to alert them to interference with their strategy of sexual selectivity. It also supports the view that sexual coercion may have been one of the recurring features of the ancestral social environment in which humans evolved.

Individual men differ in their proclivity toward rape. In one study, men were asked to imagine that they had the possibility of forcing sex on someone else against her will when there was no chance that they would get caught, no chance that anyone would find out, no risk of disease, and no possibility of damage to their reputation. In the study 35 percent indicated that there was some likelihood under these conditions, although in most cases the likelihood was slight.[48] In another study, which used a similar method, 27 percent of the men indicated some likelihood if there was no chance of getting caught.[49] Although these percentages are alarmingly high, they also indicate that most men are apparently not potential rapists.

Men who do use coercion to get sex have been shown to exhibit a distinct set of characteristics. They tend to be hostile toward women, endorse the myth that women secretly want to be raped, and show a personality profile marked by impulsiveness, hostility, and hypermasculinity, combined with a high degree of sexual promiscuity.[50] Studies of rapists show that they also have low self-esteem. Although no one knows what the origins are of the traits that make a man prone to rape, one possibility is that the most sexually coercive men are low in desirability, as reflected in the fact that rapists have lower incomes and come disproportionately from the lower classes.[51] Interviews with rapists support this view. One serial rapist, for example, reported that "I felt that my social station would make her reject me. And I didn't feel that I would be able to make this person. I didn't know how to go about meeting her. . . . I took advantage of her fright and raped her."[52] For men who lack the status, money, or other resources to attract women, coercion may represent a desperate alternative. Men scorned by women because they lack the qualities for attracting desirable mates may develop hostility toward women, an attitude that short circuits the normal empathic response and so promotes coercive sexual behavior.

In addition to personality, culture and context heavily influence the occurrence of rape. Among the Yanomamö, for example, kidnapping women from neighboring villages for mating purposes is considered an acceptable cultural practice.[53] The hundreds of thousands of rapes that occur in war contexts, especially among those who are successfully conquering an enemy, suggest that rape occurs when the costs incurred by the rapist are generally minimal or absent.[54] Perhaps by identifying and fostering conditions that inflict greater personal costs on perpetrators, the incidence of this terrible form of sexual conflict can be reduced.

The Evolutionary Arms Race

Conflicts between men and women pervade their interactions and relationships. These range from conflicts over sexual access in dating couples, to fighting over commitment and investment among married couples to sexual harassment in the workplace, date-rape, and rape on the streets. The vast majority of these conflicts can be traced directly to men's and women's evolved mating strategies. The strategies pursued by members of one sex often interfere with those of the other sex.

Both sexes have evolved psychological mechanisms, such as anger, sadness, and jealousy, that function to alert them to interference with their mating strategies. A woman's anger is evoked most intensely in the specific contexts in which a man interferes with her mating strategies, for example, if he acts condescending, abusive, or sexually aggressive toward her. A man's anger is most intensely evoked when a woman interferes with his mating strategies, for example, by spurning his advances, refusing to have sex with him, or cuckolding him.

Unfortunately, these battles create a spiraling arms race over evolutionary time. For every increment in men's ability to deceive women, women evolve comparable increments in their ability to detect deception. Better abilities to detect deception, in turn, create the evolutionary conditions for the opposite sex to develop increasingly subtle forms of deception. For every escalating test that women impose on men to gauge the depth of their commitment, men develop increasingly more elaborate strategies to mimic commitment. This development in turn favors more refined and subtle tests by women to weed out the fakers. And for every form of abuse heaped on one sex, the other evolves methods for escaping the abuse. As women evolve better and more sophisticated strategies to achieve their mating goals, men evolve increasingly sophisticated strategies to achieve theirs. Because the mating goals of the sexes interfere with each other, there is no evolutionary end to the spiral.

The adaptive emotions such as anger and psychological pain, however, help women and men to reduce the costs they experience when someone attempts to interfere with their mating strategies. In the context of dating or marriage, these emotions sometimes lead to a termination of the relationship.

8

Breaking Up

Women marry believing that their husbands will change;
Men marry believing that their wives will not change;
They're both wrong.

—Anonymous

HUMAN MATING is rarely a once-in-a-lifetime occurrence. Divorce and remarriage are so common in the United States that nearly 50 percent of all children do not live with both of their genetic parents. Stepfamilies are rapidly becoming the norm, not the exception. Contrary to some beliefs, this state of affairs does not represent a recent phenomenon, nor does it reflect a sudden decline in family values. Divorce specifically, and the dissolution of long-term mating relationships more generally, are cross-cultural universals. Among the !Kung, for example, 134 marriages out of 331 recorded ended in divorce.[1] Among the Ache of Paraguay, the average man and woman are married and divorced more than eleven times each by the time they reach the age of forty.[2]

People end committed relationships for a variety of reasons. A spouse can start imposing costs, for example, or a better opportunity for a mate can come along. Staying in a bad marriage can be costly in terms of lost resources, lost mating opportunities, physical abuse, inadequate care for children, and psychological abuse, outcomes that interfere with successful solutions to the critical adaptive problems of survival and reproduction. The acquisition of new mating opportunities, superior resources, better child care, and stauncher allies are some of the benefits that may flow to people who leave bad relationships.

Ancestral Conditions

Many mates in ancestral times became injured and died before old age. Men, for example, sustained wounds or were killed in combat between warring tribes. The paleontological record reveals fascinating evidence of aggression between men. Pieces of spears and knives have been found lodged in the remains of human rib cages. Injuries to skulls and ribs are found more frequently on male than on female skeletons, suggesting that physical combat was primarily a male activity. Perhaps most intriguing of all, more injuries are located on the left sides of skulls and rib cages, suggesting a greater prevalence of right-handed attackers. The earliest known homicide victim in the paleontological record is a Neanderthal man, who was stabbed in the chest by a right-hander roughly 50,000 years ago.[3] These highly patterned injuries cannot be explained as accidents. Instead, they demonstrate that injury and death at the hands of other people has been a recurrent hazard in human evolutionary history.

Traditional tribes today do not escape the havoc wreaked by aggression between males. Among the Ache, for example, ritual club fights occur only among men, and they often produce permanent disabilities and death.[4] A woman whose husband goes off to a club fight can never be sure that he will return intact. Among the Yanomamö tribe, a boy does not achieve full status as a man until he has killed another man. Yanomamö men display their scars proudly, often painting them bright colors to draw attention to them.[5] Wars throughout human history have been fought by men, exposing them to grave risks.

Violence at the hands of other men was not the only way an ancestral man could die. Hunting has always been a male-dominated human enterprise, and ancestral men risked injury, particularly when hunting large game, such as wild boar, bison, or buffalo. Lions, panthers, and tigers roamed the African savanna, inflicting injury on the unwary, the unskilled, or the imprudent. Accidental plunges from cliffs or falls from trees were possibilities. In human ancestral environments, since a woman's husband had a chance of dying first or becoming so seriously injured as to cripple his ability to hunt or to protect her, it would have been highly adaptive for her to assess and even court alternative mates.

Ancestral women never warred and rarely hunted. Women's gathering activities, which yielded 60 to 80 percent of the family's food resources, were far less dangerous.[6] Childbirth, however, took its toll. Without modern medical technology, many women failed to survive the dangerous journey of pregnancy and childbirth. A man left mateless by his wife's death would have had to start the search and courting process from scratch, unless he had psychological mechanisms that anticipated this possibility and caused him to lay the groundwork for securing a replacement. It would have paid for both men and women not to wait until their mate's death to start evaluating potential alternatives.

Injury, disease, or the death of a mate were not the only hazards to force ancestral mates to look elsewhere. A woman's husband could lose status within the group, be ostracized, become dominated by a rival male, prove a bad father, reveal infertility, fail as a hunter, start abusing her or her children, initiate affairs, direct resources to other women, or turn out to be impotent. A man's wife could fail at gathering food, mishandle family resources, prove to be a bad mother, be infertile, be frigid, become unfaithful, or get pregnant by another man. Either sex could contract debilitating diseases or become riddled with parasites. Life events could take a treacherous toll on a mate who had been full of vitality when initially chosen. Once a selected spouse decreased in value, alternatives would become attractive.

A mate's decline in value and potential death represented only two of the conditions that might have diverted a person's attention to alternatives. Another critical condition is an increase in one's own desirability, which opens up an array of alternatives that were previously unobtainable. A man, for example, could sometimes dramatically elevate his status by performing an unusually brave deed, such as killing a large animal, defeating another man in combat, or saving someone's child from harm. Sudden increases in a man's status opened up new mating possibilities with younger, more attractive mates or multiple mates, who could make a current mate pale by comparison. Mating options mushroomed for men who managed to boost their status. Because a woman's value as a mate was closely tied with her reproductive value, she usually could not elevate her desirability to the same extent that men could. Nevertheless, women could improve their mate value by acquiring status or power, showing unusual adeptness at dealing with crises, displaying exceptional wisdom, or having sons, daughters, or other kin who achieved elevated positions within the group. These possibilities for changes in mating value are still with us today.

Increases and decreases in the value of a mate are not the only conditions that favor the seeking of alternatives. Another important impetus to divorce was the presence of more desirable alternatives. A desirable mate who had previously been taken could suddenly become available. A previously uninterested person could develop a strong attraction. A member of a neighboring tribe could appear on the scene. And any of these people could be sufficiently desirable to warrant breaking an existing marital bond.

In sum, three major general circumstances could lead someone to leave a long-term mate: when a current mate became less desirable because of a decrease in abilities or resources or a failure to provide the reproductively relevant resources that were inherent in the initial selection, when someone experienced an increase in resources or reputation that opened up previously unobtainable mating possibilities, and when compelling alternatives became available. Because these three conditions were likely to recur with regularity among our ancestors, it is reasonable to expect that humans have evolved psychological mechanisms to evaluate the costs and benefits of existing relationships in comparison with the perceived alternatives. These mechanisms would have been attuned to changes in the value of a mate, would have continued to identify and gauge mating alternatives, and would have led to the courting of potential replacement mates.

Evolved Psychological Mechanisms

Ancestral conditions that favored the dissolution of a mateship constituted a recurrent adaptive problem over human evolutionary history and thus imposed selection pressures for the evolution of strategic solutions. People who were oblivious to a decrease in their mate's value, who were totally unprepared to remate in the event of the death of a spouse, or who failed to trade up to a higher quality mate when offered the opportunity would have been at a tremendous reproductive disadvantage compared with those who perceived and acted on these conditions.

It may be disconcerting, but people do assess and evaluate other possible mates while in a committed relationship to one mate. Married men's banter, when it does not center on sports or work, often revolves around the appearance and sexual availability of women in their milieu. Married women talk as well about which men are attractive, available, promiscuous, and high in status. These forms of discourse accomplish the goals of exchanging information and assessing the mating terrain. It pays to monitor alternatives with an eye toward mating opportunities. Those who stick it out with an undesirable mate through thick and thin may receive our admiration, but their kind would not have reproduced as successfully and are not well represented among us today. Men and women evaluate alternative mating possibilities, even if they have no immediate intention to act upon them. It pays to plan ahead.

Psychological preferences continue to operate during marriage, being directed not just at comparing the array of potential mates but at comparing those alternatives with the current mate. Men's preference for young, attractive women does not disappear once the wedding vows are declared; nor does women's attention to the status and prestige of other men. Indeed, one's mate provides a ready standard for repeated comparisons. Decisions to keep or get rid of one's mate depend on the outcome of these calculations, which may be made unconsciously.

A man whose increased status opens up better mating alternatives does not think to himself, "Well, if I leave my current wife, I can increase my reproductive success by mating with younger, more reproductively valuable women." He simply finds other women increasingly attractive and perceives that they are more attainable than before. A woman whose mate abuses her does not think to herself, "My reproductive success and that of my children will increase if I leave this cost-inflicting mate." She thinks instead that she had better get herself and her children to safety. Just as our taste preferences for sugar, fat, and protein operate without our conscious awareness of the adaptive functions they serve, so marital dissolution mechanisms operate without our awareness of the adaptive problems they solve.

People typically need a clear justification for leaving a long-term mate, one that explains the breakup to friends, to family, and even to themselves and one that preserves or minimizes the damage to their social reputation. Although some simply walk away from the relationship, this straightforward solution is rarely employed. One effective justification for expelling a mate, in evolutionary psychological terms, would be a violation of the partner's expectations for that mate, so that the partner no longer desired to maintain the relationship. Ancestral men could withhold resources or give signals that investments were being channeled to other women. Women could decrease a man's certainty of paternity by infidelities and withholding sex from her mate. Cruel, unkind, inconsiderate, malevolent, harmful, or caustic acts would be effective tactics for expelling a mate for both sexes because they violate the universal preferences men and women hold for mates who are kind and understanding. These tactics have in common the exploitation of existing psychological mechanisms in the opposite sex—mechanisms that alert people to the possibility that they have chosen a mate unwisely, that their mate has changed in unwanted ways, and that perhaps they should cut their losses.

The sex differences in benefits from long-term matings in ancestral times, whereby men's benefits came from monopolizing a woman's reproductive capacity and women's from sequestering a man's investments, have profound implications for the causes of separation and divorce. They imply that men and women evaluate changes in their mates over time by very different standards. As a woman ages from twenty-five to forty, for example, she experiences a rapid decline in her reproductive value, although other components of her mating value may increase and hence compensate for the loss. During a comparable period a man may elevate himself in status and so enjoy an unanticipated avalanche of mating opportunities. Or he may suffer losses and become desperate to keep his current mate. Thus, ancestral men and women would have been expected to break up for somewhat different reasons, which go to the core of the adaptive problems that each sex must solve to mate successfully.

A major source of evidence on breaking up comes from the most extensive cross-cultural study ever undertaken on the causes of divorce, in which the evolutionary anthropologist Laura Betzig analyzed information from 160 societies.[7] This study identified forty-three causes of conjugal dissolution recorded earlier by ethnographers who had lived in the society or by informants who resided in each society. Various constraints, such as the lack of a standard method of gathering data and incomplete data, preclude calculation of the absolute frequencies of the causes of divorce. Nonetheless, the relative frequencies are readily available, and the more societies that manifest a particular cause of divorce, the more likely it is to be a universal cause of divorce. Topping the list of causes of divorce are two key events with particular relevance to reproduction—infidelity and infertility.

Infidelity

The most powerful signal of a man's failure to retain access to a woman's reproductive capacity is her infidelity. The most powerful signal of a woman's failure to retain access to a man's resources is his infidelity. Among the forty-three categories of causes, ranging from the absence of male children to sexual neglect, adultery is the single most pervasive cause of conjugal dissolution, being cited in eighty-eight societies. Among the societies that cite adultery, there are strong sex differences in its prevalence. Although in twenty-five societies divorce follows from adultery by either partner, in fifty-four societies divorce occurs only if the wife is adulterous; in only two societies does divorce occur only following the husband's adultery. Even these two societies can hardly to be considered exceptions to the double standard, because an unfaithful wife rarely goes without punishment. In both of these cultures, men are known to thrash their wife upon discovery of her infidelity and, in some circumstances, to beat her to death. Unfaithful wives in these two cultures may not be divorced, but neither do they get off lightly.

The finding that a woman's infidelity is a more prevalent cause of divorce is especially striking because men are more likely to be unfaithful.[8] Kinsey, for example, found that 50 percent of the husbands but only 26 percent of the wives surveyed had been unfaithful. The double standard in reactions to unfaithfulness is not confined to American culture or to Western societies but is observed across the globe. Its pervasiveness stems from three possible sources. First, men have greater power to impose their will, so that women may be forced to tolerate infidelity in their husbands more often than men are forced to tolerate infidelity in their wives. Second, women worldwide may be more forgiving of their husband's sexual indiscretions because sexual infidelity per se has been less costly for women than for men over human evolutionary history, unless it was accompanied by the diversion of his resources and commitments. Third, women worldwide may more often be forced to tolerate a husband's infidelity because of the prohibitively high costs of divorce, especially if they have children that curtail their value on the mating market. For all these reasons, a wife's unfaithfulness more often causes an irrevocable rift that ends in divorce.

People's knowledge that infidelity causes conjugal dissolution may be the reason that infidelity is sometimes used intentionally to get out of a bad marriage. In a study of the breakup of mates, we asked 100 men and women which tactics they would use to get out of a bad relationship. Subsequently, a different group of 54 individuals evaluated each tactic for its effectiveness in accomplishing the goal. One common method for getting rid of an unwanted mate is to start an affair, perhaps by sleeping around in an obvious manner or arranging to be seen with a member of the opposite sex in some other questionable situation.

Sometimes an actual affair is not carried out but is merely alluded to or implied. People use such tactics as flirting with others or telling a partner that they are in love with someone else so that the mate will end the relationship. A related tactic involves mentioning that they want to date other people in order to be sure that what the two of them have is right, possibly as a means of gracefully exiting from the relationship through a gradual transition out of commitment.

So justifiable is infidelity as a cause of getting rid of a mate that people sometimes exploit it, even if no actual infidelity has occurred. In Truk, for example, if a husband wants to terminate a marriage, he has merely to spread a rumor about his wife's adultery, pretend to believe it, and leave in indignation.[9] Apparently, people are highly concerned about justifying a marital dissolution to their social networks. Pretending that an affair has occurred provides this justification, because infidelity is so widely regarded as a compelling reason for breaking up.

Infertility

Although ring doves tend to be monogamous, more so than many bird species, they experience a divorce rate of about 25 percent a season. The major cause of breaking a bond is infertility—the failure of the pair to reproduce.[10] Pairs of ring doves that produce chicks in one breeding season are highly likely to mate again for the next season; those that fail to reproduce in one season seek out alternative mates the next season.

Failure to produce children is also a leading cause of divorce for humans. Couples with no children divorce far more often than couples with two or more children. According to a United Nations study of millions of people in forty-five societies, 39 percent of divorces occur when there are no children, 26 percent when there is only a single child, 19 percent when there are two, and less than 3 percent when there are four or more. The toll on marriage caused by childlessness occurs regardless of the duration of the marriage.[11] Children strengthen marital bonds, reducing the probability of divorce, by creating a powerful commonality of genetic interest between a man and a woman. Failure to produce these small vehicles that transport the genes of both parents into the future deprives a couple of this powerful common bond.

Infertility is exceeded only by adultery as the most frequently cited cause of divorce across societies. In the cross-cultural study of conjugal dissolution, seventy-five societies reported infertility or sterility as a cause of conjugal dissolution. Of these, twelve specify that sterility by either the husband or the wife is grounds for divorce. But sterility, like adultery, appears to be strongly sex-linked. Whereas sterility ascribed exclusively to the man is cited as a cause of divorce in twelve societies, sterility ascribed exclusively to the woman is cited in thirty societies— perhaps reflecting another type of double standard in which women are blamed more than men. In the remaining twenty-one societies it is impossible to discern whether or not sterility on the part of men, women, or both was a cause of marital dissolution.

Not all societies sanction divorce. Where divorce is not sanctioned, however, provisions are often made for separating a man and woman who do not produce children. In the Andaman Islands off the southern coast of Asia, for example, a marriage is not regarded as consummated unless a child is born.[12] The trial marriage is not considered to be real or binding unless children are produced. Many villages in Japan hold off recording a marriage until long after a wedding, and frequently the marriage is not entered into the family register in the village office until the first child is born.[13] When marriages are not regarded as legally sanctioned until children are born, infertility effectively becomes a cause of marital dissolution.

Old age is linked with lower fertility, although this linkage is stronger in women than in men. Although sperm concentration per ejaculate declines somewhat with age, men in their sixties, seventies, and eighties can still sire children, and they frequently do so in many cultures. Among the Yanomamö, one particularly productive man had children who differed in age by fifty years. Among the Tiwi of Northern Australia, older men frequently monopolize women thirty or more years younger and sire children with them. Although couples in Western culture tend to be more similar in age than those among the Tiwi and Yanomamö, it is not uncommon for a man to divorce a postmenopausal wife and start a new family with a younger woman.[14]

The difference in the reproductive biology of men and women leads to the expectation that older age in a wife will lead to divorce more often than older age in a husband. Although the cross-cultural study on conjugal dissolution did not find old age to be a frequently cited cause of divorce, it is cited in eight societies, and in all eight the old age of the woman, never the man, is the cause of divorce. When men divorce, they almost invariably marry younger women.

In evolutionary terms, it makes perfect sense that infertility and infidelity are the most prevalent causes of divorce worldwide. Both represent the strongest and most direct failures to deliver the reproductive resources that provide the evolutionary raison d'être for long-term mating. People do not consciously calculate that their fitness suffers from these events. Rather, infidelity and infertility are adaptive problems that exerted selection pressure on human ancestors for a psychology attuned to reproductive failures. Just as having sex tends to lead to producing babies although the people involved may have no awareness of the reproductive logic involved, so anger leads to leaving an unfaithful or infertile mate without requiring conscious articulation of the underlying adaptive logic. The fact that couples who are childless by choice are nonetheless devastated by infidelity shows that our psychological mechanisms continue to operate in modern contexts, even those far removed from the selection pressures that gave rise to them.

Sexual Withdrawal

A wife who refuses to have sex with her husband is effectively depriving him of access to her reproductive value, although neither sex thinks about it in these terms. Since sex throughout human evolutionary history has been necessary for reproduction, depriving a man of sex may short circuit the reproductive dividends on the investment that he has expended in obtaining his wife. It may also signal that she is allocating her sexuality to another man. Men would have evolved psychological mechanisms that alerted them to this form of interference with their sexual strategies.

In the cross-cultural study on conjugal dissolution, twelve societies identify the refusal to have sex as a cause of conjugal dissolution. In all these societies the cause is ascribed exclusively to the wives' refusal, not the husbands'. The study of the breakup of mates also found sexual refusal to be a major tactic for getting rid of unwanted mates. Women describe their tactics for breaking up variously as refusing to have physical contact with their mates, becoming cold and distant sexually, refusing to let the man touch her body, and declining sexual requests. These tactics are employed exclusively by females.

The success of this tactic is illustrated by one woman's account in the study on the breakup of mates. She had complained to a friend that her repeated attempts to break off with her husband had failed. She wanted advice. Further discussion revealed that, although she seriously wanted to get rid of her husband, she never had refused his sexual advances. Her friend suggested that she try it. A week later, she reported that her husband had become enraged at her sexual refusal and, after two days, had packed his bags and left. They were divorced shortly thereafter. If women give sex to get love and men give love to get sex, then depriving a man of sex may be a reliable way to stop his love and encourage his departure.

Lack of Economic Support

A man's ability and willingness to provide a woman with resources are central to his mating value, central to her selection of him as a marriage partner, central to the tactics that men use in general to attract mates, and central to the tactics that men use to retain mates. In evolutionary terms, a man's failure to provide resources to his wife and her children should therefore have been a major sex-linked cause of marital dissolution. Men who were unable or unwilling to supply these resources negated a criterion on which they were initially selected by women as mates.

Provisioning failure by men worldwide is in fact a cause of divorce. The cross-cultural study on conjugal dissolution found that a major cause of divorce is inadequate economic support in twenty societies, inadequate housing in four societies, inadequate food in three societies, and inadequate clothing in four societies. All these causes are ascribed solely and exclusively to men. In no society does a woman's failure at providing resources constitute grounds for divorce.

The seriousness of the male's lack of economic providing is illustrated by the report of a woman in her late twenties who participated in a study of marital separation:

> My husband lost a series of jobs and was very depressed. He just couldn't keep a job. He had a job for a couple of years, and that ended, and then he had another for a year, and that ended, and then he had another. And then he was really depressed, and he saw a social worker, but it didn't seem to be helping. And he was sleeping a lot. And I think one day I just came to the end of the line with his sleeping. I think I went out one night and came back and he hadn't even been able to get out of bed to put the children to bed. I left them watching television and there they were when I came back. The next day I asked him to leave. Very forcefully.[15]

In contemporary America, when women make more money than their husbands, they tend to leave them. One study found that the divorce rate among American couples in which the woman earns more than her husband is 50 percent higher than among couples in which the husband earns more than his wife.[16] Indeed, men whose wives' careers blossom sometimes express resentment. In a study on the causes of divorce among women, one woman noted that her husband "hated that I earned more than he did; it made him feel less than a man." Women also resent husbands who lack ambition. Another woman noted: "I worked full-time, while he worked part-time and drank full-time; eventually, I realized I wanted more help getting where I'm going."[17] Men who do not fulfill women's primary preference for a mate who provides resources are jettisoned, especially when the woman can earn more than the man.

Conflict among Multiple Wives

Polygyny is a widespread practice across cultures. An analysis of 853 cultures revealed that 83 percent of them permitted polygyny. In some

West African societies, 25 percent of all older men have two or more wives simultaneously. Even in cultures in which polygyny is not legally sanctioned, it sometimes occurs. One study estimated that there are 25,000 to 35,000 polygynous marriages in the United States, mostly in western states.[18] Another study of 437 financially successful American men found that some maintained two separate families, each unknown to the other.[19]

From a woman's perspective, a major drawback of her husband's taking additional wives is that resources channeled to one wife and her children are denied to another wife and her children. Although co-wives may derive significant benefits from one another's presence, more often, one wife's gain is another wife's loss. The cross-cultural study on conjugal dissolution found polygyny to be a cause for divorce in twenty-five societies, largely because of conflict among the man's co-wives.

Conflict among co-wives may have been an adaptive problem that polygynous men in ancestral times had to solve to maintain control over their wives. The problem is how to keep all wives happy so that none defects; defection deprives the man of significant reproductive resources. Some polygynous men adopt strict rules about resource distribution, offering each wife equal attention and equal sex. Among the Kipsigis in Kenya, women of polygynous husbands have their own plots of land, which are divided equally among them by the husband.[20] Kipsigis men maintain a separate residence apart from their wives, and they alternate the days spent with each wife, carefully allocating time equally. All these tactics tend to minimize conflict among co-wives. Sororal polygyny, in which co-wives are sisters, also tends to minimize conflict, which suggests that genetic overlap creates a psychological convergence in the interests of women.[21]

Despite men's efforts to keep peace among co-wives, women in societies such as Gambia often leave their husbands when they indicate that they plan to acquire a second wife, even though polygyny is legal.[22] Wives find it difficult to share their husband's time and resources with other women.

Cruelty and Unkindness

Worldwide, one of the most highly valued characteristics in a committed mate is kindness, because it signals a willingness to engage in a cooperative alliance, which is an essential ingredient for success in long-term mating. Disagreeable people make poor mates. Having a mate who is irritable, violent, abusive, and derogatory, or who beats children, destroys possessions, neglects chores, and alienates friends imposes severe costs psychologically, socially, and physically.

Given these costs, cruelty, maltreatment, and ruthlessness rank among the most frequent causes of marital breakup in the cross-cultural study on conjugal dissolution, cited in fifty-four societies. Indeed, in all cultures these traits are exceeded only by adultery and sterility as sources of conjugal dissolution.[23] According to one study on the causes of divorce among women, 63 percent of divorced women report that their husbands abused them emotionally and 29 percent reported that their husbands abused them physically.[24]

Unkindness and psychological cruelty may in some cases be related to events that occur during the course of a marriage, particularly adultery and infertility. Sterility, for example, often sparks harsh words between mates in tribal India. One Indian husband said: "We went to each other for seven years till we were weary, and still there was no child; every time my wife's period began she abused me saying, 'Are you a man? Haven't you any strength?' And I used to feel miserable and ashamed."[25] Eventually, the couple divorced.

Adultery also provokes cruelty and unkindness. When a Quiche woman commits adultery, her husband is likely to nag, insult, scold, abuse, and even starve her.[26] Worldwide, adulterous wives are beaten, raped, scorned, verbally abused, and injured by enraged husbands.[27] Thus, some forms of unkindness are evoked by reproductively damaging events that occur within the marriage. Cruelty and unkindness, in other words, may in part be symptoms of other underlying causes of divorce. Psychological mechanisms and behavioral strategies kick in to solve costly problems imposed by one's mate.

In other cases, unkindness is a personality characteristic of one spouse that is stable over time.[28] In the study of newlywed couples, we examined the links between the personality characteristics of one spouse and the problems he or she caused the mate. The wives of disagreeable husbands express distress because such men are condescending, physically abusive, verbally abusive, unfaithful, inconsiderate, moody, insulting, and self-centered.[29] The wives of men judged to be disagreeable tend to complain that their husbands treat them as inferiors. Such men demand too much time and attention and ignore their wives' feelings. They slap them, hit them, and call them nasty names. They have sex with other women. They fail to help with the household chores. They abuse alcohol, insult their wives' appearance, and hide all their emotions so as to appear tough. Not surprisingly, spouses of disagreeable people tend to be dissatisfied with the marriage, and by the fourth year of marriage many seek separation and divorce.

Given the premium that people place on kindness in a mate, it is not surprising that one of the most effective tactics for getting rid of a bad mate is to act mean, cruel, caustic, and quarrelsome. Men and women say that effective tactics for prompting mates to depart include treating them badly, insulting them to others publicly, intentionally hurting their feelings, creating a fight, yelling without explanation, and escalating a trivial disagreement into a fight.

Cruelty and unkindness occur worldwide as a tactic for expelling a mate. Among the Quiche, when a husband wants to get rid of his wife, often because of her infidelities, he makes her position unbearable through a variety of means: "The undesired wife is nagged, insulted, and starved; her husband scolds and abuses her; he is openly unfaithful. He may marry another woman or even outrage his wife's dignity by introducing a prostitute into the house."[30] All these acts signal cruelty, the opposite of the kindness that is central to men's and women's preferences in a mate worldwide.

Implications for a Lasting Marriage

The major causes of marital dissolution worldwide are those that historically caused damage to the reproductive success of one spouse by imposing reproductive costs and interfering with preferred mating strategies. The most damaging events and changes are infidelity, which can reduce a husband's confidence in paternity and can deprive a wife of some or all of the husband's resources; infertility, which renders a couple childless; sexual withdrawal, which deprives a husband of access to a wife's reproductive value or signals to a wife that he is channeling his resources elsewhere; a man's failure to provide economic support, which deprives a woman of the reproductively relevant resources inherent in her initial choice of a mate; a man's acquisition of additional wives, which diverts resources from a particular spouse; and unkindness, which signals abuse, defection, affairs, and an unwillingness or inability to engage in the formation of a cooperative alliance.

The implications of these fundamental trends in human mating psychology for a lasting marriage are profound. To preserve a marriage, couples should remain faithful; produce children together; have ample economic resources; be kind, generous, and understanding; and never refuse or neglect a mate sexually. These actions do not guarantee a successful marriage, but they increase the odds substantially.

Unfortunately, not all damaging events or changes can be prevented. Ancestral environments imposed hostile forces that no one could control, such as infertility, old age, lack of sexual desire, disease, status slippage, ostracism, and even death. These forces could crush a mate's value irrevocably, despite the best intentions. Alternative potential mates sometimes offered to provide what was lacking, so evolution has shaped psychological mechanisms that dispose people to leave their lovers under these circumstances.

Psychological assessment mechanisms, designed to attend to the shifting circumstances of mating, cannot be easily turned off. In ancestral times, it frequently paid reproductive dividends in the event of the loss of a mate to be prepared by maintaining alternative prospects and to switch mates if a valuable trade could be arranged. Those who were caught unprepared, who failed to play in the field of possibilities, or who were unwilling to leave a reproductively damaging mate did not become our ancestors. Because the costs incurred and the benefits bestowed by a current mate must always be evaluated relative to those available from alternative mates, the psychological mechanisms of mate switching inevitably include comparisons. Unfortunately for lifelong happiness, a current mate may be sadly deficient, may fail to measure up to the alternatives, or may have declined in relative value.

Most of these hostile forces are still with us today. A mate's status can rise or fall, infertility traumatizes otherwise joyous couples, infidelities mount, and the sadness of aging turns the youthful frustration of unrequited love into the despair of unobtainable love. These events activate psychological mechanisms that evolved to deal with marital dissolution, causing people to avoid threats to their reproduction, much as our evolved fears of snakes and strangers cause people to avoid threats to their survival. These mechanisms, it seems, cannot be easily shut off. They cause people to seek new mates and sometimes to divorce repeatedly as adaptively significant events emerge over the lifetime.

9

Changes over Time

The world is full of complainers. But the fact is—nothing comes with a guarantee.

—Detective in the film *Blood Simple*

AMONG THE CHIMPANZEES at the large zoo colony in Arnhem, the Netherlands, Yeroen reigned as the dominant adult male.[1] He walked in an exaggeratedly heavy manner, and he looked larger than he really was. Only occasionally did he need to demonstrate his dominance, raising his hair on end and running full speed at the other apes, who scattered in all directions at his charge. Yeroen's dominance extended to sex. Although there were four adult males in the troop, Yeroen was responsible for nearly 75 percent of all matings when the females came into estrus.

As Yeroen grew older, however, things began to change. A younger male, Luit, experienced a sudden growth spurt and started to challenge Yeroen's status. Luit gradually stopped displaying the submissive greeting to Yeroen, brazenly showing his fearlessness. Once, Luit approached Yeroen and smacked him hard, and another time Luit used his potentially lethal canines to draw blood. Most of the time, however, the battles were more symbolic, with threats and bluffs in the place of bloodshed. Initially, all the females sided with Yeroen, allowing him to maintain his status. One by one they defected to Luit, however, as the tide turned. After two months, the transition was complete. Yeroen had been dethroned, and started to display the submissive greeting to Luit. The mating behavior followed suit. While Luit achieved only 25 percent of the matings during Yeroen's reign of power, his sexual access jumped to more than 50 percent when he took over. Yeroen's sexual access to females dropped to 0.

Although ousted from power and lacking sexual access, Yeroen's life was not over. Gradually, he formed an alliance with an upcoming male named Nikkie. Although neither Yeroen nor Nikkie dared to challenge Luit alone, together they made a formidable coalition. Over several weeks, the coalition grew bolder in challenging Luit. Eventually, a physical fight erupted. Although all the chimpanzees involved sustained injuries, the alliance of Nikkie and Yeroen triumphed. Following this victory, Nikkie secured 50 percent of the matings. But Yeroen, because of his alliance with Nikkie, now enjoyed 25 percent of the matings. His banishment from females had been temporary. Although he never again regained the dominant position, he had rallied from the setback sufficiently to remain a contender in the troop.

With humans as with chimpanzees, nothing in mating remains static over a lifetime. An individual's value as a mate changes, depending on sex and circumstances. Because many of the changes individuals experience have occurred repeatedly over human evolutionary history, posing recurrent adaptive problems for our ancestors, we have evolved psychological mechanisms designed to deal with them. A person who steadily ascends a status hierarchy may suddenly be passed by a more talented newcomer. A hunter's promise may be cut suddenly short by a debilitating injury. An older woman's son may become the chief of her tribe. An ignored introvert, long regarded as occupying the bottom rungs of desirability as a mate, may achieve renown through a dazzling invention that is useful to the group. A young married couple bursting with health may tragically discover that one of them is infertile. Ignoring change would have been maladaptive, impeding solutions to ancestral adaptive problems. We have evolved psychological mechanisms that are designed to alert us to these changes, mechanisms that motivate adaptive action.

In a sense, all mating behavior entails changes over time, from the early hormonal stirrings touched off by the onset of puberty to grandparents' attempts to influence the mating decisions of those in their family. Clarifying one's mating desires takes time. Honing one's skills of attraction takes practice. Mating is never static through life. The goal of this chapter is to describe some of the broader changes that befall men and women over the course of their mating lives—the losses and the triumphs, the uncertainties and the inevitabilities.

Changes in a Woman's Worth

Because a woman's desirability as a mate is strongly determined by cues to her reproductivity, that value generally diminishes as she gets older. The woman who attracts a highly desirable husband at age twenty will attract a less desirable husband at age forty, all else being equal. This downturn is shown in societies where women are literally purchased by men in return for a bride price, as occurs among the Kipsigis in Kenya.[2] The bride price consists of quantities of cows, goats, sheep, and Kenyan shillings that a groom or his family pays to the bride's family in exchange for the bride. A prospective groom's father initiates negotiations with the father of the prospective bride, making an initial offer of cows, sheep, goats, and shillings. The bride's father considers all competing offers. He then counters by demanding a higher bride price than was offered by any of the suitors. Negotiations can last several months. A final suitor is selected by the bride's father, and a final price is set, depending essentially on the perceived quality of the bride. The higher the reproductive value of the bride, the greater the bride price she is able to command. Older women, even if older by only four or five years, fetch a lower bride price. Several other factors lower a woman's value to a prospective husband and hence lower her price as a potential bride, such as poor physical condition or a physical handicap, pregnancy, and the prior birth of children by another man.

The Kipsigis custom of placing a premium on the age and physical condition of a woman is not unique. In Tanzania, for example, the Turu refund a portion of the bride price in the event of a divorce, and older wives command less of a refund due to the physical "depreciation of the wife's body."[3] In Uganda, the Sebei pay more for young widows than for old widows, stating explicitly that an older widow has fewer reproductive years left.[4]

The effect of aging on a woman's value as a mate shows up in the changing perceptions of attractiveness through life. In one study in Germany, thirty-two photographs were taken of women ranging in age from eighteen to sixty-four.[5] A group of 252 men and women, from sixteen to sixty years of age, then rated each photograph for its attractiveness on a 9-point scale. The age of the subjects of the photographs strongly determines judgments of female attractiveness, regardless of the age or sex of the raters. Young women command the highest ratings, old women the lowest. These age effects are even more pronounced when men do the ratings. The change in the perceived attractiveness of women as they move through life is not an arbitrary aspect of a particularly sexist culture, even though these effects undoubtedly do damage women. Rather, this change in perceptions reflects the universal psychological mechanisms in men that equate cues to a woman's youth with her value as a mate.

There are many exceptions, of course. Some women, because of their status, fame, money, personality, or social networks, are able to remain desirable as they age. The averages mask a wide variability in individual circumstances. Ultimately, a person's value as a mate is an individual matter and is determined by the particular needs of the individual making the selection. Consider the real-life case of a highly successful fifty-year-old business executive who had six children with his wife. She developed cancer and died young. He subsequently married a woman three years older than he, and his new wife devoted a major share of her effort to raising his children. To this man, a younger woman who had less experience in child rearing and who wanted children of her own would have been less valuable, and possibly would have interfered with his goal of raising his own children. A fifty-three-year-old woman may be especially valuable to a man with children who need her and less valuable to a man with no children who wants to start a family. To the individual selecting a mate, averages are less important than particular circumstances.

The same woman can have a different value to a man when his circumstances change. In the case of the business executive, after the man's children reached college age, he divorced the woman who had raised them, married a twenty-three-year-old Japanese woman, and started a second family. His behavior was ruthless and not very admirable, perhaps, but his circumstances had changed. From his individual perspective, the value of his second wife lowered precipitously when his children were grown, and the attractiveness of the younger woman increased to accompany his new circumstances.

Although averages can obscure individual circumstances, they do give the broad outlines of the lifetime trends of many people. Furthermore, they suggest adaptive problems that have shaped the human psychology of mating. From the wife's perspective, as her direct reproductive value declines with age, her reproductive success becomes increasingly linked with nurturing her children, the vehicles by which her genes travel into the future. From her husband's perspective, her parenting skills constitute a valuable and virtually irreplaceable resource. Women often continue to provide economic resources, domestic labor, and other resources, many of which decline less dramatically with age than her reproductive capacity, and some of which increase. Among the Tiwi tribe, for example, older women can become powerful political allies of their mates, offering access to an extended network of social alliances, and even helping their husbands acquire additional wives.[6] But from the perspective of other men on the mating market, an older woman's value as a prospective mate if she reenters the mating market, is generally low, not only because her direct reproductive value has declined but also because her efforts may already be monopolized by the care of her children and eventually her grandchildren. These changes reverberate through a marriage.

Loss of Desire

One of the most prominent changes within marriage over time occurs in the realm of sex. The study of newlywed couples showed that with each passing year, men increasingly complain that their wives withhold sex. Although only 14 percent of men complain that their newlywed brides have refused to have sex during the first year of marriage, 43 percent, or three times as many, of the men express this feeling four years later. Women's complaints that their husbands refuse to have sex with them increase from 4 percent in the first year to 18 percent in the fifth year. Both men and women increasingly charge their partners with refusing sex, although more than twice as many men as women voice this complaint.

One indication of the lessened sexual involvement of married people with their spouses over time is the decline in the frequency of intercourse. When married women are less than nineteen years old, intercourse occurs roughly eleven or twelve times per month.[7] By age thirty it drops to nine times per month, and by age forty-two to six times per month, or half the frequency of married women half their age. Past age fifty, the average frequency of intercourse among married couples drops to once a week. These results may reflect a lessened interest by women, by men, or most likely by both.

Another indication of the reduction in sexual involvement with age comes from a Gallup poll measuring the extent of sexual satisfaction and the frequency of sexual intercourse over time among married couples.[8] The percentage of couples having intercourse at least once a week declines from nearly 80 percent at age thirty to roughly 40 percent by age sixty. Sexual satisfaction shows a similar decline. Nearly 40 percent of the couples report "very great satisfaction" with their sex lives at age thirty, but only 20 percent voice this level of satisfaction by age sixty.

The arrival of a baby has a significant impact on the frequency of sex. In one study, twenty-one couples kept daily records of the frequency of intercourse over a period of three years, starting with the first day of marriage.[9] The rates of intercourse a year after the marriage were half what they had been during the first month. The arrival of a baby depresses the frequency of sex even more, when the rate of intercourse averages about a third of what it had been during the first month of marriage. Although more extensive studies over longer time periods are needed to confirm this finding, it suggests that the birth of a baby has a longlasting effect on marital sex, as mating effort shifts to parental effort.

The effect of the length of a marriage on sexual intercourse appears to be influenced by a woman's physical appearance. According to a study of more than 1,500 married individuals, men and women respond differently to the normal changes in physical appearance that accompany aging.[10] As women age, husbands show less sexual interest in them and experience less happiness with their sexual relationship. This effect is especially strong, however, for husbands who perceive that their wives have markedly declined in physical attractiveness. Other research confirms that after the early years of marriage, husbands lose more sexual interest than wives do in their spouses.[11] Men's sexual attraction is more sensitive than women's to declines in the physical appearance of an aging mate.

Lowered Commitment

Not only do aging men and women become increasingly unhappy about their sex lives with their spouses, they also become increasingly distressed with their partners' failure to show affection and attention, which suggests a lowered commitment to the relationship. Women are more distressed by declining affection over time than are men. Whereas only 8 percent of newlywed women complain about their partner's failure to express love, 18 percent of women voice this complaint by the time they are four years into the marriage. In comparison, only 4 percent of newlywed men are upset about their wives' failure to express love, which doubles to 8 percent by the fourth year of marriage. Whereas 64 percent of newlywed women complain that their husbands sometimes fail to pay attention when they speak, 80 percent of women are disturbed by this behavior by the fourth and fifth years of marriage. Fewer husbands overall show distress about their partners' inattentiveness, but the increase in this complaint over time parallels that of their wives, rising from 18 percent to 34 percent during the first four years of marriage.

Another indication of the withdrawal of commitment over time is reflected in ignoring a spouse's feelings. Among newlywed women, 35 percent express distress about having their feelings ignored, whereas four years later this figure has jumped to 57 percent. The comparable figures for complaints by men are 12 percent in the first year and 32 percent in the fourth. These changes signify a gradual diminution of commitment to a spouse over time, which occurs for both sexes but is more problematic for women than for men.

While women are more disturbed about men's increasing failure to show commitment through affection and attention, men are more distressed about the growing demands for commitment from their wives. Whereas 22 percent of newlywed men complain that their wives demand too much of their time, 36 percent of husbands express upset about this demand by the fourth year of marriage. The comparable figures for women are only 2 percent and 7 percent. Similarly, 16 percent of newlywed men express distress over their wives' demands for attention, whereas 29 percent voice this complaint in the fourth year of marriage. The comparable figures for women are only 3 percent and 8 percent. Thus, while both sexes show increasing distress over their partners' demands for commitment, more men than women are troubled by these changes.

These changes are accompanied by a shift in the way a man guards his mate, which is another index of commitment to the relationship. In evolutionary terms, a man's efforts to guard his mate should be most intense when his mate is youngest and hence most reproductively valuable, because failure to retain a mate carries the most severe reproductive penalties when the woman has the highest value. The age of a husband, however, would not necessarily govern the intensity of a woman's efforts to keep him. The value of a man as a mate does not necessarily decline from age twenty to forty, as it does for a woman, because his capacity to accrue resources often increases with age. Thus, the intensity of a woman's efforts to retain a mate would be linked less to a man's age than to his effectiveness at providing her with valuable resources.

These different behaviors of men and women are confirmed by a study I conducted of methods used by husbands and wives to keep their mates.[12] Using a group of newlywed couples ranging in age from twenty to forty, I explored the frequency of nineteen tactics, which ranged from positive inducements, such as bestowing gifts and lavishing attention, to negative inducements, such as threats and violence. The use of these tactics was then correlated with factors such as the age of the tactician, the age of the mate, and the length of the relationship. The frequency or intensity of the husbands' efforts is a direct function of the age of their wives. Wives in their middle to late thirties are guarded significantly less intensely than are wives in their early to middle twenties. The husbands of younger wives tend especially to perform acts that signal to other men to stay away. A man married to a younger woman may tell other men outright that his wife is already taken, show physical affection when other men are around, or ask her to wear rings and other ornaments that signal a committed status. Husbands of younger women, more often than those of older women, may glower at other men who pay attention to their wives or threaten them with bodily harm. In contrast, efforts devoted by wives to keeping older husbands are just as frequent as efforts devoted to keeping younger husbands. Regardless of the husband's age, women show equal vigilance, monopolization of time, and appearance enhancement tactics. The intensity of women's efforts to guard their mates is therefore unrelated to the age of the man, showing a marked contrast to men's reliance on a woman's age to modulate the intensity of their guarding.

The most plausible explanation for this sex difference is the decrease in a women's reproductive capacity with age. If declines in mate guarding were merely related to the fact that people simply get tired when they get older, as all of their functions senesce, then the degree of mate guarding would be directly related to the age of the person doing the guarding. But as the study on keeping a mate showed, neither the age of the man nor the age of the woman is a good indicator of their efforts to hold on to a mate. These efforts decline only trivially with the age of the tactician. And if the decrease in men's guarding zeal were related to the length of the relationship, guarding it would dwindle as the relationship got older. But as the study showed, the length of the relationship is not related to the intensity of the guarding efforts. In short, the most plausible way to account for the effect of a woman's age on the intensity of a man's efforts to guard her is that women of differing ages differ in their desirability, and men therefore devote less effort to guarding an older wife than a younger wife.

The population of the Caribbean island of Trinidad exhibits this pattern of behavior.[13] As shown by observations of 480 individuals at regular intervals, the anthropologist Mark Flinn found that men whose wives are fecund (young and not pregnant at the time) spend more time with their mates, get into more fights with their mates, and get into more fights with rival men. In contrast, men whose wives are infecund (older, pregnant, or having just given birth) spend less time with their mates and get along better with other men. Flinn concludes that the reproductive potential of a man's mate is the key determinant of the intensity of his mate guarding.

In Middle Eastern societies that encourage the practice of sequestering women, postpubescent women are veiled and concealed most heavily when they are youngest, and these practices are relaxed as women age.[14] Homicidal rages of husbands worldwide over real or suspected infidelities occur most often if they have young wives, regardless of the age of the husband. Wives who are less than twenty years old are more than twice as likely as women who are more than twenty to be killed by a husband in a jealous rage.[15] These are just a few of the extreme strategies that men use to prevent other men from gaining sexual access to young wives. As their wives get older, the intensity of men's efforts to control their mates lessens.

Changes in Frequency of Extramarital Affairs

As men's intense mate guarding lessens, women become less constrained by their husbands in their sexual behavior with other men. It has been said that "monogamy is the Western custom of one wife and hardly any mistresses."[16] Reliable information on extramarital affairs is difficult to come by. The question on this subject caused more people to decline to participate in Alfred Kinsey's study of sex than did any other question, and more people refused to answer it than any other question. A shroud of secrecy surrounds extramarital sex, despite the multitude of studies on the subject.

The statistics on the incidence of extramarital sex must therefore be regarded as conservative, in that extramarital affairs tend to be underreported. The Kinsey report suggested that the actual incidence of affairs is probably at least 10 percent higher than reported. Another study of 750 spouses found that the incidence may be even higher. Whereas only 30 percent of these people initially admitted to extramarital affairs, under subsequent intensive scrutiny an additional 30 percent revealed that they had had extramarital sex, bringing the total to approximately 60 percent.[17]

The incidence of extramarital sex by women shows a marked trend with age. The behavior is rare among the youngest wives, being acknowledged by only 6 percent of wives at ages sixteen to twenty and about 9 percent of them at ages twenty-one to twenty-five. The incidence of extramarital affairs goes up to 14 percent of women at ages twenty-six to thirty and hits a peak of 17 percent of women between ages thirty-one and forty. After the late thirties and early forties, extramarital sex by women declines steadily, acknowledged by 6 percent of women at ages fifty-one to fifty-five and only 4 percent of them at ages fifty-six to sixty. Thus, there is a curvilinear relationship between age and affairs for women: affairs are low when women are both most and least reproductively valuable, but high toward the end of their reproductive years.

A similar curvilinear age trend is found for women's orgasm. Kinsey tabulated the percentage of women's total sexual activity to orgasm, whatever the source, including marital sex, masturbation, and affairs.

For women, orgasms from extramarital affairs again show a curvilinear trend with age. Such orgasms represent only 3 percent of women's total orgasms between ages twenty-one and twenty-five, nearly triple to 11 percent toward the end of women's reproductive years at ages thirty-six to forty-five, and drop again to only 4 percent after menopause from ages fifty-six to sixty.

There are a number of reasons why women's extramarital affairs and orgasms might peak toward the end of their reproductive years. Women at this time are less likely to be so intensely guarded by their husbands and thus are better able to take advantage of existing sexual opportunities than their younger counterparts. Older women also suffer fewer costs inflicted at the hands of a jealous husband, and therefore the deterrents to a tempting extramarital involvement might be less potent.[18] Because the penalties for being caught philandering are lower, older women may feel freer to pursue their extramarital desires.

Affairs may also signal an effort by women to switch mates before their own reproductive value has plummeted. Support for this idea comes from a study of 205 married individuals who had affairs. Fully 72 percent of women but only 51 percent of men are motivated by emotional commitment or long-term love rather than sexual desires in their extramarital dalliances.[19] Another study found that men who have affairs are twice as likely as women to think of the involvement as purely sexual, devoid of emotional attachments.[20] Yet another study found that only 33 percent of women who have affairs believe that their marriages are happy, whereas 56 percent of men who have extramarital sex consider their marriages to be happy.[21] More men than women who are happily married can engage in extramarital sex without emotional involvement and without the feeling that their marriages are unsatisfactory. The fact that women who have affairs are more likely to be unhappy in their marriages and more likely to be emotionally involved with the extramarital partner suggests that they may be using their affairs for the purpose of changing mates.

Men's patterns of extramarital sex differ from those of women. Men engage in sex outside marriage both more often and more consistently than women over their lifetime. The desires of married people provide a window on men's greater desire for extramarital sex. In one study, 48 percent of American men express a desire to engage in extramarital sex; the comparable figure for women is only 5 percent.[22] In another study of marital happiness among 769 American men and 770 American women, 72 percent of men, but only 27 percent of women, admit that they sometimes experience a desire for extramarital intercourse.[23] A study of working-class Germans reveals similar tendencies: 46 percent of married men but only 6 percent of married women acknowledge that they would take advantage of a casual sexual opportunity with someone attractive if it was provided.[24]

These desires often translate into actual affairs. In the Kinsey report on the lifetime incidence of extramarital coitus from age sixteen through age sixty, affairs by husbands surpass those by wives at every age.[25] Fully 37 percent of married men in the youngest age bracket of sixteen to twenty report at least one affair, in contrast to a mere 6 percent of comparably aged wives. The incidence of affairs by husbands remains relatively constant over the years, with only a slight downward trend in the later years.

These affairs are not occasional trifles for the men who have sex outside their marriages. Instead, affairs make up a significant proportion of the men's sexual outlets at every age throughout their life. Extramarital sex comprises about a fifth of these men's sexual outlets between ages sixteen and thirty-five. It rises steadily to 26 percent at ages thirty-six to forty, 30 percent at ages forty-one to forty-five, and 35 percent at ages forty-six to fifty. For men who engage in extramarital sex with companions and prostitutes, these forms of sex become increasingly important with age and occur at the expense of sex with their wives, which becomes a smaller and smaller fraction of their total. Given our knowledge of men's evolved sexual psychology, it is likely that the increase in the importance of extramarital sex for these men results from boredom at repeating sex with the same partner or from a wife's decreasing sexual attractiveness to the husband as a result of her increasing age.

The proportion of men and women who have affairs over their lifetimes depends upon the nature of the mating system. In polygamous mating systems, for example, where many men are left mateless and most fertile women are married, the percentages of men and women having affairs must be different from the percentages in presumptively monogamous societies. Bachelors who seek sex have only married women to choose from. Furthermore, it is historically and cross-culturally common for a few high-ranking men to cuckold a large number of low-ranking men, as when Roman emperors such as Julius Caesar were permitted by law sexual access to other men's wives.[26] Under these conditions, the percentage of women having affairs would necessarily be greater than the percentage of men having affairs.

The main point about our evolved sexual strategies is not that men inevitably have more affairs than women or that infidelity is invariably expressed in men's behavior. Rather, men's sexual psychology disposes them to seek sexual variety, and men seek extramarital sex when the costs and risks are low. Women also seek short-term sex, including extramarital sex, but their desires, fantasies, and motivations for this form of sex are less intense on average than are men's. Mark Twain observed that "many men are goats and can't help committing adultery when they get a chance; whereas there are numbers of men who, by temperament, can keep their purity and let an opportunity go by if the woman lacks in attractiveness."[27] Extramarital sex remains a larger component of men's desires throughout life.

Menopause

A critical change that accompanies shifts in women's sexual activities over their lifetime is the cessation of their capacity for direct reproduction, which reaches zero at menopause. One of the amazing facts about women's lifetime development is that menopause occurs so long before life is over. Reproduction completely terminates for most women by the time they reach fifty, even though many women live well into their seventies and beyond. This situation contrasts sharply with that of all other primate species. Even in long-lived mammals, the postreproductive phase for females represents only 10 percent or less of their total lifespan. Only 5 percent of elephants, for example, reach age fifty-five, but female fertility at that age is still 50 percent of the maximum observed at the peak of fertility.[28]

Other female functions decline gradually with age. Heart and lung efficiency, for example, is nearly 100 percent of capacity in the early twenties, and declines to only 80 percent by the age of fifty.[29] In contrast, fertility peaks in the early twenties but is close to zero percent by the time a woman reaches fifty. The steep decline in women's fertility, compared with all other bodily functions, begs for explanation.

At one point in history, women themselves were blamed for menopause, due to "many excesses introduced by luxury, and the irregularities of the passions."[30] Today, one theory to account for this puzzling phenomenon is that women's postreproductive phase has been artificially lengthened as a result of better nutrition and health care. According to this view, our human ancestors would have rarely lived long past menopause, if they reached it at all. This explanation appears highly unlikely, however, because the increase in the average human lifespan is due mainly to a decline in infant mortality. Ancestral people who lived to reach age twenty typically enjoyed a maximum lifespan nearly identical to our own, or roughly seventy to eighty years. Indeed, there is no evidence that medical technology has altered the maximum lifetime of humans at all.[31] In addition, the view that menopause is an incidental byproduct of longer lives cannot explain why women's reproductive function declines sharply, whereas all of women's other vital capacities decline only gradually, as if they were designed for a longer lifetime. Selection would be unlikely to favor efficient body functions into the fifties and sixties if ancestral humans did not live beyond fifty. Furthermore, the longer-life view cannot explain the differences between the sexes whereby men's fertility fades only gradually, while women's declines precipitously.[32]

A more likely explanation for women's long postreproductive phase is that menopause is a female adaptation that prompts the shift from mating and direct reproduction to parenting, grandparenting, and other forms of investing in kin. This explanation, called the grandmother hypothesis, depends on the assumption that continuing to produce children would actually have interfered with an ancestral woman's reproductive success as compared to investing in her existing children and other genetic relatives. It also assumes that older women would have been particularly valuable to their children and grandchildren. Older women, for example, tend to acquire wisdom and knowledge about health practices, kin relations, and stress management that are unavailable to younger women. They also tend to increase their control over resources and their ability to influence other people. These increased powers and skills can be channeled toward children, grandchildren, and the entire extended network of a woman's genetic clan.[33]

A preliminary test of the grandmother hypothesis among the Ache Indians suggests that, for this group, the reproductive benefits provided by the shift from direct reproduction to grandparental investment may not be high enough to outweigh the reproductive costs to women of their lost capacity to produce children directly.[34] Nevertheless, the grandmother hypothesis of menopause squares with common observations of the increased investment of women in their kin as they age and so remains a viable possibility, awaiting more extensive tests.

Another hypothesis for women's menopause is that there is a trade-off between rapid reproduction relatively early in life and more extended reproduction over the lifespan. Producing many high-quality children early may in effect wear out a woman's reproductive machinery, so that menopause is not in itself an adaptation but is rather an incidental byproduct of early and rapid breeding.[35] In this view, it becomes critical to identify the conditions that would have allowed ancestral women the opportunity to reproduce early and rapidly.

Early reproduction and births at short intervals, or at three to four years on average, may occur in women because ancestral women could often rely on food and protection offered by an investing mate. The

tremendous parental resources that men channel to their children and
mates may have created the propitious conditions for early and rapid
reproduction. Chimpanzee and gorilla females, in contrast, must do all
the provisioning by themselves and thus cannot space children so
closely. In these species, females space out their reproduction over
nearly all of their adult lives by having one offspring every five or six
years. The change in women's lives that produces a cessation of direct
reproduction and a shift to investing in genetic relatives may therefore
be directly linked to the high levels of parental investment by men.
Since men's investment can be traced, in turn, to the active choosing by
women of men who show the ability and willingness to invest, the reproductive changes that occur over women's lives are intimately linked with
the mating relations that occur between the sexes.

Changes in a Man's Worth

While women's desirability as mates declines steeply with age, the
same does not apply to men's. The reason is that many of the key qualities that contribute to a man's value are not as closely or as predictably
linked with age. These components include a man's intelligence, cooperativeness, parenting proclivities, political alliances, kin networks, coalitions, and, perhaps most important, ability and willingness to provide
resources to a woman and her children.

Men's value in supplying resources, indicated by cues such as income
and social status, shows a markedly different distribution with age than
women's reproductive value. There are two important differences
between the sexes: men's resources and social status typically peak much
later in life than women's reproductive value, and men differ more
markedly from one another in the resources and social status they
accrue. Men's resources and status sometimes plummet, sometimes
remain constant, and sometimes skyrocket with increasing age, whereas
women's reproductive value declines steadily and inexorably with age.

For men, a distinction must be drawn between social status and the
accrual of resources to understand their lifetime value as mates. In
ancestral hunter-gatherer societies, limited hunting capacities and the
short shelf life of killed game constrained how much meat men could
accumulate. Furthermore, men in current hunter-gatherer societies do
not vary widely in the amount of land they hold or the amount of meat
they store.[36] Indeed, although men vary in hunting ability, some cultures,
such as the Ache, share their meat communally, so that individual men
do not vary widely in the direct resources they derive from the hunt.

In societies where meat is shared communally, however, skillful hunters do experience a greater reproductive success than poor hunters. This can happen in a society in which hunters do not apportion their own kill for two reasons. Men who are good hunters obtain more extra-marital matings than men who are poor hunters because women prefer to have sex with the better hunters. Also, the children of good hunters are better nurtured by other members of the group than are the children of poor hunters. Although the men do not vary in their meat resources per se, they do vary in their social status derived from hunting, which gives them sexual access to desirable women and seems to promote better care for their children.[37] Thus, status and possession of resources are separate qualities.

The advent of agriculture roughly ten thousand years ago and the invention of cash economies permitted the stockpiling of resources far beyond what was possible among our hunter-gatherer ancestors. The differences in tangible resources between a Rockefeller and a panhandler are much greater than those between the highest-ranked head man among the Ache and the lowest-ranked older male who is no longer able to hunt. The same may not be true for social status. Although cash economies have amplified the differences in men's resources, the status differences of contemporary men are not necessarily greater than the status differences among our ancestors.

Although social status is harder to measure than income, contemporary hunter-gatherer societies around the world provide clues to the distribution of social status by age. In no known culture do teenage boys enjoy the highest status. Among the Tiwi tribe, men are typically at least thirty years old, and may often be middle aged, before they are in a position of sufficient status to acquire a wife or two.[38] Young Tiwi men lack the political alliances to garner much status and hence a wife.

Among the !Kung, the decade of the twenties is spent refining skills and acquiring knowledge and wisdom about hunting.[39] Not until a !Kung man is in his thirties does he come into his own in taking down large game for the group. Among the Ache Indians, male prestige is also linked to hunting ability, which does not peak until the middle to late twenties and carries into the thirties or beyond.[40] Among both the !Kung and Ache, men older than sixty typically become unable to hunt successfully, stop carrying bows and arrows, and show a considerable decline in their political status and ability to attract younger wives. Status among the Ache males may peak somewhere between twenty-five and fifty, corresponding closely with their hunting prowess.[41] Older Ache, Yanomamö, and Tiwi men garner respect, status, and awe from younger men because they have survived so many club fights, spear fights, and ax fights. Men maintain status well into middle age if they survive the onslaught of aggression from other men that long.

Similar trends tied to age are observed in contemporary Western societies. One indication of men's resources over their lifetime in contemporary Western society is actual monetary income. Unfortunately, no worldwide statistics are available on men's and women's resources as a function of age. A particular income distribution by age in the United States, however, has been found repeatedly over the years. For example, the distribution of men's mean income in the United States in the year 1987, broken down by age, shows that income tends to be quite low among men in their teens and early twenties. In the decade between the ages of twenty-five and thirty-four, men's income attains only two-thirds of its eventual peak. Not until the decades from ages thirty-five to fifty-four does men's income in the United States achieve its peak. From age fifty-five on, men's income declines, undoubtedly because some men retire, become incapacitated, or lose the ability to command their previous salaries.[42] These income averages conceal great variability, because some men's resources continue to increase throughout their old age, whereas other men remain poor throughout their lives.

Because older men tend to have more status and resources than younger men, men and women of the same age differ on average in their value as mates. In the same decade between the ages of fifteen and twenty-four when women peak in fertility and reproductive value, men's income and status are typically the lowest that they will be in their adult lives. When most women between the ages of thirty-five and forty-four are rapidly approaching the end of their reproductive years, most men in the same decade are just approaching the peak of their earning capacity. To the extent that the central ingredient of a woman's desirability is her reproductive value and of a man's is his resource capacity, men and women of comparable age are not typically comparable in desirability.

Greater variability, which is the other critical difference between the value of women and men as mates at different ages, renders age per se a less important factor for men in mating. Men's occupational status in Western societies ranges from janitor and gas station attendant to company president and successful entrepreneur. Men at the same age vary in income from the nickels and dimes of a panhandler to the billionaire bank books of a Rockefeller or Getty. Between the ages of twenty and forty, men diverge dramatically in their ability to accrue resources.

These trends, however, fail to reveal the tremendous variability in the individual circumstances of women who do the choosing. From a woman's perspective, the particular circumstances, not the averages, carry the most weight. Some middle-aged women prefer older men not because of the men's resources but because of the women's belief that older men value them more than do men their own age. Among the Aka of Africa, for example, men who achieve high status and garner many resources during their lives contribute little to the direct care of their children when they marry. In contrast, Aka men who attain only low status and few resources for a wife and children compensate by spending more time directly caring for the children.[43] One key indicator of a father's investment, for example, is how many minutes a day he spends holding an infant, which is an expensive activity in terms of both calories consumed and other activities forgone. Holding protects the infant from environmental dangers, temperature changes, accidents, and aggression from others. Aka men who maintain positions of status in the group hold their infants an average of thirty minutes per day. Men who lack positions of status, in contrast, hold their infants more than seventy minutes per day. Although women typically prefer men with status and resources, a man's willingness to parent constitutes a valuable resource that can partially compensate for the lack of other qualities.

Some women, because of the tremendous economic resources they command, may not need to select a man based on his external acquisitions. The desirability of men must be evaluated by means of the psychological mechanisms of women, and these mechanisms are highly sensitive to circumstances. This is not to deny the importance of average trends; indeed, selection has produced such trends over thousands of generations of human evolutionary history. Our evolved psychological mechanisms include not only those that promote mating choices that are specific and typical of each sex, but also mechanisms that tailor our choices over our lifetime to the individual circumstances in which we find ourselves.

Earlier Death of Men

Human mating mechanisms account for the puzzling finding that men die faster and earlier than women in all societies. Selection has been harder on men than on women in this respect. Men live shorter lives than women and die in greater numbers of more causes at every point in the life cycle. In America, for example, men die on average six to eight years earlier than women. Men are susceptible to more infections than women and die of a greater variety of diseases than women. Men have more accidents than women, including falls, accidental poisonings, drownings, firearm accidents, car crashes, fires, and explosions. Males suffer a 30 percent higher mortality rate from accidents during the first four years of life and a 400 percent higher mortality from accidents by the time they reach adulthood.[44] Men are murdered nearly three times as often as women. Men die taking risks more often than women and commit suicide more often than women. The ages between sixteen and twenty-eight, when intrasexual competition reaches a strident pitch, seem especially bad for men. During those ages, men suffer a mortality rate nearly 200 percent higher than women.

The reason for men's higher mortality, like that of males of many mammalian species, stems directly from their sexual psychology, and in particular from their competition for mates. The use of risky tactics of competition becomes greater as the differences in reproductive outcome become greater. Where some males monopolize more than one female, there are tremendous reproductive benefits to being a winner and tremendous reproductive penalties for being a loser. The red deer is a case in point. Male deer who grow larger bodies and larger antlers experience greater mating success on average than their smaller counterparts. They are able to best their intrasexual competitors in head-to-head competition. But their success comes at a cost to their survival. Precisely the same traits that give them their mating success lead to a greater likelihood of dying. During a cold winter with scarce resources, for example, the male is more likely to die because of a failure to obtain enough food for his larger body. Larger size may also make the male more susceptible to predation and less agile at escape. To these possibilities must be added the risk of dying directly through intrasexual combat. All these risks follow from the sexual strategies of red deer, which generally pay off in the competition for mates but which also generally result in a shorter lifetime for males than for females.

As a rule, throughout the animal kingdom, the more polygynous the mating system, the greater the differences between the sexes in terms of mortality.[45] Polygynous mating selects for males who take risks—risks in competing with other males, risks in securing the resources desired by females, and risks in exposing themselves while pursuing and courting females. Even in a mildly polygynous mating system like our own, where some men acquire multiple partners through serial marriage and affairs and others are left mateless, competition among men and selection by women of men who are high in status and resources are ultimately responsible for the evolution in males of risk-taking traits that lead to successful mating at the expense of a long life.

Because the reproductive stakes are higher for men than for women, more men than women risk being shut out of mating entirely. Bachelors who are mateless for life are more numerous than spinsters in every society. In America in 1988, for example, 43 percent of men but only 29 percent of women had never been married by the age of twenty-nine.[46] By the age of thirty-four, 25 percent of men but only 16 percent of women had never been married. These sex differences reach extremes in highly polygynous cultures such as the Tiwi, where literally all women are married, a few men have as many as twenty-nine wives, and therefore many men are consigned to bachelorhood.[47]

This adaptive logic suggests that the greater risk taking, and hence greater death rate, should occur among men who are at the bottom of the mating pool and who therefore risk getting shut out entirely. And that is in fact the case. Men who are unemployed, unmarried, and young are greatly overrepresented in risky activities, ranging from gambling to lethal fights.[48] Among homicides in Detroit in 1972, for example, 41 percent of adult male offenders were unemployed, compared with an unemployment rate of 11 percent for the whole city. Sixty-nine percent of the male victims and 73 percent of the male perpetrators were unmarried, compared with an unmarried rate of 43 percent in the entire city. These homicides were also disproportionately concentrated between the ages of sixteen and thirty. In short, men low in desirability, as indicated by being unemployed, unmarried, and young, seem especially prone to risk taking, which sometimes crosses the line and becomes lethal. The point is not that killing per se is necessarily an adaptation but rather that men's evolved sexual psychologies are designed to respond to particular conditions by increasing the amount of risk they are willing to take.

In ancestral times, the great reproductive gains that risk-taking men generally achieved and the reproductive oblivion that usually awaited more cautious men have selected for traits that yielded success in competition among males at the expense of success at longevity. In the currencies of survival and longevity, selection via intrasexual competition has been hard on men.

The Marriage Squeeze

The earlier mortality of men is one critical factor among several that produces a serious imbalance between the number of men relative to the number of women on the mating market—an imbalance that gets more severe with time. This phenomenon is referred to as the marriage squeeze because some women get squeezed out of the mating market due to the lack of available men for them. Many factors affect the relative numbers. Rates of infant, childhood, adolescent, and adult mortality differ, with males continuing to die at a faster rate throughout the life-span. Men emigrate more often than women, leaving behind a sexual imbalance. Baby booms also cause imbalances because the many women born during the boom have fewer men from whom to choose, since they typically select men older than they, who come from the smaller cohort born before the baby boom. From men's perspective, those born prior to the baby boom have a relatively large pool of women to select from, since they tend to choose younger women who were born during the boom period. Far more men than women are imprisoned, further imbal-ancing the ratio between the sexes on the mating market. And wars end men's lives far more often than women's lives, creating a surplus of women on subsequent mating markets.

Divorce and remarriage patterns over the lifetime are other key causes of the marriage squeeze. Men who divorce tend to remarry women who are increasingly younger than they are. Furthermore, more men than women remarry, and this sex difference grows larger through the lifetime. Women who are divorced, for example, find it much more difficult to obtain a second marriage partner than do men. Among Cana-dians, the remarriage probability is 83 percent for divorced men between the ages of twenty and twenty-four, and 88 percent for divorced men between the ages of twenty-five and twenty-nine.[49] The compara-ble remarriage rates for women are only 61 percent for the ages of twenty to twenty-four and 40 percent for the ages of twenty-five to twenty-nine. In the United States, 76 percent of women between the ages of fourteen and twenty-nine remarry after a divorce, but the figure drops to 56 percent between thirty and thirty-nine, 32 percent between forty and forty-nine, and only 12 percent between fifty and seventy-five.[50]

These remarriage patterns are not quirks of North American coun-tries but rather emerge in every country for which there is adequate information. In one study of 47 countries, age affects women's chances of remarriage more than men's.[51] For the ages of twenty-five to twenty-nine, the differences in remarriage by sex are slight, because young women maintain high desirability as potential mates. By the ages of fifty to fifty-four, however, the sexes diverge remarkably in their remarriage rates. In that age bracket in Egypt, for example, four times as many men as women remarry; in Ecuador, nine times as many men as women remarry; and in Tunisia, nineteen times as many men as women remarry.

The estimated marital opportunities of black women of different ages in the United States in 1980 illustrate these cumulative effects. Adoles-cent women at the peak of their reproductive value have the greatest marital opportunities. At this age, there are 108 men for every 100 women. By the late twenties, however, the ratio has shifted. By ages twenty-six to twenty-eight, for example, there are only 80 men for every 100 women. The ratio continues to decline as the women's reproductive value declines. When women reach ages thirty-eight to forty-two, there are only about 62 men for every 100 women. This means that 38 women out of every 100 in this age group will potentially have no husband. The marital opportunities for women continue to worsen as they age, reaching dramatic imbalances of as few as 40 men for every 100 women past the age of sixty.[52]

The marriage squeeze as women age is in large measure an outcome of the sexual psychology of men and women. At the heart of this squeeze is the sharp decline in female reproductive value with age, which caused selection to favor ancestral men who preferred younger women as mates and to favor ancestral women who preferred older men with resources as mates. Ultimately, women and men share responsibility for the marriage squeeze. Young, healthy, and attractive women act on their desires for older, resource-laden mates, monopolizing the men who might otherwise serve as mates for older women. Men with status and resources try to fulfill their preferences for young, healthy, attractive women. And because ancestral women's preferences for men with resources created a selection pressure for greater male competitiveness and risk taking, men die at a faster rate than women, thereby exacerbating the scarcity of men.

Changes in the proportion of men to women throughout life cause predictable changes in men's and women's sexual strategies. The degree of selectivity is the first strategy to shift. When there is a surplus of men, fewer men can be highly selective, and they must settle for a less desirable mate than they would otherwise attract if the sexes were more in balance. A low ratio of men, in contrast, restricts women's selectivity, because there are fewer men from whom to choose. These ratios thus affect the degree to which both sexes can realize their ideal preferences.

Low proportions of males also cause a destabilization of marriage. An excess of women relative to available men means that many women lack the ability to secure strong commitments from men. Men with many available women can pursue casual sexual liaisons with aplomb and dispatch. Changes in the ratios of men to women within the United States through history confirm this fact, because periods of increasing divorce, as between 1970 and 1980, correspond closely to periods when there is a surplus of women on the mating market.[53]

In the late 1980s, in contrast, divorce rates among new marriages were lower than in the previous decade, coinciding with an increase in the ratio of males.[54] At that time American women's marital happiness was also higher than their husbands', whereas it had fallen below their husbands' marital happiness during the preceding fifteen years when there was a shortage of men.[55] The number of men pursuing business careers doubled between 1973 and the late 1980s, coinciding with the shift from a low to a high ratio of males and suggesting that men were becoming more concerned with their economic success. Men's willingness to invest directly in care for their children can also be expected to increase at such times, though no evidence yet exists on this point. Men should strive to become kinder and gentler to fulfill women's mating preferences when there are relatively few available women.

A dearth of available men also causes women to take greater responsibility for providing resources. One reason is that women are not able to count on provisioning from men. Furthermore, increasing economic assets may represent a woman's strategy to increase her desirability, analogous to the dowry competition in traditional societies. Throughout history, female participation in paid employment has increased during periods of low ratios of men to women. When during the 1920s foreign-born women in the United States outnumbered foreign-born men because of a change in the immigration laws, the participation of these women in the labor force abruptly rose.[56] The existence of fewer investing men causes women to take a greater responsibility for securing their own resources.

Women in mating environments of few men also intensify their competition with each other by enhancing their appearance, increasing their health-promoting behavior, and even offering sexual resources to attract men. The sexual revolution in the United States in the late 1960s and the 1970s, for example, involved a change in which many women abandoned their sexual reserve and engaged in sexual relationships without requiring serious male commitment. This shift in sexual mores coincided with a period of low numbers of older men for the baby boom women. Increased competition among females with regard to their appearance, as shown by such trends as the rise of the diet industries, the mushrooming of the women's make-up and make-over industries, and the increase in cosmetic plastic surgery—including tummy tucks, breast implants, and facelifts—also occurred in this time of a shortage of men.

When there are more men competing for fewer women, the balance of power shifts to women. Women can more easily exact what they want from men, and men in turn become more competitive with one another to attract and retain desirable women. Marriages are more stable, because men are more willing to offer commitment and are less willing to leave a marriage. Men have fewer available alternatives and cannot easily pursue casual sexual goals when women are scarce. Men therefore increasingly compete to fulfill women's preferences for a long-term mate, especially by striving for resources and showing a willingness to invest parentally.

Not all changes that occur during periods of high ratios of men, however, benefit women. An important drawback is their potential for increasing violence toward women. During periods of male surplus, great numbers of men are excluded from mating because there are not enough women to go around. Furthermore, men who can attract a mate under these conditions jealously guard the woman against rivals. Married women in turn have more alternatives and so the threat of leaving gains greater credibility. This circumstance may evoke sexual jealousy in husbands, promoting threats and violence to control wives and increased violence against men who threaten to lure a mate away.[57]

The existence of large numbers of men who are unable to attract a mate may also increase sexual aggression and rape. Violence is often the recourse of people who lack resources that would otherwise elicit voluntary compliance with their wishes.[58] Rape is perpetrated more often by marginal men who lack the status and resources that women seek in long-term mates.[59] Furthermore, the likelihood of war is apparently higher in societies with a high ratio of males than in societies with a low ratio of males, which supports the notion that competition among males is exacerbated at times of a surplus of males.[60]

Changes in the ratio of men to women throughout life cause corresponding shifts in mating strategies. Young men often live in a world where available women are in scarce supply, because women prefer mature men with greater status and resources. Young men's strategies reflect these local conditions of female scarcity, because they engage in highly risky competition strategies, committing the vast majority of violent crimes of sexual coercion, robbery, battery, and murder.[61] In one study, for example, 71 percent of the men arrested for rape were between the ages of fifteen and twenty-nine.[62] These are crimes of coercion against women whom men cannot attract or control through positive incentives.

As men mature into their thirties and forties, the ratio between the sexes typically tilts in their favor, if they have survived risks and attained positions of reasonable status. They have a wider pool of potential women to choose from, and they enjoy a higher value on the mating market than they did in their youth. They are more able to attract multiple mates, whether through casual sex, extramarital sex, serial marriage, or polygyny. Men of any age who have little desirability as mates, however, do not enjoy this advantage, and some men are shut out of mating entirely. Women experience an increasingly skewed sex ratio as they age and are more often forced to compromise their mating strategies by lowering their standards, increasing their level of intrasexual competition, and securing more resources on their own. These changes over time all result from our evolved mating strategies.

The Prospects for Lifetime Mating

Human mating behavior changes over a lifetime, from the internal stirrings of puberty through the final bequest of resources to a surviving spouse. Both sexes have evolved psychological mechanisms designed to solve the problems posed by change over time—mechanisms that are sensitive to shifts in reproductive value, shifts in status and resources, and shifts in mating opportunities. The changes befall women and men differently, and some of these changes are unpleasant. Women start puberty two years sooner than men, but their capacity for reproduction stops two or three decades before men's. The urgency that some childless women feel as their remaining years of potential reproduction wane—the increasingly loud ticking of the biological clock—is not caused by an arbitrary custom dictated by a particular culture, but rather reflects a psychological mechanism attuned to reproductive reality.

A woman's reproductive value over time affects not only her own sexual strategies but also those of the men in her social environment, including her husband and other potential mates. When women are young, their husbands guard them intensely, clinging tightly to the valuable reproductive resource they have successfully secured. The intense guarding closes off a woman's opportunities for affairs and often is seen as a sign of a man's commitment. The sex life of many couples starts out electrifying, and is perhaps made more so by the presence of interested rivals. With each passing year, however, the frequency of intercourse declines as women's reproductive value declines. Episodes of intense jealousy gradually wane. Men become increasingly dissatisfied, and they show less affection to their wives. Women deplore these declines in attention from their mates, complaining increasingly about being neglected. Simultaneously, men express mounting distress about the demands of their mates for time and attention.

As women get older, men loosen the grip of guarding, and a higher and higher proportion of women pursue extramarital affairs, reaching a maximum as women approach the end of their reproductive years.

Whereas for men, affairs are motivated mainly by the desire for sexual variety, for women affairs are motivated more by emotional goals and may represent an effort to switch mates while they are still reproductively capable. Women seem to know that their desirability on the mating market will be higher if they leave their husbands sooner rather than later. After menopause, women shift their effort toward parenting and grandparenting, aiding the survival and reproduction of their descendants rather than continuing to reproduce directly. Women pay for their reproductive strategy of early and rapid reproduction in the currency of a shorter period of fertility.

Changes in men over a lifetime, like those of male chimpanzees, are more variable in the currency of mating and reproduction. Men who increase their status and prestige remain highly desirable over the years. Men who fail to accrue resources and status become increasingly sidelined in the field of mating. Roughly half of all married men pursue some extramarital mating over their lifetime, and for those who do, liaisons occur at the expense of sex with their wives. Furthermore, many men continue throughout life to compete for new mates, divorcing older wives and marrying younger women. Long attributed by traditional scientists to the fragile male ego, to psychosexual immaturity, to "male menopause," or to a culture of youth, men's effort to mate with younger women as they age instead reflects a universal desire that has a long evolutionary history.

One startling byproduct of the differences in mating strategies of the sexes over the lifetime is that men die at an earlier age than women. This is a predictable consequence of the greater risk taking and intrasexual competition of men in the pursuit of status and resources that brings about success in mating. As men are gradually leeched from the mating pool, the ratio of men to women becomes increasingly skewed, resulting in a surfeit of women. For women who reenter the mating market, the marriage squeeze becomes tighter and tighter with each passing year. Both sexes have evolved mechanisms designed to shift strategies depending on changes in the sex ratio.

Given all the changes that befall men and women over their lifetimes, it is remarkable that in fact 50 percent of them manage to remain together through thick and thin. The lifelong convergence of interests between two individuals who share no genes may be the most remarkable feat in the evolutionary story of human mating. Just as we have evolved mechanisms that draw us into conflict, we have evolved mechanisms that enable us to live harmoniously with the other sex. The international study, for example, found that as men and women age, they place less value on physical appearance in a mate and more value on enduring qualities such as dependability and having a pleasing disposition—qualities important for the success of a marriage and critical for the investment in children. The mechanisms that promote this strategic harmony between the sexes, just as much as the mechanisms that produce strife, stem from the adaptive logic of human mating.

10

Harmony between the Sexes

Everything that every individual has ever done in all of human history and prehistory establishes the minimum boundary of the possible. The maximum, if any, is completely unknown.

— John Tooby and Leda Cosmides, *The Adapted Mind*

A CENTRAL MESSAGE of human sexual strategies is that mating behavior is enormously flexible and sensitive to social context. Our complex psychological mechanisms, designed by a long history of evolution, give us a versatile behavioral repertoire for solving the adaptive problems of mating. With this repertoire, we can tailor our mating decisions to personal circumstances in order to fulfill our desires. Thus, in the sexual arena, no behavior is inevitable or genetically preordained—neither infidelity nor monogamy, neither sexual violence nor sexual tranquility, neither jealous guarding nor sexual indifference. Men are not doomed to have affairs because of an insatiable lust for sexual variety. Women are not doomed to scoff at men who are unwilling to make a commitment. We are not conscripted slaves to sex roles dictated by evolution. Knowledge of the conditions that favor each mating strategy gives us the possibility of choosing which to activate and which to leave dormant.

Understanding why sexual strategies have developed and what functions they were designed to serve provides a powerful fulcrum for changing behavior, just as understanding the adaptive functions of physiological mechanisms affords insights for change. Just because humans have developed physiological mechanisms that make us grow calluses as a response to repeated rubbing on the skin, for example, it is not inevitable that humans must develop calluses. We can avoid friction on the skin to prevent their occurrence. Similarly, knowing that jealousy functions to protect paternity for men and the commitment of a mate for women brings into focus the conditions most likely to trigger jealousy in each sex, such as cues to sexual infidelity and emotional infidelity. In principle, we can create relationships that minimize jealousy, just as we can create environments that minimize friction.

Throughout this book I have used empirical studies of human mating as the building blocks for a theory of sexual behavior. Although I have not hesitated to speculate, the discussion has been anchored in evidence. Now I will go beyond the findings to describe what I see as their broader implications for social interactions in general, and for relations between men and women in particular.

Differences between the Sexes

Insight into the relations between men and women must penetrate the riddle of sexual similarities and sexual differences. Because both sexes have faced many of the same problems over evolutionary history, the sexes share many adaptive solutions. Both sexes sweat and shiver to regulate body temperature. Both sexes place a tremendous value on intelligence and dependability in a lifetime mate. Both seek mates who are cooperative, trustworthy, and loyal. And both sexes desire mates who will not inflict catastrophic costs on them. We are all of one species, and recognition of our shared psychology and shared biology is one step toward producing harmony between the sexes.

Against the backdrop of these shared adaptations, sexual differences stand out in stark relief and demand explanation. Men and women differ in their psychology of mating solely and specifically in the domains where they have faced different adaptive problems over the course of evolution. Because ancestral women bore the brunt of nourishing their infants, women rather than men have lactating breasts. Because fertilization occurs internally within women, ancestral men confronted the reproductive problem of uncertainty over their fatherhood. As a consequence, men have evolved particular mate preferences for sexual loyalty, a psychology of jealousy centered on sexual infidelity, and a predisposition to withdraw commitment when cuckolded, which differ from the adaptive mechanisms of women.[1]

Some of these sexual differences may be unpleasant. Women dislike being treated as sex objects or valued for qualities largely beyond their control, such as youth and beauty. Men dislike being treated as success objects or valued for the size of their wallet and the importance of their status in a competitive world. It is painful to be the wife of a man whose desire for sexual variety leads him to sexual infidelity. It is painful to be the husband of a woman whose desire for emotional closeness leads her to seek intimacy with another man. For both sexes it is distressing to be regarded as undesirable merely because one does not possess qualities that the opposite sex prefers in a mate.

To assume that men and women are psychologically the same, as was generally done in traditional social science, goes against what is now known about our evolved sexual psychology. Given the power of sexual selection, under which each sex competes for access to desirable mates of the other sex, it would be astonishing to find that men and women were psychologically identical in aspects of mating about which they have faced different problems of reproduction for millions of years. At this point in history, we can no longer doubt that men and women differ in their preferences for a mate: primarily for youth and physical attractiveness in one case, and for status, maturity, and economic resources in the other. Men and women also differ in their proclivities for casual sex without emotional involvement, in their desire for sexual variety, and in the nature of their sexual fantasies. Men and women face different forms of interference with their preferred sexual behavior and so differ in the kinds of events that trigger powerful emotions such as anger and jealousy. Men and women differ in their tactics to attract mates, to keep mates, and to replace mates. These differences between the sexes appear to be universal features of our evolved selves. They govern the relations between the sexes.

Some people rail against these differences, denying that they exist or wishing that they would cease to exist. But wishes and denials will not make psychological sex differences disappear, any more than they will make beard growth or breast development disappear. Harmony between men and women will be approached only when these denials are swept away and we squarely confront the differing desires of each sex.

A Feminist Viewpoint

The evolution of sexual differences has unavoidable implications for feminism, as noted by feminist evolutionists such as Patricia Gowaty, Jane Lancaster, and Barbara Smuts. According to the tenets of many feminists, patriarchy—defined roughly as the control of resources by men and the physical, psychological, and sexual subordination of women—is a major cause of the battle between the sexes. Oppression through subordination and the control of resources is said to be motivated by men's desire to control women's sexuality and reproduction.

Human sexual strategies bear out major elements of this feminist viewpoint. Men indeed tend to control resources worldwide. Men do oppress women not only through their control of resources but sometimes through sexual coercion and violence. Men's efforts to control women do center on women's sexuality and reproduction. And women, as well as men, often participate in perpetuating this oppression.[2]

An evolutionary perspective on sexual strategies provides valuable insights into the origins and maintenance of men's control of resources and men's attempts to control women's sexuality. A startling consequence of sexual strategies, for example, is that men's dominant control of resources worldwide can be traced, in part, to women's preferences in choosing a mate.[3] These preferences, operating repeatedly over thousands of generations, have led women to favor men who possess status and resources and to disfavor men who lack these assets. Ancestral men who failed to acquire such resources failed to attract women as mates.

Women's preferences thus established a critical set of ground rules for men in their competition with one another. Modern men have inherited from their ancestors psychological mechanisms that not only give priority to resources and status but also lead men to take risks to attain resources and status. Men who fail to give these goals a high personal priority and fail to take calculated risks to best other men also fail to attract mates.

One of men's key strategies is to form coalitions with other men. These organized alliances give men the power to triumph over other men in their quest for resources and sexual access. In animals, strong coalitions are seen among baboons, chimpanzees, and dolphins.[4] Male bottlenose dolphins, for example, form coalitions to herd females and thereby gain greater sexual access than would be possible by operating alone.[5] Among chimpanzees, our closest primate relative, males form alliances to increase their chances of victory in physical contests with other chimpanzees, their status in the group hierarchy, and their sexual access to females. Rarely can a male chimpanzee become the dominant member of the troop without the aid of male allies. Solitary males without coalition partners are at great risk of being brutally attacked and sometimes killed by males from other groups.[6]

Human males, too, form alliances for gaining resources such as large game, power within the extended group, ways to defend against the aggression of other coalitions of men, and sexual access to women.[7] The survival and reproductive benefits derived from these coalitional activities constituted tremendous selection pressure over human evolutionary history for men to form alliances with other men. Since ancestral women did not hunt large game, declare war on other tribes, or attempt to forcibly capture men from neighboring tribes, they did not experience equivalent selection pressure to form coalitions.[8] Although women do form coalitions with other women for the care of kin, these are weakened whenever a woman leaves her kin group to live with her husband and his clan. The combination of strong coalitions among men and relatively weak coalitions among women, according to Barbara Smuts, may have contributed historically to men's dominance over women.[9] Women's preferences for a successful, ambitious, and resourceful mate and men's competitive mating strategies evolved together. These strategies include risk taking, status striving, derogation of competitors, coalition formation, and an array of individual efforts aimed at besting other men on the dimensions that women desire. The intertwining of these co-evolved mechanisms in men and women created the conditions for men to dominate in the domain of resources.

The origin of male control over resources is not simply an incidental historical footnote of passing curiosity. Rather, it has a profound bearing on the present, because it reveals some of the primary causes of men's continuing control of resources. Women today continue to want men who have resources, and they continue to reject men who lack resources. These preferences are expressed repeatedly and invariably in dozens of studies conducted on tens of thousands of individuals in scores of countries worldwide. They are expressed countless times in everyday life. In any given year, the men whom women marry earn more than men of the same age whom women do not marry. Women who earn more than their husbands seek divorce at double the rate of women whose husbands earn more than they do. Furthermore, men continue to form alliances and compete with other men to acquire the status and resources that make them desirable to women. The forces that originally caused the resource inequality between the sexes, namely women's preferences and men's competitive strategies, are the same forces that contribute to maintaining resource inequality today.[10]

Feminists' and evolutionists' conclusions converge in their implication that men's efforts to control female sexuality lie at the core of their efforts to control women. Our evolved sexual strategies account for why this occurs, and why control of women's sexuality is a central preoccupation of men.[11] Over the course of human evolutionary history, men who failed to control women's sexuality—for example, by failing to attract a mate, failing to prevent cuckoldry, or failing to keep a mate—experienced lower reproductive success than men who succeeded in controlling women's sexuality. We come from a long and unbroken line of ancestral fathers who succeeded in obtaining mates, preventing their infidelity, and providing enough benefits to keep them from leaving. We also come from a long line of ancestral mothers who granted sexual access to men who provided beneficial resources.

Feminist theory sometimes portrays men as being united with all other men in their common purpose of oppressing women.[12] But the evolution of human mating suggests that this scenario cannot be true, because men and women compete primarily against members of their own sex. Men strive to control resources mainly at the expense of other men. Men deprive other men of their resources, exclude other men from positions of status and power, and derogate other men in order to make them less desirable to women. Indeed, the fact that nearly 70 percent of all homicides are inflicted by men on other men reveals the tip of the iceberg of the cost of competition to men.[13] The fact that men on average die six years earlier than women is further testimony to the penalties men pay for this struggle with other men.

Women do not escape damage inflicted by members of their own sex.[14] Women compete with each other for access to high-status men, have sex with other women's husbands, and lure men away from their wives. Women slander and denigrate their rivals, especially those who pursue short-term sexual strategies. Women and men are both victims of the sexual strategies of their own sex, and so can hardly be said to be united with members of their own sex for some common goal.

Moreover, both men and women benefit from the strategies of the opposite sex. Men lavish resources on certain women, including their wives, their sisters, their daughters, and their mistresses. A woman's father, brothers, and sons all benefit from her selection of a mate with status and resources. Contrary to the view that men or women are united with all members of their own sex for the purpose of oppressing the other sex, each individual shares key interests with particular members of each sex and is in conflict with other members of each sex. Simple-minded views of a same-sex conspiracy have no foundation in reality.

Although today men's sexual strategies contribute to their control over resources, the origins of their strategies cannot be divorced from the evolution of women's desires. This analysis does not imply that we should blame women for the fact that men control resources. Rather, if harmony and equality are to be achieved, women and men both must be recognized as linked together in a spiraling co-evolutionary process. This process started long ago with the evolution of desire and continues to operate today through our strategies of mating.

Diversity in Mating Strategies

Differences in the desires of men and women represent an important part of the diversity within the human species, but there is tremendous variability within each sex as well. Although more men than women are inclined to pursue purely casual sexual relationships, some men remain exclusively monogamous for life and some women find casual sex preferable to monogamy. Some men seek women for their economic resources and some women seek men for their looks, despite trends to the contrary. These differences within each sex cannot be dismissed as statistical flukes. They are crucial to understanding the rich repertoire of human mating strategies.

Sexual diversity hinges on the individual circumstances that favor each person's choice of one strategy over another within their repertoire—a choice that may not be consciously articulated. For example, Aka men favor a mating strategy of high parental investment under circumstances in which they lack economic resources.[15] !Kung women favor serial mating under circumstances in which they are sufficiently desirable to continue attracting men who are willing to invest.[16] No mating strategies, however deeply rooted in our evolved psychology, are invariably expressed regardless of context. Knowledge of the critical social contexts that foster each sexual strategy aids our understanding of the diversity of mating behaviors within and between the sexes.

Knowledge of this diversity leads one to scrutinize certain value judgments for the selfish interests that may be driving them. In Western society, lifelong monogamy is often held up to be the ideal. Anyone who does not conform to this practice is regarded as deviant, immature, sinful, or a failure. Such a judgment may turn out to be a manifestation of the underlying sexual strategies of the person who upholds it. It is often in the best interests of a woman, for example, to convince others of the ideal of lifelong love. Promiscuous women can pose a threat to monogamous women, siphoning off the resources, attention, and commitment of their husbands. It is often in the best interests of a man to convince others to adopt a monogamous strategy, even if he fails to follow it himself. Promiscuous men usurp single men's mating opportunities and threaten to cuckold married men. The values we espouse about sexuality are often manifestations of our evolved mating strategies.

Casual sexual strategies of both sexes are deeply founded in human evolutionary history. Evolutionary accounts that emphasize the sexually indiscriminate male and the sexually coy female overstate the case. Just as men have the capacity for commitment as part of their strategic repertoire, women have the capacity for casual sex within theirs, and they in fact pursue casual sex when they perceive that it is to their advantage to do so. The benefits to women of casual sex remain the least explored and most ignored arena of human mating.

For a century after Darwin proposed the theory of sexual selection, it was vigorously resisted by male scientists, in part because they presumed that women were passive in the mating process. The proposal that women actively select their mates and that these selections constitute a powerful evolutionary force was thought to be science fiction rather than scientific fact. In the 1970s, scientists gradually came to accept the profound importance of female choice in the animal and insect world. In the 1980s, scientists began to document within our own species the active strategies that women pursue in choosing and competing for mates. But in the 1990s, many scientists continue to insist that women have but a single mating strategy—the pursuit of a permanent mate.

Scientific evidence suggests otherwise. The fact that women who are engaged in casual sex as opposed to committed mating change their mating desires to favor a man's extravagant life style and physical attractiveness tells us that women have specific psychological mechanisms designed for temporary mating. The fact that women who have extramarital affairs choose men who are higher in status than their husbands tells us that women have specific psychological mechanisms designed for temporary mating. And the fact that women shift to brief liaisons under predictable circumstances, such as a dearth of men capable of investing in them or an unfavorable ratio of women to men, tells us that women have specific psychological mechanisms designed for temporary mating.

People often decry the frequent switching of mates and promiscuous activities. And it often serves their interests to foster this view of morality in others. From a scientific point of view, however, taking the long view over evolutionary time, there is no moral justification for placing a premium on a single strategy within the collective human repertoire. Our human nature is found in the diversity of our sexual strategies. Recognition of the rich diversity of desires within the human repertoire takes us one step closer to harmony.

Cultural Variation in Mating Behavior

Cultural variation represents one of the most fascinating and mysterious aspects of human diversity. Members of different societies differ dramatically on some qualities, as in their desire for virginity in a marriage partner. In China, for example, nearly every individual, both male and female, views virginity as indispensable in a mate. Nonvirgin Chinese are virtually unmarriageable. In Scandinavian countries such as Sweden and Norway, chastity is unimportant in a mate. This kind of cultural variability poses a puzzle for all theories of human mating.

Evolutionary psychology focuses on early experiences, parenting practices, and other environmental factors to explain variability in mating strategies. The psychologist Jay Belsky and his colleagues, for example, argue that harsh, rejecting, and inconsistent child-rearing practices, erratically provided resources, and marital discord foster in children a mating strategy of early reproduction and rapid turnover.[17] In contrast, sensitive, supportive, and responsive child rearing, combined with reliable resources and spousal harmony, foster in children a mating strategy of commitment marked by delayed reproduction and stable marital bonds. Children growing up in uncertain and unpredictable environments, in short, learn that they cannot rely on a single mate. They therefore opt for a sexual life that starts early and that inclines them to seek immediate resources from multiple, temporary mates. In contrast, children who grow up in stable homes with predictably investing parents opt for a strategy of permanent mating because they expect to attract a stable, high-investing mate. The evidence from children of divorced homes supports this theory. Such children reach puberty earlier, engage in intercourse earlier, and have more numerous sex partners than their peers from intact homes.

The sensitivity of mating strategies to early experiences may help to explain the differences in the value placed on chastity across cultures. In China, for example, marriages are lasting, divorce is rare, and parents invest heavily in their children over extended periods. In Sweden, many children are born out of wedlock, divorce is common, and fewer fathers invest consistently over time. Chinese and Swedes may select different sexual strategies from the human repertoire because of these early developmental experiences. Although the significance of early experiences requires further testing, the evidence so far reinforces the view that men and women both have casual and committed mating strategies within their repertoires. The particular strategy they choose from this menu depends partly on their early experiences, which vary from culture to culture.

Differences between the promiscuous Ache and the relatively monogamous Hiwi also illuminate the cultural variability of human sexual strategies. The different ratios of males to females in these two tribes may be the critical factor in eliciting a different sexual strategy. Among the Ache, there are approximately 1.5 women for every man. Among the

Hiwi, there are more men than women, although precise numbers are not available. The prevalence of available Ache women creates sexual opportunities for Ache men not experienced by Hiwi men. Ache men seize these opportunities, as evidenced by the high frequency of mate switching and casual affairs. Ache men can pursue a temporary sexual strategy more successfully than Hiwi men can. Hiwi women are better able than Ache women are to secure a high investment from men who must provide resources to attract and retain a mate.[18]

Evolved mating mechanisms are central to understanding differences among cultures in sexual strategies. Cultures differ in the sexual opportunities available, the resources provided by their ecology, the ratio of men to women, and the extent to which they foster permanent versus temporary mating. Our evolved psychological mechanisms are attuned to these cultural inputs. Cultural variations in mating behavior thus reflect differences in the choices made from the whole repertoire of possible human sexual strategies, based in part on cultural input. Every living human has inherited the complete repertoire from successful ancestors.

Competition and Conflict in the Mating Arena

An unpleasant fact of human mating is that desirable partners are always outnumbered by those who desire them. Some men demonstrate a superior ability to accrue resources; because women typically desire these men, women compete with each other to attract them. Only women high in desirability, however, succeed. Women of striking beauty are desired by many men, but only a few men succeed in attracting them. The combined qualities of kindness, intelligence, dependability, athleticism, looks, and economic prospects occur in the same person only rarely. Most of us must settle for someone who has less than the full complement of desirable characteristics.

These stark facts create competition and conflict within each sex that can be avoided only by opting out of the mating game entirely. The fundamental desires of mating, however, are not easily extinguished. The quest to fulfill these desires catapults people headlong into the arena of competition with members of their own sex. People do not always recognize competition in its many guises. A man or women buying the latest facial cream may not construe this attention to skin as competition. A woman or man getting pumped up on the latest fitness machine or working late into the night may not construe these actions as competition. But as long as people have mating desires and as long as people differ in the qualities desired by the opposite sex, competition among people of the same sex will be an inevitable aspect of human mating.

Conflict between the sexes is likewise not easily banished. Some men show a thoughtless insensitivity to women's sexual psychology. Men sometimes seek sex sooner, more frequently, more persistently, or more aggressively than women want. Charges of sexual harassment and coercion are almost exclusively levied by women against men because of fundamental differences in the mating strategies of the two sexes. Men's strategies conflict with women's desires, causing anger and distress. Analogously, women spurn men who lack the desired qualities, causing frustration and resentment among the men who are rejected. Women thus interfere with men's sexual strategies as much as men interfere with women's, although they do so in less brutal and coercive ways.

Conflict within couples is also impossible to eliminate entirely. Although some couples live harmonious, happy lives together, no couple experiences a complete absence of conflict. The conditions that trigger conflict are often unavoidable. A man who gets laid off from his job because of factors that are beyond his control may find that his wife wants a divorce because he no longer provides the resources on which she based her mating decision. A woman with encroaching wrinkles, through no fault of her own, may find that her professionally successful husband desires younger women. Some conflict between the sexes is impossible to eliminate because the conditions that foster it cannot be avoided.

The fact that conflicts between men and women originate from our evolved mating psychology is disturbing to some people, in part because it contradicts widely-held beliefs. Many of us have learned the traditional view that these conflicts are reflections of a particular culture whose practices perturb the natural harmony of human nature. But the anger that women feel when sexually coerced and the rage that men feel when cuckolded arise from our evolved mating strategies, and not from capitalism, culture, or socialization. Evolution operates by the ruthless criterion of reproductive success, no matter how repugnant we may find the strategies produced by that process, and no matter how abhorrent the consequences of those strategies may be.

An especially pernicious manifestation of conflict between members of the same sex is warfare, which has been a recurrent activity throughout human history. Given men's tendency to take physical risks in their pursuit of the resources needed for success at mating, it comes as no surprise that warfare is almost exclusively a male activity. Among the Yanomamö, there are two key motives that spur men to declare war on another tribe—a desire to capture the wives of other men or a desire to recapture wives that were lost in previous raids. When the American anthropologist Napoleon Chagnon explained to his Yanomamö informants that his country declared war for ideals such as freedom and democracy, they were astonished. It seemed silly to them to risk one's life for anything other than capturing women.[19]

The frequency of rape during wars throughout the course of human recorded history suggests that the sexual motives of the Yanomamö men may not be either strange or atypical.[20] Men worldwide share the same evolved psychology. The fact that there has never in history been a single case of women forming a war party to raid neighboring villages and capture husbands tells us something important about the nature of sex differences—that men's mating strategies are often more brutal and aggressive than women's.[21] The sexual motivation underlying violence also reveals the close connection between conflict *within* a sex and conflict *between* the sexes.

In everyday life, the war between the sexes occurs not on the literal battlefield but between individual men and women interacting with each other socially—in the workplace, at parties, and at home. The selective exclusion of mates, for example, does not affect all people, only those who lack the desired characteristics. Sexual jealousy is a cost inflicted not by all men on all women but rather by particular men, such as those lower in desirability than their partners, in particular circumstances, such as instances of infidelity, on particular women, such as spouses rather than casual sex partners. Sexual coercion, to take another example, is perpetrated only by some men. Most men are not rapists, and most would be unlikely to commit rape even if there were no risk of getting caught.[22]

There is no solidarity among all men or all women that creates conflict between the sexes. Rather, members of one sex generally favor a common set of strategies which differs from the typical strategies pursued by members of the other sex. It is possible to speak of conflict between the sexes because the ways in which men and women typically conflict result from the strategies they share with their own sex. Still, we must recognize that no man or woman is fundamentally united with his or her own sex nor fundamentally at odds with members of the opposite sex.

We are empowered now, perhaps more than at any previous time in human evolutionary history, to shape our future. The fact that abuse and other abhorrent behaviors stem from our mating strategies does not justify their perpetuation. By employing the evolved mechanisms that are sensitive to personal costs, such as our fear of ostracism and sensitivity to reputational damage, we may be able to reduce the expression of the more brutal aspects of our human repertoire.

Cooperation between the Sexes

Men and women have always depended on each other for passing their genes on to future generations. Marital unions are characterized by a complex web of long-term trust and reciprocity that appears to be unparalleled in other species. In this sense, cooperation between the sexes reaches a pinnacle among humans. Our strategies for cooperation define human nature as much as our capacity for culture or our consciousness.

Sexual strategies provide us with some of the conditions that facilitate the achievement of lifelong love. Children, the shared vehicles by which genes survive the journey to future generations, align the interests of a man and a woman and foster permanent bonds of marriage. Parents share in the delights of producing new life and nurturing their children to maturity. They marvel together as the gift of their union partakes of life's reproductive cycle. But children also create new sources of conflict, from disputes about dividing the daytime child care to reduced opportunities for nighttime sexual harmony. No blessing is unmixed.

Sexual fidelity also promotes marital harmony. Any possibility of infidelity opens up a chasm of conflicting interests. Infidelity disrupts marital bonds and leads to divorce. Monogamy encourages prolonged trust between a man and a woman. If a woman is unfaithful, she may benefit by obtaining extra material resources or better genes to pass on to her children. But the benefits that flow to her through infidelity come at a cost to her husband in a reduced certainty of paternity and a destruction of trust. A man's infidelity may satisfy his quest for sexual variety or give him a momentary euphoria that mimics that of a polygynous man. But these benefits come at a cost to his wife as a portion of her husband's love and investment is diverted to a rival. Lifelong sexual fidelity promotes harmony between a man and a woman, but it comes at a price for both sexes in relinquished opportunities.

Fulfilling each other's evolved desires is the key to harmony between a man and woman. A woman's happiness increases when the man brings more economic resources to the union and shows kindness, affection, and commitment. A man's happiness increases when the woman is more physically attractive than he is, and when she shows kindness, affection, and commitment.[23] Those whose fulfill each other's desires have more fulfilling relationships. Our evolved desires, in short, provide the essential ingredients for solving the mystery of harmony between the sexes.

The multiplicity of our desires may be the most powerful tool for promoting harmony. It is a crowning achievement of humankind that two unrelated individuals can bring all of their individual resources into a lifelong alliance characterized by love. This happens because of the remarkable resources that each person brings to the relationship, the tremendous benefits that flow to those who cooperate, and the sophisticated psychological machinery that we have for forming beneficial alliances with others. Some of these resources tend to be linked to a person's sex, such as the female's reproductive viability or the male's provisioning capacity. But mating resources typically transcend these reproductive essentials to include such capacities as protection from danger, deterrence of enemies, formation of alliances, tutoring of children, loyalty in times of absence, and nurturance in times of sickness. Each of these resources fulfills one of the many special desires that define our human nature.

A profound respect for the other sex should come from the knowledge that we have always depended on each other for the resources required for survival and reproduction. Similarly, we have always depended on each other for the fulfillment of our desires. These facts may be responsible for the unique feeling of completeness people experience when they become entwined in the intoxicating grip of love. A lifelong alliance of love is a triumphant achievement of human mating strategies.

Today we are confronted with novel sexual circumstances not encountered by any of our ancestors, including reliable contraception, fertility drugs, artificial insemination, telephone sex, video dating services, breast implants, tummy tucks, "test tube" babies, sperm banks, and AIDS. Our ability to control the consequences of our mating behavior has reached proportions that are unprecedented in human evolutionary history and have been attained by no other species on earth. But we confront these modern novelties with an ancient set of mating strategies that worked in ancestral times and in places that are irretrievably lost. Our mating mechanisms are the living fossils that tell us who we are and where we came from.

We are the first species in the known history of three and a half billion years of life on earth with the capacity to control our own destiny. The prospect of designing our destiny remains excellent to the degree that we comprehend our evolutionary past. Only by examining the complex repertoire of human sexual strategies can we know where we came from. Only by understanding why these human strategies have evolved can we control where we are going.

11

Women's Hidden Sexual Strategies

. . . to an extraordinary degree, the predilections of the investing sex—females—potentially determine the direction in which the species will evolve. For it is the female who is the ultimate arbiter of when she mates and how often and with whom.
—Sarah Blaffer Hrdy, *The Woman That Never Evolved*

WOMEN'S MATING STRATEGIES show complexities that defy efforts at easy understanding. The challenge is not merely penetrating the puzzle of what women want; it's revealing the strategies that women have evolved to achieve their desires. Hidden within their bodies, concealed within their minds, reside bewildering intricacies of sexuality that cry out for understanding. Some strategies remain secret for an excellent evolutionary reason—they cannot be implemented successfully if their true design is revealed. But humans want to know. We feel a deep desire to understand women. Men seem more transparent by comparison, but this may be misleading. The principle of co-evolution tells us that men are unlikely to stay evolutionarily still while women evolve increasingly sophisticated strategies. Women's mating adaptations are mirrored in the counter-adaptations of men, just as men's adaptations are mirrored in the counter-adaptations of women.

This chapter explores four evolutionary enigmas that have been the focus of recent empirical research on women's strategies of human mating: Does the female orgasm serve a specific function? Why do women have affairs? Are women's sexual strategies linked to the menstrual cycle? Can men detect when women ovulate?

Is Female Sexual Orgasm an Adaptation?

In one episode of the popular HBO show *Six Feet Under,* Brenda, an attractive, emotionally troubled, sexually adventurous woman, is engaged to be married to Nate. Their sex life is miles away from story-book bliss. At the beginning of one episode, while waiting for a stop-light to change to green, she looks over at a rugged man in the pickup truck in the adjacent lane. He looks back. In the next scene, they embrace in frenetic sex in his pickup truck. She is visibly turned on, be-coming flushed with passion. As Brenda approaches the brink of orgasm, we discover that the sexual encounter was a product of pure fantasy. Back in reality, the light turns green and she lurches away from the intersection, alone in her own car. Later that night, she urges her fiancé to go outside and pretend to be an intruder breaking into her house. Nate declines. Instead, they make love softly. The scene ends with Nate on top of her, gently moving back and forth, while murmuring "I love you." Brenda urges him to do it "harder," but Nate continues his soft and too-tender lovemaking. Her reaction is frustra-tion and irritation rather than arousal and orgasm. The scene fades.

Women's sexual orgasm has puzzled, frightened, delighted, dis-turbed, and mystified men for centuries. It's been defined as "a highly variable peak in sexual experience accompanying involuntary, rhythmic contractions of the outer third of the vagina—and frequently of the uterus, rectal sphincter, and the urethral sphincter as well—and the concomitant release of vasocongestion and muscular tension associated with intense sexual arousal."[1] To understand the phenomenology of fe-male orgasm, consider these descriptions by women experiencing them:

> A heightened feeling of excitement with severe muscular tension, espe-cially through the back and legs, rigid straightening of the body for about 5 seconds, and a strong and general relaxation and a very tired relieved feeling.

> Combinations of waves of very pleasurable sensations and mounting of tensions, culminating in a fantastic sensation and release of tension.

> Begins with tensing and tingling in anticipation, rectal contractions starting a series of chills up the spine. Tingling and buzzing sensations grow suddenly to explosion in genital area, some sensations of dizzying and weakening—almost loss of conscious sensation, but not really. Explo-sion sort of flowers out to varying distance from genital area, depending on intensity.[2]

These descriptions highlight the more dramatic episodes. For some women, orgasm is described more as a slower deep drumming sensation followed by a gentle release.

The female orgasm varies considerably across women. In one fairly typical study, 15 percent of the women reported always experiencing orgasm from sexual intercourse, 48 percent reported orgasm most of the time, 19 percent sometimes, 11 percent occasionally, and 7 percent never.[3] Roughly comparable findings, using somewhat different methods and samples, have been reported by Terman, Kinsey, Hunt, Chester, Fisher, Hite, and more recently Laumann and Gagnon. Our fascination with female orgasm flows partly from its uncertainty and unpredictability: "Unlike the unicorn, which is specially interesting precisely because it does not exist . . . and the male orgasm, which exists with monotonous regularity . . . the female orgasm definitely exists and yet inspires interest, debate, polemics, ideology, technical manuals, and scientific and popular literature solely because it is so often absent."[4]

What makes some women easily orgasmic and others less so? What makes a woman orgasmic with one man and sexually frustrated with another?[5] Scientists of all stripes have puzzled over these questions, exploring many facets of women's sexual orgasm—the relationship circumstances in which it occurs, subjective experiences, physiological responses, psychological precursors, and emotional aftermath. The central *evolutionary* question that galvanizes inquiry is one that combines all these aspects: Has the female sexual orgasm evolved for a particular function?

At one end of the debate are two unlikely theoretical companions, evolutionary anthropologist Donald Symons and the late evolutionary paleontologist Steven J. Gould. Symons, in 1979, subsequently endorsed by Gould in 1987, argued that female orgasm, unlike male orgasm, has *not* evolved for a specific function.[6] Male orgasm and the accompanying ejaculation, in contrast, seems obviously functional—well designed for propelling sperm deeply into the female reproductive tract, facilitating successful conception. Peak sexual pleasure occurs at ejaculation, linking male orgasm with the greatest likelihood of successful conception. Female orgasm, however, is not necessary for conception. According to Symons, there is no solid evidence that female orgasm contains any special design features that led orgasmic female ancestors to out-reproduce their non-orgasmic competitors. Therefore, it is unlikely to be an adaptation. Instead, Symons suggests, female orgasm is analogous to male nipples. Both are functionless byproducts of developmental compromises in mammalian prenatal development. Just as humans possess the genetic potential for either functional female nipples or functionless male nipples, they also possess the genetic potential for functional male orgasm or functionless female orgasm. Which sex-typical mechanism actually develops, and which is suppressed, according to this argument, is mediated by hormonally driven genetic switches that occur at various stages of development. Males and females are not separate entities, but rather "are variants upon a single ground plan, elaborated later in embryology."[7] The female orgasm, in short, is a non-adaptive developmental by-product of the male orgasm, which is a sexual adaptation.

Gould expressed impatience with those who proposed possible functions of female orgasm. He chastised evolutionary anthropologist Sarah Hrdy, for example, for telling "adaptive stories" and developing "fanciful theories" when she advanced the hypothesis that female orgasm functions as a paternity confusion device designed to evoke support from multiple males. Symons has offered a more careful consideration of the arguments and evidence. He marshaled four distinct lines of argument for the by-product explanation of female orgasm. First, he suggested that there is no compelling evidence that non-human female primates experience orgasm during intercourse, although many have the *capacity* to experience orgasm when stimulated in certain ways such as rubbing the clitoris. Second, female orgasm is not necessary for successful conception; pregnancies occur worldwide in women who do not experience sexual climax. Third, female orgasm is highly variable. Unlike male orgasm, which is a reliable outcome of sexual intercourse, female orgasm sometimes occurs and sometimes is like the unicorn. Fourth, in some cultures orgasm is apparently entirely unknown. Symons cites this ethnographic summary of the evidence to support this last argument:

> In most of the societies for which there are data, it is reported that men take the initiative and, without extended foreplay, proceed vigorously toward climax without much regard for achieving synchrony with the woman's orgasm. Again and again, there are reports that coitus is primarily completed in terms of the man's passions and pleasures, with scant attention paid to the woman's response. If women do experience orgasm, they do so passively.[8]

He also points out that women in Western cultures tend not to mention orgasm as the *primary* reason for their enjoyment of sexual intercourse; instead more women emphasize *emotional intimacy* as the core reason for enjoying sex and often single out the moment of penetration as the most pleasurable moment.

Since the publication of Symons's classic treatise on the evolution of human sexuality in 1979, new research suggests that females in some non-human primate species may in fact experience orgasm during intercourse.[9] Researchers studying stumptail macaque monkeys, for example, have secured telemetric recordings of female uterine contractions during copulation. Interestingly, these physiological contractions occur simultaneously with the display of the "climax facial expression." This facial expression bears a close resemblance to the male macaque "ejaculation face." When the uterine contractions stop, the female climax facial expressions stop within 10 seconds. Although researchers obviously cannot interview female monkeys to obtain evidence about their subjective feelings, the close correlation between the physiological contractions and facial expressions points to the existence of an orgasmic experience in these female primates. Similar responses have been observed in female chimpanzees. In short, some recent evidence suggests that the capacity for female orgasm during intercourse may have originated early in the primate lineage.

The primate evidence does not speak directly to the question of whether human female orgasm is functional or a functionless by-product. Indeed, if all female primates have the capacity for orgasm, then it's possible that nothing evolved *specifically in humans* to serve a particular function. In order to demonstrate adaptation, we must turn to evidence required of all hypothesized adaptations—species-typicality, specificity, economy, and precision of purpose for solving a particular adaptive problem. This evidence begins with the cross-cultural record.

Arguments that hinge on the cross-cultural ethnographic evidence remain problematic, especially in the domain of sexuality. Most anthropologists have been males, as have been most of their native informants. Women understandably may be reluctant to discuss details of their sexual experiences with a foreign male anthropologist. Often, researchers simply fail to seek information about the nuances of women's mating behavior. These factors may have led to inaccurate ethnographic assessments of the prevalence of female orgasm.

Consider the cultures sometimes cited as evidence of the absence of female orgasm. For example, one informant among the Muria of India, a culture viewed as lacking female orgasm, provided this report: *"When he is on her, she puts his organ in its place with her hand. She says nothing, nor does he. They are very quiet. He must do it hard: unless you sweat, unless your rut leaves you, you are not satisfied. She says, 'push on, push on.' She won't let him go till she is satisfied."*[10] This seems like female desire for orgasm, despite the culture being cited as an example of its absence. In ethnographies conducted by female anthropologists, reports of orgasms are more common. In the book *Nisa: The Life and Words of a !Kung Woman*, Margorie Shostak provides this report:

> Sometimes the woman finishes first and the man, after. Sometimes they finish together. Both ways are equally good. The only way it is bad is when the woman hasn't finished and the man has. . . . All women know sexual pleasure. Some women, those who really like sex, if they haven't finished and the man has, will wait until the man has rested, then get up and make love to him. Because she wants to finish, too. She'll have sex with the man until she is satisfied. Otherwise she could get sick.[11]

Although one can probably find ethnographies to support a range of views, the key point is that there have been no *systematic* studies of women across cultures aimed at determining with greater confidence whether societies exist in which female orgasm is entirely unknown or not experienced.[12] As one author concluded, "obtaining information on the existence of female orgasm has not been a high priority among ethnographers."[13]

Variability of female orgasm within and across cultures is sometimes cited as evidence for the by-product explanation of female orgasm. Variability, rather than uniformity, however, is precisely what is expected according to several adaptationist hypotheses. Evidence for adaptation is typically sought in universality of design, not universality of manifest expression. Callus-producing mechanisms are universal human adaptations, but there is much individual and cultural variability in the thickness and distribution of calluses. An adaptation can be *designed* to be variable in its manifestation *in order to produce* a reliable, precise, and efficient function. Indeed, functional signals cease to be of value when they are either uniformly present or uniformly absent.[14] If orgasm functions as a signal, as several adaptationist hypotheses suggest, then variability is an absolutely necessary part of the design of women's orgasm.

Five Possible Functions of Female Orgasm

At least five distinct adaptive functions have been proposed for the female orgasm. The first and most common is the *hedonic hypothesis*—Girls just want to have fun. The hedonic hypothesis proposes that orgasm motivates women to have intercourse throughout their cycle, increasing the likelihood of successful conception.[15] Orgasm makes sex more fun for women, propelling them to do it more often. Thus, orgasmic women may have historically out-reproduced anorgasmic women by engaging in more frequent sex and consequently producing more numerous children. Since this hypothesis implies high uniformity across women in orgasmic experience, the criterion of universality of design applies; the well-documented empirical variability renders this hypothesis unsupported or at best incomplete. Furthermore, although the hedonic hypothesis explains why women like sex, it fails to explain why orgasm and its specific design features, such as rising tension, sudden climax, peak of pleasure, and specific muscular contractions, are required for this enjoyment.

A second adaptive function has been called the *Mr. Right hypothesis*, which posits that female orgasm serves as a mate selection device. As science journalist Natalie Angier notes, "female orgasm is the ultimate expression of female choice . . . a woman's way of controlling the terms of the underground debate."[16] By choosing a man with whom she is orgasmic, a woman is presumed to be selecting a man who will stick around and invest in her and her children. Perhaps a man's sensitivity to a woman's desires, his ability to read her needs, and effort to ensure her sexual satisfaction auger well for his future as a good husband and a good dad. Variability in female orgasm, especially when the same woman is differentially orgasmic with different men, is indispensable for serving the hypothesized mate choice function.

Whereas the Mr. Right hypothesis focuses on the information value a woman's orgasm provides her, the *paternity confidence hypothesis* focuses on the signal value her orgasm provides to her partner.[17] It tells the man that she is sexually satisfied with him, and hence will not be motivated to seek sexual gratification elsewhere. As a consequence, her orgasm furnishes a sign of her sexual fidelity. If she climaxes, it tells him that she will stay rather than stray. The function of a woman's fidelity signal is the effect it has on her mate's behavior—an increase in the likelihood that he will remain committed to her and invest in her children.

A fourth function is captured by the *paternity confusion hypothesis,* initially proposed more than two decades ago by evolutionist Sarah Hrdy in the context of her work with langur monkeys and macaques.[18] According to this view, female orgasm evolved to promote promiscuous mating. Mating with a variety of different males clouded the identity of the true genetic father. By promoting paternal uncertainty, a female could reduce the odds that any male in the group might kill her offspring—after all, the infant might be his own. The confusion might also increase positive investments from several males, giving her benefits beyond what she could secure from a single male.

Symons points out an important conceptual problem with the paternity confusion hypothesis.[19] It assumes that males can assess paternity. As a consequence, why wouldn't males decrease their investment as the likelihood of their paternity decreases? And if they do, why would it be advantageous for a female to secure one unit of investment from five males rather than five units of investment from one male? In addition to this conceptual problem, there have been no empirical tests of the paternity confusion hypothesis in humans, and recently Hrdy herself appears to have abandoned it.[20]

Some evolutionary biologists have advanced the *sperm retention hypothesis* of female orgasm, already described in Chapter 4. According to this hypothesis, female orgasm functions to draw sperm into the cervix and uterine cavity, increasing the odds of conception.[21] Although the precise physiological mechanism by which this might work is not known, it potentially could occur in one of three ways: if the female orgasm causes the cervix to dip lower into the pool of seminal fluid the male deposits; if orgasm lengthens the amount of time the cervix remains dipped into this pool; or if female contractions cause the cervical mucus to draw the sperm up into the uterine cavity.[22]

Evolutionary scientists have devised studies and assembled available empirical evidence to sort through these competing hypotheses. As a background for evaluating this evidence, it's worth noting that many women believe that sex can be extremely enjoyable without orgasm at all. A recent study in Great Britain, for example, revealed that 71 percent of women believe that sex *without* orgasm can be truly satisfying for the woman. Interestingly, 10 percent more men than women believe that the female orgasm is necessary for her full enjoyment, suggesting that it might be a greater preoccupation of men than of women.[23]

Daniel Rancour-Laferriere favors the Mr. Right hypothesis, which he labels the "domestic bliss function." A *Redbook* study of 100,000 women found that they were most likely to be orgasmic, both before and after marriage, if sex occurred in the context of a stable committed relationship. Roughly 77 percent of the women who experienced a sequence of one-night stands reported that they *never* attained orgasm. In contrast, among women having regular sex with a committed partner, only 23 percent reported never reaching orgasm.[24] The classic Kinsey study more than half a century ago found that married women are more likely to experience orgasms than their non-married peers.[25] And the well-controlled 1994 *Sex in America* survey found that whereas more than two-thirds of all single women usually *fail* to reach orgasm during sexual encounters, roughly 75 percent of married women usually or always climax.[26] All these findings suggest that orgasm is most frequent in long-term committed mating. This is consistent with the Mr. Right hypothesis, although it also could be attributed to the effect of practice, or trial and error with a single partner, and hence is not definitive evidence for special design for the mate selection function.

Married women who experience more frequent orgasms report being happier with their marriages than women who experience less frequent orgasms. This finding supports the Mr. Right hypothesis only if it is amended to state that orgasm functions not just in initial mate choice, but also in decisions to remain with an already chosen mate.[27] One study of 6,000 English women affirms the continued link between orgasm and marital quality. Whereas only 3 percent of women who were often or always orgasmic with their husbands expressed an interest in extramarital sex, 10 percent of women on the low end of the orgasm scale reported interest in having sexual affairs with other men.[28] In Kinsey's study, among the 6,927 women who were having extramarital affairs, 42 percent indicated more frequent orgasms with their affair partner than with their husband; only 24 percent indicated more frequent orgasms with their husbands, and the remaining 34 percent indicated equal frequency. Interestingly, 94 percent of the married women who experienced frequent orgasms with their husbands reported that they still loved their husbands as much now as during their newlywed year. Sixty-one percent of the less orgasmic women reported feeling comparable emotions of spousal love. So although love and orgasm are linked, orgasm is not a necessary condition for love. Furthermore, the direction of causality cannot be determined from any of these studies. Perhaps a happy marriage leads to more frequent female orgasms rather than the other way around. Perhaps some men are especially kind to their partners, especially physically attracted them, or especially in love with them, and consequently put more effort into ensuring their wife's sexual satisfaction, leading to a link between love and orgasm.

In short, the Mr. Right hypothesis receives some empirical support, but not in the form originally proposed. Female orgasm may play a role in domestic bliss, as the Mr. Right hypothesis suggests. But the absence of orgasm may motivate extramarital sex, which suggests a more sinister function.

Rather than being used to select Mr. Right for matrimonial paradise, female orgasm may have evolved, in part, as a mechanism for genetic cuckoldry—a sperm selection device for choosing which male will end up fertilizing her nutrient-rich eggs. One hint of this comes from a study of non-human primates—Japanese macaque monkeys.[29] Alfonso Troisi and Monica Carosi studied 240 copulations among a group of 16 males and 26 females. Female orgasms, indicated by the female clutching, muscular body spasms, and vocalizations, occurred in 33 percent of these copulations. As in humans, longer copulation time and a larger number of pelvic thrusts increased the probability of female orgasm. But the fascinating finding was that females proved to be more orgasmic with the socially dominant males, especially when a low-ranked female copulated with a high-ranking male.

Roughly analogous studies of humans have focused on the links between male qualities such as symmetrical features and physical attractiveness and female orgasm. Chapter 3 noted that genetic abnormalities and environmental insults can produce physical asymmetries in the body and face. Many biologists view symmetry as a marker of heritable fitness, suggesting genetic quality. In a study of 86 heterosexual couples, Randy Thornhill and his colleagues found that women with more symmetrical partners reported significantly more copulatory orgasms than women with more asymmetrical partners.[30] An even larger study of 388 women, some residing in Germany and others in the United States, found a similar effect—women mated to more physically attractive men reported a higher likelihood of orgasm during their most recent sexual encounter.[31] These findings provide some support for the male selection component of the Mr. Right hypothesis, in that women are more orgasmic with men of high genetic and phenotypic quality. These studies are all problematic, however, because the causal direction of effect cannot be determined—perhaps attractive and symmetrical men have more sexual experience, leading to more opportunities to learn to become better lovers. Furthermore, female orgasm in these recent studies was *not* linked with the woman having greater love for her partner, greater investment in the relationship, or her perceptions of the man's love and investment—all of which appear to go against the domestic bliss version of the Mr. Right hypothesis.

So what's going on? A key to this mystery appears to be the link between female orgasm and sperm retention, combined with a hidden side of female sexuality—women's sexual infidelities. Recall that Kinsey found that women were almost twice as likely to achieve more orgasms with their affair partners as with their husbands. A recent British study found that women have more frequent high-sperm-retention orgasms (those that occur within two minutes after the male orgasm) with their affair partners than with their husbands.[32] The clincher, however, may be the *timing* of lunchtime romance at the No-Tell Motel: Women who have affairs appear to time their sexual liaisons to coincide with the most fertile phase of their cycle—prior to or at ovulation. Indeed, rate of sexual intercourse with an affair partner during peak fertility is three times as high as the rate that occurs during the low-fertile post-ovulatory phase.[33]

A solution to the mystery of the female orgasm is finally beginning to emerge. Female orgasmic capacity *originally* may have arisen as a by-product, as Symons and Gould contended. But evolution appears to have adaptively modified female orgasm to influence *when* and *with whom* it occurs. The evidence points to the Mr. Right hypothesis, but not in the version originally formulated. Orgasm appears to function as a selection device to choose which man will end up fertilizing her eggs, a man who is not necessarily her husband. Women are more orgasmic with regular mates who have good genetic quality, as indexed by anatomical measures of symmetry and judgments of physical attractiveness. But *if* they are having affairs, women preferentially choose affair partners of high genetic quality and then experience more frequent sexual orgasms in the context of their liaisons. For women having affairs, orgasm may facilitate a mating strategy of getting the best of both worlds—investment from one man who provides parenting and resources for her children, and good genes from another man who provides little investment, but who increases the genetic quality of her children.

Although my reading of scientific evidence leads me to conclude that the female orgasm shows at least some design hallmarks of adaptation, skeptics of this conclusion—advocates of the by-product hypothesis—still have plenty of ammunition to work with. No current adaptationist hypothesis, for example, can explain why there appear to be huge cultural differences in the occurrence of female orgasm. Furthermore, we must admit to the possibility that the female orgasm may be neither 100 percent adaptation nor 100 percent by-product, but rather contains certain features that are by-products combined with some adaptive modification.

On a final note, a striking omission from evolutionary theorizing about the possible functions of female orgasm is how such functions have affected *men's* sexual strategies.[34] If female orgasm functions as a Mr. Right detector or to increase the odds of conception with a particular man, selection should favor the co-evolution of adaptations in men to increase the probability of a partner achieving sexual climax. Men might be predicted to have adaptations designed to (a) detect female orgasm, (b) not be fooled by female faking of orgasm, (c) withhold their own ejaculation until the female orgasms, and (d) ejaculate immediately following female orgasm. No evidence exists for these hypothesized co-evolved adaptations—a challenge for future researchers with the fortitude to enter the scientific debate about the possible functions of female orgasm.

Why Do Women Have Affairs?

A recent study of the sexual fantasies of 349 individuals found a remarkable result—87 percent reported having vivid sexual fantasies about *someone other than their regular partner* within the past two months.[35] The study also revealed a marked sex difference—18 percent more men than women reported these extra-pair fantasies. Nonetheless, a whopping 80 percent of women reported experiencing recent sexual fantasies about someone outside of their current romantic relationship. Women also have frequent sexual fantasies about their current partner. In fact, the majority of sexual fantasies by both sexes—64 percent of women's and 54 percent of men's—center on their current partner. Yet 34 percent of women's erotic daydreams focused on someone else. Why?

One hint comes from the function of sexual fantasies: ". . . the mind is adapted to cope with the rare, the complex, and the future . . . the function of the mind is to cause behavior; even if only one impulse in a thousand is consummated, the function of lust nonetheless is to motivate sexual intercourse."[36] Fantasies provide a window into the mating mind, but they do far more than that; they motivate us to act on our desires when an opportunity arises and the moment is right.

Is there any evidence that sexual fantasies motivate affairs? Consider these statistics. Men's sexual fantasies about other women were *not* significantly linked to whether or not they have cheated on their partner—54 percent of the faithful men's fantasies were about an extra-pair partner, compared with 55 percent of unfaithful men's fantasies. In contrast, whereas only 30 percent of faithful women's sexual fantasies focused on someone else, more than 53 percent of unfaithful women's fantasies centered on extra-pair partners. Direction of causality, of course, cannot be determined with certainty from these findings. Perhaps infidelity causes women to have more fantasies rather than fantasies leading to affairs. The results nonetheless are consistent with the idea that women's extra-pair sexual fantasies encourage them to seek sex in the arms of a lover.

Why women seek dangerous liaisons, from an evolutionary perspective, continues to confound scientists for two reasons. The first is that, compared to men, women can rarely increase their direct reproductive output by having additional sex partners. Whereas men historically could achieve direct increases in reproductive success by adding sex partners, women could not. The nine-month investment required of pregnancy prevents women from having more than one child per year, whether they have one, a dozen, or a hundred sex partners.

The second deterrent to women's wandering eyes is the avalanche of costs they incur from infidelity. If a woman has an affair, she risks being abandoned by her mate. Men frequently divorce women caught having sex with other men (see Chapter 8). Even if they are not abandoned, women risk physical and psychological abuse at the hands of jealous partners. Women damage their social reputations as a result of sexual indiscretions. They risk impairing their mate value should they need to go back out onto the mating market. They endanger the success of their children, since cuckolded men might abandon their children or curtail investment in them. They risk contracting sexually transmitted diseases from affair partners. And, as if all these costs were not enough, affairs also require time, energy, and effort—precious resources that might be better allocated to other adaptive tasks. Why would women go through all the effort and risk incurring so many costs merely to obtain a few moments of sexual gratification and the presumably trivial addition of another man's superfluous sperm? What benefit possibly could be so substantial that it outweighs all of the costs women might incur?

Many hypotheses have been advanced to answer these questions. Chapter 4 explored the viability of the *resource accrual hypothesis* and the *protection hypothesis* in the context of short-term mating strategies. Women can and often do receive food, gifts, and sometimes money from affair partners, supporting the resource accrual hypothesis.[37] The protection hypothesis, however, is more questionable. Not only is there no evidence that women actually receive protection from affair partners, but women risk violence when their regular partners observe, or even merely suspect, infidelity.[38] It strains credulity to think that women would risk inciting violence from a jealous husband in order to gain physical protection from an affair partner who is likely to be far less invested in her.

Recent studies point to more compelling potential benefits that women can accrue from affairs. One benefit is already apparent from the evidence on female sexual orgasm—the *good genes hypothesis*. The economics of the mating market dictate that women can secure genes from an affair partner that are superior to those of her regular partner, at least in principle. A highly desirable man is often willing to have a brief encounter with a less desirable woman, as long as she does not burden him with entangling commitments. Indeed, if there were no costs, an optimal female mating strategy, in the ruthless currency of reproductive fitness, would be to secure reliable investments from her husband and superior genes from an affair partner. Sexual flings can provide her with better genes, more diverse genes, and "sexy son genes," all of which could increase the viability and reproductive success of her children. So although ancestral women rarely could have increased their direct reproductive output through affairs, they could have increased their eventual reproductive success through the genetic superiority of their children—a reproductive advantage to women that comes at a cost to their cuckolded husbands.[39]

One source of evidence supporting the "good genes" explanation for women's affairs comes from studies of the rates of genetic cuckoldry. These studies, which use either blood grouping methods or DNA fingerprinting, are diabolically difficult to conduct, and potentially explosive in outcome. Few have been published. Of those published, estimates of genetic cuckoldry range from 1 to 30 percent, with the average hovering around 10 percent. A study in Switzerland, for example, found only 1 percent genetic non-paternity, whereas a study conducted in Monterey, Mexico, discovered a 12 percent genetic non-paternity rate.[40] A female colleague of mine who wishes to remain anonymous told me that she discovered a 10 percent genetic cuckoldry rate, using DNA fingerprinting technology, in a study she was conducting on the genetics of breast cancer in the United States. So perhaps 10 percent of the readers of these pages have genetic fathers different from their putative fathers, products of their mother's clandestine infidelities. These studies, while not directly supporting the good genes hypothesis, lend support to a necessary condition for it to be correct—the historical siring of children through men other than the woman's regular partner.

The good genes hypothesis has been tested in a fascinating study conducted by Steve Gangestad and Randy Thornhill.[41] They asked this key question: What are the qualities of the men who women select as extra-pair sexual partners? They examined several variables, including sexual experience, age, socio-economic status, expected income, and attachment style. They also measured two indicators of genetic quality—physical symmetry, as measured by calipers, and physical attractiveness. Recall that symmetry is hypothesized to be a heritable marker of fitness, signaling the absence of genes that perturb development or the presence of genes that facilitate resistance to environmental insults. Symmetrical men also tend to be more muscular, vigorous, larger in size, more physically healthy, more mentally healthy, and slightly higher in tested intelligence than their less symmetrical peers.[42] The most important finding was this: *Women choose symmetrical men as affair partners more than asymmetrical men*. Furthermore, these symmetrical men tended to have more sexual liaisons with women already in relationships than their more lopsided peers. Women who choose symmetrical men, in essence, may be selecting partners with genes that ultimately increase the survival and reproductive success of their children.

Beyond securing good genes, the leverage to switch to alternative mates is another important benefit women can reap from affairs. The *mate switching hypothesis* of affairs has several variants. One is that the affair may be used as leverage to get out of an unrewarding or cumbersome relationship, perhaps by inducing the husband to break up with her, or as Donald Symons notes, "to divest herself of her present husband and acquire a better one." Second, having an affair may permit a "trial run" with another man to secure information about how compatible they are or how much he is willing to invest in her—information that may be difficult to obtain without some level of intimate involvement. Affairs also might allow a woman to evaluate how desirable she is on the mating market, although this information can usually be obtained through less costly means such as flirting or simply observing the number and desirability of the men who show signs of sexual or romantic interest.

Recent research yields promising support for the mate switching hypothesis. Heidi Greiling and I conducted four studies to explore this and other hypotheses about the benefits women gain from affairs.[43] In one study, we asked 58 women to evaluate the *likelihood* of receiving each of 28 potential benefits from affairs. The list ranged from "She would improve her skills of attraction and seduction" to "She would receive money, free dinners, or clothing." The top-rated item proved to be sexual gratification, possibly pointing to the centrality of orgasm in affairs. Many of the most highly rated benefits, however, centered on mate switching:

- Finding a partner more desirable than the current partner.
- Making it easier to break up with the current partner.
- Being able to replace the current partner.
- Discovering other potential partners who were interested in her.
- Clarifying the characteristics she believed to be important in a long-term marriage partner.
- Becoming better able to evaluate accurately what other potential partners thought about her.

In a second study, we asked 101 women to judge 47 circumstances on whether each would increase the likelihood of her becoming sexually involved with someone other than her current partner. These circumstances ranged from "Finding out that one's current partner is having an affair" to "Current partner cannot hold down a job." Again, women judged the mate switching circumstances to be highly likely to trigger an affair:

- Feeling that she could find someone with whom she would be more compatible than her current partner.
- Meeting someone who is willing to spend a lot of time with her.
- Meeting someone who is better looking than current partner who seems interested in her.

This last circumstance may also indirectly support the "good genes" hypothesis of affairs, given that physical attractiveness is partly heritable.

Heidi Greiling and I conducted a third study of women who had an active history of short-term mating to discover their perceptions of the benefits of affairs. Again, mate switching emerged prominently. Sexually experienced women judged "discovering other available partners through her affair partner" and "discovering other partners who were interested in her" to be huge benefits of affairs—sentiments not shared by their more monogamous peers.

Our fourth study revealed a hidden benefit of women's affairs—*a boost to women's self-esteem*. We asked 53 women to rate *how beneficial* each of 81 potential benefits would be if they were received from an affair partner. These benefits topped the list:

- Her affair partner made her feel better about herself than any partner had ever done.
- She felt good about herself because her partner respected her.
- Because the affair partner was interested in the details of her life, she felt good about herself when with him.
- Her affair partner made her feel important.
- Her affair partner made her feel intelligent.
- Her affair partner made her feel beautiful.
- Her affair partner made her feel sexy.

Why would these self-esteem benefits loom so large in women's affairs? Self-esteem is multifaceted and undoubtedly serves many functions.[44] One function may be linked to mate switching. Over the long course of a mateship that has grown stale with boredom, the sudden surge in self-esteem a woman draws from another sex partner is like a wonder drug. It tells her that she is desirable, intelligent, interesting, and sexy. It fills her with optimism that there are better partners out there. It gives her the confidence to jettison an existing mate. It gives her the power to risk leaving the security blanket of a current relationship and throw herself back into the mating market. Since men rarely tolerate wives discovered to be sharing beds with other men, an affair may provide the added incentive to extricate herself from the entanglements of marriage. Whether or not she ends up with her affair partner may be irrelevant. She now feels attractive and has the confidence to know that others will sense her desirability. The boost in self-esteem, in short, gives her the psychological self-assurance she needs to switch mates.

A final clue to the mate switching function of women's affairs comes from an investigation into the attachment styles of women who actually tend to have affairs. Attachment styles are ways people approach relationships—orientations that are presumed to be established in childhood as a consequence of the nature of one's relationship with the mother and other caregivers. Psychologists have identified three distinct attachment styles. Those with a *secure attachment style* find it easy to get close to others, trust that others will be there for them, find it easy to reciprocate by having others depend on them, and tend to form mature, anxiety-free romantic relationships. Those with an *avoidant attachment style* are uncomfortable with psychological closeness, find it hard to trust others, and avoid being dependent on them. They tend to push away those who try to get close to them. Those with an *anxious/ambivalent attachment style* have deep insecurity about whether or not others really love them. They want to get close to others and merge with a loved one, but feel that others are reluctant to get truly intimate with them. They feel that their desire for togetherness can scare someone away.

Which attachment style is more linked with having affairs? Secure attachment is unrelated to affair probability—secure women are neither more nor less likely to have an affair.[45] The other two styles, however, are definitely correlated with extra-pair sex. Avoidant women are *less* likely to have an affair; perhaps they avoid intimacy with their long-term mates and have no desire to seek it in others. Anxious/ambivalent women, however, are *more* likely to have affairs. It's as though the combination of an urgent thirst for intimacy, combined with a fear of abandonment from a primary mate, leads them into the arms of other men. If the perceptions of these women are accurate—perhaps based on past experience with being abandoned—then affairs may be a strategy to simultaneously avoid the pain of desertion while seeking with another man the psychological intimacy they so desperately need. Affairs for anxious/ambivalent women, in short, may serve a mate switching function.

We now have at least partial answers to why women have affairs. Clues to the functions of affairs are revealed by which women have them, the circumstances in which they have them, the benefits they are likely to receive, and the nature of the men who women chose to be affair partners. For women who stay with their primary partners, affairs are likely to serve a "good genes" function: obtaining investment from one man and superior DNA from another. For other women, affairs serve a mate switching function: They give women the boost in self-esteem they need to propel themselves out of one relationship in their quest for intimacy in another.

Do Women's Menstrual Cycles Influence Sexual Strategies?

A joke circulating around the psychological community runs as follows: "*A recent study showed that the kind of male face a woman finds attractive can differ depending on where a woman is in her menstrual cycle. For instance, if she is ovulating, she is attracted to men with rugged, masculine features. If she is about to menstruate, on the other hand, she is more prone to be attracted to a man with scissors shoved in his temple.*"

Women's menstrual cycles evoke fascination, but until recently few scientific studies had been conducted to explore their effects on mating strategies. The dearth of studies is largely due to two factors. First, the studies are difficult to do. They ideally require repeated measurements of women's cycles, which are hard to assess accurately without the proper technology. Second, the field lacked compelling theories that might predict which mating changes, if any, would be expected. Evolutionary psychologists, biologists, and anthropologists are now beginning to fill the gaps.

The first question on many people's minds is this: When do women most want sex? An answer is finally emerging. In one study, ovulation was determined by basal body temperature, which rises just prior to ovulation. Over twenty-four months, women recorded an "X" on a daily chart whenever they experienced sexual desire.[46] These X's were then plotted on a graph across the 28-day menstrual cycle. Women's sexual desire increased steadily as ovulation approached, rising to a sharp peak just before ovulation, which occurs on the 14th day of the cycle.

Desire then steadily marched downhill as women approached the infertile period of menstruation. Although women can and sometimes do desire sex throughout their ovulation cycle, and some studies indicate a slight increase in desire just before menstruation, the largest and most methodologically sound studies show a clear peak in sexual desire during the mid-follicular phase—just prior to ovulation when they are most likely to be fertile.[47] Although conventional wisdom in biology is that "ovulation is concealed or cryptic," ancient sexual yearnings seem to awaken in women precisely when they are most likely to conceive.

Exactly what these signals reveal has been the subject of a flurry of recent research. One study used a nationally marketed ovulation detector to measure the surge in luteinizing hormones that occurs just prior to ovulation (roughly 24 to 48 hours before) in a sample of 51 women.[48] The participating women completed questionnaires at two times—once during their most fertile follicular phase and once at their least fertile luteal phase. Among the questions were probes about sexual desires and sexual fantasies they had about men other than their current romantic partner:

- "Felt strong sexual attraction toward someone other than a curent partner."
- "Fantasized about sex with a stranger, acquaintance, or past partner."
- "Felt sexually aroused by the sight of someone very physically attractive [other than a primary current partner]."
- "Felt sexually aroused by the scent of someone [other than a primary current partner]."

The researchers also asked about attractions to, and fantasies about, their current partner. Women at the most fertile phase experienced more frequent fantasies about other men and felt the strongest sexual arousal in response to other men. Women's desires and fantasies for other men were at least 65 percent higher during their fertile phase. In contrast, women showed no differences across the cycle in sexual attraction to their primary partner. Women's sexual strategy of extra-pair sexual involvement, apparently, is intimately coupled with ovulation.

The Macho Male Hypothesis

If women with regular partners experience sexual attraction to other men just before ovulation, the next logical question is: What are the qualities of the men they are attracted to? Two psychologists from the United Kingdom have explored this question, using sophisticated computer technology to generate facial images.[49] They created digital photographs, which they subsequently manipulated to make more "masculine" or more "feminine." Women's jaws, for example, tend to be smaller than men's jaws, and men's brow ridges are more prominent than women's brow ridges. Photographs can be digitally altered to appear more masculine or more feminine by manipulating these features. A sample of 139 women then evaluated five photographs, varying in masculinity–femininity: 50 percent feminized, 30 percent feminized, 0 percent (neither feminized nor masculinized), 30 percent masculinized, and 50 percent masculinized. Women were instructed to choose *the one* they found the most attractive. The women were classified into two groups, a "high conception risk" group and a "low conception risk" group, based on their reports about the timing of their last menses (admittedly a less accurate procedure than basal body temperature or assays of luteinizing hormone). The results were astonishing. Women in the *least* fertile phase of their cycle were most attracted to the face that was slightly feminized. In sharp contrast, women in the *most* fertile phase of their cycle were drawn to the face that was 30 percent masculinized. Similar findings have been replicated among Japanese participants.[50]

Why would ovulating women prefer masculine faces? The theory behind this effect is that the masculinity of the face is a reliable physical marker of immunocompetence. Testosterone production, which is responsible for producing masculinized features, turns out to compromise the immune system. Only men who are extremely healthy can "afford" to crank out a lot of testosterone during the critical adolescent period of their development when their facial shape approaches mature adult form. Men who are less reproductively fit cannot withstand the assault of testosterone to their less robust systems, and so suppress the amount of testosterone their bodies produce during development. Only males in extremely good condition can bear the costs of producing above-average secondary sexual characteristics.

The end result is that somewhat masculinized faces signal heritable fitness—a healthy immune system that can be passed down to children. In essence, women's preference for masculinized faces at ovulation reveals a preference for "good genes" that are sometimes better secured from affair partners than from regular mates. Women judge the less masculine faces, preferred during their least fertile days of the month, as a signal of cooperativeness, honesty, and good parenting qualities. Women may find these "good guy" qualities most attractive in regular mates since they indicate the long-term provisioning of her and her children. So nice guys may indeed finish first—but only when their partners are not ovulating.

Evolutionary psychologist Victor Johnston and his colleagues have taken this work a step farther by developing a sophisticated experimental tool in the form of a 1200-frame Quick Time movie.[51] The computer program allows a person to search through a multidimensional space containing hundreds of faces that vary in masculinity, femininity, and other features. Participants use a slider control and single-frame buttons to move back and forth through the 1200-frame movie in order to locate the frame containing the desired target, such as the "most attractive for a short-term mate." In two different sessions Johnston tested 42 women between the ages of 18 and 35 who were not taking birth control pills—once during the fertile follicular phase and once during the less fertile post-ovulation phase. Ovulation was computed by counting backward 14 days from the onset of menses. Although women vary in the length of their menstrual cycle, most of the variation occurs between the onset of menses and ovulation. In contrast, ovulation almost always occurs 14 days before the next menses, regardless of length of the total cycle.

Johnston and his colleagues made three important discoveries. First, women overall, regardless of their menstrual phase, preferred faces in the more masculine direction over average faces. This result directly contradicts the UK study reported above, which found that women prefer slightly more feminine male faces when they are least likely to conceive. Further research is needed to clarify the discrepancies between the two studies. Second, when women were in the high-risk-of-conception phase, they preferred even more masculine faces than those they preferred during their low-risk phase—a finding that fully replicated both the UK and Japanese studies. In quantitative terms, the observed shift averaged 29 frames in the masculine direction, from frame number 299 to frame number 270. Third, women who scored low on a psychological test of "masculinity" showed an especially strong preference shift across their cycle—from frame 298 during the low-risk time to frame 245, a full 53-frame shift in the masculine direction. This group of low-masculine women also found the masculine-looking males to be especially desirable as short-term mating partners.

Johnston argues that masculine features are primarily a consequence of pubertal hormones. High levels of testosterone produce long, broad lower jaws, stronger brow ridges, and more pronounced cheekbones—hormone markers that signal good health. Indeed, when women were asked to choose the "healthiest" face, their choices were indistinguishable from their judgments of the "most attractive" face. In sum, women appear to be attracted to healthy immunocompetent men, especially when fertile and especially for short-term mating, as a means of securing good genes that can be passed down to their children.

The Scent of Symmetry

Anecdotal reports suggest that bad smell can be a sexual kill-switch, and empirical studies show that many women spontaneously report that scent is central to sexual desire.[52] The importance of chemical signals in human mating—the detection of odors, and possibly pheromones, through the olfactory mechanisms—has been championed recently by James Kohl, Karl Grammer, and others.[53] The term "pheromone" combines two Greek words: *hormon,* which means to stimulate or excite, and *pherein,* which means to carry. Pheromones are chemical messengers secreted by one person's body that produce physiological and behavioral changes in another person. Pheromones are secreted by the apocrine glands in the skin, as well as by the mouth, feet, and vagina. Although apocrine glands emerge in utero, they become functional only at puberty, pointing to their potential importance in human mating.

Women not only have a keener sense of smell than men, but their olfactory acuity peaks at or just prior to ovulation. Could this spike have an evolved function? Steve Gangestad and Randy Thornhill asked men who varied in physical symmetry to wear the same T-shirts during two nights without showering or using deodorants.[54] They instructed the men not to eat any spicy foods—no peppers, garlic, onions, and so on. After two days, they collected the T-shirts and then brought women into the lab to smell them. Women rated each T-shirt on how good or bad it smelled. They were not aware of the purpose of the study, nor did they know any of the men who had contributed T-shirts. The fascinating finding was that women judged the T-shirts worn by symmetrical men as more pleasant smelling (or for some women, less unpleasant), but only if they happened to be in the ovulation phase of their menstrual cycle. Ovulating women think symmetrical men smell sexy, or at least sexier than less symmetrical men. Future research is likely to reveal other important functions of body odor on human mating, although these effects may be muted in modern societies where people bathe daily and expunge their natural smells with deodorants.[55]

In the eighteenth century, the French philosopher Montesquieu wrote that "Man is the only animal who eats when he is not hungry, drinks when he is not thirsty, and makes love in all seasons." The general thrust of his remarks may be correct across the four seasons of the year, but women's cycles have subtle sexual rhythms over monthly seasons. Although women's ovulation is not accompanied by the genital swellings common among female chimpanzees in estrus, the cycle is far from silent in directing women's sexual strategies.

Can Men Detect When Women Ovulate?

If so many aspects of women's mating strategies are influenced by ovulation—sexual desire, sexual fantasies about other men, attraction to the scent of symmetrical men, and preferences for masculine faces—the intriguing next question is whether men can detect it. Conventional scientific wisdom says they can't. According to Donald Symons, "The most straightforward prediction I could have made, based on simple reproductive logic and the study of nonhuman animals, would have been that . . . men will be able to detect when women are ovulating and will find ovulating women most sexually attractive. Such adaptations have been looked for in the human male and have never been found." [56]

There are compelling adaptive reasons, however, why they should exist.[57] First, men who could detect when women ovulate could channel their seduction tactics and sexual overtures toward women at this time, thus maximizing their chances of successful fertilization and reproduction. Second, they could avoid the opportunity costs they would incur by curtailing expenditure of mating effort on women who are not ovulating. Third, men's tactics of mate guarding would be maximally beneficial when directed toward a mate who is ovulating. At no other time would lapses in vigilance prove more costly.

These adaptive benefits for men, if they could detect when women ovulate, would have been operative over the vast expanse of time in which humans evolved—an insight derived from a keen observation by evolutionist Margie Profet.[58] Consider these reasonable assumptions about the conditions of ancestral women, based on data from more traditional cultures. Women's reproductive span of fertility would have averaged roughly 26 years, from age 16 to 42. During many of those years, perhaps 92 percent of the time, a woman would have been either pregnant or lactating. Breast feeding and pregnancy suppress ovulation. Thus, the number of ovulatory episodes our ancestral mothers actually experienced may have been only a few dozen during their entire lives! The rarity of these monumental events would have amplified the intensity of selection pressure on men favoring ovulation-detection adaptations. Those men who missed these rare events bit the evolutionary dust.

Ovulation, in short, is a critical event in the temporal flow of a mating life. It is the point around which the precious few reproductive events can occur. There is no doubt that women's ovulation has become *relatively* cryptic; it's not the florid event that it is for our chimpanzee relatives. Women evolved adaptations to mute their signals of ovulation, either in the service of long-term mating or to facilitate the success of clandestine affairs, or both. On the other hand, it would defy reproductive logic if men stood evolutionarily still while signs of ovulation got driven underground. Co-evolution, in principle, would favor the evolution of adaptations in men to detect increasingly subtle signals. Or have women truly won this co-evolutionary arms race?

Several years ago, I predicted that conventional wisdom about the total inability of men to detect ovulation would be overturned.[59] The prediction stemmed partly from an analysis of the adaptive problems men would successfully solve by its detection, from sexual overtures to mate guarding. In part, the prediction stemmed from informal interviews with male colleagues. One man, for example, told me a story about going to a party one day and encountering a woman whom he had previously scarcely noticed. This day she seemed to be glowing, positively radiating sexuality. He couldn't take his eyes off of her. When he happened to see her a week later, his momentary attraction had receded. He wondered whether it was something in his mind, or something about her, that had caused this temporal shift. Although many women report bad and good hair days, I began to wonder whether some of the seemingly profound fluctuations in attractiveness might flow from the ovulation cycle.

Recent research has begun to explore these oscillations. In the most well controlled study to date, evolutionary psychologists Devendra Singh and Matt Bronstad had 17 women wear white cotton T-shirts at different phases of their menstrual cycle to obtain body odor.[60] Women secrete "copulins," or vaginal fatty acids that differ over the ovulatory cycle. Most copulins are produced at ovulation, and then steadily decline over the course of the luteal phase as women approach menstruation. Women also secrete odors from the apocrine sweat glands located in the skin, concentrated in places such as the areola of the breasts. Fifty-two men, who had no knowledge of the purpose of the study and did not know any of the women, rated each T-shirt on "pleasantness" and "sexiness." Men found the odors of the T-shirts from the follicular phase to smell the sexiest and most pleasant, giving them an average rating of 7.76, nearly seven points higher than the ratings given to the shirts from the luteal phase. Similar findings have been discovered among pair-bonded couples, when the body odors were collected from saliva, vagina, and underarms, as well as in studies of men who do not know the women who provided the sample odors.[61]

Other circumstantial evidence points to cues that men can potentially detect—signals known to be linked with sexual attraction. Women's skin color varies over the menstrual cycle, being lightest near ovulation.[62] The skin also becomes vascularized near ovulation, more suffused with blood in a way that corresponds to what men subjectively experience as a woman appearing to "glow." Women also become more symmetrical in soft tissue such as breasts and ears at ovulation.[63] Margie Profet has speculated that high levels of circulating estrogens may decrease women's waist-to-hip ratio. All these cues, from skin changes to symmetry to waist-to-hip ratio, are *potentially* observable and *known* to be sexually attractive to men. Given their relative subtlety, of course, they would be most visible to men with whom the women have daily contact—a circumstance that would have applied to many in the small group living conditions of our evolutionary past.

In addition to sights and scents, women change their behavior when ovulating. Evolutionary psychologist Karl Grammer stationed observers in singles bars to evaluate the tightness of their clothing to record how often women were touched by men.[64] A second member of the research team approached each woman as she left the bar, photographed her, and secured information on her point in the menstrual cycle. Grammer digitized the photographic images, and a computer program calculated the proportion of skin each woman revealed.

For non-pill-taking women, men in the singles bar initiated touching with ovulating women more than with non-ovulating women. Ovulating women also displayed more sexual signals than non-ovulating women, as evidenced by wearing tighter blouses and shorter skirts, and generally showing a greater amount of skin. So it may not be the case that men are so adept at discerning when women ovulate, but rather that ovulating women feel sexier and display more sexual signals designed to attract men. Another study supports this interpretation— women near ovulation *initiated* sexual encounters with their partners more than women at other phases of the cycle.[65]

A final clue to the enigma of ovulation comes from how intensely men guard their romantic partners.[66] Women near ovulation report that their partners ratchet up their levels of *proprietariness* (e.g., "Got angry if he saw me walking alone with another man"), *time monopolization* (e.g., "Spent as much free time with me as he could so I couldn't see other men"), and *spoiling* (e.g., "Tried to be as nice as he could to please me"). The most dramatic shift occurred for *vigilance*. When their partners were ovulating, men were more likely to call them unexpectedly to see who they were with, look through their personal belongings, and question them about what they were doing while they were apart. In short, men may devote considerably more effort to guarding their partners when they are ovulating.

Precisely why these links occur, however, cannot be determined with finality from this study. Since the reports of men's behavior came from the women themselves, it is possible that the women became more sensitive to their partner's mate guarding when they were ovulating, especially if they experienced attraction toward other men. Women might be more likely to notice and report men's mate guarding, rather than men being more likely to notice signals of women's ovulation and ratchet up their mate guarding. Alternatively, men might be picking up on signals of women's sexual flirtatiousness or restlessness, triggering increased mate guarding. Finally, it's possible that men perceive their partners as more attractive and desirable when they are ovulating than when they are not ovulating—circumstances already known to prompt more intense male mate guarding.[67] Future studies must tease apart this fascinating finding to determine whether it's due to men's perceptions of women's physical changes, their detection of women's behavioral changes, or whether the effect resides in women's increased sensitivity to men's mate guarding at ovulation.

The assumption of cryptic ovulation has been central to many evolutionary scenarios about what led to unique features of human mating—sex throughout the cycle, the formation of long-term pair-bonds, and the emergence of heavy male parental investment. And it is undoubtedly true that ovulation in humans is mostly concealed, at least compared with closely related primates such as chimpanzees. The recent evidence, however, calls into question the long-held view that ovulation is totally concealed. Women emit subtle visual and olfactory signals when ovulating. Men perceive these signals as sexy. Women experience greater sexual desire when ovulating and more sexual fantasies about men other than their regular partners. They wear tighter clothes, show more skin, and initiate more sex. And men ramp up their efforts to guard their partners precisely at this time. Given the monumental importance of ovulation for reproduction, and the relatively few episodes of ovulation that ancestral women would have experienced, it would be astonishing if women and men had failed to evolve specific mating strategies to grapple with the adaptive challenges posed by this critical event.

Mating research is now entering an "ovulation revolution." Future work is destined to discover other facets of mating strategies that are tethered to the menstrual cycle. Do women intentionally flirt with other men during this period, evoking jealousy and greater male–male intrasexual competition? Do men become more sexually insistent during this time? Do women who are having affairs become especially adept at deceiving their regular partners while ovulating to evade their increased vigilance? Are women who are unmated most likely to "put themselves on the mating market" when ovulating, since they will be able to attract the most desirable men at this time? Do men genuinely feel more love for their partners when they are ovulating? Do men experience more doubts about their relationships when their partners are not ovulating? Within the next decade, we will have answers to all of these intriguing questions.

12

Mysteries of Human Mating

THIS CHAPTER EXPLORES a medley of mating mysteries—those that continue to baffle scientists, those for which we now have clear answers, and those that are so disturbing that dispassionate scientific inquiry is nearly impossible. The first mystery is homosexuality, which seems on the surface to defy evolutionary logic. If evolution creates bodies built for reproduction, why would it equip some minds with desires that seem contrary to procreative purpose?

A second mystery is rape, a topic surrounded by controversy, politics, high emotions, and discouragingly few systematic studies. When *Desire* was first published, little scientific information existed on this abhorrent scourge of the mating world. New evidence and fresh arguments require us to revisit whether rape is an evolved sexual strategy of men, a functionless by-product of other adaptations, or a pathology of modern society. Of equal practical and theoretical importance is whether women have evolved *anti-rape* adaptations—strategies designed to prevent forced intercourse.

New scientific light also shines on other enigmas of mating: Are humans biased in reading the sexual minds of the opposite sex? Why do people "mate poach"? When do friends become rivals? And can men and women ever be "just friends"? Recent scientific studies offer substantive answers to these perplexing questions.

What About Homosexuality?

"Heterosexual orientation is a paradigmatic psychological adaptation," according to Michael Bailey, one of the world's renowned scientists who study sexual orientation. His reasoning is compelling. Among sexually reproducing species, males and females must mate with each other for successful reproduction. Any orientation that lowers the likelihood of successful reproduction will be ruthlessly weeded out. Although controversy surrounds estimates, most scientists converge on the finding that roughly 96 to 98 percent of all men and 98 to 99 percent of all women have a *primary* orientation toward heterosexuality, precisely the sort of canalization expected from a species-typical adaptation.

The persistence of a small percentage of primarily or exclusively lesbian women and homosexual men, however, poses a genuine evolutionary puzzle. In the several hundred public lectures I've given on human sexual strategies, the question "What about homosexuality?" is by far the most frequently asked. It's a mystery of human mating and an empirical enigma for evolutionary theory.[1] The riddle is made more intriguing by two known facts. First, a number of twin studies show that sexual orientation is moderately heritable, suggesting a partial genetic basis.[2] Second, a handful of other studies show beyond a reasonable doubt that homosexual men have a decisively lower rate of reproduction than heterosexual men.[3] How can a sexual orientation that is partly inherited continue to persist in the face of continual selection against it?

One early evolutionary explanation of homosexuality, initially advanced by E. O. Wilson, is the *kin altruism theory*.[4] According to this theory, genes for homosexual orientation can evolve and be maintained because, although homosexuals tend to have low direct reproductive output, they increase their reproductive fitness by investing heavily in their genetic relatives, such as their sister's or brother's children. This view has been elaborated by theorists who argue that male homosexuals are those with poor heterosexual mating prospects, and so the fitness costs of foregoing direct reproduction are not large. If you can't attract mates, the theory suggests, why not forget about heterosexual mating entirely and channel your resources to your relatives who are reproducing? The kin altruism theory of homosexuality has two pieces of indirect evidence going for it. First, gay males tend to be born later in birth order and often have older brothers, suggesting the presence of viable kin as potential foci of kin investment. Second, homosexual men, on average, tend to be more empathic and feminine than heterosexual men, inclinations that might be linked with greater altruism.

The kin altruism theory, however, encounters serious conceptual and empirical problems. To start with, the theory fails to explain why people would be sexually attracted to members of their own sex to begin with. If selection favors mechanisms designed to deliver benefits to genetic relatives, why build in potentially costly homosexual desires? Why not simply design a kin altruist to be asexual?[5] Second, it is not clear that being *generally* more empathic would translate into altruism *specifically* directed toward genetic relatives, a key prediction that requires confirmation for the theory to hold water. Third, even granting for the sake of argument the problematic premises of the theory, the amount of altruistic investment toward relatives would have to be unusually large to compensate for the loss of direct reproduction.

The hard hand of empirical data is the final arbiter of scientific theories, and psychiatrist David Bobrow and evolutionary psychologist Michael Bailey have conducted a critical test. Using samples of homosexual and heterosexual men matched for age, education, and ethnicity, they explored the patterns and magnitude of investment in kin. They assayed generosity toward family members, both financial and emotional; avuncular tendencies, such as the willingness to channel gifts, cash, and psychological support to nieces and nephews; and general feelings of closeness toward genetic relatives. The results proved conclusive—they found no evidence for the key prediction made by the kin altruism theory of homosexuality. Gay men did not differ at all from heterosexual men in their likelihood of funneling resources toward kin. Indeed, homosexual men reported being somewhat more estranged from their genetic relatives relative to heterosexual men, contrary to the kin altruism theory. Barring some radical new conceptual refinement or reversal of the empirical findings, the kin altruism theory of sexual orientation can be safely consigned to the scientific graveyard.

That still leaves us with the puzzle of the origins and persistence of homosexuality. Several new theories have recently been proposed to fill the gap. One is by evolutionary psychologist Frank Muscarella, who argues that we should focus on the functions of *homoerotic behavior,* same-sex sexual conduct involving pleasurable genital contact, rather than on homosexual orientation. Muscarella proposes a specific function for homoerotic behavior—alliance formation—a function also articulated by several evolutionary primatologists.[6] According to *alliance-formation theory*, homoerotic behavior evolved to strengthen same-sex bonds—relationships that historically were particularly valuable for adolescent males. By allying themselves with men higher in status, adolescent males could potentially gain access to resources, protect themselves from aggressive males, boost themselves up the status hierarchy, and ultimately gain greater sexual access to women. Proclivities for same-sex sexual behavior evolved, according to this theory, because of the alliance benefits they provided their practitioners.

The alliance-formation theory contains several virtues, such as a focus on the functions of actual homosexual behavior (sometimes ignored by theories of homosexual orientation) and an emphasis on a cross-species comparative framework (same-sex sexual contact is not limited to humans, but has been observed in non-human primates). The theory nonetheless encounters several conceptual and empirical problems. First, it would seem to predict that homosexual behavior would be *universal* across cultures and commonly practiced by a majority within each culture. Although it might explain practices in a minority of cultures, such as ancient Greece and certain New Guinean tribes, there is no evidence that the majority of young men in most cultures routinely gratify older men sexually. Second, if it's adaptive to form alliances, selection should favor individuals who form alliances in the least costly manner. Why not just form an alliance and cut out the costs of sex? Indeed, same-sex *non-sexual* alliances are quite common among humans as well as among non-human primates, suggesting that such alliances do not require sexual involvement.[7] Third, the alliance-formation theory does not explain why men or women would have an *exclusive* homosexual orientation—a far deeper evolutionary puzzle than homosexual activity that does not impede heterosexual reproduction. Finally, there is no evidence that men who engage in homosexual behavior actually gain the alliance benefits the theory posits, such as increased status or subsequent sexual access to women.

Another new theory has been proposed by economist Edward Miller—*the nice-guy theory* of homosexuality.[8] His point of departure is that neither homosexuality nor homoerotic behavior per se is an adaptation, contrary to the basic claims of prior theories. Rather, homosexuality is a relatively rare by-product of genes designed for another function—the production of "feminine" traits such as empathy, sensitivity, tender-mindedness, and kindness. According to Miller, the possession of these "good guy" traits makes men highly attractive to women because men with these qualities make better parents and better providers than those with more macho qualities. If many different genes contribute to nice-guy qualities, men will naturally vary in the number of such genes they possess. Most men will possess a moderate number, tempering their masculinity to an optimal mix of masculinity–femininity that is attractive to women. But some men, say two or three or four percent, happen to draw from the genetic lottery an unusually large number of these "feminine" traits, which tilt their brain circuits in the homosexual direction. Genes that have these effects can thrive evolutionarily, in principle, because most of the time they lead to greater reproduction when they inhabit the bodies of heterosexual men. The genes are favored because, on average, women found their developmental outcomes more attractive. Homosexual orientation, in short, is the occasional by-product of nice-guy genes that thrive in general because women favor them.

The nice-guy theory of homosexuality, unfortunately, also encounters conceptual and empirical difficulties. Conceptually, given the reproductive costs of homosexual preference, why wouldn't selection have favored modifier genes that allowed niceness to coexist with heterosexuality? The theory can only work if the only way for evolution to make men nice is to load them up with feminine genes. Is it really plausible that there are no nice heterosexuals? Empirically, although there is some evidence that gay men are slightly more empathic and sensitive, and less aggressive, on average, than heterosexual men, there is no evidence that women prefer to mate with men with these "feminine" traits rather than men with more "masculine" traits such as assertiveness and boldness.[9] The nice-guy theory, like many other theories of homosexual orientation, also fails to explain lesbianism.

Existing theories of homosexuality, in short, contain fundamental conceptual and empirical problems, so the explanatory search continues. There was initial excitement about the possible discovery of a so-called "gay gene" on the X chromosome at segment Xq28, but this finding has not been replicated in other studies.[10] Others have suggested that homosexuality might be a by-product of novel modern environments, produced by a discrepancy between the conditions in which humans evolved and unusual features of modern society. Although this possibility cannot be ruled out, no one has specified what those discrepant environmental circumstances might be. Furthermore, it's important to bear in mind that "the attraction to reproductive partners of a reproductively feasible sex seems so critical to evolutionary fitness that one would expect these attractions to be strongly buffered against social effects that could generate a preference for exclusive sexual relations with members of the same sex."[11]

Another recent theory may win the "controversial theory of the year" award—that male homosexual orientation might *not* have a primary genetic basis at all, but rather might be a side effect of infectious disease agents, which could be spread through sexual or non-sexual means.[12] The infectious agent theory has not been subjected to any empirical tests, and detailed predictions have yet to be outlined. The findings of moderate heritability of sexual orientation would seem to contradict a strong version of the infectious agent theory, since the theory invokes environmental rather than genetic means of transmission. Recent twin studies, however, have found only a 20 to 30 percent twin concordance rate for homosexuality—that is, lower heritability than previously suspected—which suggests that the infectious agent theory cannot be ruled out by the heritability findings. Similarly, the occurrence of early developmental crystallization of sexual orientation *prior to* the commencement of sexual activity would rule out the hypothesis of *sexual* transmission of the relevant infectious agent, although these findings would not eliminate the possibility of *non-sexual* means of transmission. Final evaluation of the infectious agent theory of male homosexuality must await more detailed predictions and corresponding empirical tests. Its authors correctly note that "The critical weaknesses of the alternative hypotheses [of homosexuality] draw attention to the need for rigorous testing of any hypothesis that has a sound theoretical basis, even if we find the hypothesis disturbing or disorienting."[13]

The next decade will undoubtedly witness greater scientific attention to the nature, origins, and consequences of homosexuality. Progress in solving the evolutionary mystery of homosexuality will be hastened by attending to the important point, articulated by theorists such as Mike Bailey, Frank Muscarella, and James Dabbs: *Homosexuality is not a singular phenomenon.* Lesbianism and male homosexuality, for example, have quite different natures and developmental trajectories. Male sexual orientation tends to be highly canalized and appears early in development, whereas female sexuality appears to be far more flexible over the life span. For example, male sexual orientation tends to be bimodally distributed—most men are either strongly heterosexual or strongly homosexual, with relatively few bisexuals in between. Women's sexual orientation, by contrast, varies more smoothly along a continuum from highly heterosexual through a series of bisexual gradations to a preference for same-sex partners.

Another difference is that women appear able to switch orientations more easily, evidence of greater flexibility of sexuality. Anecdotally, there is the "LUG phenomenon" found in women's colleges—Lesbian Until Graduation. The actress Anne Heche lived for several years in a lesbian relationship with comedienne and actress Ellen Degeneres. After they broke up, Anne Heche married a man, and recently had a child with him. Similarly, some women start out getting married, have children, and then in middle age switch to a lesbian lifestyle. Although some men "come out of the closet" after a socially prescribed marriage to someone to whom they are not sexually attracted, men's primary sexual orientation appears to be set relatively early in life and rarely changes from one sex to the other. Future theories of homosexuality would do well to respect the different natures of lesbianism and male homosexuality, and not try to make one theory fit both.

Future theories might also attend to the recent work conducted on large individual differences *within* those currently classified as "lesbian" and "gay." For example, mate preferences vary across lesbians who describe themselves as "butch" as opposed to "femme."[14] Butch lesbians tend to be more masculine, dominant, and assertive, whereas femme lesbians tend to be more sensitive, cheerful, and feminine. The differences are more than merely psychological. Butch lesbians, compared to their femme peers, have higher levels of circulating testosterone, more masculine waist-to-hip ratios, more permissive attitudes toward casual sex, and less desire to have children.[15] Femme lesbians place greater importance than butch lesbians on financial resources in a potential romantic partner and experience sexual jealousy over rivals who are more physically attractive. Butch lesbians place less value on financial resources when seeking partners, but experience greater jealousy over rival competitors who are more financially successful. The psychological, morphological, and hormonal correlates imply that "butch" and "femme" are not merely arbitrary labels, but rather reflect genuine individual differences.

Despite the recent theoretical and empirical attention to understanding and explaining homosexual orientation and same-sex sexual behavior, their origins remain scientific mysteries. Progress may accelerate with the realization of the possibility that there may be no single theory that can fully explain both gay males and lesbians, much less one that can explain the profound individual differences among those with a same-sex sexual orientation.

Are Men Really More Interested in Casual Sex?

A recent memo circulated via email on how to attract a mate:

How to impress a woman: Compliment her, cuddle her, kiss her, love her, stroke her, tease her, comfort her, protect her, hug her, hold her, spend money on her, wine and dine her, buy things for her, listen to her, care for her, stand by her, go to the ends of the earth for her.

How to impress a man: Show up naked, bring beer.

Although this joke wildly underestimates women's desire for sexual variety, and perhaps overestimates men's, it reveals a stark difference for which there is voluminous evidence. Even the late Steven J. Gould, a frequent critic of certain segments of the field of evolutionary psychology, conceded that men and women differ in their evolved sexual strategies on this dimension.[16] Nonetheless, a few continue to question whether the sexes really differ in their desire for a variety of sex partners, hence the need for a scientific update.

A recent study of unprecedented size surveyed 281,064 college students at 421 different colleges and universities on whether they agreed or disagreed with this statement: *"If two people really like each other, it's all right for them to have sex even if they've known each other for only a very short time."*[17] Large sex differences emerged—55.2 percent of the men, but only 31.7 percent of the women, strongly or somewhat agreed with this statement. Although this study reveals general attitudes toward casual sex rather than a personal willingness to engage in it, other research provides such evidence. In a detailed study of 200 students, evolutionary psychologist Michele Surbey concluded that men showed a greater "willingness to engage in sexual intercourse across all conditions compared with women."[18] In response to the question, *"Have you ever deliberately had sex without emotional involvement?"* another study showed that 73 percent of the men, but only 27 percent of the women, gave an affirmative response.[19] Other research found that men were significantly more likely than women to describe themselves, and to be described by others, as *unfaithful, polygamous, adulterous,* and *loose,* and less likely than women to be described as *faithful, monogamous,* and *devoted.*[20]

Evolutionary psychologist David Schmitt and his colleagues conducted four studies involving 1,458 individuals of varying ages to explore the specifics of the psychology of casual sex. As in all previous studies, Schmitt found that men, far more than women, express a desire for a larger number of lifetime sexual partners, let less time elapse before seeking sexual intercourse, and express a stronger motivation to seek casual sex partners. When women were asked to judge men and men to judge women on these same qualities, precisely the same sex differences emerged. Most women know full well that men are more likely than they are to yearn for casual sex, desire a larger number of partners, and let less time go by before initiating sexual encounters.[21]

In a massive study of unprecedented scope, David Schmitt surveyed 13,551 people from 10 major world regions, including 6 continents, 13 islands, 27 languages, and 52 nations. From the small island of Fiji to the large island of Taiwan, from the south of Tanzania to the north of Norway, in every single island, continent, and culture, men expressed a substantially greater desire than women for a variety of different sex partners.[22]

Evolutionary psychologist Martie Haselton found evidence for a possible adaptation in men to facilitate the success of a short-term mating strategy—an emotional shift right after sexual intercourse.[23] She found that men with more sex partners experienced a sharp decline in how sexually attractive they found their partner immediately following intercourse, whereas neither women nor men with less sexual experience showed this decline. If further work verifies the attraction-reduction effect, it may support the hypothesis that men have yet another psychological adaptation designed to promote the success of a casual sexual strategy—one that motivates either a hasty post-copulatory departure in order to minimize investment in any one woman or, alternatively, a roving eye within the context of an existing long-term mateship.

Women, of course, engage in short-term mating, but the motives that drive men and women into the arms of strangers differ. Psychologist Pamela Regan found that 44 percent of women, but only 9 percent of men, listed "to increase the probability of long-term commitment" as a motive for engaging in short-term sexual encounters. Here are three women's accounts, in their own words:

- "I was going through a very insecure period where I wanted to have a relationship. At the time I thought that a one-night stand would be the right way to at least start developing one."
- "The reason I engaged in a short-term sexual encounter is that I had hoped to have a long-term relationship with the man I was with."
- "Because when a guy wants to have sex with me, it makes me feel pretty. It makes me feel like he really likes me and cares about me . . . I hope that if I have sex with the guy right away then the relationship will last longer and he will stick around."

Men are more likely to mention pure sexual desire as the motivating reason for casual sex:

- "My reasoning at the time was purely physical. Having sex is enjoyable and I was attracted to this person."
- "All I wanted to do was to have sex with her. I didn't want anything else, a relationship or dating or anything, just the sex."
- "I think that the reason that I have engaged in short-term sexual encounters is because I can—to prove it to myself and to everyone else. . . . By having sex, I feel like I've accomplished a goal."[24]

Nor is it true that people who pursue casual sex are somehow maladjusted or psychologically pathological. Women and men who have experienced many different sexual partners are just as emotionally stable as those who have had only a few, one, or none.[25] Indeed, men who have had many sexual partners score higher on self-esteem than men with a history of fewer sex partners.[26]

An interesting new twist on the well-documented sex difference in the desire for a variety of sexual partners centers on what happens as men and women age. Psychologist Eugene Mathes studied three age samples of men and women—teens, twenties, and thirties.[27] Although men desired a larger number of sex partners than women within each of the three ages, the sex difference diminished with increasing age. The diminution was mostly due to changes in men. The older men in the study expressed a lower desire for sexual variety than the younger men in the study, whereas women's desires were more constant across the age groups. To the extent that conflicts between the sexes are due to men's persistent desire for casual sex (see Chapter 7), these results may be welcome news for the prospect of between-sex harmony over the life span.

On a final note, the controversy over the sex difference in men's and women's reports of how many sexual partners they have actually experienced appears to have been resolved. Historically, many self-report surveys have found that men report a greater number of sexual partners than women, which is mathematically impossible. Given an equal sex ratio in the mating pool, the average number of actual sex partners must be identical for the sexes. Scientists have advanced several hypotheses to explain the sex difference in reported numbers—perhaps men exaggerate, perhaps women underestimate, perhaps the sexes have different definitions of what counts as sex. Although these factors may contribute in small measure, the real reason turns out to be something simpler: Women who are prostitutes are underrepresented in sex surveys. Men, of course, are the primary customers of prostitutes (see Chapter 4). Prostitutes typically have sex with a large number of men—in one study an average of 694 per year. When the underrepresented professional sex workers are factored in, the apparent discrepancy between the sexes in reported number of partners disappears.[28] The fact that the *number of sex partners* must be mathematically identical for the sexes, of course, does not negate the existence of a profound sex difference in *sexual desire* for a variety of different partners.

Women and men alike have a menu of sexual strategies ranging from casual sex to lifelong monogamy and everything in between. Attempts to reduce the complexity of human mating to a singular strategy, such as long-term mating, reflect ideology or romanticism rather than empirical reality. Both sexes pursue short-term mating, and there are compelling adaptive reasons why this is part of the mating menu of both sexes. It is now as established as any psychological finding can be that men worldwide experience a greater desire for sexual variety, on average, than women. Some find that desire loathsome. Some wish that it did not exist, and so try to argue that it does not exist—what I have called "the anti-naturalistic fallacy" and what Steven Pinker has recently called "the moralistic fallacy."[29] Some bemoan the pain it inflicts on those who are pursuing long-term committed relationships. When it comes to the desire for casual sex, men and women may not come from entirely different planets. But it's foolhardy to think that they are sexually identical.

Can Women and Men Be "Just Friends"?

In the popular movie *When Harry Met Sally*, Sally, played by Meg Ryan, and Harry, played by Billy Crystal, have the following conversation:

Harry: You realize, of course, that we can never be friends.

Sally: Why not?

Harry: Men and women can't be friends because the sex part always gets in the way.

Sally: That's not true! I have a number of men friends and there is no sex involved.

Harry: No, you don't.

Sally: Yes, I do.

Harry: No, you don't.

Sally: Yes, I do!

Harry: You only think you do.

Sally: You're saying that I'm having sex with these men without my knowledge?

Harry: No. What I'm saying is that they all want to have sex with you. . . . Because no man can be friends with a woman that he finds attractive. He always wants to have sex with her.

Sally (smugly, thinking she has won the argument): So you're saying that a man can be friends with a woman he finds unattractive.

Harry (thinks it over): No, you pretty much want to nail them too.

A female colleague came into my office with tears streaming down her face. She had developed a friendship with a man on her coed softball team. Over the course of several months, they confided in each other, offered each other advice, and developed a warm, close relationship. One day, while sharing a beer after a game, she joyfully told her friend the good news—her boyfriend had proposed marriage, and she had accepted. Rather than expressing delight for her, the friend grew sullen and distant. The next day he emailed her and told her that he did not wish to be friends with her. He was distraught that she was planning to marry. How could she have led him on like that? Surely, she must have known about the depth of his feelings for her? My colleague asked me how this could have happened. She had thought that they were such good friends. She had never concealed the fact that she had a boyfriend. Her friend quit the team shortly thereafter. To this day, he has refused to have any contact with her.

Until recently, the psychology of opposite-sex friendship has remained unexplored. Evolutionary psychologist April Bleske has taken the lead to fill this gap.[30] Bleske defines an opposite-sex friend as a close and important member of the opposite sex who is *not* a romantic partner. She explored what people perceive to be the *benefits* of opposite-sex friendships, the perceived frequency of receiving these benefits, the *costs* of these friendships, and the *frequency* with which people incur these costs. Bleske also requested information on perceptions about the *reasons for initiating* the friendship, how much *sexual attraction* existed between the friends, and whether or not any *sexual interactions* had taken place.

In a case of science imitating art, fascinating sex differences emerged precisely along the lines of the argument between Billy Crystal and Meg Ryan in *When Harry Met Sally*. Men evaluated the potential for sexual access to their opposite-sex friends as 100 percent more beneficial than did women. Men were nearly twice as sexually attracted as women to their opposite-sex friends. Men also expressed almost twice as strong a desire to have sex with their opposite-sex friends than women. Interestingly, when Bleske separated her sample into those who were single and those who were already in committed romantic relationships, the sex differences remained exactly the same. Already mated men felt just as sexually attracted to, and desired to have sex with, their female friends as single men—and both desires were twice as strong as those expressed by women. Single or mated, unattached or committed—it doesn't seem to matter to men when it comes to sexual desire for their female friends.

An even more surprising finding occurred when Dr. Bleske asked participants *how sexually attracted their opposite-sex friends were to them*. Women slightly underestimated how attracted their friends were to them. Whereas men's sexual attraction to their female friends came in at 5.3 on a 7-point scale, women's perceptions of how attracted their male friends were to them came in at 4.7. Men's perceptions of how attracted their opposite-sex friends were to them, however, proved to be more off base. Men viewed their female friends as moderately sexually attracted to them, averaging 4.7; but in fact, women expressed only a 3.6 level of attraction to their male friends. In other words, men erroneously see their female friends as moderately sexually attracted to them, despite the fact that, for many of these women, sex was not even on the radar screen. Finally, men were 62 percent more likely than women to cite "because of a lack of sex" as a reason for breaking up an opposite-sex friendship and 65 percent more likely to cite "because of a loss of attraction." Bleske's studies confirmed the experience of my female colleague—men are more likely to end a friendship when it becomes clear that sex is not part of the picture.

So can men and women be "just friends"? Both Meg Ryan and Billy Crystal were perhaps correct from their own sexes' point of view. Women like to have male friends—they offer companionship, sharing, protection in times of need, information about the opposite sex, and even a boost to their self-esteem. Men too gain much from their female friends, including companionship, information, and sometimes even contacts with potential mates. But many men and only some women harbor sexual desires for their opposite-sex friends. Sometimes these desires are consummated—20 percent report having had sex with an opposite-sex friend. But "friends with privileges," "friends with benefits," or, as they sometimes say in New York, "kissing friends" are in the minority. Most women do not reciprocate their male friend's sexual yearnings, despite the fact that men sometimes delude themselves that their female friends do. When misperceptions surface, as happened with my colleague, they can lead to an unpleasant end for men and women who start out as "just friends." For others, opposite-sex friends sometimes turn into lifelong lovers, as eventually happened in the movie *When Harry Met Sally*.

Friends as Rivals

Many nearest and dearest friends, of course, are of the same sex. Same-sex friends occupy a unique position in the constellation of our social lives. They can offer a bounty of benefits—protection in times of need, valuable information, connections to people with prestige, advice in times of trouble. As noted in Ecclesiastes 6:

For some man is a friend for his own occasion, and will not abide in the day of thy trouble. . . . If thou be brought low, he will be against thee, and will hide from thy face. . . . A faithful friend is a strong defense: and he that hath found such a one hath found himself a treasure. Nothing doth countervail a faithful friend.

Friends can also hurt you in ways no enemy can. Friends have special knowledge of our strengths and vulnerabilities. They are familiar with our habits—when we are at work, when we are out of town, when we are sick, when we are weak. They typically know our mates and know when our mating bonds become weakened by inner turmoil or bumpy patches. Because friends, like mates, are often similar to each other in desirability, values, and interests, they simultaneously share both similarity to, and proximity with, our mates. Similarity and propinquity are fundamental laws of mating, twin forces that often draw our friends and mates together. Friends are positioned better than anyone else to become sexual Trojan Horses—under the guise of friendship they can unleash a hidden agenda of mate poaching.

Evolutionary psychologists April Bleske and Todd Shackelford have pioneered the exploration of mate poaching, promiscuity, and deceit in same-sex friendships.[31] They asked 169 men and women to record memorable instances in which they had deceived a friend or been deceived by a friend, simultaneously supplying the motive for deception. By far the most frequent memories involved mating-related deception—lies of commission or omission about mate poaching, mate rivalry, and a mate's sexual infidelity. Here are a few examples:

- "I did not tell my friend that I had sex with his partner."
- "My friend did not tell me that she had sex with my ex-boyfriend."
- "I did not tell my friend that the woman he liked actually liked me."
- "My friend did not tell me that my wife had cheated on me."

The severity of the problem of friend deception dictates that people choose their friends wisely. Women seem especially aware of same-sex sexual deception, reporting greater distress than men when friends show signs of sexual availability. Women judge sexually free women to be so undesirable because they realize that available women can pose a great threat to their committed relationships. Given the attraction many men harbor for sexual opportunities, available women can lure a man into a casual fling, wreaking havoc with long-term love. These relationship dynamics set a co-evolutionary arms race in motion. Some women deceive their female friends on precisely this dimension—they intentionally lowball the amount of sexual experience they have had in order to avoid seeming like a sexual threat.

True friends enrich life. Without them, existence would probably seem empty. But friends are in a position to betray. And when a friend deceives you and poaches your mate, you experience the double cost of deception—you risk losing a friend and a romantic partner with a single stroke.

The Specter of Mate Poaching

Desirable mates are always in short supply. Glamorous, interesting, attractive, socially skilled people are heavily courted and rapidly removed from the mating pool. Those who succeed in attracting the "9's" and "10's" tend to hold on, escalating the effort they allocate to mate guarding.[32] Transitions between relationships are brief for the beautiful. In modern monogamous societies, for those left on the sidelines of the dance, mate shortages get more severe with each passing year. In traditional polygynous societies, where most desirable women marry shortly after puberty, single men suffer the most. How can a person find a desirable mate when all these factors conspire to take the attractive out of the mating market?

One un-pretty solution to this recurrent quandary is mate poaching. Although many regard efforts to lure someone out of an existing mateship as loathsome, it has a long recorded history.[33] One of the earliest written records of mate poaching is a biblical account of King David and Bathsheba. One day King David happened to spy the beautiful Bathsheba, wife of Uriah, bathing on the roof of a neighboring house. David's passion for her consumed him. He succeeded in seducing her, and consequently Bathsheba became pregnant. King David set out to destroy Uriah by sending him to the battle front and commanding his troops to retreat, exposing him to mortal danger. After Uriah was killed, King David married Bathsheba. Although their first child died, their union proved fruitful, and they went on to produce four children.

David Schmitt and I discovered that 60 percent of men and 53 percent of women admitted to having attempted to lure someone else's mate into a committed relationship. Although more than half of these attempts failed, nearly half succeeded. Similarity between the sexes in long-term poaching attempts contrasted with efforts designed for brief sexual encounters—60 percent of the men, but only 38 percent of the women, reporting attempting to lure someone else's mate into a casual sexual encounter. Far higher percentages of both sexes said that others had attempted to entice them to leave an existing relationship—93 percent of the men and 82 percent of the women for long-term love, and 87 percent of the men and 94 percent of the women for a brief sexual encounter. Somewhat smaller percentages report someone attempting to poach their mate, suggesting that poaching ploys are often initiated away from the prying eyes of the unsuspecting "victim." Roughly a third of the sample—35 percent of the men and 30 percent of the women—reported that a partner had been *successfully* taken away from them by a mate poacher. Mate poaching, in short, is clearly a common mating strategy. Although many attempts fail, nearly a third appear to succeed. David Schmitt has replicated these basic findings in a massive cross-cultural study involving more than 30 nations.[34] Mate poaching has probably been successful often enough to have evolved as a distinct sexual strategy.

People poach for many of the same reasons that they want to mate to begin with—to find emotional intimacy, experience passionate sex, secure protection, gain resources, enhance social status, fall in love, or have children. But mate poachers perceive additional benefits unique to the context of mate poaching. One is *gaining revenge against a rival* by stealing the rival's mate. Vengeance as an evolved motive could only have evolved, of course, if it served an adaptive function, such as inflicting a cost on a rival that lowered the rival's relative reproductive success or deterring other potential rivals from inflicting costs. Another benefit is *securing access to a pre-approved mate,* one who has already established credibility by passing another's screening criteria. Although enticing a mate who is already "taken" can provide these benefits, it sometimes comes with a price tag. Mate poachers risk violence—injury or even death—at the hands of the jealous partner. Poachers also incur damage to their social reputation if branded as a deceiver. They may be shunned when word of their deceit gets around, impairing their ability to attract other potential mates. Furthermore, even if the mate poacher is successful, it might be potentially costly to have a mate who is revealed to be potentially poachable, thus requiring more expensive mate guarding.

Schmitt and I found that many of the tactics used to attract mates in other contexts are also effective for the purpose of poaching—enhancing appearance, displaying resources, showing kindness, presenting a sense of humor, revealing empathy, and so on. Two tactics, however, are specially tailored to enticing mates from others. The first is *temporal invasion,* acts such as changing one's schedule in order to be around the target more than the target's current partner, or dropping by when the current partner is off at work or out of town.

The second is *driving a wedge*—insinuating oneself into the existing mateship and actively promoting a breakup. One way to drive a wedge is to boost the target's self-esteem, conveying messages that enhance their self-perceptions of their own desirability. At the same time, the poacher might communicate that the target is not appreciated by their regular partner: "He doesn't treat you well" or "You deserve better" or "You're too good for him." The simultaneous boost in self-esteem combined with the contrast of feeling underappreciated is sometimes enough to succeed in widening a small crack in a relationship. Through this double-pronged strategy, the mate poacher frees up an already taken mate, and sits waiting in the wings when it happens.

Defending Against Sexual Treachery— Jealousy and Mate Guarding

Sexual treachery pervades human mating. Both sexes experience sexual fantasies about other partners. Women fantasize about strangers more when ovulating. They seek affairs with men more desirable than their regular partners. If they have sexual liaisons, women are more likely to experience sexual orgasm with their affair partners. Friends sometimes become sexual rivals. Mate poachers hover and pounce, disrupting previously harmonious mateships. Given all this deceit and duplicity, it would defy evolutionary logic if selection had not sculpted powerful defenses to guard against them.

Genetic cuckoldry looms as an ever-present threat to men. Internal fertilization guarantees that women are certain that their children are genetically their own. The phrase "Mama's baby, papa's maybe" captures this sexual asymmetry. Since a sexual infidelity historically jeopardized a man's paternity, men's jealousy should focus heavily on signals of *sexual* betrayal, a topic explored in Chapter 6. Infidelities by men, in contrast, pose an equally dangerous reproductive risk for women—the loss of the man's time, attention, energy, parenting, investment, and commitment. Women's jealousy, as a consequence, should focus heavily on signals of these kinds of losses, such as a partner becoming *emotionally* involved with another woman. Sexual and emotional infidelity in a partner, of course, are correlated in nature.[35] People tend to become emotionally involved with those with whom they have sex. And people often become sexually involved with those they are emotionally close to. But not always. Sex can occur without emotional involvement, as in a one-night stand or a spring break fling. People can get emotionally involved without any sex, as occurs in at least some opposite-sex friendships. Both forms of infidelity, of course, are extremely upsetting to both sexes, and both can signal the dramatic loss of reproductively valuable resources.[36]

When forced to choose which form of infidelity is more upsetting, however, large sex differences emerge consistently. Men are more likely than women to become distressed by sexual infidelity; women are more likely than men to become distressed by emotional infidelity (see Chapter 6). These fundamental sex differences have now been replicated by many different scientists in many diverse cultures— China (David Geary), Sweden (Michael Wiederman), the Netherlands (Bram Buunk and Pieternel Dijkstra), Germany (Alois Angeitner and Victor Oubaid), Japan (Mariko Hasegawa and Toshikazu Hasegawa), and Korea (Jae Choe).[37]

Sex differences in the design of the jealousy defense also have been revealed in other facets of the mating game using a panoply of scientific methods. Todd Shackelford and his colleagues, for example, found that men more than women report that they would be more likely to *terminate* a relationship over a sexual infidelity; women are more likely than men to *forgive* a one-time sexual transgression.[38] Actual divorce statistics reported in Chapter 8 verify this sex difference. Robert Pietrzak of Clark University recently found the fundamental sex differences in jealousy using four different measures of physiological distress. When imagining an emotional infidelity, for example, women's skin conductance, heart rate, electromyographic activity, and body temperature all shoot up—physiological events that are highly correlated with the subjective reports of actual distress.[39] Men show greater physiological distress when imagining a partner trying out different sexual positions with a rival.

The evolutionary origins of these sex differences, of course, have been challenged, and alternative hypotheses to account for them have been proposed. There have been two lines of argument marshaled against the evolutionary explanation. One line attempts to dismiss the sex differences entirely by arguing that they are artifacts of one particular method.[40] The weight of the scientific evidence, however, shows that the sex differences are quite robust across diverse methods ranging from forced choice formats to physiological recordings to spontaneously reported jealousy-inducing events.[41] A second line of argument attempts to provide an alternative explanation by proposing that sex differences in jealousy exist, but they are attributable to the "beliefs" men and women hold about the likelihood of one type of infidelity given that the other has occurred.[42] Systematic empirical tests of this alternative explanation by diverse groups of investigators, however, have consistently failed to support it.[43] In one study, for example, researchers asked 234 participants to imagine that their worst nightmare had occurred—their partner had become both sexually *and* emotionally involved with someone else. They then asked participants to state *which aspect* of the betrayal they found more upsetting. Sixty-three percent of the men, but only 13 percent of the women, found *the sexual aspect* of the infidelity to be more upsetting. In contrast, 87 percent of the women found *the emotional aspect* of the infidelity to be more upsetting. These sex differences have now been found in Korea and Japan.

In summary, the evolutionary hypothesis of sex-linked design differences in the jealousy defense mechanism has withstood a number of empirical tests. It parsimoniously accounts for a constellation of findings that no other theory can. It accounts for sex differences in distress responses to the original infidelity dilemmas. It accounts for the component of the betrayal that is more upsetting when both have occurred. It explains why these sex differences occur both psychologically and physiologically. It explains why the sex differences are found across a wide variety of cultures, including those that are sexually liberal, such as Sweden and the Netherlands, as well as those that are more sexually conservative, such as China and Korea. And it explains why sexual infidelity by a woman is more likely to lead to breakups, violence, and divorce than a sexual infidelity by a man.

Defenses against threats of infidelity, of course, do not end with the emotional response we call jealousy. Evolutionary psychologists have discovered many other design features that characterize this critical defense against betrayal. One such design feature centers on *which rivals* are perceived to be the most threatening. Dutch, Korean, and American people ranked eleven rival qualities according to which would be most upsetting.[44] The rival characteristics ranged from "having a better sense of humor than you" to "being a more skilled sexual partner than you." Men in all three cultures, more than women, reported that they would experience greater distress when a rival surpassed them on the dimensions of *financial prospects, job prospects,* and *physical strength.* Women in all three cultures, more than men, reported greater distress when a rival had *a more attractive face* or *a more desirable body.*

A study of 107 newlywed married couples explored predictors of the intensity of effort a person allocated to mate guarding.[45] Men married to young and physically attractive women mate guarded most intensely. They were more likely than other men to conceal their mates, display emotional outbursts at the slightest signals of infidelity, and threaten other men with violence. Examples of the specific actions these men performed include:

- Refusing to take her to the party where other men were present.
- Insisting that she spend all her free time with him.
- Yelling at her for talking to another man.
- Telling her that he would die if she ever left him.
- Derogating another man's intelligence.
- Staring coldly at the other guy who was looking at her.

Just as a woman's youth and physical attractiveness figure heavily in men's initial mate preferences, they also determine the intensity of effort men devote to holding on.

Women's mate guarding, in contrast, was not at all determined by their husbands' physical appearance or his age. Rather, it was affected by husband's income and how determined he was to climb the status hierarchy. Women married to men with abundant resources and status were more likely than other women to ramp up their level of vigilance, express emotional distress at the slightest hint of a partner's wandering eye, put extra effort into enhancing their appearance, and show more submissiveness in the service of holding on to their partner. Specific acts by these mate-guarding women include:

- Staying close by his side when they were at the party.
- Threatening to break up if he ever cheated on her.
- Making herself "extra attractive" to maintain his interest.
- Telling him that she would change to please him.
- Asking him to wear a ring to signify that he was taken.

Just as women's desire for men who have status and resources influences initial mate selection, these same qualities continue to influence the effort women devote to keeping the men they have attracted.

The defense we call jealousy is an evolved solution for the problem of the successful maintenance of a relationship because of the ever-present possibility of sexual betrayal or emotional defection. In a hazardous world where rivals lurk in the guise of friends, partners harbor passions for other people, and infidelity threatens to destroy what would have been lifelong love, it is not surprising that evolution has forged elaborate strategies to detect and fend off these threats. But there may be an even darker threat to women and their partners, a threat so abhorrent that even broaching the topic raises everyone's emotional temperature—the threat of rape.

Do Men Have Adaptations to Rape?

It was her first fraternity party. The beer flowed freely and she had much more to drink than she had planned. It was hot and crowded and the party spread out all over the house, so that when three men asked her to go upstairs, she went with them. They took her into a bedroom, locked the door and began to undress her. Groggy with alcohol, her feeble protests were ignored as the three men raped her. When they finished, they put her in the hallway, naked, locking her clothes in the bedroom. (Small eastern liberal arts college)[46]

A thousand miles away, a woman in the Amazonian jungle bordering Brazil and Venezuela experienced a similar fate:

The tug-of-war went on for ten minutes or so while I watched, my blood rising as instinct told me to put a stop to it. The boys would drag Roobemi [an Amazonian Indian woman] a few yards, then the old ladies would get a better purchase and drag her back as she struggled to keep her balance, her head tossing this way and that. . . . "Sister-in-law, what are they doing to her?" I asked. "Oh," she said, smiling at me, "they're taking her out into the forest." "What for?" "They're going to rape her," came the answer. . . . With a concerted heave, the teenagers pulled her free. . . . Howling in victory, they ran down the trail, yanking her along. . . . This kind of thing went on. If a woman left her village and showed up somewhere unattached, chances were she'd be raped. She knew it, they knew it. It was expected.[47]

Rapes occur in all cultures. "All Mehinaku women live in fear of rape," according to anthropologist Thomas Gregor, who lived among Brazilian Amazonian Indian groups.[48] Among the Yanomamö of Venezuela, according to Kenneth Good, whose own Yanomama wife was raped, "I know there isn't a Yanomama woman who hasn't been raped."[49] On the distant island of Samoa, once touted by Margaret Mead as a utopian paradise, rape rates are between two and five times as high as those within the United States: "Rape is greatly feared by Samoan girls, and is viewed with deadly seriousness by the family of any girl actually assaulted."[50] Although rape rates vary tremendously by culture—extremely low in Norway, for example, and relatively high in the United States—there are no known cultures where rape is entirely absent.

Nor is rape absent among non-human primates. Among orangutans, primatologists have long observed individual differences among males.

While some males develop from adolescence into mature adult size and form (198 pounds on average), other males remain in a state commonly called "arrested development." These males remain small for many years and they do not act like the large adult males. They do not hold territory, make loud noises, or get into fights with the mature males. The original interpretation by primatologists was that these arrested males remain in this state of immaturity because of environmental stress to avoid competing with the higher-ranking adult males.

Researchers have made three discoveries that overturned this view.[51] First, the levels of stress hormones turned out not to be higher in arrested development males. Second, although physically immature in many respects, such as lacking full beards and a large sac at the throat to facilitate loud vocalizations, arrested development males have fully functioning sperm and testes. They are neither stressed nor reproductively immature. Third, although arrested males avoid direct competition with the full-sized adult males and keep a low profile when in their presence, they often stalk females, sometimes for days, and forcibly copulate with them. Primatologists infer rape from the fact that the females do everything in their power to avoid these copulations. They flee, emit loud guttural sounds, and attempt to bite the males, behaviors they do not perform when copulating with a mature adult male. In field work conducted in Borneo, anthropologist John Mitani observed a total of 151 copulations by arrested males; 144 were forced. In contrast, copulations involving mature adult males were rarely forced. It's important to emphasize that orangutans may be unique among primates. What looks like a distinct orangutan rape strategy that is frequently implemented by one subgroup of males has *not* been observed among other primates closer to humans, such as bonobos or common chimpanzees. Nonetheless, the orangutan findings point to the *possibility* that rape can evolve in some species under some conditions.

Controversy about this possibility erupted in the year 2000 when biologist Randy Thornhill and anthropologist Craig Palmer published a book called *A Natural History of Rape: Biological Bases of Sexual Coercion*.[52] Although evolutionary theories of human rape had been published for two decades preceding its publication (see Chapter 7), their book proved to be a flash point. The authors outlined two competing theories of rape, one endorsed by each author. Randy Thornhill proposed the theory that men have *evolved rape adaptations*—specialized psychological mechanisms for forcing sex on unwilling women as a reproductive strategy. Craig Palmer proposed instead that *rape is a byproduct* of other evolved mechanisms, such as the male desire for sexual variety, a desire for low-cost consensual sex, a psychological sensitivity to sexual opportunities, and the general capacity of men to use physical aggression to achieve a wide variety of goals.

The *rape-as-adaptation* theory proposes six specialized adaptations that may have evolved in the male mind:

- Assessment of the vulnerability of potential rape victims (e.g., during warfare, or in non-warfare contexts where a woman lacks the protection of husband or kin).
- A context-sensitive "switch" that motivates rape in men who lack sexual access to consenting partners (e.g., "loser" males who cannot obtain mates through regular channels of courtship).
- A preference for maximally fertile rape victims, as contrasted with a preference in marriage contexts for more reproductively valuable, but perhaps less immediately fertile, partners (see Chapter 3).
- An increase in sperm counts of rape ejaculates compared with those occurring in consensual sex.
- Sexual arousal in men specifically to the use of force or to signs of female resistance to consensual sex.
- Context-specific marital rape in circumstances where sperm competition might exist (e.g., when there is evidence or suspicion of female infidelity).

Unfortunately, evidence bearing on these hypothesized adaptations is either absent or ambiguous. Rape is common in war, clearly a context where women are often vulnerable, but so is theft, looting, and property damage. Are there specialized adaptations for all these behaviors, or are they instead by-products of other psychological mechanisms or merely the output of more general cost–benefit evaluation mechanisms? Decisive studies have not yet been conducted.

Convicted rapists come disproportionately from lower socioeconomic groups, supporting what's been termed the "mate deprivation hypothesis." But this finding could be caused by lower report rates when the rape occurs by men from higher social groups, or from the greater ability of privileged men to evade arrest and conviction because of expensive attorneys. Or perhaps women raped by high-status men might be less likely to press charges, given the lower odds of being believed and obtaining justice.

There is also direct evidence *against* the mate deprivation hypothesis of rape. In a study of 156 heterosexual men, average age of 20, evolutionary psychologist Martin Lalumiere and his colleagues measured the use of sexual coercion with items such as: "Have you ever had sexual intercourse with a woman even though she didn't really want to because you used some degree of physical force?"[53] Separately, they measured mating success. Men who scored high on mating success *also* scored high on sexual aggression. Men who have had a lot of sexual partners were *more* likely to report using force. Furthermore, men who evaluated their future earning potential as high reported using more, not less, physical coercion in their mating tactics. Although additional studies are needed, we can tentatively conclude that a simple version of the mate deprivation theory of rape is false.

These results, however, do not rule out a more complex hypothesis—perhaps men have evolved two kinds of context-specific rape adaptations, one contingent on when they experience mating failure and one when the costs are so low that they can get away with it, as might occur among the upper socio-economic stratum of society.[54] There is no current evidence to suggest that this is the case, nor is there evidence against it.

Rape victims tend to be disproportionately concentrated among young, reproductive-age women. Most studies show peak victim rates for women in their 20's, and typically 70 percent or more of the victims fall between age 16 and 35.[55] That rapists disproportionately victimize young fertile women, however, is not decisive evidence for or against any theory of rape—this finding can be attributed to men's evolved preference for cues to fertile women in regular mating contexts rather than a rape-specific adaptation (see Chapter 7). Critics of the rape-adaptation hypothesis also point out that many non-fertile women also get raped. A few studies find that nearly a third of all rape victims are girls younger than 11 or post-reproductive women older than 45, and these are difficult to reconcile with rape-adaptation theory.

One source of evidence that many scientists believe to be relevant to theories of rape is the pregnancy rate that follows from rape. If rape evolved as a reproductive strategy, it must historically have resulted in reproduction some of the time. Modern rape-pregnancy rates, of course, are not necessarily relevant to whether rape resulted in pregnancy in the past; routine modern contraceptive devices may reduce current rape-pregnancy rates below those that occurred in ancestral times. Thus, it is all the more startling that a recent study discovered that pregnancy rates resulting *from penile–vaginal rape among reproductive-age women* are extraordinarily high—6.42 percent—compared to a consensual per-incident rate of only 3.1 percent.[56] This finding can be partially explained by selection bias in the victims whom rapists target—young fertile women. Nonetheless, even controlling for age, the authors find a rape-pregnancy rate that is roughly 2 percent higher than the consensual-sex pregnancy rate. This counterintuitive finding, *if it turns out to be replicable,* cries out for some kind of explanation.

Jonathan and Tiffani Gottschall offer a hypothesis anchored in the premise that men who court women using normal mating strategies are "at the mercy of discriminating females," whereas rapists are not. Rapists, although constrained by opportunity and the defense mechanisms of women, nonetheless can and do choose victims who would otherwise refuse to mate with them. Thus, rapists might choose women who, in addition to being young, are especially physically attractive. Since attractive women are more fecund (see Chapter 3), this may partially explain the unusually high rape-pregnancy rate.

The rape-pregnancy findings, however, do not directly support the rape-as-adaptation hypothesis. We already know that men are attracted to features that correlate with fertility (e.g., cues to youth and health) in consensual mating contexts, and so no specialized rape adaptation is required to explain these results (see Chapter 7). The rape-pregnancy findings do, however, contradict the "argument from inconceivable conception," according to which some opponents of the rape-adaptation hypothesis have claimed that rape cannot have evolved because it so rarely leads to conception.[57]

Finally, there is some evidence that marital rapes are more likely when the husband is concerned about a potential sexual infidelity, as well as during or immediately following a breakup.[58] This finding suggests the possibility of rape as a sperm competition adaptation. Nonetheless, the direction of causality is unclear—perhaps women are more likely to break up with partners who tend to force them into unwanted sex. In short, a conclusion reached by Donald Symons more than two decades ago appears to be apt today: "I do not believe that available data are even close to sufficient to warrant the conclusion that rape itself is a facultative adaptation in the human male."[59]

Absence of evidence, however, is not evidence of absence. The fact that investigations into the causes of rape are so ideologically charged has thwarted thorough research into this abhorrent phenomenon. The Thornhill–Palmer book has been castigated, denounced, and ridiculed more than any other book in the recent history of science. Although the book contains flaws, best articulated by two balanced reviews, one by Massimo Pigliucci and one by the evolutionary legal scholar Owen Jones,[60] its authors should be commended for showing the scientific bravery to advance competing theories of rape, and to assemble the available evidence bearing on them. It is unfortunate that many have rushed to condemn the authors for advancing the theoretical *possibility* that men have evolved rape adaptations. The denunciation has had the unintended effect of shutting down careful scientific studies that might be conducted to determine the actual causes of rape, preventing the acquisition of the knowledge base needed to deal with this pervasive problem.

My speculation is that scientific progress will advance when theorists distinguish different types of rape, rather than viewing sexual coercion as a singular entity. Consider date rape, stranger rape, warfare rape, rape by husbands, homosexual rape, and rape of stepdaughters by stepfathers. The causes of one type of rape may differ substantially from the causes of others. Date rape, for example, may be partly a by-product of the modern conditions of living, where young women live in social circumstances often devoid of the close protection of extended kin—a known deterrent to violence against women. Serial stranger rapists often manage to avoid detection owing to the unusual modern conditions of geographic mobility and anonymous urban living. The limited geographical mobility and small group living of our ancestors would have rendered certain kinds of stranger rape virtually impossible. Rape in the context of warfare, in contrast, appears to have a cross-cultural prevalence and historical depth that may have favored selection for rape. Some kinds of rape may be caused by pathology or dysfunction of evolved mechanisms; others may be by-products; still others may be caused by specific rape adaptations. Lumping all instances of forced sex under a single label "rape" may impede progress in discovering the unique underlying causal conditions that lead to each distinct type of crime.

Have Women Evolved Anti-Rape Defenses?

> I have never been free of the fear of rape. From a very early age, I, like most women, have thought of rape as part of my natural environment—something to be feared and prayed against like fire or lightning. I never asked why men raped; I simply thought it one of the many mysteries of human nature. (Susan Griffin)[61]

Although the rape controversy has focused primarily on what motivates men to force sex on women, almost lost in the furor is theoretical attention to the psychology of rape victims. There is one point about victim psychology, however, on which all sides of the debate agree: *Rape is an abhorrent atrocity that typically inflicts heavy costs on victims.* We need no formal theory to arrive at this insight. Nonetheless, it is important to determine *why* rape is experienced as extraordinarily traumatic.

From an evolutionary perspective, the costs of rape begin with the fact that it circumvents female choice, a core component of women's sexual strategy. A raped woman risks untimely pregnancy with a man she has not chosen—a man who imposes himself against her will, a man who is unlikely to invest in her children, a man who may have genes inferior to those she would otherwise have chosen. A raped woman risks being blamed, punished, or abandoned by her regular mate, who may suspect that it was consensual or that she somehow brought it on herself. The costs of being raped are dramatically illustrated in a recent case in Pakistan:

> Zafran Bibi, a 26-year-old devout Muslim residing in Pakistan, was sentenced to death by stoning. Her crime was adultery, punishable by death according to Islamic law. The evidence: A child born more than a year after her husband had abandoned her, but had not yet divorced her. This was no ordinary adultery. Zafran Bibi had been raped by her brother-in-law, she testified. That did not matter. The birth of the illegitimate child proved adultery, according to the judge. Her accusation that her brother-in-law had raped her was tantamount to a criminal confession.[62]

Raped women suffer psychologically. They experience fear, humiliation, embarrassment, anxiety, depression, rage, and fury. They feel guilty, used, violated, and polluted. Women view forced sex as more upsetting to them than any of at least 147 other things that a man can do to hurt a woman, more upsetting even than savage non-sexual beatings at the hands of a man.[63] Raped women also suffer in the aftermath. Some victims fear leaving their houses, avoid contact with men, isolate themselves socially, and live in a psychological prison with no apparent reprieve.

On top of the psychological torment, raped women suffer socially. As the case of Zafran Bibi illustrates, victims are sometimes held responsible for the crime perpetrated on them. They experience damage to their reputations. They suffer a loss in perceived desirability on the mating market. Their kin may reject or ostracize them for bringing shame on their family. They sometimes become socially shunned. Whatever the causes of rape, no one except the clueless and callused doubts the appalling damage it inflicts on the victim.

Given these often catastrophic costs, *if* rape has occurred throughout human history, it would defy evolutionary logic if selection had not fashioned defenses in women to prevent its occurrence. This is a separate issue from that of whether men have evolved adaptations to rape. Women could have evolved anti-rape adaptations, in principle, even if

rape has been entirely a by-product of non-rape mechanisms. We lack
a videotape of the past, and so can never determine with absolute certainty whether rape was frequent enough to have forged a female anti-
rape psychology. But we can assemble available historical and
cross-cultural evidence to make some educated guesses. Written history dating back to the Bible brims with episodes of rape, and even
specifications by religious leaders about the conditions under which
men can take women by force. For example, the Sages of the Talmud,
codified by Maimonides, provide this injunction:

> A soldier in the invading army may, if overpowered by passion, cohabit with
> a captive woman . . . [but] he is forbidden to cohabit a second time before
> he marries her. . . . Coition with her is permitted only at the time when she
> is taken captive . . . he must not force her in the open field of battle . . . that
> is, he shall take her to a private place and cohabit with her.[64]

Although no systematic studies have been conducted on the occurrence and frequency of rape among traditional societies across cultures,
an informal review of published ethnographies reveals that rape is reported in many. Indeed, the cross-cultural evidence is replete with
cases of rape, from the Amazonian jungle of Brazil to the more peaceful
!Kung San of Botswana. The Semai of central Malaysia were frequently
victimized by Malay raiders, who would ambush them, kill the men, and
take the women by force.[65] The Amazonian peoples studied by Thomas
Gregor have special words for both rape, *antapai,* and gang rape,
aintyawakakinapai. Rapes in war occurred as far back as there are written records, as amply documented by Susan Brownmiller in her classic
treatise *Against Our Will.* Genghis Khan, more than 800 years ago,
talked with relish about the gratification received through rape:

> The greatest pleasure is to vanquish your enemies, to chase them before
> you, to rob them of their wealth, to see their near and dear bathed in
> tears, to ride their horses and sleep on the white bellies of their wives and
> daughters (Genghis Khan, 1167–1227)[66]

Evolutionary anthropologist Barbara Smuts summarizes the cross-
cultural evidence in this way: "Although the prevalence of male violence against women varies from place to place, cross cultural surveys
indicate that societies in which men rarely attack or rape women are
the exception, not the norm."[67]

Evolutionary scientists such as Tara Chavanne, Gordon Gallup, Patricia Gowaty, Sarah Mesnick, Craig Palmer, Sandra Petralia, Barbara

Smuts, Nancy Thornhill, Randy Thornhill, and Margo Wilson have been at the forefront in articulating potential evolved defenses against rape. Hypothesized anti-rape adaptations include:

- Psychological pain upon rape that motivates avoiding rape in the future.
- Formation of alliances with other males as "special friends" for protection.
- Formation of female–female coalitions for protection.
- Specialized fears that motivate women to avoid situations in which they might be in danger of rape.
- The shunning of risky activities during ovulation to decrease the odds of sexual assault when they are most likely to conceive.

The first clue to the possibility that women have evolved adaptations to prevent being raped comes from two studies that analyzed the distribution of rapes across the female menstrual cycle. In one study of 785 rape victims, proportionately fewer women were raped during mid-cycle, defined as days 10–22 (an unfortunately wide and hence imprecise interval).[68] Another study found that ovulating women were less often victims of sexual assault.[69] To explore these patterns, Tara Chavanne and Gordon Gallup studied risk-taking among 300 undergraduate women.[70] Women indicated whether they had engaged in each of 18 activities that varied in their risk in making someone vulnerable to sexual assault. Going to church and watching television were examples of low-risk activities. Going to a bar and walking in a dimly lit area were examples of high-risk activities.

For women taking birth control pills, Chavanne and Gallup found no effect of sexual cycle on risk-taking. Among women not taking the pill, however, ovulating women showed a decrease in risk-taking activities. The authors argue that risk-avoidance is a candidate for an anti-rape adaptation, and are able to successfully rule out several alternative explanations for the reduction in risk-taking. For example, this reduction in risk-taking is not a reflection of a reduction in sexual receptivity at ovulation; in fact, women usually peak in sexual receptivity at mid-cycle when with consensual partners. The mid-cycle risk-avoidance also cannot be attributed to a decrease in women's general activity level, since pedometer-recorded activity level in women tends to increase during ovulation.[71] In short, ovulating women appear to avoid behaviors that put them at increased risk of rape, suggesting the possibility of *specialized risk-avoidance* as an anti-rape adaptation.

Many women *routinely* engage in risk-avoidance maneuvers to avoid putting themselves in harm's way.[72] In one study of urban women, 41 percent reported "isolation tactics," such as not going out on the street at night, and 71 percent reported using "street-savvy tactics," such as wearing shoes that enable running away should they be attacked. Another study in Seattle found that 67 percent of the women avoided certain dangerous locations of the city, 42 percent reported not going out unaccompanied, and 27 percent sometimes refused to answer their door. A study of Greek women reported that 71 percent avoided venturing out alone at night, and 78 percent shunned dangerous locations within the city. Women also show wariness around men who talk about sex a lot, men who are sexually aggressive, and men who have a reputation for sleeping with a lot of women. Women report choosing public places for dates with men they don't know well. They intentionally avoid giving mixed sexual signals to certain men. They sometimes carry mace, whistles, or weapons. And they sometimes limit their drinking around men they don't know well.[73]

These risk-avoidance strategies may be learned prudence measures, much like installing a burglar alarm after reading about a rash of burglaries in the neighborhood. Alternatively, risk-avoidance may be motivated, in part, by a *specialized fear of rape*—a second potential anti-rape adaptation that induces women to avoid contexts conducive to sexual assault. Evidence for this specialized fear comes from a strong positive correlation between women's reports of rape-fear and their reports of how many different behavioral precautions they take to avoid rape.[74] Women who are fearful of rape, more than women who experience less fear, avoid being alone with men they don't know well, decline rides from men, leave when a man comes on too strong sexually, avoid outdoor activities when alone, and exercise caution in their drinking. One New Zealand study found that young women experience more fear of sexual assault than older women; older women's fears were more likely to center on being robbed or burgled than on being raped.[75] Women residing in neighborhoods where there was a high incidence of rape report more fear than those living in safer neighborhoods. These studies, of course, cannot determine whether women have evolved a specialized fear of rape contingent on their age and vulnerability, or whether these fears are expressions of more general mechanisms such as a rational appraisal of danger combined with fear mechanisms possessed by all people.

Psychologists Susan Hickman and Charlene Muehlenhard found that women were more fearful of being raped by strangers than by acquaintances. This difference occurred despite the fact that stranger-rape is rare, accounting for only 10–20 percent of all rapes, compared with acquaintance-rape, which is far more common, roughly 80–90 percent.[76] Hickman and Muehlenhard conclude that women's fears do not match the realities of rape. An alternative interpretation is that women's apprehensions are actually effective: Stranger fear motivates precautionary behaviors, lowering the real incidence of stranger rape below what it would have been without these functional fears. According to this view, women's stranger-fears are functional in preventing rape.

Sarah Mesnick and Margo Wilson have explored a third potential anti-rape adaptation, which they call the *bodyguard hypothesis*. According to this hypothesis, women form heterosexual pair-bonds with men in part for the purpose of reducing their risk of sexual aggression from other men.[77] According to the bodyguard hypothesis, women should be especially attracted to physically large and socially dominant men in contexts in which they are at risk of sexual aggression. To test the bodyguard hypothesis, Wilson and Mesnick studied 12,252 women, each interviewed over the phone by trained female interviewers. Questions about sexual assault began with: *"Has a male stranger ever forced you or attempted to force you into any sexual activity by threatening you, holding you down or hurting you in some way?"* Subsequent questions dealt with unwanted sexual touching: *"*[Apart from this incident you have just told me about], *has a male stranger ever touched you against your will in any sexual way, such as unwanted touching, grabbing, kissing, or fondling?"*[78] The statistical analyses focused on sexual victimizations that occurred within the 12 months prior to the interview, and excluded sexual assaults by husbands or boyfriends.

A total of 410 unmarried and 258 married women reported experiencing one or more of these sexual violations. Marital status proved to have a dramatic effect on sexual victimization. Among women in the youngest age bracket of 18–24, 18 out of 100 unmarried women reported sexual victimization by a stranger, whereas only 7 out of every 100 married women reported sexual victimization. Messick and Wilson conclude that their results support the bodyguard hypothesis, although they acknowledge that they have not identified the causal mechanism by which married women are less likely to be raped than comparably aged single women. The lower rape rates among married than single women might reflect lifestyle differences—single women might spend more time in public places rather than at home, making them more vulnerable to predatory rapists. It might reflect individual differences in mating strategies, whereby single women might be more likely to pursue short-term matings that place them in contexts where they are exposed to greater danger of sexual coercion. Or it might reflect the deterrent effects of husbands on potential rapists, as the bodyguard hypothesis suggests. The bodyguard hypothesis requires more direct tests: Are women especially likely to choose large, physically imposing men when living in social circumstances that indicate a relatively higher risk of rape? Are women with such men less likely to be raped?

A fourth hypothesized anti-rape adaptation is *specialized psychological pain*, recently articulated in the Thornhill–Palmer book. According to this hypothesis, the psychological trauma women experience from rape motivates them to avoid similar recurrences in the future. Evidence for this hypothesis comes from a study that purports to show that the women who experience the most intense pain and psychological trauma are (a) young and fertile women rather than pre-pubescent or post-menopausal, (b) married rather than single, and (c) vaginally raped rather than orally or anally raped. Furthermore, (d) women who experience the most visible signs of physical violence during rape experience the least psychological pain, presumably because they would be less likely to be blamed or suspected of complicity in the rape. An advocate of the psychological pain hypothesis might have added an additional prediction—(e) that women raped by men low in mate value (e.g., unattractive, low socio-economic status) will experience more psychological trauma than women raped by men higher in mate value (e.g., more attractive, higher in status).

Biologist Jerry Coyne, a vocal critic of the Thornhill–Palmer book, argues that the evidence for the pain hypothesis is considerably weaker than its authors suggest.[79] Coyne correctly questions the problematic methodology—for example, the girls under the age of 12 were helped in answering questions about pain and trauma by their caretakers, which makes their responses not strictly comparable to women who reported their psychological states directly. Furthermore, no significant differences were found between reproductive-aged and post-reproductive-aged women, contradicting the specialized pain hypothesis.

Regardless of these points of theoretical and empirical contention, one thing is startlingly clear—good evidence is lacking on the specifics of women's defenses against rape. Research is urgently needed on women's anti-rape strategies and their relative effectiveness, whether or not such strategies ultimately turn out to be specialized evolved adaptations or products of more general cognitive and emotional mechanisms.

Cognitive Biases in Sexual Mind Reading

Humans live in an uncertain social world. We must make inferences about others' intentions and emotional states. How attracted is he to her? How committed is she to him? Does that smile signal sexual interest or mere friendliness? Some states, such as smoldering passions for other people, are intentionally concealed, rendering uncertainty greater and inferences more tortuous. We are forced to make inferences about intentions and concealed deeds using a chaos of cues that are only probabilistically related to the deeds' occurrence. An unexplained scent on one's romantic partner, for example, could signal betrayal or an innocuous olfactory acquisition from a casual conversation.

In reading the minds of others, there are two ways to go wrong. You can infer a psychological state that is not there, such as assuming sexual interest when it is absent. Or you can fail to infer a psychological state that is there, such as remaining oblivious to another's true romantic yearnings. According to a new approach pioneered by evolutionary psychologist Martie Haselton, called Error Management Theory, it would be exceedingly unlikely that the cost–benefit consequences of the two types of errors would be identical across their many occurrences.[80] We intuitively understand this in the context of smoke alarms, which are typically set to be hypersensitive to any hint of smoke. The costs of the occasional false alarm are trivial compared with the catastrophic costs of failing to detect a real house fire. Error Management Theory extends this logic to cost–benefit consequences in evolutionary fitness, and in particular to reading the mating minds of the opposite sex.

According to Error Management Theory, asymmetries in the cost–benefit consequences of mind-reading inferences, if they recur over evolutionary time, created selection pressures that produced predictable *cognitive biases*. Just as smoke alarms are "biased" to produce more false positives than false negatives, Error Management Theory predicts that evolved mind-reading mechanisms will be biased to produce more of one type of inferential error than another. Martie Haselton and I have explored two potential mind-reading biases. The first is the *sexual over-perception bias*, whereby men possess mind-reading biases designed to minimize the costs of missed sexual opportunities. The theory provides a cogent explanation for why men appear to falsely infer that a woman is sexually interested in him when she merely smiles, touches his arm, or happens to stop at the local bar for a drink (see Chapter 4).

The second is the *commitment skepticism bias* in women. According to this hypothesis, women have evolved an inferential bias designed to underestimate men's actual level of romantic commitment to her early in courtship. This bias functions to minimize the costs of being sexually deceived by men who feign commitment in order to pursue a strategy of casual sex. If men give flowers or gifts to women, for example, the recipients tend to *underestimate* the extent to which these offerings signal commitment compared with "objective" outside observers. Of course, there are good reasons for women's commitment skepticism. Men motivated to seek casual sex frequently attempt to deceive women about their commitment, social status, and even fondness for children—domains of deception about which women are well aware.[81]

A third bias is linked to sexual jealousy—false inferences about a partner's infidelity.[82] Men and women sometimes harbor false suspicions that a partner is unfaithful when he or she is in fact the paragon of loyalty. The bias gets activated in contexts that historically have been linked to infidelity—when a partner is sexually dissatisfied, after a sudden decline in sex drive, or with an increasing gap in the mate value of the two partners.

Error Management Theory offers a fresh perspective on human mating problems by suggesting that certain types of errors reflect functional adaptations rather than actual flaws in the psychological machinery. It provides new insights into why men and women get into certain types of conflict—for example, men's sexual over-perception bias leading to unwanted sexual come-ons. Knowledge of these biases and the evolutionary logic by which they came about may help men and women to read each other's mating minds more accurately.

Miscellaneous Mysteries

A number of other mysteries of human mating remain. Do humans have adaptations to *sperm competition*? One research project has failed to find evidence of the "Kamikaze sperm" hypothesized to destroy the sperm of other males (see Chapter 4).[83] On the other hand, other research has verified at a psychological level hypothesized sperm competition adaptations. Todd Shackelford, for example, found that as the time spent apart from their mates increased, hence opening a window of opportunity for rival males to copulate with their wives, men found their partners more sexually attractive and experienced a greater desire to have sex with them immediately.[84] This effect occurred as a function of time spent apart, even when time since last copulation was controlled statistically. Given the known non-trivial incidence of women's sexual affairs, we can anticipate more research attention to possible sperm competition adaptations, both physiological and psychological.

Mating is not solely influenced by desires; aversions also play a role. Although this book focuses primarily on the evolution of desire, there is a prime case of the lack of desire—*incest-avoidance* produced by the absence of attraction to genetic relatives. The first to document this was the sociologist Edward Westermarck, in his classic 1891 treatise *The History of Human Marriage*.[85] Since then, the sexual aversion to genetic relatives has been dubbed the Westermarck Effect. Two selective forces may have led to this near-universal aversion—the costs of inbreeding and the advantages of outbreeding. Inbreeding produces children who possess pairs of deleterious recessive genes, yielding depressed levels of intelligence and increased incidence of congenital abnormalities. Outbreeding, by producing more genetically variable offspring, may help to combat parasites and pathogens.[86]

Voluminous evidence supports the hypothesis that people are not merely *not* sexually attracted to close genetic relatives, but experience sexual aversions to them, and even emotional disgust if forced to imagine having sex with them.[87] Studies conducted in China, Israel, and North America find conclusively that growing up in close proximity with someone usually inhibits sexual attraction to that person. Recent research by evolutionary psychologists Irene Bevc and Irwin Silverman has found that the sexual aversion experienced between siblings who have grown up together centers especially on genital intercourse—precisely the event that would lead to the costs of inbreeding and missing the benefits of outbreeding.[88] Future research will likely center on identifying the precise mechanisms by which incest-avoidance operates, such as olfactory imprinting or kinship recognition devices, as well as the potentially disastrous genetic and psychological consequences that have been linked with violations of the incest taboo.[89]

Another mystery centers on the psychology of mate value. Considerable evidence now suggests that men and women higher in overall desirability are more discriminating and impose higher standards in their mate selection preferences than those lower in desirability.[90] Evolutionary psychologist Norman Li has developed an ingenious "budget allocation" method whereby he can vary the number of "mating dollars" each person has; in other words, he varies (albeit artificially) their level of desirability.[91] When mating budgets are tight, that is, when one's level of desirability is relatively low, people tend to go for what Li calls the "necessities" of mating. For women, intelligence, financial resources, work ethic, and sense of humor top the list of necessities. For men, physical attractiveness is a necessity. When budgets get larger, that is, when one's mate value increases, more "luxuries" of mating come into play. After certain levels of the necessities are reached in intelligence, attractiveness, and resources, people spend their "surplus" mating dollars on obtaining mates who are especially creative or who have interesting personalities.

We now know the relatively obvious implications of individual differences in market value. The "8's" and the "10's" can be more exacting and are better able to pursue the sexual strategies they prefer. The "4's" and the "6's" have plenty of potential mates available, but they must settle for less. Future work will focus on the more subtle implications of mate value: Does a woman's mate value vary predictably as a function of her ovulation cycle, peaking near ovulation and dipping thereafter? Do women show more *monthly variability* in mate value than do men, corresponding to intuitions about good and bad hair days, since women are in fact more reproductively valuable when ovulating than when not ovulating? Over longer time periods, do men show more dramatic oscillations in mate value, corresponding to spectacular public successes and catastrophic falls in social status? Within mating relationships, how do these daily, monthly, and longer-term fluctuations affect the relative balance of power, feelings of love, and sexual fantasies about others? These questions cry out for exploration, and undoubtedly will be answered within the next decade.

The Centrality of Mating in Social Life

Evolution by selection has sculpted mating mechanisms that are complex, elaborate, and sometimes mysterious. The quest for successful mating is central to many human endeavors, from the formation of friendships to the derogation of competitors, from the pursuit of prestige to the motivation for murder. The evolution of language lies behind verbal signals used in attraction, humor, courtship, and sexual gossip. Large game hunting and the physical and psychological evolution it required enabled greater provisioning in courtship. War evolved in part in the quest for mates and the resources needed to attract and retain them. Even the motivation for creative cultural displays may have evolved in the service of signaling fitness to potential mates.[92] Our anatomy, physiology, psychology, and cultural traditions have been finely honed by the mating successes and failures of our hominid ancestors.

No social relationship remains untouched by mating. Men misread women's smiles in the service of sexual exploitation. Women remain skeptical of men's commitment signals to avoid sexual victimization. Fathers guard their daughters to influence mate choice, and daughters manipulate their fathers to mate with the men they love. Both sexes deploy deceptive signals. Men and women experience great difficulty being "just friends." Same-sex allies sometimes turn into Trojan horses. Mate poachers lurk behind smiling faces. Sometimes, thankfully, we find lifelong love. As individuals, mating permeates much of what we do. As a species, it defines who we are.

Notes

CHAPTER 1: ORIGINS OF MATING BEHAVIOR

1. Jankowiak and Fisher 1992.
2. Beach and Tesser 1988; Sternberg 1988.
3. Darwin 1859, 1871.
4. Major proponents of evolutionary psychology include Cosmides and Tooby (1987), Daly and Wilson (1988), Pinker (1994), Thornhill and Thornhill (1990a), Symons (1979), and Buss (1989a, 1991a).
5. Rozin 1976.
6. Collias and Collias 1970.
7. Le Boeuf 1974.
8. Vandenberg 1972.
9. Smuts 1987; Lindburg 1971; Seyfarth 1976.
10. Thornhill and Alcock 1983.
11. Daly, Wilson, and Weghorst 1982; Symons 1979; Buss, Larsen, Westen, and Semmelroth 1992.
12. Erickson and Zenone 1976.
13. Betzig 1989.
14. Thornhill 1980a.
15. Buss and Schmitt 1993.
16. Symons 1987.
17. Low 1989.
18. Guttentag and Secord 1983; Kim Hill, personal communication, 1991.
19. Daly and Wilson 1988.
20. Chagnon 1988.

CHAPTER 2: WHAT WOMEN WANT

1. Trivers 1972; Williams 1975.

2. Trivers 1985.
3. Trivers 1972.
4. Yosef 1991.
5. Draper and Harpending 1982; Belsky, Steinberg, and Draper 1991.
6. Smuts, in press.
7. Hudson and Henze 1969; McGinnis 1958; Hill 1945.
8. Buss 1989a.
9. Kenrick, Sadalla, Groth, and Trost 1990.
10. Wiederman, in press.
11. Buss 1989a.
12. Betzig 1986; Brown, and Chai-yun n.d.
13. Betzig 1986.
14. Hill 1945; Langhorne and Secord 1955; McGinnis 1958; Hudson and Henze 1969; Buss and Barnes 1986.
15. Langhorne and Secord 1955.
16. Buss 1989a.
17. Buss 1989a.
18. Jencks 1979.
19. Hart and Pilling 1960.
20. Kim Hill, personal communication, May 17, 1991; Don Symons, personal communication, July 10, 1990.
21. McCrae and Costa 1990; Gough 1980.
22. Jankowiak, Hill, and Donovan 1992.
23. Martin Whyte, personal communication, 1990.
24. Townsend 1989; Townsend and Levy 1990; Wiederman and Allgeier 1992; Buss 1989a.
25. Buss 1989a; Willerman 1979; Kyle-Heku and Buss, unpublished; Jencks 1979.
26. Langhorne and Secord 1955.
27. Buss and Schmitt 1993; Betzig 1989.
28. Buss 1991b.
29. Jencks 1979.
30. Herrnstein 1989; Brown 1991; Brown and Chai-yun, n.d.
31. Barkow 1989.
32. Hill, Rubin, and Peplau 1976.
33. Buss 1984, 1985, n.d.
34. Buss 1987b; Buss et al. 1990.
35. Buss and Barnes 1986; Kenrick, Groth, Trost, and Sadalla 1993; Thibeau and Kelley 1986.
36. Trivers 1985.
37. Buss and Schmitt 1993.
38. Jackson 1992.
39. Brown and Chai-yun n.d.
40. Ellis 1992, 279–281.
41. Gregor 1985, 35, 96.
42. Buss et al. 1990.

43. Ford and Beach 1951.
44. Hamilton and Zuk 1982.
45. Farrell 1986, 50.
46. Jankowiak and Fisher 1992; Sprecher, Aron, Hatfield, Cortese, Potapova, and Levitskaya 1992.
47. Buss 1988c.
48. Sprecher et al. 1992.
49. Thiessen, Young, and Burroughs, in press.
50. Harrison and Saeed 1977.
51. Wiederman, in press.
52. Buss 1991b.
53. Buss 1991b.
54. Buss and Barnes 1986.
55. Secord 1982; Ardener, Ardener, and Warmington 1960.
56. Wiederman and Allgeier 1992; Townsend 1989.
57. Buss 1989a.

CHAPTER 3: MEN WANT SOMETHING ELSE

1. Hill and Hurtado, in press.
2. Symons 1979, 271.
3. Symons 1979; Williams 1975.
4. Hill 1945; McGinnis 1958; Hudson and Henze 1969; Buss 1989a.
5. Symons 1989, 34–35.
6. Hart and Pilling 1960; see also Buss 1989a.
7. Kenrick and Keefe 1992.
8. Guttentag and Secord 1983; Low 1991.
9. Buss 1989a.
10. Hart and Pilling 1960.
11. Orions and Heerwagen 1992; Symons 1979.
12. Ford and Beach 1951.
13. Malinowski 1929, 244.
14. Jackson 1992.
15. Berscheid and Walster 1974; Langlois, Roggman, Casey, Ritter, Rieser-Danner, and Jenkins 1987.
16. Langlois, Roggman, and Reiser-Danner 1990; Cross and Cross 1971.
17. Cunningham, Roberts, Richards, and Wu 1989.
18. Thakerar and Iwawaki 1979; Morse, Reis, Gruzen, and Wolff 1974; Cross and Cross 1971; Jackson 1992.
19. Langlois and Roggman 1990.
20. Gangestad and Thornhill, in press.
21. Ford and Beach 1951.
22. Rosenblatt 1974.
23. Symons 1979.
24. Rozin and Fallon 1988.

25. Singh, 1993, in press a, b.
26. Langhorne and Secord 1955.
27. Hill 1945; McGinnis 1958; Hudson and Henze 1969; Buss 1985, 1989a; Buss and Barnes 1986.
28. Buss 1987a.
29. Buss, in preparation a.
30. Low 1979.
31. Buss 1987a.
32. Buss, in preparation b.
33. Symons 1979.
34. Posner 1992.
35. Wilson 1975, 1978.
36. Ruse 1988.
37. Jankowiak, Hill, and Donovan 1992.
38. Deaux and Hanna 1984.
39. Tripp 1975; Hoffman 1977; Symons 1979, 295.
40. Blumstein and Schwartz 1983.
41. Voland and Engel 1990; Borgerhoff Mulder 1988; Røskraft, Wara, and Viken 1992.
42. Betzig 1992.
43. Elder 1969; Taylor and Glenn 1976; Udry and Eckland 1984.
44. Grammer 1992.
45. Wolf 1991.
46. Kenrick, Neuberg, Zierk, and Krones, in press.
47. Kenrick, Gutierres, and Goldberg 1989.
48. Alexander and Noonan 1979; Daniels 1983; Strassman 1981.
49. Alexander and Noonan 1979.
50. Hill 1945; McGinnis 1958; Hudson and Henze 1969; Buss, in preparation a.
51. Dickemann 1981.
52. Posner 1992.
53. Buss 1989a.
54. Tooby and Cosmides 1989a, 39.
55. Thompson 1983; Weiss and Slosnerick 1981.
56. Buss and Schmitt 1993.
57. Buss 1989b.
58. Symons 1987.

CHAPTER 4: CASUAL SEX

1. Clark and Hatfield 1989.
2. Smith 1984.
3. Smith 1984.
4. Smith 1984; Short 1979.
5. Baker and Bellis, in press a.

6. Baker and Bellis, in press b.
7. Baker and Bellis, in press c.
8. Symons 1979, 207.
9. Buss and Schmitt 1993.
10. Buss and Schmitt 1993.
11. Bermant 1976.
12. James 1981; Kinsey, Pomeroy, and Martin 1953; Symons 1979.
13. Anthanasiou, Shaver, and Travis 1970; Hite 1987; Hunt 1974.
14. Thompson 1983; Lawson 1988.
15. Symons 1979.
16. Elwin 1968, 47.
17. Schapera 1940, 193.
18. Gregor 1985, 84, 72.
19. Kinsey, Pomeroy, and Martin 1948, 589.
20. Ellis and Symons 1990.
21. Hunt 1974.
22. Wilson 1987, 126.
23. Barclay 1973, 209.
24. Ellis and Symons 1990, 544.
25. Barclay 1973, 211.
26. Ellis and Symons 1990.
27. Gladue and Delaney 1990; Nida and Koon 1983; Pennybaker, Dyer, Caulkins, Litowixz, Ackerman, and Anderson 1979.
28. Symons 1979.
29. Saghir and Robins 1973.
30. Ruse 1988.
31. Symons 1979, 300.
32. Burley and Symanski 1981; Smith 1984; Symons 1979.
33. Thornhill 1992a; Welham 1990.
34. Buss and Schmitt 1993; Small 1992; Smith 1984; Smuts 1985; Barkow 1989; Thornhill 1992a; Wilson and Daly 1992.
35. Malinowski 1929, 269.
36. Buss and Schmitt 1993.
37. Burley and Symanski 1981.
38. Janus and Janus 1993.
39. Buss and Schmitt 1993.
40. Buss and Schmitt 1993.
41. Smuts 1991.
42. Biocca 1970.
43. Smuts 1985.
44. Smith 1984, 614.
45. Colwell and Oring 1989.
46. Greiling 1993; see also Spanier and Margolis 1983, and Terman 1938.
47. Symons 1979; Baker and Bellis, in press, c; see also Gangestad 1989; Gangestad and Simpson, 1990.
48. Fisher 1958.

49. Buss and Schmitt 1993; Kenrick et al. 1993.
50. Symons 1979.
51. Daly and Wilson 1988.
52. Kim Hill personal communication, 1991.
53. Muehlenhard and Linton, 1987.
54. Hill and Hurtado, in press.
55. Daly and Wilson 1988.
56. Wilson and Daly 1992.
57. Holmes and Sherman 1982.
58. Draper and Belsky 1990; Moffitt, Caspi, and Belsky 1990.
59. Frayser 1985; Gregor 1985.
60. Secord 1983; Pedersen 1991.
61. Gaulin and Schlegel 1980.
62. Hill and Kaplan 1988; Kim Hill, personal communication, 1991.
63. Posner 1992.
64. Betzig 1992.

CHAPTER 5: ATTRACTING A PARTNER

1. Kevles 1986.
2. Buss 1988a; Schmitt and Buss, in preparation.
3. Buss and Dedden, 1990.
4. Cloyd 1976.
5. Hill, Nocks, and Gardner 1987; Townsend and Levy, in preparation.
6. Holmberg 1950, 58.
7. Ovid 1982, 199.
8. Tooke and Camire 1991.
9. La Cerra, Cosmides, and Tooby 1993.
10. Schmitt and Buss, in preparation.
11. Margulis and Sagan 1991, 103; Trivers 1985, 395; Thornhill and Alcock 1983.
12. Allan and Fishel 1979, 150.
13. Chagnon 1988.
14. Barkow 1989.
15. Cloyd 1976, 300.
16. Kiesler and Baral 1970; Stroebe 1977.
17. Cloyd 1976; Nesse 1990.
18. Howard 1981.
19. Schmitt and Buss, in preparation.
20. Schmitt and Buss, in preparation.
21. Dawkins 1976; Symons 1979; Buss and Chiodo 1991.
22. Allan and Fishel 1979, 152.
23. Buss, in preparation, b.
24. Graziano, Jensen-Campbell, Shebilske, and Lundgren, in press.
25. Wolf 1991, 11.

26. Buss and Dedden 1990.
27. Barth 1987.
28. Buss 1988a; Schmitt and Buss, in preparation.
29. Hatfield and Rapson 1993.
30. Hatfield, Walster, Piliavin, and Schmidt 1973.
31. Kim Hill, personal communication, 1991.
32. Cashdan 1993.
33. Hill, Nocks, and Gardner 1987.
34. Allan and Fishel 1979, 137; 139.
35. Abbey 1982.
36. Givins 1978.
37. Daly and Wilson 1988; Guttentag and Secord 1983; Pedersen 1991.

CHAPTER 6: STAYING TOGETHER

1. Thornhill and Alcock 1983.
2. Alcock 1981.
3. Alexander 1962.
4. Thornhill and Alcock 1983.
5. Abele and Gilchrist 1977; Parker 1970.
6. Buss 1988b; Buss and Barnes 1986; Kenrick, Groth, Trost, and Sadalla, 1993.
7. Alexander and Noonan 1979; Daly, Wilson, and Weghorst 1982.
8. Shettel-Neuber, Bryson, and Young 1978; Buss, in preparation c.
9. Daly and Wilson 1988, 182.
10. Safilios-Rothschild 1969, 78–79.
11. White 1981.
12. Buunk and Hupka 1987.
13. Teisman and Mosher 1978.
14. Francis 1977.
15. Buss et al. 1992.
16. Gottschalk 1936.
17. Buunk and Hupka 1987.
18. Chimbos 1978, 54.
19. Daly and Wilson 1988, 196.
20. Miller 1980.
21. Daly, Wilson, and Weghorst 1982.
22. Lobban 1972; Tanner 1970; Bohannan 1960.
23. Lobban 1972.
24. Daly, Wilson, and Weghorst 1982.
25. Daly and Wilson 1988.
26. Buss 1988b.
27. Buss, in preparation d.
28. Shettel-Neuber, Bryson, and Young 1978.
29. Dickemann 1981.

30. Betzig, in preparation, 17.
31. Dass 1970, 78.
32. Saletore 1978, 64; Saletore 1974, 61.
33. Van Gulik 1974, 17.
34. Cienza de Leon 1959, 41.
35. Smuts and Smuts 1993.
36. Daly and Wilson 1988; Russell 1990; Margo Wilson 1989 and personal communication.
37. Hosken 1979.
38. Daly, Wilson, and Weghorst 1982; Hosken 1979, 2.
39. Miller 1980.
40. Handy 1923, cited in Daly and Wilson, 1988, 204.
41. Rasmussen 1931.
42. Wilson and Daly 1992, 311.

CHAPTER 7: SEXUAL CONFLICT

1. Buss 1989b.
2. Byers and Lewis 1988.
3. Saal, Johnson, and Weber 1989; see Abbey 1982 for comparable results.
4. Abbey and Melby 1986.
5. Abbey 1982; Saal, Johnson, and Weber 1989.
6. Semmelroth and Buss, unpublished data.
7. Ellis and Symons 1990; Hazan 1983.
8. Thornhill and Thornhill 1990a, 1990b.
9. Buss 1989b.
10. Semmelroth and Buss, unpublished data.
11. Zahavi 1977.
12. Zahavi 1977.
13. Blumstein and Schwartz 1983.
14. Trivers 1985.
15. Cassell 1984, 155.
16. Semmelroth and Buss, unpublished data.
17. Semmelroth and Buss, unpublished data.
18. Daly and Wilson 1988.
19. Margo Wilson 1989 and personal communication.
20. Whitehurst 1971.
21. Rounsaville 1978.
22. Hilberman and Munson 1978.
23. Daly and Wilson 1988; Russell 1990.
24. Chagnon 1983.
25. Studd and Gattiker 1991, 251.
26. Terpstra and Cook 1985.
27. Studd and Gattiker 1991.

28. Studd and Gattiker 1991.
29. Terpstra and Cook 1985.
30. Terpstra and Cook 1985.
31. Gutek 1985.
32. Studd and Gattiker, in preparation.
33. Gutek 1985; Studd and Gattiker 1991; Quinn 1977.
34. Koss and Oros 1982.
35. Muehlenhard and Linton 1987.
36. Gavey 1991.
37. Russell 1990.
38. Malamuth, Heavey, and Linz 1993; Thornhill and Thornhill 1992.
39. Thornhill 1980a, 1980b.
40. Malamuth 1992; Thornhill and Thornhill 1992.
41. Mazur 1992.
42. Thornhill and Thornhill 1983.
43. Thornhill and Thornhill 1992; see also Clark and Lewis 1977.
44. Byers and Lewis 1988; McCormick 1979; Muehlenhard and Linton 1987.
45. Muehlenhard and Linton 1987.
46. Daly and Wilson 1988; Thornhill and Thornhill 1992.
47. Thornhill and Thornhill 1990a, 1990b.
48. Malamuth 1981.
49. Young and Thiessen 1992.
50. Malamuth 1986; Malamuth, Sockloskie, Koss, and Tanaka 1991.
51. Thornhill and Thornhill 1983.
52. Freemont 1975, 244–246.
53. Chagnon 1983.
54. Brownmiller 1975.

CHAPTER 8: BREAKING UP

1. Howell 1979.
2. Kim Hill, personal communication, 1991.
3. Daly and Wilson 1988; Trinkaus and Zimmerman 1982.
4. Hill and Hurtado, in press.
5. Chagnon 1983.
6. Tooby and DeVore 1987.
7. Betzig 1989.
8. Daly and Wilson 1988.
9. Gladwin and Sarason 1953, 128.
10. Erickson and Zenone 1976.
11. Fisher 1992.
12. Radcliffe-Brown 1922.
13. Beardsley et al. 1959.
14. Chagnon 1983; Hart and Pilling 1960; Buss 1989a.

15. Weiss 1975, 19.
16. Cherlin 1981; Fisher 1992; Whyte 1990.
17. Bowe 1992, 200.
18. Seiler 1976.
19. Cuber and Harroff 1965.
20. Borgerhoff Mulder 1985, 1988.
21. Murdock and Wilson 1972.
22. Ames 1953.
23. Betzig 1989.
24. Bowe 1992.
25. Elwin 1949, 70.
26. Bunzel 1952, 132.
27. Daly and Wilson 1988.
28. McCrae and Costa 1990.
29. Buss 1991b.
30. Bunzel 1952, 132.

CHAPTER 9: CHANGES OVER TIME

1. de Waal 1982.
2. Borgerhoff Mulder 1988.
3. Schneider 1964, 53.
4. Goldschmidt 1974.
5. Henss 1992.
6. Hart and Pilling 1960.
7. Udry 1980.
8. Greeley 1991.
9. James 1981.
10. Margolin and White 1987.
11. Pfeiffer and Davis 1972.
12. Buss, in preparation d.
13. Flinn 1988.
14. Dickemann 1979.
15. Daly and Wilson 1988.
16. Byrne 1988.
17. Green, Lee, and Lustig 1974.
18. Daly and Wilson 1988.
19. Spanier and Margolis 1982.
20. Thompson 1984.
21. Glass and Wright 1985.
22. Johnson 1970.
23. Terman 1938.
24. Sigusch and Schmidt 1971.
25. Kinsey, Pomeroy, and Martin 1948, 1953.
26. Betzig 1992.

27. Quoted in Symons 1979, 166.
28. Hill and Hurtado 1991; Jones 1975; Croze, Hillman, and Lang 1981.
29. Hill and Hurtado 1991.
30. Utian 1980, cited in Pavelka and Fedigan 1991.
31. Alexander 1990.
32. Hill and Hurtado 1991.
33. Alexander 1990; Dawkins 1976; Hill and Hurtado 1991; Williams 1957.
34. Hill and Hurtado 1991.
35. Hill and Hurtado 1991.
36. Hill and Hurtado, in press.
37. Kaplan and Hill 1985a; Kaplan, Hill, and Hurtado 1984; Hill and Hurtado 1989; Hill and Kaplan 1988.
38. Hart and Pilling 1960.
39. Shostak 1981.
40. Kim Hill, personal communication, 1991.
41. Hill and Hurtado, in press.
42. Jencks 1979.
43. Hewlett 1991.
44. Trivers 1985.
45. Daly and Wilson 1988; Trivers 1985.
46. U.S. Bureau of the Census 1989.
47. Hart and Pilling 1960.
48. Wilson and Daly 1985.
49. Kuzel and Krishnan 1979.
50. Mackey 1980; U.S. Bureau of the Census 1977.
51. Chamie and Nsuly 1981.
52. Guttentag and Secord 1983, 204–205.
53. Pedersen 1991.
54. Pedersen 1991.
55. Markman, Stanley, and Storaasili 1991.
56. Gaulin and Boster 1990; Pedersen 1991.
57. Flinn 1988.
58. Wilson 1989, 53.
59. Thornhill and Thornhill 1983.
60. Divale and Harris 1976.
61. Daly and Wilson 1988.
62. Thornhill and Thornhill 1983.

CHAPTER 10: HARMONY BETWEEN THE SEXES

1. Baker and Bellis, in press c; Buss and Schmitt 1993; Betzig 1989.
2. Gowaty 1992; MacKinnon 1987; Smuts, in press; Ortner 1974; Ortner and Whitehead 1981; Daly and Wilson 1988.

3. Buss 1989a.
4. Hall and DeVore 1965; de Waal 1982.
5. Conner, Smolker, and Richards 1992.
6. Nishida and Goodall 1986; Goodall 1986.
7. Alexander 1987; Chagnon 1983.
8. Tooby and Cosmides 1989b.
9. Smuts, in press.
10. This analysis of resource inequality, of course, does not deny the exis-
    tence of other contributing causes such as the sexist practice of giving
    women and men unequal pay for the same work.
11. Smuts, in press.
12. Brownmiller 1975.
13. Daly and Wilson 1988; Smuts 1992.
14. Buss and Dedden 1990; Hrdy 1981.
15. Hewlett 1991.
16. Shostak 1981.
17. Belsky, Steinberg, and Draper 1991.
18. Kim Hill, personal communication, 1992.
19. Chagnon 1983, personal communication, 1991.
20. Brownmiller 1975.
21. Tooby and Cosmides 1989.
22. Malamuth 1981; Young and Thiessen 1992.
23. Weisfeld, Russell, Weisfeld, and Wells 1992.

CHAPTER 11: WOMEN'S HIDDEN
SEXUAL STRATEGIES

1. Symons 1979, 75.
2. Bancroft 1989.
3. Tavris and Sadd 1977.
4. Symons 1979, 86.
5. One woman reader pointed out that men are variable as well in
   ease of orgasm and in variability across sexual partners—topics
   that have been insufficiently explored.
6. Symons 1979; Gould 1987.
7. Gould 1987, 16.
8. Davenport 1977, 149.
9. Slob and van der Werff ten Bosch 1991; Dixon 1998; Baker and
   Bellis 1995.
10. Elwin 1968, 131.
11. Shostak 1981, 286–287.
12. Rancour-Laferriere 1985.
13. Rancour-Laferriere 1985, 79.

14. Rancour-Laferriere 1985, 70.
15. Rancour-Laferriere 1985, 105.
16. Angier 1999, 74.
17. Alexander and Noonan 1979, 449.
18. Hrdy 1999.
19. Symons 1982.
20. Hrdy 1999, 223.
21. Fox, Wolff, and Baker 1970 initially proposed this hypothesis; recently, it has been studied by a number of scientists, notably Baker and Bellis 1995.
22. Baker and Bellis 1995.
23. Welling, Field, Johnson, and Wadsworth 1994.
24. Tavris and Sadd 1977.
25. Kinsey et al. 1953.
26. Michael, Gagnon, Laumann, and Kolata 1994.
27. Fisher 1973; Terman 1938.
28. Chesser 1957.
29. Troisi and Carosi 1998.
30. Thornhill, Gangestad, and Comer 1995.
31. Shackelford, Weekes-Shackelford, LeBlanc, Bleske, Euler, and Hoier 2000.
32. Baker and Bellis 1995.
33. Baker and Bellis 1995.
34. Thanks go to Don Symons for pointing this out.
35. Hicks and Leitenberg 2001.
36. Symons 1979, 206–207.
37. Greiling and Buss 2000.
38. See Buss 2000 for a review of this evidence.
39. One issue that calls this reasoning into question is: Why wouldn't women have evolved to recognize the genes that lead a man to be a good provider and good father, rather than just genes that lead a man to be good at short-term sexual conquests?
40. Cerda-Flores, Barton, Marty-Gonzalez, Rivas, and Chakraborty 1999; Sasse, Muller, Chakraborty, and Ott 1994; MacIntyre and Sooman 1991.
41. Gangestad and Thornhill 1997.
42. Thornhill and Gangestad, in press.
43. Greiling and Buss 2000.
44. Kirkpatrick and Ellis 2001.
45. Gangestad and Thornhill 1997.
46. Stanislaw and Rice 1988; see also Regan 1996.
47. See Gangestad and Cousins, in press, for a review and conclusions.
48. Gangestad, Thornhill, and Garver, in press.
49. Penton-Voak and Perrett 2000.

50. Penton-Voak, Perrett, Castles, Kobayashi, Burt, Murray, and Minamisawa 1999.
51. Johnston, Hagel, Franklin, Fink, and Grammer 2001.
52. Regan and Berscheid 1995.
53. Kohl, Atzmueller, Fink, and Grammer 2001.
54. Gangestad and Thornhill 1998; this result has also been found by Rikowski and Grammer 1999.
55. Another study suggesting the importance of odor found that women prefer the scents of men with dissimilar MHC (major histocompatibility) genotypes (see Wedekind, Seeback, Bettens, and Paepke 1995).
56. Symons 1987, 133.
57. Buss 1999, 145.
58. Margie Profet, personal communication, cited in Symons 1995, 90–91.
59. Buss 1999.
60. Singh and Bronstad 2001.
61. Poran 1994; Kuukasjarvi, Eriksson, Koskela, Mappes, and Rantala, under review; see also Doty, Ford, Preti, and Huggins 1975; Thornhill and Gangestad 1999, however, failed to find these results using a different set of methods.
62. Van den Berghe and Frost 1986.
63. Manning and Scutt 1996.
64. Grammer 1996.
65. Gangestad and Cousins, in press.
66. Gangestad, Thornhill, and Carver, in press.
67. Buss and Shackelford 1997.

CHAPTER 12: MYSTERIES OF HUMAN MATING

1. Bobrow and Bailey 2001.
2. See Rahman and Wilson, in press, for a recent summary; although most studies point to moderate heritability roughly 50%, some studies find only 20–30% concordance for homosexual orientation among monozygotic identical twins, which would suggest a slightly more modest role for heritable influence.
3. See Bobrow and Bailey 2001, Muscarella 2000, and McKnight 1997 for summaries.
4. Wilson 1975.
5. Dobrow and Bailey 2001.
6. Kirkpatrick 2000; Parish 1994; Vasey 1995.
7. de Waal 1989; Wrangham 1999.
8. Miller 2000; see also McKnight 1997.

9. Rahman and Wilson, in press.
10. See Hamer and Copeland 1998 for a summary of early efforts to identify "the gay gene." See Rice, Anderson, Rische, and Ebers 1999 for failure to replicate, and Bailey et al. 1999 for a related failure to find evidence of maternal transmission. See Rahman and Wilson, in press, for a compromise position suggesting that most studies confirm that an X-linked gene influences male sexual orientation.
11. Cochran, Ewald, and Cochran 2000, 437–438.
12. Cochran, Ewald, and Cochran 2000.
13. Cochran, Ewald, and Cochran 2000, 438.
14. Bailey, Kim, Hills, and Linsenmeier 1997; Bassett, Pearcey, and Dabbs 2001.
15. Singh, Vidaurri, Zambarano, and Dabbs 1999.
16. Gould 1997.
17. Cooperative Institutional Research Program, University of California, Los Angeles, 2001.
18. Surbey and Conohan 2000, 367.
19. Townsend, Kline, and Wasserman 1995.
20. Schmitt and Buss 2000.
21. Schmitt, Shackelford, Duntley, Tooke, and Buss 2001.
22. Schmitt, under review.
23. Haselton and Buss 2001.
24. Regan and Dreyer 1999.
25. Schmitt et al. 2001.
26. Walsh 1991; Schmitt et al. 2001.
27. Mathes, King, Miller, and Reed 2002.
28. Brewer et al. 2000.
29. Pinker 2002.
30. Bleske and Buss 2000, 2001.
31. Bleske and Shackelford 2001.
32. Buss and Shackelford 1997.
33. Schmitt and Buss 2001.
34. Schmitt 2001.
35. Buss et al. 1992.
36. Buss 2000.
37. Buunk et al. 1996; Wiederman and Kendall 1999; Geary et al. 1995; Buss et al. 1999.
38. Shackelford, Buss, and Bennett 2002.
39. Pietrzak et al. 2002; sex differences have been replicated now by dozens of different investigators worldwide, and now constitute one of the most well-established psychological sex differences in the scientific literature. Even critics of the evolutionary interpretation have successfully replicated the sex differences, using both physiological and psychological measures (e.g., Harris 2000).

40. DeSteno, Bartlett, Braverman, and Salovey, in press.
41. See Buss 2000 for an extensive summary; see also Pietrzak et al. 2002 for the best multi-method study yet conducted.
42. DeSteno and Salovey 1996; Harris and Christenfeld 1996.
43. Cramer, Abraham, Johnson, and Manning-Ryan 2001–2002; Buss et al. 1999; Pietrzak et al. 2002.
44. Buss, Shackelford, Choe, Buunk, and Dijkstra 2000.
45. Buss and Shackelford 1997.
46. Sanday 1990, 3.
47. Good 1991, 102.
48. Gregor 1985, 103.
49. Good 1991, 199.
50. Freeman 1984.
51. Maggioncalda and Sapolsky 2002; Mitani 1985.
52. Thornhill and Palmer 2000.
53. Lalumiere et al. 1996.
54. Thornhill and Palmer 2000.
55. Thornhill and Thornhill 1983.
56. Gottschall and Gottschall, in press; most studies that compare rape-pregnancy rates with pregnancy rates from consensual sex are confounded in various ways. Some collapse across all categories of rape, such as forced oral sex, anal sex, and penile–vaginal rape, and compare them with penile–vaginal rape resulting from consensual sex. Most fail to factor in the widespread use of emergency contraception given to rape victims, e.g., the "morning after pill." The Gottschall study is the first to provide systematic controls for these variables.
57. See Jones 1999, who provided the label for this objection to rape-as-adaptation theories.
58. Russell 1990.
59. Symons 1979, 284.
60. The most level-headed evaluation of the weaknesses and strengths of the Thornhill–Palmer book may be found in the reviews by Owen Jones 2001 and Massimo Pigliucci 2002.
61. Griffin 1971; cited in Hickman and Muehlenhard 1997.
62. S. Mydans, *Austin American Statesman*, March 24, 2002, p. A25.
63. Buss 1989.
64. Hartung, n.d.
65. Gilmore 1990.
66. Royle 1989.
67. Smuts 1992, 1.
68. Rogel 1976. This finding appears to contradict the Gotschall study, which found a surprisingly high rape-pregnancy rate; future research must resolve the apparent opposition of these two findings.

69. Morgan 1981.
70. Chavanne and Gallup 1998.
71. Morris and Udry 1970.
72. Studies summarized by Hickman and Muehlenhard 1997.
73. Hickman and Muehlenhard 1997.
74. Hickman and Muehlenhard 1997.
75. Pawson and Banks 1993.
76. Hickman and Muehlenhard 1997.
77. Wilson and Mesnick 1997.
78. Wilson and Mesnick 1997, 507.
79. Coyne 2000. Although the Coyne review draws attention to certain weaknesses of the Thornhill–Palmer book, his review is marred by the frequent use of ad hominem remarks and deep conceptual confusion about the logic of evolutionary psychology.
80. Haselton and Buss 2000; Haselton, in press; Haselton and Buss, in press.
81. Keenan, Gallup, Goulet, and Kulkarni 1997.
82. Buss 2000, 2001.
83. Moore, Martin, and Birkhead 1999.
84. Shackelford, LeBlanc, Weekes-Shackelford, Bleske-Rechek, Euler, and Hoier 2002.
85. Westermarck 1891.
86. Hamilton 1982.
87. Lieberman 2002.
88. Bevc and Silverman 2000.
89. Schneider and Hendrix 2000; Immerman and Mackey 1997.
90. Pawlowski and Dunbar 1999.
91. Li and Bailey 2002.
92. Miller 2000.

Bibliography

Abbey, A. (1982). Sex differences in attributions for friendly behavior: Do males misperceive females' friendliness? *Journal of Personality and Social Psychology 32*, 830–838.

Abbey, A., & Melby, C. (1986). The effects of nonverbal cues on gender differences in perceptions of sexual intent. *Sex Roles, 15*, 283–298.

Abele, L., & Gilchrist, S. (1977). Homosexual rape and sexual selection in acanthocephalan worms. *Science, 197*, 81–83.

Alcock, J. (1981). Seduction on the wing. *Natural History, 90*, 36–41.

Alexander, R. D. (1962). Evolutionary change in cricket acoustical communication. *Evolution, 16*, 443–467.

Alexander, R. D. (1987). *The biology of moral systems.* New York: Aldine de Gruyter.

Alexander, R. D. (1990). *How did humans evolve? Reflections on the uniquely unique species* (Special Publication No. 13). Ann Arbor: The University of Michigan, Museum of Zoology.

Alexander, R. D., & Noonan, K. M. (1979). Concealment of ovulation, parental care, and human social evolution. In N. A. Chagnon & W. Irons (Eds.), *Evolutionary biology and human social behavior: An anthropological perspective* (pp. 402–435). North Scituate, MA: Duxbury Press.

Allan, N., & Fishel, D. (1979). Singles bars. In N. Allan (Ed.), *Urban life styles* (pp. 128–179). Dubuque, IA: William C. Brown.

Ames, D. (1953). *Plural marriage among the Wolof in Gambia.* Ph.D. dissertation, Northwestern University, Evanston, Illinois.

Ardener, E. W., Ardener, S. G., & Warmington, W. A. (1960). *Plantation and village in the Cameroons.* London: Oxford University Press.

Athanasiou, R., Shaver, P., & Tavris, C. (1970, July). Sex. *Psychology Today,* pp. 37–52.

Baker, R .R., & Bellis, M. A. (in press a). Human sperm competition: Ejaculate adjustment by males and the function of masturbation. *Animal Behavior, 45*.

Baker, R. R., & Bellis, M. A. (in press b). Human sperm competition: Ejaculate manipulation by females and a function for the female orgasm. *Animal Behavior, 45.*

Baker, R. R., & Bellis, M. A. (in press c). *Sperm competition: Copulation, masturbation, and infidelity.* London: Chapman and Hall.

Barclay, A. M. (1973). Sexual fantasies in men and women. *Medical Aspects of Human Sexuality, 7,* 205–216.

Barkow, J. (1989). *Darwin, sex, and status.* Toronto: University of Toronto Press.

Barth, J. (1987). *The sot-weed factor.* Garden City, NY: Anchor Books.

Beach, S. T., & Tesser, A. (1988). Love in marriage: A cognitive account. In R. J. Sternberg & M. L. Barnes (Eds.), *The psychology of love* (pp. 330–358). New Haven: Yale University Press.

Beardsley, R. K., Hall, J. W., & Ward, R. E. (1959). *Village Japan.* Chicago: University of Chicago Press.

Becker, G. S., Landes, E. M., & Michael, R. T. (1977). An economic analysis of marital instability. *Journal of Political Economy, 85,* 1141–1187.

Belsky, J., Steinberg, L., & Draper, P. (1991). Childhood experience, interpersonal development, and reproductive strategy: An evolutionary theory of socialization. *Child Development, 62,* 647–670.

Bermant, G. (1976). Sexual behavior: Hard times with the Coolidge effect. In M. H. Siegel & H. P. Ziegler (Eds.), *Psychological research: The inside story* (pp. 76–103). New York: Harper & Row.

Berscheid, E., & Walster, E. (1974). Physical attractiveness. In L. Berkowitz (Ed.), *Advances in experimental social psychology* (pp. 157–215). New York: Academic Press.

Betzig, L. (1986). *Despotism and differential reproduction: A Darwinian view of history.* Hawthorne, NY: Aldine de Gruyter.

Betzig, L. (1989). Causes of conjugal dissolution: A cross-cultural study. *Current Anthropology, 30,* 654–676.

Betzig, L. (1992). Roman polygyny. *Ethology and Sociobiology, 13,* 309–349.

Betzig, L. (in preparation). Why monogamy? Submitted to *Behavioral and Brain Sciences.*

Biocca, E. (1970). *Yanomama: The narrative of a white girl kidnapped by Amazonian Indians.* New York: E. P. Dutton.

Blumstein, P., & Schwartz, P. (1983). *American couples.* New York: William Morrow.

Bohannan, P. (1960). *African homicide and suicide.* Princeton: Princeton University Press.

Borgerhoff Mulder, M. (1985). Polygyny threshold: A Kipsigis case study. *National Geographic Research Reports, 21,* 33–39.

Borgerhoff Mulder, M. (1988). Kipsigis bridewealth payments. In L. L. Betzig, M. Borgerhoff Mulder, & P. Turke (Eds.), *Human reproductive behavior* (pp. 65–82). New York: Cambridge University Press.

Bowe, C. (1992). Everything we think, feel, and do about divorce. *Cosmopolitan, 212* (2), 199–207.

Brown, D. E. (1991). *Human universals.* Philadelphia: Temple University Press.

Brown, D. E., & Chai-yun, Y. (n.d.). *"Big Man:" Its distribution, meaning and origin.* Unpublished manuscript, Department of Anthropology, University of California, Santa Barbara.

Brownmiller, S. (1975). *Against our will: Men, women, and rape.* New York: Bantam Books.

Bunzel, R. (1952). *Chichicastenango.* New York: J. J. Augustin.

Burley, N., & Symanski, R. (1981). Women without: An evolutionary and cross-cultural perspective on prostitution. In R. Symanski, *The immoral landscape: Female prostitution in Western societies* (pp. 239–274). Toronto: Butterworths.

Buss, D. M. (1984). Toward a psychology of person-environment (PE) correlation: The role of spouse selection. *Journal of Personality and Social Psychology, 47,* 361–377.

Buss, D. M. (1985). Human mate selection. *American Scientist, 73,* 47–51.

Buss, D. M. (1987a). Sex differences in human mate selection criteria: An evolutionary perspective. In C. Crawford, D. Krebs, & M. Smith (Eds.), *Sociobiology and psychology: Ideas, issues, and applications* (pp. 335–352). Hillsdale, NJ: Erlbaum.

Buss, D. M. (1987b). Selection, evocation, and manipulation. *Journal of Personality and Social Psychology, 53,* 1214–1221.

Buss, D. M. (1988a). The evolution of human intrasexual competition. *Journal of Personality and Social Psychology, 54,* 616–628.

Buss, D. M. (1988b). From vigilance to violence: Mate guarding tactics. *Ethology and Sociobiology, 9,* 291–317.

Buss, D. M. (1988c). Love acts: The evolutionary biology of love. In R. J. Sternberg & M. L. Barnes (Eds.), *The psychology of love* (pp. 100–118). New Haven, CT: Yale University Press.

Buss, D. M. (1989a). Sex differences in human mate preferences: Evolutionary hypotheses tested in 37 cultures. *Behavioral and Brain Sciences, 12,* 1–49.

Buss, D. M. (1989b). Conflict between the sexes: Strategic interference and the evocation of anger and upset. *Journal of Personality and Social Psychology, 56,* 735–747.

Buss, D. M. (1991a). Evolutionary personality psychology. *Annual Review of Psychology, 42,* 459–491.

Buss, D. M. (1991b). Conflict in married couples: Personality predictors of anger and upset. *Journal of Personality, 59,* 663–688.

Buss, D. M. (n.d.). *Contemporary worldviews: Spousal assortment or convergence?* Department of Psychology, University of Michigan, Ann Arbor.

Buss, D. M. (in preparation a). *Cross-generational preferences in mate selection.* Department of Psychology, University of Michigan, Ann Arbor.

Buss, D. M. (in preparation b). *Human prestige criteria.* Department of Psychology, University of Michigan, Ann Arbor.

Buss, D. M. (in preparation c). *Humiliation, anger, sadness, and abandonment: Emotional reactions to sexual infidelity.* Department of Psychology, University of Michigan, Ann Arbor.

Buss, D. M. (in preparation d). *Mate guarding in married couples: A four year longitudinal study.* Department of Psychology, University of Michigan, Ann Arbor.

Buss, D. M., Abbott, M., Angleitner, A., Asherian, A., Biaggio, A., Blanco-VillaSeñor, A., Bruchon-Schweitzer, M., Ch'u, Hai-yuan, Czapinski, J., DeRaad, B., Ekehammar, B., Fioravanti, M., Georgas, J., Gjerde, P., Guttman, R., Hazan, F., Iwawaki, S., Janakiramaiah, N., Khosroshani, F., Kreitler, S., K. Lachenicht, L., Lee, M., Liik, K., Little, B., Lohamy, N., Makim, S., Mika, S., Moadel-Shahid, M., Moane, G., Montero, M., Mundy-Castle, A. C., Little, B., Niit, T., Nsenduluka, E., Peltzer, K., Pienkowski, R., Pirttila-Backman, A., Ponce De Leon, J., Rousseau, J., Runco, M. A., Safir, M. P., Samuels, C., Sanitioso, R., Schweitzer, B., Serpell, R., Smid, N., Spencer, C., Tadinac, M., Todorova, E. N., Troland, K., Van den Brande, L., Van Heck, G., Van Langenhove, L., & Yang, Kuo-Shu. (1990). International preferences in selecting mates: A study of 37 cultures. *Journal of Cross-Cultural Psychology, 21,* 5–47.

Buss, D. M., & Barnes, M. F. (1986). Preferences in human mate selection. *Journal of Personality and Social Psychology, 50,* 559–570.

Buss, D. M., & Chiodo, L. A. (1991). Narcissistic acts in everyday life. *Journal of Personality, 59,* 179–216.

Buss, D. M., & Dedden, L. A. (1990). Derogation of competitors. *Journal of Social and Personal Relationships, 7,* 395–422.

Buss, D. M., Larsen, R. J., Westen, D., & Semmelroth, J. (1992). Sex differences in jealousy: Evolution, physiology, and psychology. *Psychological Science, 3,* 251–255.

Buss, D. M., & Schmitt, D. P. (1993). Sexual strategies theory: An evolutionary perspective on human mating. *Psychological Review, 100,* 204–232.

Buunk, B., & Hupka, R. B. (1987). Cross-cultural differences in the elicitation of sexual jealousy. *Journal of Sex Research, 23,* 12–22.

Byers, E. S., & Lewis, K. (1988). Dating couples' disagreements over desired level of sexual intimacy. *Journal of Sex Research, 24,* 15–29.

Byrne, R. (1988). *1,911 best things anybody ever said.* New York: Fawcett Columbine.

Cashdan, E. (1993). Attracting mates: Effects of paternal investment on mate attraction strategies. *Ethology and Sociobiology, 14,* 1–24.

Cassell, C. (1984). *Swept away: Why women confuse love and sex.* New York: Simon & Schuster.

Cattell, R. B., & Nesselroade, J. R. (1967). *"Likeness" and "completeness" theories examined by 16 personality factor measures on stably and unstably married couples.* (Advanced Publication No. 7). Urbana: University of Illinois, Laboratory of Personality and Group Analysis.

Chagnon, N. (1983). *Yanomamö: The fierce people* (3rd ed.). New York: Holt, Rinehart & Winston.

Chagnon, N. (1988). Life histories, blood revenge, and warfare in a tribal population. *Science, 239,* 985–992.

Chamie, J., & Nsuly, S. (1981). Sex differences in remarriage and spouse selection. *Demography, 18,* 335–348.

Cherlin, A. J. (1981). *Marriage, divorce, remarriage.* Cambridge: Harvard University Press.

Chimbos, P. D. (1978). *Marital violence: A study of interspouse homicide.* San Francisco: R & E Research Associates.

Cienza de Leon, P. (1959). *The Incas.* Norman: University of Oklahoma Press.

Clark, L., & Lewis, D. (1977). *Rape: The price of coercive sexuality.* Toronto: Women's Educational Press.

Clark, R. D., & Hatfield, E. (1989). Gender differences in receptivity to sexual offers. *Journal of Psychology and Human Sexuality, 2,* 39–55.

Cloyd, J. W. (1976). The market-place bar: The interrelation between sex, situation, and strategies in the pairing ritual of *Homo Ludens. Urban Life, 5,* 293–312.

Collias, N. E., & Collias, E. C. (1970). The behavior of the West African village weaverbird. *Ibis, 112,* 457–480.

Colwell, M. A., & Oring, L. W. (1989). Extra-pair mating in the spotted sandpiper: A female mate acquisition tactic. *Animal Behavior, 38,* 675–684.

Connor, R. C., Smolker, R. A., & Richards, A. F. (1992). Two levels of alliance formation among male bottlenose dolphins (*Tursiops sp.*). *Proceedings of the National Academy of Sciences, 89,* 987–990.

Cosmides, L., & Tooby, J. (1987). From evolution to behavior: Evolutionary psychology as the missing link. In J. Dupre (Ed.), *The latest on the best: Essays on evolution and optimality* (pp. 277–306). Cambridge, MA: MIT Press.

Cosmides, L., & Tooby, J. (1989). Evolutionary psychology and the generation of culture: 2. Case study: A computational theory of social exchange. *Ethology and Sociobiology, 10,* 51–97.

Cross, J. F., & Cross, J. (1971). Age, sex, race, and the perception of facial beauty. *Developmental Psychology, 5,* 433–439.

Croze, H. A., Hillman, A. K., & Lang, E. M. (1981). Elephants and their habitats: How do they tolerate each other? In C. W. Fowler & T. D. Smith (Eds.), *Dynamics of large mammal populations.* New York: Wiley.

Cuber, J. F., & Harroff, P. B. (1965). *Sex and the significant Americans: A study of sexual behavior among the affluent.* New York: Penguin Books.

Cunningham, M. R., Roberts, T., Richards, T., & Wu, C. (1989). *The facial-metric prediction of physical attractiveness across races, ethnic groups, and cultures.* Unpublished manuscript, Department of Psychology, University of Louisville, Kentucky.

Daly, M., & Wilson, M. (1988). *Homicide.* Hawthorne, NY: Aldine de Gruyter.

Daly, M., Wilson, M., & Weghorst, S. J. (1982). Male sexual jealousy. *Ethology and Sociobiology, 3,* 11–27.

Daniels, D. (1983). The evolution of concealed ovulation and self-deception. *Ethology and Sociobiology, 4,* 69–87.

Darwin, C. (1859). *On the origin of the species by means of natural selection, or preservation of favoured races in the struggle for life.* London: Murray.

Darwin, C. (1871). *The descent of man and selection in relation to sex.* London: Murray.

Dass, D. J. (1970). *Maharaja.* Delhi: Hind.

Dawkins, R. (1976). *The selfish gene.* Oxford: Oxford University Press.

Deaux, K., & Hanna, R. (1984). Courtship in the personals column: The influence of gender and sexual orientation. *Sex Roles, 11,* 363–375.

de Waal, F. (1982). *Chimpanzee politics: Power and sex among apes.* Baltimore: John Hopkins University Press.

Dickemann, M. (1979). The ecology of mating systems in hypergynous dowry societies. *Social Science Information, 18,* 163–195.

Dickemann, M. (1981). Paternal confidence and dowry competition: A biocultural analysis of purdah. In R. D. Alexander & D. W. Tinkle (Eds.), *Natural selection and social behavior: Recent research and new theory* (pp. 417–438). New York: Chiron Press.

Divale, W., & Harris, M. (1976). Population, warfare, and the male supremacist complex. *American Anthropologist, 78,* 521–538.

Draper, P., & Belsky, J. (1990). Personality development in evolutionary perspective. *Journal of Personality, 58,* 141–162.

Draper, P., & Harpending, H. (1982). Father absence and reproductive strategy: An evolutionary perspective. *Journal of Anthropological Research, 38,* 255–273.

Elder, G. H., Jr. (1969). Appearance and education in marriage mobility. *American Sociological Review, 34,* 519–533.

Ellis, B. J. (1992). The evolution of sexual attraction: Evaluative mechanisms in women. In J. Barkow, L. Cosmides, & J. Tooby (Eds.), *The adapted mind: Evolutionary psychology and the generation of culture* (pp. 267–288). New York: Oxford University Press.

Ellis, B. J., & Symons, D. (1990). Sex differences in sexual fantasy: An evolutionary psychological approach. *Journal of Sex Research, 27,* 527–556.

Elwin, V. (1949). *The Muria and their Ghotul.* Bombay: Oxford University Press.

Elwin, V. (1968). *The kingdom of the young.* London: Oxford University Press.

Erickson, C. J., & Zenone, P. G. (1976). Courtship differences in male ring doves: Avoidance of cuckoldry? *Science, 192,* 1353–1354.

Farrell, W. (1986). *Why men are the way they are.* New York: Berkley Books.

Fisher, H. (1992). *Anatomy of love.* New York: Norton.

Fisher, R. A. (1958). *The genetical theory of natural selection,* 2nd edition. New York: Dover.

Flinn, M. (1988). Mate guarding in a Caribbean village. *Ethology and Sociobiology, 9,* 1–28.

Ford, C. S., & Beach, F. A. (1951). *Patterns of sexual behavior*. New York: Harper & Row.

Francis, J. L. (1977). Toward the management of heterosexual jealousy. *Journal of Marriage and the Family, 10*, 61–69.

Frayser, S. (1985). *Varieties of sexual experience: An anthropological perspective*. New Haven: HRAF Press.

Freemont, J. (1975). Rapists speak for themselves. In D. E. H. Russell, *The politics of rape: The victim's perspective* (pp. 241–256). New York: Stein and Day.

Gangestad, S. W. (1989). The evolutionary history of genetic variation: An emerging issue in the behavioral genetic study of personality. In D. M. Buss & N. Cantor (Eds.), *Personality: Recent trends and emerging directions*. New York: Springer.

Gangestad, S. W., & Simpson, J. A. (1990). Toward an evolutionary history of female sociosexual variation. *Journal of Personality, 58*, 69–96.

Gangestad, S. W., & Thornhill, R. (in press). Facial attractiveness, developmental stability, and fluctuating asymmetry. *Ethology and Sociobiology*.

Gaulin, S. J. C., & Boster, J. S. (1990). Dowry as female competition. *American Anthropologist, 92*, 994–1005.

Gaulin, S. J. C., & Schlegel, A. (1980). Paternal confidence and paternal investment: A cross-cultural test of a sociobiological hypothesis. *Ethology and Sociobiology, 1*, 301–309.

Gavey, N. (1991). Sexual victimization prevalence among New Zealand university students. *Journal of Consulting and Clinical Psychology, 59*, 464–466.

Givins, D. B. (1978). The nonverbal basis of attraction: Flirtation, courtship, and seduction. *Psychiatry, 41*, 336–359.

Gladue, B. A., & Delaney, J. J. (1990). Gender differences in perception of attractiveness of men and women in bars. *Personality and Social Psychology Bulletin, 16*, 378–391.

Gladwin, T., & Sarason, S. B. (1953). *Truk: Man in paradise*. New York: Wenner-Gren Foundation for Anthropology Research.

Glass, D. P., & Wright, T. L. (1985). Sex differences in type of extramarital involvement and marital dissatisfaction. *Sex Roles, 12*, 1101–1120.

Goldschmidt, W. (1974). The economics of bridewealth among the Sebei in East Africa. *Ethnology, 13*, 311–333.

Goodall, J. (1986). *The chimpanzees of Gombe: Patterns of behavior*. Cambridge, MA: Harvard University Press.

Gottschalk, H. (1936). *Skinsygens problemer* [Problems of jealousy]. Copenhagen: Fremad.

Gough, H. G. (1980). *Manual for the California Psychological Inventory*. Palo Alto, CA: Consulting Psychologists Press.

Gowaty, P. A. (1992). Evolutionary biology and feminism. *Human Nature, 3*, 217–249.

Grammer, K. (1992). Variations on a theme: Age dependent mate selection in humans. *Behavioral and Brain Sciences, 15*, 100–102.

Graziano, W. G., Jensen-Campbell, L. A., Shebilske, L. J., & Lundgren, S. R. (in press). Social influence, sex differences, and judgments of beauty: Putting the "interpersonal" back in interpersonal attraction. *Journal of Personality and Social Psychology.*

Greeley, A. M. (1991). *Faithful attraction: Discovering intimacy, love, and fidelity in American marriage.* New York: Tom Doherty Associates.

Green, B. L., Lee, R. R., & Lustig, N. (1974, September). Conscious and unconscious factors in marital infidelity. *Medical Aspects of Human Sexuality, 87–91, 97–98, 104–105.*

Gregor, T. (1985). *Anxious pleasures: The sexual lives of an Amazonian people.* Chicago: University of Chicago Press.

Greiling, H. (1993, June). *Women's short-term sexual strategies.* Paper presented at the Conference on Evolution and the Human Sciences, London School of Economics Centre for the Philosophy of the Natural and Social Sciences, London, England.

Gutek, B. A. (1985). *Sex and the workplace: The impact of sexual behavior and harassment on women, men, and the organization.* San Francisco: Jossey-Bass.

Guttentag, M., & Secord, P. (1983). *Too many women?* Beverly Hills, CA: Sage.

Hall, K., & DeVore, I. (1965). Baboon social behavior. In I. DeVore (Ed.), *Primate behavior* (pp. 53–110). New York: Holt.

Hamilton, W. D., & Zuk, M. (1982). Heritable true fitness and bright birds: A role for parasites? *Science, 218,* 384–387.

Handy, E. S. C. (1923). *The native culture in the Marquesas* (Bulletin No. 9.) Honolulu: Bernice A. Bishop Museum.

Harrison, A. A., & Saeed, L. (1977). Let's make a deal: An analysis of revelations and stipulations in lonely hearts' advertisements. *Journal of Personality and Social Psychology, 35,* 257–264.

Hart, C. W., & Pilling, A. R. (1960). *The Tiwi of North Australia.* New York: Holt, Rinehart & Winston.

Hatfield, E., & Rapson, R. L. (1993). *Love, sex, and intimacy: Their psychology, biology, and history.* New York: HarperCollins.

Hatfield, E., Walster, G. W., Piliavin, J., & Schmidt, L. (1973). Playing hard-to-get: Understanding an elusive phenomenon. *Journal of Personality and Social Psychology, 26,* 113–121.

Hazan, H. (1983). *Endless rapture: Rape, romance, and the female imagination.* New York: Scribner's.

Henss, R. (1992). *Perceiving age and attractiveness in facial photographs.* Unpublished manuscript, Psychologisches Institüt, University of the Saarland, Germany.

Herrnstein, R. (1989, May). IQ and falling birth rates. *Atlantic Monthly,* pp. 73–79.

Hewlett, B. S. (1991). *Intimate fathers.* Ann Arbor: University of Michigan Press.

Hilberman, E., & Munson, K. (1978). Sixty battered women. *Victimology, 2,* 460–470.

Hill, C. T., Rubin, Z., & Peplau, L. A. (1976). Breakups before marriage: The end of 103 affairs. *Journal of Social Issues, 32,* 147–168.

Hill, E. M., Nocks, E. S., & Gardner, L. (1987). Physical attractiveness: Manipulation by physique and status displays. *Ethology and Sociobiology, 8,* 143–154.

Hill, K., & Hurtado, A. M. (1989). Hunter-gatherers of the new world. *American Scientist, 77,* 437–443.

Hill, K., & Hurtado, A. M. (1991). The evolution of premature reproductive senescence and menopause in human females. *Human Nature, 2,* 313–350.

Hill, K., & Hurtado, A. M. (in press). *Demographic/life history of Ache foragers.* Hawthorne, NY: Aldine de Gruyter.

Hill, K., & Kaplan, H. (1988). Tradeoffs in male and female reproductive strategies among the Ache (parts 1 and 2). In L. Betzig, M. Borgerhoff Mulder, & P. Turke (Eds.), *Human reproductive behavior* (pp. 277–306). New York: Cambridge University Press.

Hill, R. (1945). Campus values in mate selection. *Journal of Home Economics, 37,* 554–558.

Hite, S. (1987). *Women and love: A cultural revolution in progress.* New York: Knopf.

Hoffman, M. (1977). Homosexuality. In F. A. Beach (Ed.), *Human sexuality in four perspectives* (pp. 164–169). Baltimore: Johns Hopkins University Press.

Holmberg, A. R. (1950). *Nomads of the long bow: The Siriono of Eastern Bolivia.* Washington, DC: U.S. Government Printing Office.

Holmes, W. G., & Sherman, P. W. (1982). The ontogeny of kin recognition in two species of ground squirrels. *American Zoologist, 22,* 491–517.

Hosken, F. P. (1979). *The Hosken Report: Genital and sexual mutilation of females* (2nd ed., rev.). Lexington, MA: Women's International Network News.

Howard, R. D. (1981). Male age-size distribution and male mating success in bullfrogs. In R. D. Alexander & D. W. Tinkle (Eds.), *Natural selection and social behavior* (pp. 61–77). New York: Chiron Press.

Howell, N. (1979). *Demography of the Dobe !Kung.* New York: Academic Press.

Hrdy, S. B. (1981). *The woman that never evolved.* Cambridge, MA: Harvard University Press.

Hudson, J. W., & Henze, L. F. (1969). Campus values in mate selection: A replication. *Journal of Marriage and the Family, 31,* 772–775.

Hunt, M. (1974). *Sexual behavior in the 70's.* Chicago: Playboy Press.

Jackson, L. A. (1992). *Physical appearance and gender: Sociobiological and sociocultural perspectives.* Albany: State University of New York Press.

James, W. H. (1981). The honeymoon effect on marital coitus. *Journal of Sex Research, 17,* 114–123.

Jankowiak, W. R., & Fisher, E. F. (1992). A cross-cultural perspective on romantic love. *Ethnology, 31,* 149–155.

Jankowiak, W. R., Hill, E. M., & Donovan, J. M. (1992). The effects of sex and sexual orientation on attractiveness judgments: An evolutionary interpretation. *Ethology and Sociobiology, 13,* 73–85.

Janus, S. S., & Janus, C. L. (1993). *The Janus Report on sexual behavior.* New York: Wiley.

Jencks, C. (1979). *Who gets ahead? The determinants of economic success in America.* New York: Basic Books.

Johnson, R. E. (1970). Some correlates of extramarital coitus. *Journal of Marriage and the Family, 32,* 449–456.

Jones, E. C. (1975). The post-reproductive phase in mammals. In P. van Keep & C. Lauritzen (Eds.), *Frontiers of hormone research* (vol. 3, pp. 1–20). Basel: Karger.

Kaplan, H., & Hill, K. (1985a). Food sharing among Ache foragers: Tests of explanatory hypotheses. *Current Anthropology, 26,* 223–245.

Kaplan, H., & Hill, K. (1985b). Hunting ability and reproductive success among male Ache foragers. *Current Anthropology, 26,* 131–133.

Kaplan, H., Hill, K., & Hurtado, M. (1984). Food sharing among the Ache hunter-gatherers of eastern Paraguay. *Current Anthropology, 25,* 113–115.

Kenrick, D. T., Groth, G. E., Trost, M. R., & Sadalla, E. K. (1993). Integrating evolutionary and social exchange perspectives on relationships: Effects of gender, self-appraisal, and involvement level on mate selection. *Journal of Personality and Social Psychology, 64,* 951–969.

Kenrick, D. T., Gutierres, S. E., & Goldberg, L. (1989). Influence of erotica on ratings of strangers and mates. *Journal of Experimental Social Psychology, 25,* 159–167.

Kenrick, D. T., & Keefe, R. C. (1992). Age preferences in mates reflect sex differences in reproductive strategies. *Behavioral and Brain Sciences, 15,* 75–133.

Kenrick, D. T., Neuberg, S. L., Zierk, K. L., & Krones, J. M. (in press). Contrast effects as a function of sex, dominance, and physical attractiveness. *Personality and Social Psychology Bulletin.*

Kenrick, D. T., Sadalla, E. K., Groth, G., & Trost, M. R. (1990). Evolution, traits, and the stages of human courtship: Qualifying the parental investment model. *Journal of Personality, 58,* 97–116.

Kevles, B. (1986). *Females of the species.* Cambridge, MA: Harvard University Press.

Kiesler, S. B., & Baral, R. L. (1970). The search for a romantic partner: The effects of self-esteem and physical attractiveness on romantic behavior. In K. J. Gergen & D. Marlow (Eds.), *Personality and social behavior* (pp. 155–165). Reading, MA: Addison-Wesley.

Kinsey, A. C., Pomeroy, W. B., & Martin, C. E. (1948). *Sexual behavior in the human male.* Philadelphia: Saunders.

Kinsey, A. C., Pomeroy, W. B., & Martin, C. E. (1953). *Sexual behavior in the human female.* Philadelphia: Saunders.

Koss, M. P., & Oros, C. J. (1982). Sexual experiences survey: A research instrument investigating sexual aggression and victimization. *Journal of Consulting and Clinical Psychology, 50,* 455–457.

Kyl-Heku, L., & Buss, D. M. (unpublished.). *Tactics of hierarchy negotiation.* Department of Psychology, University of Michigan, Ann Arbor.

La Cerra, P., Cosmides, L., and Tooby, J. (1993, August). *Psychological adaptations in women for assessing a man's willingness to invest in offspring.* Paper presented at the Fifth Annual Meeting of the Human Behavior and Evolution Society, Binghamton, New York.

Langhorne, M. C., & Secord, P. F. (1955). Variations in marital needs with age, sex, marital status, and regional composition. *Journal of Social Psychology, 41,* 19–37.

Langlois, J. H., & Roggman, L. A. (1990). Attractive faces are only average. *Psychological Science, 1,* 115–121.

Langlois, J. H., Roggman, L. A., Casey, R. J., Ritter, J. M., Rieser-Danner, L. A., & Jenkins, V. Y. (1987). Infant preferences for attractive faces: Rudiments of a stereotype. *Developmental Psychology, 23,* 363–369.

Langlois, J. H., Roggman, L. A., & Reiser-Danner, L. A. (1990). Infants' differential social responses to attractive and unattractive faces. *Developmental Psychology, 26,* 153–159.

Lawson, A. (1988). *Adultery: An analysis of love and betrayal.* New York: Basic Books.

Le Boeuf, B. J. (1974). Male-male competition and reproductive success in elephant seals. *American Zoology, 14,* 163–176.

Lindburg, D. G. (1971). The rhesus monkey in northern India: An ecological and behavioral study. In L. A. Rosenblum (Ed.), *Primate behavior* (vol. 2). New York: Academic Press.

Lobban, C. F. (1972). *Law and anthropology in the Sudan (an analysis of homicide cases in Sudan)* (African Studies Seminar Series No. 13). Sudan Research Unit, Khartoum University.

Low, B. S. (1979). Sexual selection and human ornamentation. In N. A. Chagnon & W. Irons (Eds.), *Evolutionary biology and human social behavior.* Boston: Duxbury Press.

Low, B. S. (1989). Cross-cultural patterns in the training of children: An evolutionary perspective. *Journal of Comparative Psychology, 103,* 313–319.

Low, B. S. (1991). Reproductive life in nineteenth century Sweden: An evolutionary perspective on demographic phenomena. *Ethology and Sociobiology, 12,* 411–448.

Mackey, W. C. (1980). A sociobiological perspective on divorce patterns of men in the United States. *Journal of Anthropological Research, 20,* 419–430.

MacKinnon, C. (1987). *Feminism unmodified.* Cambridge: Harvard University Press.

Malamuth, N. M. (1981). Rape proclivity among males. *Journal of Social Issues, 37,* 138–157.

Malamuth, N. M (1986). Predictors of naturalistic sexual aggression. *Journal of Personality and Social Psychology, 50,* 953–962.

Malamuth, N. M. (1992). Evolution and laboratory research on men's sexual arousal: What do the data show and how can we explain them? *Behavioral and Brain Sciences, 15,* 394–396.

Malamuth, N. M., Heavy, C., & Linz, D. (1993). Predicting men's antisocial behavior against women: The "interaction model" of sexual aggression. In N. G. Hall & R. Hirshman (Eds.), *Sexual aggression: Issues in etiology, assessment, treatment, and policy.* New York: Hemisphere.

Malamuth, N. M., Sockloskie, R., Koss, M., & Tanaka, J. (1991). The characteristics of aggressors against women: Testing a model using a national sample of college women. *Journal of Consulting and Clinical Psychology, 59,* 670–681.

Malinowski, B. (1929). *The sexual life of savages in North-Western Melanesia.* London: Routledge.

Margolin, L., & White, L. (1987). The continuing role of physical attractiveness in marriage. *Journal of Marriage and the Family, 49,* 21–27.

Margulis, L., & Sagan, D. (1991). *Mystery dance: On the evolution of human sexuality.* New York: Summit Books.

Markman, H. S., Stanley, S., & Storaasili, R. (1991). *Destructive fighting predicts divorce: Results from a 7-year follow-up.* Unpublished manuscript, Department of Psychology, University of Denver.

Mazur, A. (1992). The evolutionary psychology of rape and food robbery. *Behavioral and Brain Sciences, 15,* 397.

McCormick, N. B. (1979). Come-ons and put-offs: Unmarried students' strategies for having and avoiding sexual intercourse. *Psychology of Women Quarterly, 4,* 194–211.

McCrae, R. R., & Costa, P. T., Jr. (1990). *Personality in adulthood.* New York: Guilford Press.

McGinnis, R. (1958). Campus values in mate selection. *Social Forces, 35,* 368–373.

Miller, D. J. (1980). *Battered women: Perceptions of their problems and their perception of community response.* Unpublished MSW thesis, University of Windsor, Ontario.

Moffitt, T., Caspi, A., & Belsky, J. (1990, March). *Family context, girls' behavior, and the onset of puberty: A test of a sociobiological model.* Paper presented at the biennial meetings of the Society for Research in Adolescence, Atlanta, Georgia.

Morse, S. J., Reis, H. T., Gruzen, J., & Wolff, E. (1974). The "eye of the beholder": Determinants of physical attractiveness judgments in the U.S. and South Africa. *Journal of Personality, 42,* 528–542.

Muehlenhard, C. L., & Linton, M. A. (1987). Date rape and sexual aggression in dating situations: Incidence and risk factors. *Journal of Counseling Psychology, 2,* 186–196.

Murdock, G. P., & Wilson, S. F. (1972). Settlement patterns and community organization: Cross-cultural codes 3. *Ethnology, 11,* 254–297.

Nesse, R. M. (1990). Evolutionary explanations of emotions. *Human Nature, 1,* 261–289.

Nida, S. A., & Koon, J. (1983). They get better looking at closing time around here, too. *Psychological Reports, 52,* 657–658.

Nishida, T. (1983). Alpha status and agonistic alliance in wild chimpanzees (*Pan troglodytes schweinfurhii*). *Primates, 24,* 318–336.

Orions, G. H., & Heerwagen, J. H. (1992). Evolved responses to landscapes. In J. Barkow, L. Cosmides, & J. Tooby (Eds.), *The adapted mind: Evolutionary psychology and the generation of culture* (pp. 555–579). New York: Oxford University Press.

Ortner, S. B. (1974). Is female to male as nature is to culture? In M. Z. Rosaldo & L. Lamphere (Eds.), *Woman, culture, and society* (pp. 67–88). Stanford: Stanford University Press.

Ortner, S. B., & Whitehead, H. (1981). *Sexual meanings: The cultural construction of gender and sexuality.* New York: Cambridge University Press.

Ovid (1982). *The erotic poems* (Peter Green, Tran.). New York: Penguin Books.

Parker, G. A. (1970). Sperm competition and its evolutionary consequences in the insects. *Biological Reviews, 45,* 525–568.

Pavelka, M. S., & Fedigan, L. M. (1991). Menopause: A comparative life history perspective. *Yearbook of Physical Anthropology, 34,* 13–38.

Pedersen, F. A. (1991). Secular trends in human sex ratios: Their influence on individual and family behavior. *Human Nature, 3,* 271–291.

Pennybaker, J. W., Dyer, M. A., Caulkins, R. S., Litowixz, D. L., Ackerman, P. L., & Anderson, D. B. (1979). Don't the girls get prettier at closing time: A country and western application to psychology. *Personality and Social Psychology Bulletin, 5,* 122–125.

Pfeiffer, E., & Davis, G. C. (1972). Determinants of sexual behavior in middle and old age. *Journal of the American Geriatrics Society, 20,* 151–158.

Posner, R. A. (1992). *Sex and reason.* Cambridge, MA: Harvard University Press.

Quinn, R. E. (1977). Coping with Cupid: The formation, impact, and management of romantic relationships in organizations. *Administrative Science Quarterly, 22,* 30–45.

Radcliffe-Brown, A. R. (1922). *The Andaman Islanders.* Cambridge: Cambridge University Press.

Rasmussen, K. (1931). *The Netsilik Eskimos: Social Life and Spiritual Culture.* Copenhagen: Gyldendalske Boghandel, Nordisk Forlag.

Rhode, D. L. (Ed.). (1990). *Theoretical perspectives on sexual difference.* New Haven: Yale University Press.

Rosenblatt, P. C. (1974). Cross–cultural perspective on attractiveness. In T. L. Huston (Ed.), *Foundations of interpersonal attraction* (pp. 79–95). New York: Academic Press.

Røskaft, E., Wara, A., & Viken, A. (1992). Reproductive success in relation to resource-access and parental age in a small Norwegian farming parish during the period 1700–1900. *Ethology and Sociobiology, 13,* 443–461.

Rounsaville, B. J. (1978). Theories in marital violence: Evidence from a study of battered women. *Victimology, 3,* 11–31.

Rozin, P. (1976). Psychological and cultural determinants of food choice. In T. Silverstone (Ed.), *Appetite and food intake* (pp. 286–312). Berlin: Dahlem Konferenzen.

Rozin, P., & Fallon, A. (1988). Body image, attitudes to weight, and misperceptions of figure preferences of the opposite sex: A comparison of men and women in two generations. *Journal of Abnormal Psychology, 97,* 342–345.

Ruse, M. (1988). *Homosexuality: A philosophical inquiry.* Oxford: Basil Blackwell.

Russell, D. E. H. (1990). *Rape in marriage.* Bloomington: University of Indiana Press.

Saal, F. E., Johnson, C. B., & Weber, N. (1989). Friendly or sexy? It may depend on whom you ask. *Psychology of Women Quarterly, 13,* 263–276.

Safiliolos-Rothschild, C. (1969). Attitudes of Greek spouses toward marital infidelity. In G. Neubeck (Ed.), *Extramarital relations* (pp. 78–79). Englewood Cliffs, NJ: Prentice Hall.

Saghir, M., & Robins, E. (1973). *Male and female homosexuality.* Baltimore: Williams and Wilkins.

Saletore, R. N. (1974). *Sex life under Indian rulers.* Delhi: Hind Pocket Books.

Saletore, R. N. (1978). *Sex in Indian harem life.* New Delhi: Orient paperbacks.

Schapera, I. (1940). *Married life in an African tribe.* London: Faber & Faber.

Schmitt, D. P., & Buss, D. M. (in preparation). *Sexual strategies: Mate competition tactics in temporal perspective.* Department of Psychology, University of Michigan, Ann Arbor.

Schneider, H. K. (1964). A model of African indigenous economy and society. *Comparative Studies in Society and History, 7,* 37–55.

Secord, P. F. (1982). The origin and maintenance of social roles: The case of sex roles. In W. Ickes & E. S. Knowles (Eds.), *Personality, roles, and social behavior* (pp. 33–53). New York: Springer.

Seiler, M. (1976, February 9). Monogamy is "unnatural," man with 9 wives says. *Los Angeles Times,* pt. 2, p. 1.

Semmelroth, J., & Buss, D. M. (unpublished). *Studies on conflict between the sexes.* Department of Psychology, University of Michigan, Ann Arbor, Michigan.

Seyfarth, R. M. (1976). Social relationships among adult female baboons. *Animal Behavior, 24,* 917–938.

Shettel-Neuber, J., Bryson, J. B., & Young, C. E. (1978). Physical attractiveness of the "other person" and jealousy. *Personality and Social Psychology Bulletin, 4,* 612–615.

Short, R. V. (1979). Sexual selection and its component parts, somatic and genital selection, as illustrated by man and great apes. *Advances in the Study of Behavior, 9,* 131–158.

Shostak, M. (1981). *Nisa: The life and words of a !Kung woman.* Cambridge, MA: Harvard University Press.

Sigusch, V., & Schmidt, G. (1971). Lower-class sexuality: Some emotional and social aspects in West German males and females. *Archives of Sexual Behavior, 1,* 29–44.

Singh, D. (1993). Adaptive significance of waist-to-hip ratio and female physical attractiveness. *Journal of Personality and Social Psychology, 65,* 293–307.

Singh, D. (in press a). Body shape and female attractiveness: Critical role of waist-to-hip ratio. *Human Nature.*

Singh, D. (in press b). Is thin really beautiful and good? Relationship between waist-to-hip ratio and female attractiveness. *Personality and Individual Differences.*

Small, M. (1992). The evolution of female sexuality and mate selection in humans. *Human Nature, 3,* 133–156.

Smith, R. L. (1984). Human sperm competition. In R. L. Smith (Ed.), *Sperm competition and the evolution of mating systems* (pp. 601–659). New York: Academic Press.

Smuts, B. B. (1985). *Sex and friendship in baboons.* New York: Aldine de Gruyter.

Smuts, B. B. (1987). Sexual competition and mate choice. In B. B. Smuts, D. L. Cheney, R. M. Seyfarth, R. W. Wrangham, & T. T. Struhsaker (Eds.), *Primate societies* (385–399). Chicago: University of Chicago Press.

Smuts, B. B. (1992). Male aggression against women: An evolutionary perspective. *Human Nature, 3,* 1–44.

Smuts, B. B. (in press). The origins of patriarchy: An evolutionary perspective. In A. Zagarell (Ed.), *Origins of gender inequality.* Kalamazoo, MI: New Issues Press.

Smuts, B. B., & Smuts, R. W. (1993). Male aggression against female primates: Evidence and theoretical implications. In P. J. B. Slater, J. S. Rosenblatt, M. Milinski, & C. T. Snowden (Eds.), *Advances in the study of behavior.* New York: Academic Press.

Spanier, G. B., & Margolis, R. L. (1983). Marital separation and extramarital sexual behavior. *Journal of Sex Research, 19,* 23–48.

Sprecher, S., Aron, A., Hatfield, E., Cortese, A., Potapova, E., & Levitskaya, A. (1992). *Love: American style, Russian style, and Japanese style.* Paper presented at the Sixth International Conference on Personal Relationships, Orono, Maine.

Sternberg, R. J. (1988). *The triangle of love.* New York: Basic Books.

Strassman, B. I. (1981). Sexual selection, parental care, and concealed ovulation in humans. *Ethology and Sociobiology, 2,* 31–40.

Stroebe, W. (1977). Self-esteem and interpersonal attraction. In S. W. Duck

(Ed.), *Theory and practice in interpersonal attraction* (pp. 79–104). London: Academic Press.

Studd, M. V., & Gattiker, U. E. (1991). The evolutionary psychology of sexual harassment in organizations. *Ethology and Sociobiology, 12,* 249–290.

Studd, M. V., & Gattiker, U. E. (in preparation). *Evolutionary psychology of sexual harassment: Effect of initiator profile and social context on response of recipients of sexual advances in the workplace.* Faculty of Management, University of Lethbridge, Alberta.

Symons, D. (1979). *The evolution of human sexuality.* New York: Oxford University Press.

Symons, D. (1987). If we're all Darwinians, what's the fuss about? In C. B. Crawford, M. F. Smith, D. L. Krebs (Eds.), *Sociobiology and psychology: Ideas, issues, and applications* (121–146). Hillsdale, NJ: Erlbaum.

Symons, D. (1989). The psychology of human mate preferences. *Behavioral and Brain Sciences, 12,* 34–35.

Tanner, R. E. S. (1970). *Homicide in Uganda, 1964: Crime in East Africa.* Uppsala: Scandinavian Institute of African Studies.

Taylor, P. A., & Glenn, N. D. (1976). The utility of education and attractiveness for females' status attainment through marriage. *American Sociological Review, 41,* 484–498.

Teisman, M. W., & Mosher, D. L. (1978). Jealous conflict in dating couples. *Psychological Reports, 42,* 1211–1216.

Terman, L. M. (1938). *Psychological factors in marital happiness.* New York: McGraw-Hill.

Terpstra, D. E., & Cook, S. E. (1985). Complainant characteristics and reported behaviors and consequences associated with formal sexual harassment charges. *Personnel Psychology, 38,* 559–574.

Thakerar, J. N., & Iwawaki, S. (1979). Cross-cultural comparisons of interpersonal attraction of females toward males. *Journal of Social Psychology, 108,* 121–122.

Thibeau, J. W., & Kelly, H. H. (1986). *The social psychology of groups* (2nd ed.). New Brunswick, NJ: Transaction Books.

Thiessen, D., Young, R. K., & Burroughs, R. (in press). Lonely hearts advertisements reflect sexually dimorphic mating strategies. *Ethology and Sociobiology.*

Thompson, A. P. (1983). Extramarital sex: A review of the research literature. *Journal of Sex Research, 19,* 1–22.

Thompson, A. P. (1984). Emotional and sexual components of extramarital relations. *Journal of Marriage and the Family, 46,* 35–42.

Thornhill, N. W. (1992a, August). *Female short-term sexual strategies: The self-esteem hypothesis.* Paper presented at the Human Behavior and Evolution Society, Albuquerque, New Mexico.

Thornhill, N. W. (1992b). *Human inbreeding* (Research Report No. 20/92). Research Group on Biological Foundations of Human Culture, Center for Interdisciplinary Research, University of Bielefeld, Germany.

Thornhill, N. W., & Thornhill, R. (1990a). An evolutionary analysis of psychological pain following rape: 1. The effects of victim's age and marital status. *Ethology and Sociobiology, 11,* 155–176.

Thornhill, N. W., & Thornhill, R. (1990b). An evolutionary analysis of psychological pain following rape: 2. The effects of stranger, friend, and family-member offenders. *Ethology and Sociobiology, 11,* 177–193.

Thornhill, R. (1980a). Mate choice in *Hylobittacus apicalis* (Insecta: Mecoptera) and its relation to some models of female choice. *Evolution, 34,* 519–538.

Thornhill, R. (1980b). Rape in *Panorpa* scorpionflies and a general rape hypothesis. *Animal Behavior, 28,* 52–59.

Thornhill, R., & Alcock, J. (1983). *The evolution of insect mating systems.* Cambridge, MA: Harvard University Press.

Thornhill, R., & Thornhill, N. (1983). Human rape: An evolutionary analysis. *Ethology and Sociobiology, 4,* 63–99.

Thornhill, R., & Thornhill, N. (1992). The evolutionary psychology of men's coercive sexuality. *Behavioral and Brain Sciences, 15,* 363–421.

Tooby, J., & Cosmides, L. (1989a). The innate versus the manifest. How universal does universal have to be? *Behavioral and Brain Sciences, 12,* 36–37.

Tooby, J., & Cosmides, L. (1989b). Evolutionary psychology and the generation of culture: 1. Theoretical considerations. *Ethology and Sociobiology, 10,* 29–49.

Tooby, J., & Cosmides, L. (1990). On the universality of human nature and the uniqueness of the individual: The role of genetics and adaptation. *Journal of Personality, 58,* 17–68.

Tooby, J., & Cosmides, L. (1992). Psychological foundations of culture. In J. Barkow, L. Cosmides, & J. Tooby (Eds.), *The adapted mind: Evolutionary psychology and the generation of culture* (pp. 19–136). New York: Oxford University Press.

Tooby, J., & DeVore, I. (1987). The reconstruction of hominid behavioral evolution through strategic modeling. In W. G. Kinzey (Ed.), *The evolution of human behavior: Primate models* (pp. 183–237). New York: State University of New York Press.

Tooke, J., & Camire, L. (1991). Patterns of deception in intersexual and intrasexual mating strategies. *Ethology and Sociobiology, 12,* 345–364.

Townsend, J. M. (1989). Mate selection criteria: A pilot study. *Ethology and Sociobiology, 10,* 241–253.

Townsend, J. M., & Levy, G. D. (1990). Effects of potential partners' physical attractiveness and socioeconomic status on sexuality and partner selection. *Archives of Sexual Behavior, 371,* 149–164.

Townsend, J. M., & Levy, G. D. (in preparation). *Effects of potential partner's costume and physical attractiveness on sexuality and partner selection: Sex differences in reported preferences of university students.* Department of Anthropology, Syracuse University, New York.

Trinkaus, E., & Zimmerman, M. R. (1982). Trauma among the Shanidar Neanderthals. *American Journal of Physical Anthropology, 57,* 61–76.

Tripp, C. A. (1975). *The homosexual matrix.* New York: Signet.

Trivers, R. (1972). Parental investment and sexual selection. In B. Campbell (Ed.), *Sexual selection and the descent of man* (pp. 136–179). New York: Aldine de Gruyter.

Trivers, R. (1985). *Social evolution.* Menlo Park, CA: Benjamin/Cummings.

Udry, J. R. (1980). Changes in the frequency of marital intercourse from panel data: *Archives of Sexual Behavior, 9,* 319–325.

Udry, J. R., & Eckland, B. K. (1984). Benefits of being attractive: Differential payoffs for men and women. *Psychological Reports, 54,* 47–56.

U.S. Bureau of the Census (1977). *Marriage, divorce, widowhood, and remarriage by family characteristics: June, 1975* (Current Population Reports Series P-20, 312). Washington, DC: U.S. Government Printing Office.

U.S. Bureau of the Census (1989). *Marital status and living arrangements, March 1988.* Washington, DC: U.S. Government Printing Office.

Utian, W. H. (1980). *Menopause in modern perspective: A guide to clinical practice.* New York: Appleton-Century-Crofts.

Vandenberg, S. (1972). Assortative mating, or who marries whom? *Behavior Genetics, 2,* 127–158.

Van Gulik, R. H. (1974). *Sexual life in ancient China.* London: E. J. Brill.

Voland, E., & Engel, C. (1990). Female choice in humans: A conditional mate selection strategy of the Krummerhörn women (Germany 1720–1874). *Ethology, 84,* 144–154.

Weisfeld, G. E., Russell, R. J. H., Weisfeld, C. C., & Wells, P. A. (1992). Correlates of satisfaction in British marriages. *Ethology and Sociobiology, 13,* 125–145.

Weiss, D. L., & Slosnerick, M. (1981). Attitudes toward sexual and nonsexual extramarital involvements among a sample of college students. *Journal of Marriage and the Family, 43,* 349–358.

Weiss, D. S. (1975). *Marital separation.* New York: Basic Books.

Welham, C. V. J. (1990). Incest: An evolutionary model. *Ethology and Sociobiology, 11,* 97–111.

White, G. L. (1981). Some correlates of romantic jealousy. *Journal of Personality, 49,* 129–147.

Whitehurst, R. N. (1971). Violence potential in extramarital sexual responses. *Journal of Marriage and the Family, 33,* 683–691.

Whyte, M. K. (1990). Changes in mate choice in Chengdu. In D. Davis & E. Vogel (Eds.), *China on the eve of Tiananmen.* Cambridge, MA: Harvard University Press.

Wiederman, M. W. (in press). Evolved gender differences in mate preferences: Evidence from personal advertisements. *Ethology and Sociobiology.*

Wiederman, M. W., & Allgeier, E. R. (1992). Gender differences in mate selection criteria: Sociobiological or socioeconomic explanation? *Ethology and Sociobiology, 13,* 115–124.

Willerman, L. (1979). *The psychology of individual and group differences.* San Francisco: Freeman.

Williams, G. C. (1957). Pleiotropy, natural selection, and the evolution of senescence. *Evolution, 11,* 398–411.

Williams, G. C. (1975). *Sex and evolution.* Princeton, NJ: Princeton University Press.

Wilson, E. O. (1975). *Sociobiology: The new synthesis.* Cambridge, MA: Harvard University Press.

Wilson, E. O. (1978). *On human nature.* Cambridge, MA: Harvard University Press.

Wilson, G. D. (1987). Male-female differences in sexual activity, enjoyment, and fantasies. *Personality and individual differences, 8,* 125–126.

Wilson, M. (1989). Conflict and homicide in evolutionary perspective. In R. Bell & N. Bell (Eds.), *Sociobiology and the social sciences* (pp. 45–62). Lubbock: Texas Tech University Press.

Wilson, M., & Daly, M. (1985). Competitiveness, risk taking, and violence: The young male syndrome. *Ethology and Sociobiology, 6,* 59–73.

Wilson, M., & Daly, M. (1992). The man who mistook his wife for a chattel. In J. Barkow, L. Cosmides, & J. Tooby (Eds.), *The adapted mind: Evolutionary psychology and the generation of culture* (pp. 289–322). New York: Oxford University Press.

Wolf, N. (1991). *The beauty myth.* New York: William Morrow.

Yosef, R. (1991, June). Females seek males with ready cache. *Natural History,* p. 37.

Young, R. R., & Thiessen, D. (1992). The Texas rape scale. *Ethology and Sociobiology, 13,* 19–33.

Zahavi, A. (1977). The testing of a bond. *Animal Behaviour, 25,* 246–247.

References for Chapters 11 and 12

Angier, N. (1999). *Woman: An intimate geography.* Boston: Houghton Mifflin Company.

Bailey, J. M., Kim, P. Y., Hills, A., & Linsenmeier, J. A. W. (1997). Butch, femme, or straight acting? Partner preferences of gay men and lesbians. *Journal of Personality and Social Psychology, 73,* 960–973.

Bailey, J. M., Pillard, R. C., Dawood, K., Miller, M. B., Farrer, L. A., Trivedi, S., & Murphy, R. L. (1999). A family history study of male sexual orientation using three independent samples. *Behavior Genetics, 29,* 79–86.

Baker, R. R., & Bellis, M. (1995). *Human sperm competition.* London: Chapman Hall.

Bancroft, J. (1989). *Human sexuality and its problems.* Edinburgh: Churchill Livingston.

Bassett, J., Pearcey, S., & Dabbs, J. M., Jr. (2001). Jealousy and partner preference among butch and femme lesbians. *Psychology, Evolution, and Gender*, 3(2), 155–165.

Bevc, I., & Silverman, I. (2000). Early separation and sibling incest: A test of the revised Westermarck theory. *Evolution and Human Behavior*, 21, 151–161.

Bleske, A. L., & Buss, D. M. (2000). Can men and women be just friends? *Personal Relationships*, 7, 131–151.

Bleske, A. L., & Buss, D. M. (2001). Opposite sex friendship: Sex differences and similarities in initiation, selection, and dissolution. *Personality and Social Psychology Bulletin*, 27, 1310–1323.

Bleske, A. L., & Shackelford, T. K. (2001). Poaching, promiscuity, and deceit: Combating mating rivalry in same-sex friendships. *Personal Relationships*, 8, 407–424.

Bobrow, D., & Bailey, J. M. (2001). Is male homosexuality maintained via kin selection? *Evolution and Human Behavior*, 22, 361–368.

Brewer, D. D., Potterat, J. J., Garrett, S. B., Muth, S. Q., Roberts, J. M., Kasprzyk, D., Montano, D. E., & Darrow, W. W. (2000). Prostitution and the sex discrepancy in reported number of sexual partners. *Proceedings of the National Academy of Science*, 97, 12385–12388.

Buss, D. M. (1999). *Evolutionary psychology: The new science of the mind*. Boston: Allyn & Bacon.

Buss, D. M. (2000). *The dangerous passion: Why jealousy is as necessary as love and sex*. New York: Free Press.

Buss, D. M. (2001). Cognitive biases and emotional wisdom in the evolution of conflict between the sexes. *Current Directions in Psychological Science*, 10, 219–223.

Buss, D. M., & Shackelford, T. K. (1997). From vigilance to violence: Mate retention tactics in married couples. *Journal of Personality and Social Psychology*, 72, 346–361.

Buss, D. M., Shackelford, T. K., Choe, J., Buunk, B., & Dijkstra, P. (2000). Distress about rivals: Reactions to intrasexual competitors in Korea, the Netherlands, and America. *Personal Relationships*, 7, 235–243.

Buss, D. M., Shackelford, T. K., Kirkpatrick, L. A., Choe, J., Hasegawa, M., Hasegawa, T., & Bennett, K. (1999). Jealousy and the nature of beliefs about infidelity: Tests of competing hypotheses about sex differences in the United States, Korea, and Japan. *Personal Relationships*, 6, 125–150.

Buunk, A. P., Angleitner, A., Oubaid, V., & Buss, D. M. (1996). Sex differences in jealousy in evolutionary and cultural perspective: Tests from the Netherlands, Germany, and the United States. *Psychological Science*, 7, 359–363.

Cerda-Flores, R. M., Barton, S. A., Marty-Gonzalez, L. F., Rivas, F., & Chakraborty, R. (1999). Estimation of nonpaternity in the Mexican population of Nuevo Leon: A validation study with blood group markers. *American Journal of Physical Anthropology*, 109, 281–293.

Chavanne, T. J., & Gallup, G. G., Jr. (1998). Variation in risk taking behavior among female college students as a function of the menstrual cycle. *Evolution and Human Behavior*, 19, 27–32.

Chesser, E. (1957). *The sexual, marital and family relationships of the English woman*. New York: Roy.

Cochran, G. M., Ewald, P. W., & Cochran, K. D. (2000). Infectious causation of disease: An evolutionary perspective. *PBM*, 43, 406–448.

Cooperative Institutional Research Program, University of California, Los Angeles (2001). *The American freshman: National norms for fall 2001*.

Coyne, J. A. (2000). Of vice and men. Review of R. Thornhill & C. Palmer, *A natural history of rape: Biological bases of sexual coercion. The New Republic*, April 3, pp. 27–34.

Cramer, R. E., Abraham, W. T., Johnson, L. M., & Manning-Ryan, B. (2001–2002). Gender differences in subjective distress to emotional and sexual infidelity: Evolutionary or logical inference explanation? *Current Psychology*, 20, 327–336.

Davenport, W. H. (1977). Sex in cross-cultural perspective. In F. A. Beach (Ed.), *Human sexuality in four perspectives* (pp. 115–163). Baltimore: The Johns Hopkins University Press.

DeSteno, D. A., & Salovey, P. (1996). Evolutionary origins of sex differences in jealousy: Questioning the "fitness" of the model. *Psychological Science*, 7, 367–372.

DeSteno, D., Bartlett, M. Y., Braverman, J., & Salovey, P. (in press). Sex differences in jealousy: Evolutionary mechanism or artifact of measurement? *Journal of Personality and Social Psychology*.

Dixon, A. F. (1998). *Primate sexuality*. New York: Oxford University Press.

Doty, R. L., Ford, M., Preti, G., & Huggins, G. R. (1975). Changes in the intensity and pleasantness of human vaginal odors during the menstrual cycle. *Science*, 190, 1316–1318.

Fisher, S. (1973). *The female orgasm: Psychology, physiology, and fantasy*. New York: Basic Books.

Fox, C. A., Wolff, H. S., & Baker, J. A. (1970). Measurement of intravaginal and intra-uterine pressures during human coitus by radiotelemetry. *Journal of Reproductive Fertility*, 22, 243–251.

Freeman, D. (1984). *Margaret Mead and Samoa: The making and unmaking of an anthropological myth*. Middlesex, England: Penguin.

Gangestad, S. W., & Cousins, A. J. (in press). Adaptive design, female mate preferences, and shifts across the menstrual cycle. *Annual Review of Sex Research*.

Gangestad, S. W., & Thornhill, R. (1997). The evolutionary psychology of extrapair sex: The role of fluctuating asymmetry. *Evolution and Human Behavior*, 18, 69–88.

Gangestad, S. W., & Thornhill, R. (1998). Menstrual cycle variation in women's preferences for the scent of symmetrical men. *Proceedings of the Royal Society of London B*, 265, 927–933.

Gangestad, S. W., Thornhill, R., & Garver, C. (in press). Changes in women's sexual interest and their partners' mate retention tactics across the menstrual cycle: Evidence for shifting conflicts of interest. *Proceedings of the Royal Society of London*.

Geary, D. C., Rumsey, M., Bow-Thomas, C. C., & Hoard, M. K. (1995). Sexual jealousy as a facultative trait: Evidence from the pattern of sex differences in adults from China and the United States. *Ethology and Sociobiology*, 16, 355–383.

Gilmore, D. D. (1990). *Manhood in the making: Cultural concepts of masculinity*. New Haven: Yale University Press.

Good, K. (1991). *Into the heart*. New York: Simon & Schuster.

Gottschall, J., & Gottschall, T. (in press). Are per-incident rape-pregnancy rates higher than per-incident consensual pregnancy rates? *Human Nature*.

Gould, S. J. (1987). Freudian slip. *Natural History*, 2(87), pp. 14–21.

Gould, S. J. (1997). Evolutionary psychology: An exchange. *New York Review of Books*, 44, 53–58.

Grammer, K. (1996). *The human mating game: The battle of the sexes and the war of signals*. Paper presented to the Human Behavior and Evolution Society Annual Meeting, Northwestern University, Evanston, Illinois, June 29.

Greiling, H., & Buss, D. M. (2000). Women's sexual strategies: The hidden dimension of extra-pair mating. *Personality and Individual Differences*, 28, 929–963.

Griffin, S. (1971). Rape: The all-American crime. *Ramparts*, 10, 26–36.

Hamer, D. H., & Copeland, P. (1998). *Living with our genes: Why they matter more than you think*. New York: Doubleday.

Hamilton, W. D. (1982). Pathogens as causes of genetic diversity in their host populations. In R. M. Anderson & R. M. May (Eds.), *Population biology of infectious diseases* (pp. 269–296). New York: Springer Verlag.

Harris, C. R. (2000). Psychophysiological responses to imagined infidelity: The specific innate modular view of jealousy reconsidered. *Journal of Personality and Social Psychology*, 78, 1082–1091.

Harris, C. R., & Christenfeld, N. (1996). Gender, jealousy, and reason. *Psychological Science*, 7, 364–366.

Hartung, J. (n.d.). *Rape: Biblical roots of the long leash on women*. Unpublished manuscript.

Haselton, M. G. (in press). The sexual overperception bias: Evidence of a systematic bias in men from a survey of naturally occurring events. *Journal of Research in Personality*.

Haselton, M. G., & Buss, D. M. (in press). Biases in social judgment: Design flaws or design features? In J. Forgas, W. von Hippel, and K. Williams (Eds.), *Responding to the social world: Explicit and implicit processes in social judgments and decisions*. Cambridge: Cambridge University Press.

Haselton, M. G., & Buss, D. M. (2000). Error Management Theory: A new perspective on biases in cross-sex mind reading. *Journal of Personality and Social Psychology*, 78, 81–91.

Haselton, M. G., & Buss, D. M. (2001). The affective shift hypothesis: The functions of emotional changes following sexual intercourse. *Personal Relationships*, 8, 357–369.

Hickman, S. E., & Muehlenhard, C. L. (1997). College women's fears and precautionary behaviors relating to acquaintance rape and stranger rape. *Psychology of Women Quarterly*, 21, 527–547.

Hicks, T. V., & Leitenberg, H. (2001). Sexual fantasies about one's partner versus someone else: Gender differences in incidence and frequency. *The Journal of Sex Research*, 38, 43–50.

Hrdy, S. B. (1999). *Mother nature*. New York: Pantheon Books.

Immerman, R. S., & Mackey, W. C. (1997). An additional facet of the incest taboo: A protection of the mating-strategy template. *The Journal of Genetic Psychology*, 158, 151–164.

Johnston, V. S., Hagel, R., Franklin, M., Fink, B., & Grammer, K. (2001). Male facial attractiveness: Evidence for hormone-mediated adaptive design. *Evolution and Human Behavior*, 22, 251–267.

Jones, O. D. (1999). Sex, culture, and the biology of rape: Toward explanation and prevention. *California Law Review*, 87, 827–941.

Jones, O. D. (2001). Realities of rape: Of science and politics, causes and meanings. *Cornell Law Review*, 86, 1386–1422.

Keenan, J. P., Gallup, G. G., Jr., Goulet, N., & Kulkarni, M. (1997). Attributions of deception in human mating strategies. *Journal of Social Behavior and Personality*, 12, 45–52.

Kirkpatrick, L. A., & Ellis, B. J. (2001). Evolutionary perspectives on self-evaluation and self-esteem. In M. Clark & G. Fletcher (Eds.), *The Blackwell handbook of social psychology, Vol. 2: Interpersonal processes*. Oxford: Blackwell Publishers.

Kirkpatrick, R. C. (2000). The evolution of human homosexual behavior. *Current Anthropology*, 41, 385–413.

Kohl, J. V., Atzmueller, M., Fink, B., & Grammer, K. (2001). Human pheromones: Integrating neuroendocrinology and ethology. *Neuroendocrinology Letters*, 22, 309–321.

Kuukasjarvi, S., Eriksson, C. J. P., Koskela, E., Mappes, T., & Rantala, M. J. (under review). *Is ovulation truly concealed in women?* Manuscript under editorial review.

Lalumiere, M. L., Chalmers, L. J., Quinsey, V. L., & Seto, M. C. (1996). A test of the mate deprivation hypothesis of sexual coercion. *Ethology and Sociobiology*, 17, 299–318.

Li, N., & Bailey, J. M. (2002). The necessities and luxuries of mate preferences. *Journal of Personality and Social Psychology*, 82, 947–955.

Lieberman, D. (2002). *The psychological mechanisms mediating the development of a sexual aversion between siblings*. Paper presented to the Annual Meeting of the American Psychological Society, New Orleans, June 7.

MacIntyre, S., & Sooman, A. (1991). Nonpaternity and prenatal genetic screening. *Lancet*, 338, 869–871.

Maggioncalda, A. N., & Sapolsky, R. M. (2002). Disturbing behaviors of the orangutan. *Scientific American*, 286, 60–65.

Manning, J. T., & Scutt, D. (1996). Symmetry and ovulation in women. *Human Reproduction*, 11, 2477–2480.

Mathes, E. W., King, C. A., Miller, J. K., & Reed, R. M. (2002). An evolutionary perspective on the interaction of age and sex differences in short-term sexual strategies. *Psychological Reports*, 90, 949–956.

McKnight, J. (1997). *Straight science: Homosexuality, evolution and adaptation*. New York: Routledge.

Michael, R. T., Gagnon, J. H., Laumann, E. O., & Kolata, G. (1994). *Sex in America: A definitive survey*. New York: Little Brown.

Miller, E. M. (2000). Homosexuality, birth order and evolution: Toward an equilibrium reproductive economics of homosexuality. *Archives of Sexual Behavior*, 29, 1–34.

Miller, G. (2000). *The mating mind*. New York: Doubleday.

Mitani, J. (1985). Mating behaviour of male orangutans in the Kutai Game Reserve, Indonesia. *Animal Behaviour*, 33, 392–402.

Moore, H. D. M., Martin, M., & Birkhead, T. R. (1999). No evidence for killer sperm or other selective interactions between human spermatozoa in ejaculates of different males *in vitro*. *Proceedings of the Royal Society of London B*, 266, 2343–2350.

Morgan, J. B. (1981). *Relationship between rape and physical damage during rape and phase of sexual cycle during which rape occurred*. Unpublished doctoral dissertation, University of Texas at Austin.

Morris, N. M., & Udry, J. R. (1970). Variations in pedometer activity during the menstrual cycle. *Obstetrics and Gynecology*, 35, 199–201.

Muscarella, F. (2000). The evolution of homoerotic behavior in humans. *Journal of Homosexuality*, 40, 51–77.

Parish, A. R. (1994). Sex and food control in the "uncommon chimpanzee": How bonobo females overcome a phylogenetic legacy of male dominance. *Ethology and Sociobiology*, 15, 157–179.

Pawlowski, B., & Dunbar, R. I. M. (1999). Impact of market value on human mate choice decisions. *Proceedings of the Royal Society of London B*, 266, 281–285.

Pawson, E., & Banks, G. (1993). Rape and fear in a New Zealand city. *Area*, 25, 55–63.

Penton-Voak, I. S., & Perrett, D. I. (2000). Female preference for male faces changes cyclically: Further evidence. *Evolution and Human Behavior*, 21, 39–48.

Penton-Voak, I. S., Perrett, D. I., Castles, D. I., Kobayashi, T., Burt, D. M., Murray, L. K., & Minamisawa, R. (1999, June). Menstrual cycle alters face preference. *Nature*, 399, 741–742.

Pietrzak, R., Laird, J. D., Stevens, D. A., & Thompson, N. S. (2002). Sex differences in human jealousy: A coordinated study of forced-choice, continuous rating-scale, and physiological responses on the same subjects. *Evolution and Human Behavior*, 23, 83–94.

Pigliucci, M (2002). Rape, sex and the research of evolutionary psychology. *Skeptic*, 9, 96–98.

Pinker, S. (1997). *How the mind works*. New York: Norton.

Pinker, S. (2002). *The blank slate: The modern denial of human nature*. New York: Viking.

Poran, N. S. (1994). Cyclic attractivity of human female odours. *Advances in Bioscience*, 93, 555–560.

Rahman, Q., & Wilson, G. D. (in press). Born gay? The psychobiology of human sexual orientation. *Personality and Individual Differences*.

Rancour-Laferriere, D. (1985). *Signs of the flesh: An essay on the evolution of human sexuality*. New York: Mouton de Gruyter.

Regan, P. C. (1996). Rhythms of desire: The association between menstrual cycle phases and female sexual desire. *The Canadian Journal of Human Sexuality*, 5, 145–156.

Regan, P. C., & Berscheid, E. (1995). Gender differences in beliefs about the causes of male and female sexual desire. *Personal Relationships*, 2, 345–358.

Regan, P. C., & Dreyer, C. S. (1999). Lust? Love? Status? Young adults' motives for engaging in casual sex. *Journal of Psychology and Human Sexuality*, 11, 1–24.

Rice, G., Anderson, N., Rische, N., & Ebers, G. (1999). Male homosexuality: Absence of linkage to microsatellite markers at Xq28. *Science*, 284, 665–667.

Rikowski, A., & Grammer, K. (1999). Human body odor, symmetry, and attractiveness. *Proceedings of the Royal Society of London B*, 266, 869–874.

Rogel, M. J. (1976). *Biosocial aspects of rape*. Unpublished doctoral dissertation, University of Chicago.

Royle, T. (1989). *A dictionary of military quotations*. New York: Simon & Schuster.

Sanday, P. R. (1990). *Fraternity gang rape*. New York: New York University Press.

Sasse, G., Muller, H., Chakraborty, R., & Ott, J. (1994). Estimating the frequency of nonpaternity in Switzerland. *Human Heredity*, 44, 337–343.

Schmitt, D. P. (under review). *Sex differences in the desire for sexual variety: Tests from 52 nations, six continents, and 13 islands*. Manuscript under editorial review.

Schmitt, D. P. (2001). *Desire for sexual variety and mate poaching experiences across multiple languages and cultures*. Paper presented to the Annual Meeting of the Human Behavior and Evolution Society, London, June.

Schmitt, D. P., & Buss, D. M. (2000). Sexual dimensions of person description: Beyond or subsumed by the big five? *Journal of Research in Personality*, 34, 141–177.

Schmitt, D. P., & Buss, D. M. (2001). Human mate poaching: Tactics and temptations for infiltrating existing mateships. *Journal of Personality and Social Psychology*, 80, 894–917.

Schmitt, D. P., Shackelford, T. K., Duntley, J., Tooke, W., & Buss, D. M. (2001). The desire for sexual variety as a key to understanding basic human mating strategies. *Personal Relationships*, 8, 425–455.

Schneider, M. A., & Hendrix, L. (2000). Olfactory sexual inhibition and the Westermarck effect. *Human Nature*, 11, 65–91.

Shackelford, T. K., Buss, D. M., & Bennett, K. (2002). Forgiveness or breakup: Sex differences in responses to a partner's infidelity. *Cognition and Emotion*, 16, 299–307.

Shackelford, T. K., LeBlanc, G. J., Weekes-Shackelford, V. A., Bleske-Rechek, A. L., Euler, H. A., & Hoier, S. (2002). Psychological adaptations to human sperm competition. *Evolution and Human Behavior*, 23, 123–138.

Shackelford, T. K., Weekes-Shackelford, V. A., LeBlanc, G. J., Bleske, A. L., Euler, H. A., & Hoier, S. (2000). Female coital orgasm and male attractiveness. *Human Nature*, 11, 299–306.

Singh, D., & Bronstad, P. M. (2001). Female body odour is a potential cue to ovulation. *Proceedings of the Royal Society of London B*, 268, 1–5.

Singh, D., Vidaurri, M., Zambarano, R. J., & Dabbs, J. M. (1999). Lesbian erotic role identification: Behavioral, morphological, and hormonal correlates. *Journal of Personality and Social Psychology*, 76, 1035–1049.

Slob, A. K., & van der Werff ten Bosch, J. J. (1991). Orgasm in nonhuman species. In P. Kothari & R. Patel (Eds.), *Proceedings of the First International Conference on Orgasm*. Bombay: VRP.

Stanislaw, H, & Rice, F. J. (1988). Correlation between sexual desire and menstrual cycle characteristics. *Archives of Sexual Behavior*, 17, 499–508.

Surbey, M. K., & Conohan, C. D. (2000). Willingness to engage in casual sex: The role of parental qualities and perceived risk of aggression. *Human Nature*, 11, 367–386.

Symons, D. (1982). Another woman that never existed. Review of S. B. Hrdy's *The woman that never evolved*. *Quarterly Review of Biology*, 57, 297–300.

Symons, D. (1995). Beauty is in the adaptations of the beholder: The evolutionary psychology of human female sexual attractiveness. In P. R. Abramson & S. D. Pinkerton (Eds.), *Sexual nature, sexual culture* (pp. 80–118). Chicago: The University of Chicago Press.

Tavris, C., & Sadd, S. (1977). *The Redbook report on female sexuality*. New York: Delacorte Press.

Thornhill, R., & Gangestad, S. W. (in press). Do women have evolved adaptation for extra-pair copulation? In E. Voland & K. Grammer (Eds.), *Evolutionary aesthetics*. Heidelberg, Germany: Springer-Verlag.

Thornhill, R., & Gangestad, S. W. (1999). The scent of symmetry: A human sex pheromone that signals fitness? *Evolution and Human Behavior*, 20, 175–201.

Thornhill, R., & Palmer, C. (2000). *A natural history of rape: Biological bases of sexual coercion*. Cambridge, MA: MIT Press.

Thornhill, R., Gangestad, S. W., & Comer, R. (1995). Human female orgasm and mate fluctuating asymmetry. *Animal Behavior*, 50, 1601–1615.

Townsend, J. M., Kline, J., & Wasserman, T. H. (1995). Low-investment copulation: Sex differences in motivations and emotional reactions. *Ethology and Sociobiology*, 16, 25–51.

Troisi, A., & Carosi, M. (1998). Female orgasm rate increases with male dominance in Japanese macaques. *Animal Behavior*, 56, 1261–1266.

van den Berghe, P. L., & Frost, P. (1986). Skin color preferences, sexual dimorphism and sexual selection: A case of gene culture co-evolution? *Ethnic and Racial Studies*, 9, 87–113.

Vasey, P. L. (1995). Homosexual behavior in primates: A review of evidence and theory. *International Journal of Primatology*, 16, 173–204.

Vasey, P. L. (1996). Interventions and alliance formation between female Japanese macaques during homosexual consortships. *Animal Behavior*, 52, 539–551.

de Waal, F. B. M. (1989). *Peacemaking among primates*. Cambridge, MA: Harvard University Press.

Walsh, A. (1991). Self-esteem and sexual behavior: Exploring gender differences. *Sex Roles*, 25, 441–450.

Wedekind, C., Seeback, T., Betterns, F., & Paepke, A. J. (1995). MHC-dependent mate preferences in humans. *Proceedings of the Royal Society of London B*, 260, 245–249.

Wellings, K., Field, J., Johnson, A. M., & Wadsworth, J. (1994). *Sexual behaviour in Britain*. London: Penguin Books.

Westermarck, E. (1891). *The history of human marriage*. London: Macmillan.

Wiederman, M. W., & Kendall, E. (1999). Evolution, gender, and sexual jealousy: Investigation with a sample from Sweden. *Evolution and Human Behavior*, 20, 121–128.

Wilson, M., & Mesnick, S. L. (1997). An empirical test of the bodyguard hypothesis. In P. A. Gowaty (Ed.), *Feminism and evolutionary biology: Boundaries, intersections, and frontiers*. New York: Chapman & Hall.

Wrangham, R. (1999). Evolution of coalitionary killing. *Yearbook of Physical Anthropology*, 42, 1–30.

Zuk, M. (2002). *Sexual selections: What we can and can't learn about sex from animals*. Berkeley, CA: University of California Press.

Index

[faint illegible library stamp]